HIGH LEVEL

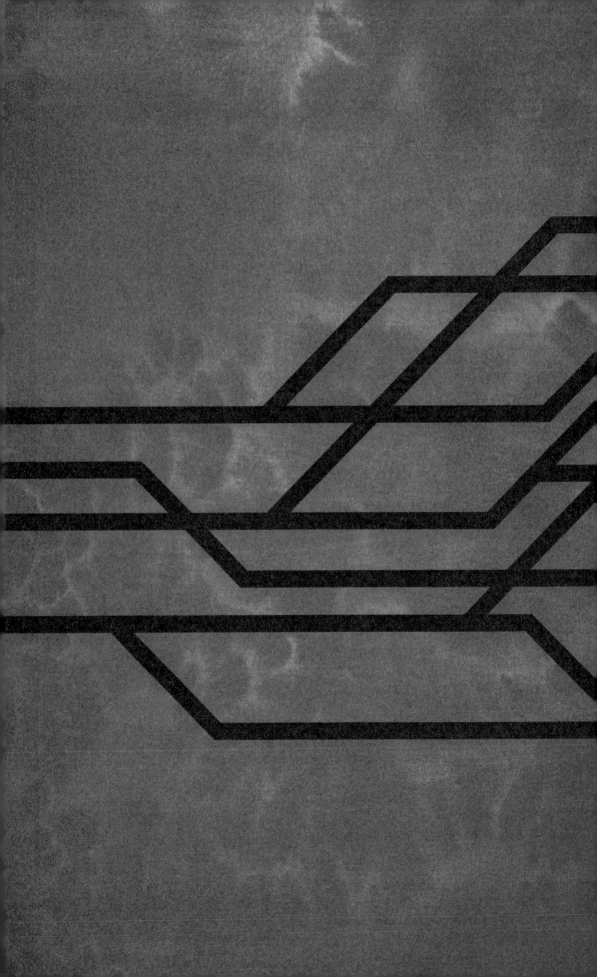

HIGH LEVEL

ROB SHERIDAN
STORY

BARNABY BAGENDA
AMANCAY NAHUELPAN
OMAR FRANCIA
ARTISTS

ROMULO FAJARDO JR.
COLORIST

NATE PIEKOS OF BLAMBOT®
LETTERER

ROB SHERIDAN
PUBLICATION and COLLECTION COVER DESIGN

BARNABY BAGENDA
COLLECTION COVER ART

ANDY KHOURI   *Editor – Original Series*
MAGGIE HOWELL   *Assistant Editor – Original Series*
JEB WOODARD   *Group Editor – Collected Editions*
ERIKA ROTHBERG   *Editor – Collected Edition*
STEVE COOK   *Design Director – Books*
ROB SHERIDAN   *Publication Design*
CHRISTY SAWYER   *Publication Production*

BOB HARRAS   *Senior VP – Editor-in-Chief, DC Comics*
MARK DOYLE   *Executive Editor, Vertigo & Black Label*

DAN DiDIO   *Publisher*
JIM LEE   *Publisher & Chief Creative Officer*
BOBBIE CHASE   *VP – New Publishing Initiatives & Talent Development*
DON FALLETTI   *VP – Manufacturing Operations & Workflow Management*
LAWRENCE GANEM   *VP – Talent Services*
ALISON GILL   *Senior VP – Manufacturing & Operations*
HANK KANALZ   *Senior VP – Publishing Strategy & Support Services*
DAN MIRON   *VP – Publishing Operations*
NICK J. NAPOLITANO   *VP – Manufacturing Administration & Design*
NANCY SPEARS   *VP – Sales*
MICHELE R. WELLS   *VP & Executive Editor, Young Reader*

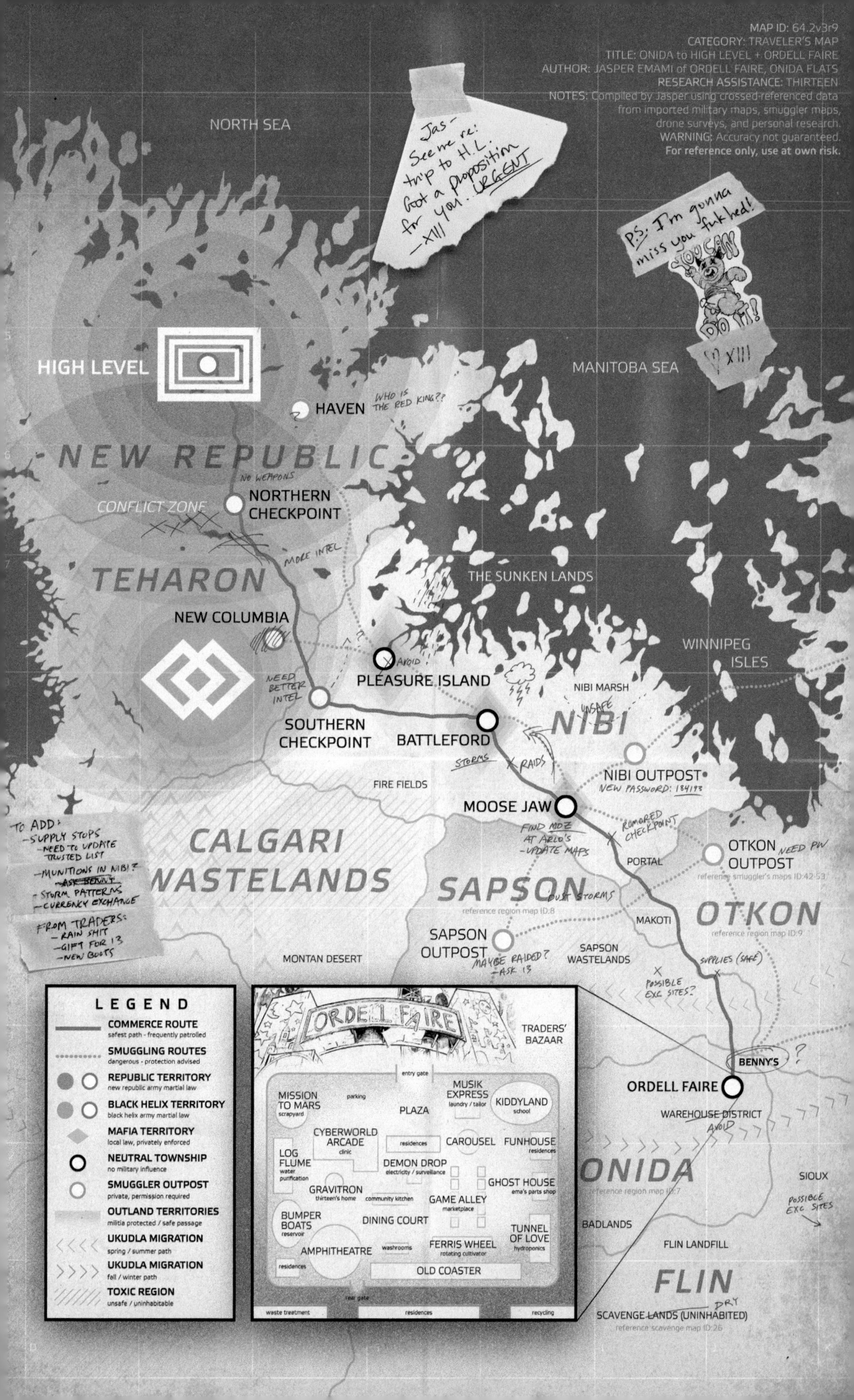

MAP ID: 64.2v3r9
CATEGORY: TRAVELER'S MAP
TITLE: ONIDA to HIGH LEVEL + ORDELL FAIRE
AUTHOR: JASPER EMAMI of ORDELL FAIRE, ONIDA FLATS
RESEARCH ASSISTANCE: THIRTEEN
NOTES: Compiled by Jasper using crossed-referenced data from imported military maps, smuggler maps, drone surveys, and personal research.
WARNING: Accuracy not guaranteed.
For reference only, use at own risk.
Jas- See me re: trip to H.L. Got a proposition for you. URGENT —XIII
P.S. I'm gonna miss you fukhed!
YOU CAN DO IT!
♡ XIII
NORTH SEA
MANITOBA SEA
HIGH LEVEL
HAVEN
WHO IS THE RED KING??
NEW REPUBLIC
NO WEAPONS
CONFLICT ZONE
NORTHERN CHECKPOINT
MORE INTEL
TEHARON
THE SUNKEN LANDS
NEW COLUMBIA
PLEASURE ISLAND
AVOID
WINNIPEG ISLES
NEED BETTER INTEL
SOUTHERN CHECKPOINT
BATTLEFORD
NIBI MARSH
UNSAFE
NIBI
STORMS
RAIDS
FIRE FIELDS
NIBI OUTPOST
NEW PASSWORD: 184193
MOOSE JAW
FIND MOZ AT ARLO'S - UPDATE MAPS
RUMORED CHECKPOINT
OTKON OUTPOST
NEED PW
PORTAL
TO ADD:
- SUPPLY STOPS
- NEED TO UPDATE TRUSTED LIST
- MUNITIONS IN NIBI?
- ASK BENNY
- STORM PATTERNS
- CURRENCY EXCHANGE
FROM TRADERS:
- RAIN SHIT
- GIFT FOR 13
- NEW BOOTS
CALGARI WASTELANDS
SAPSON
reference region map ID:8
DUST STORMS
MAKOTI
OTKON
reference region map ID:9
SAPSON OUTPOST
MAYBE RAIDED? - ASK 13
SAPSON WASTELANDS
MONTAN DESERT
SUPPLIES (SAFE)
POSSIBLE EXC SITES?
LEGEND
COMMERCE ROUTE
safest path - frequently patrolled
SMUGGLING ROUTES
dangerous - protection advised
REPUBLIC TERRITORY
new republic army martial law
BLACK HELIX TERRITORY
black helix army martial law
MAFIA TERRITORY
local law, privately enforced
NEUTRAL TOWNSHIP
no military influence
SMUGGLER OUTPOST
private, permission required
OUTLAND TERRITORIES
militia protected / safe passage
UKUDLA MIGRATION
spring / summer path
UKUDLA MIGRATION
fall / winter path
TOXIC REGION
unsafe / uninhabitable
ORDELL FAIRE
TRADERS' BAZAAR
entry gate
MISSION TO MARS
scrapyard
parking
PLAZA
MUSIK EXPRESS
laundry / tailor
KIDDYLAND
school
CYBERWORLD ARCADE
clinic
residences
CAROUSEL
FUNHOUSE
residences
LOG FLUME
water purification
DEMON DROP
electricity / surveillance
GHOST HOUSE
ema's parts shop
GRAVITRON
thirteen's home
community kitchen
GAME ALLEY
marketplace
BUMPER BOATS
reservoir
DINING COURT
TUNNEL OF LOVE
hydroponics
AMPHITHEATRE
washrooms
FERRIS WHEEL
rotating cultivator
residences
OLD COASTER
rear gate
waste treatment
residences
recycling
BENNY'S
ORDELL FAIRE
WAREHOUSE DISTRICT
AVOID
ONIDA
SIOUX
POSSIBLE EXC SITES
BADLANDS
FLIN LANDFILL
FLIN
SCAVENGE LANDS (UNINHABITED)
DRY
reference scavenge map ID:26

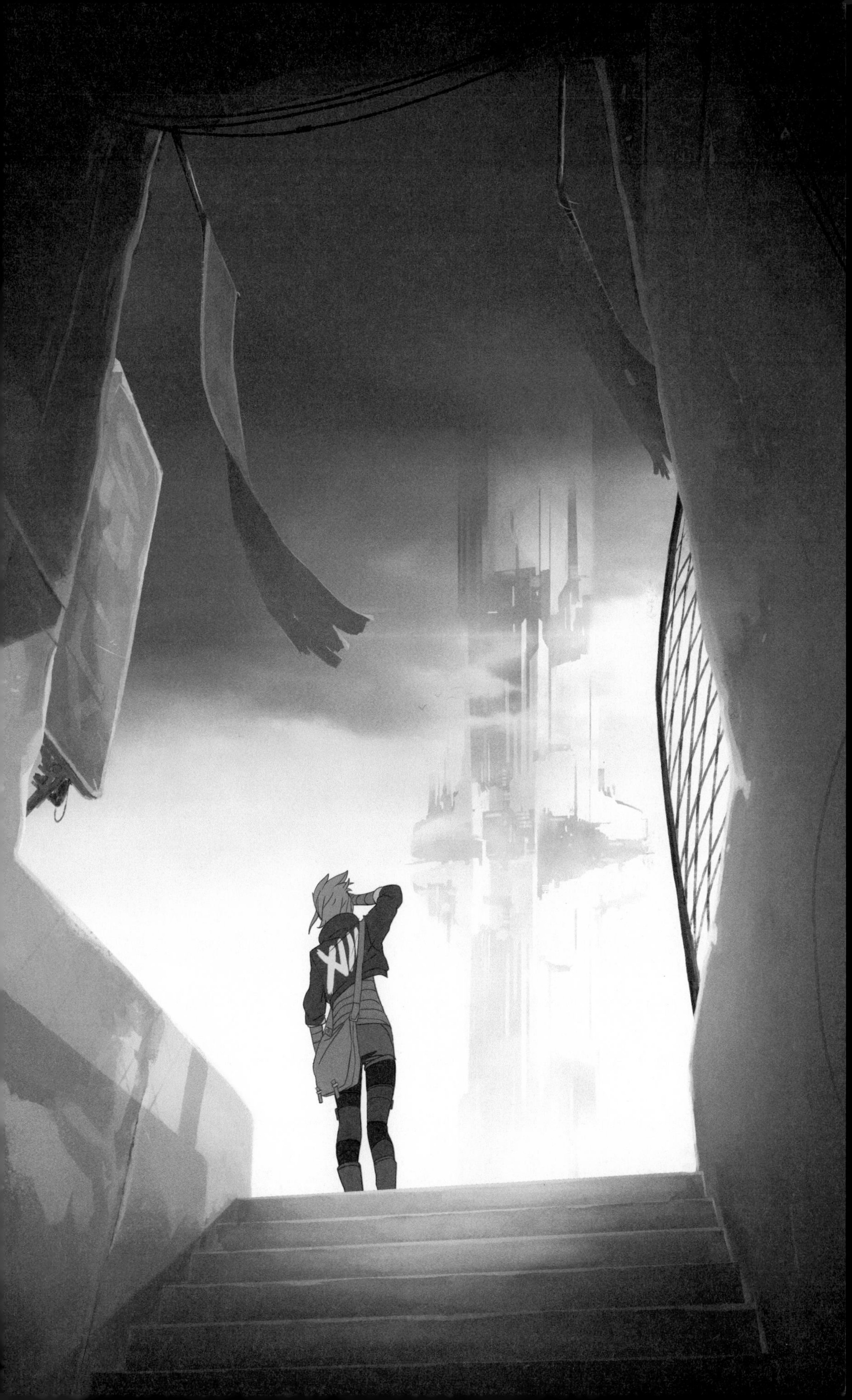

CHAPTER ONE
ONIDA

STORY
ROB SHERIDAN

ART
BARNABY BAGENDA

COLORS
ROMULO FAJARDO JR.

LETTERING
NATE PIEKOS OF BLAMBOT®

COVER
GUILLAUME OSPITAL

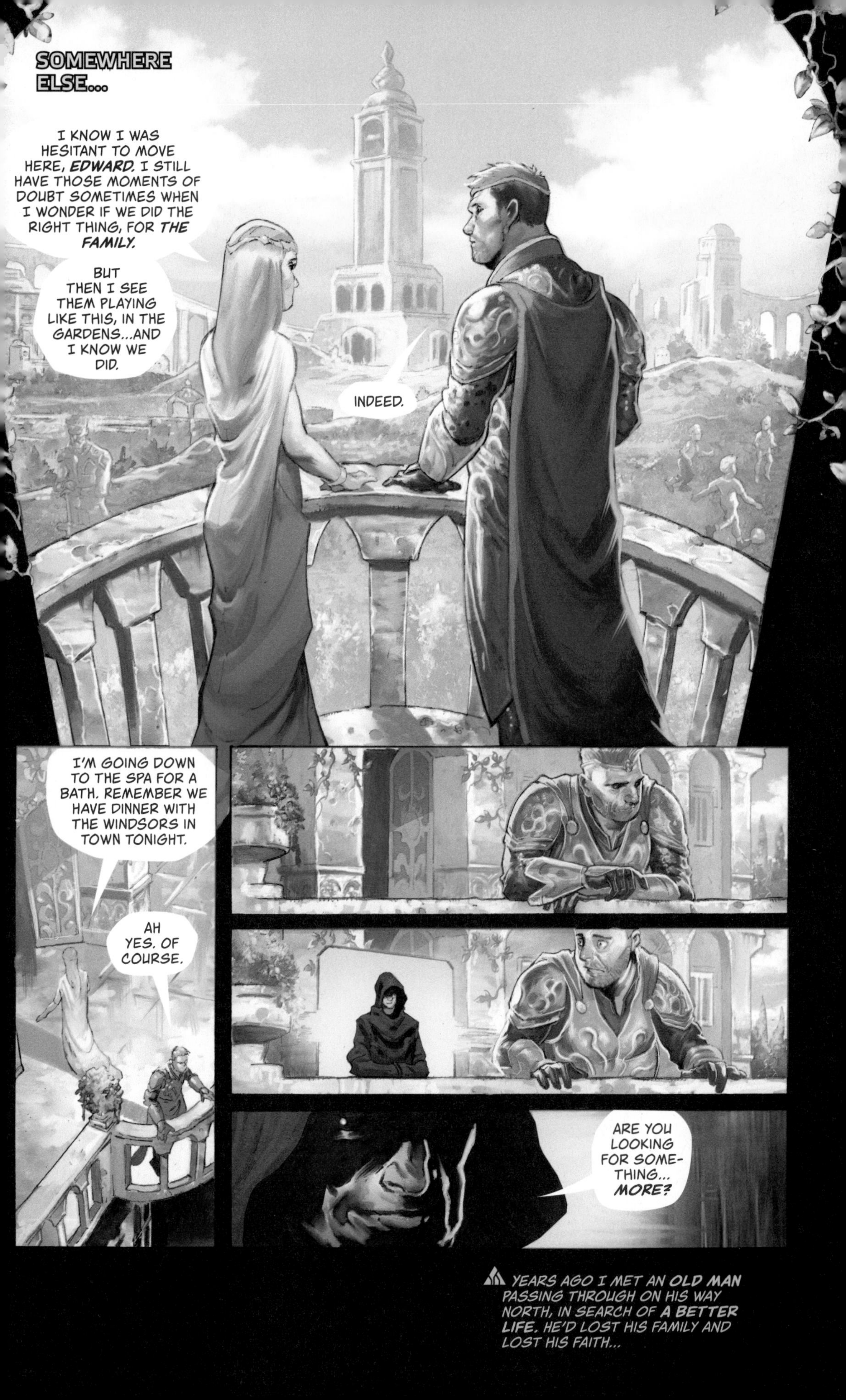
SOMEWHERE ELSE...
I KNOW I WAS HESITANT TO MOVE HERE, EDWARD. I STILL HAVE THOSE MOMENTS OF DOUBT SOMETIMES WHEN I WONDER IF WE DID THE RIGHT THING, FOR THE FAMILY.
BUT THEN I SEE THEM PLAYING LIKE THIS, IN THE GARDENS...AND I KNOW WE DID.
INDEED.
I'M GOING DOWN TO THE SPA FOR A BATH. REMEMBER WE HAVE DINNER WITH THE WINDSORS IN TOWN TONIGHT.
AH YES. OF COURSE.
ARE YOU LOOKING FOR SOME-THING... MORE?
YEARS AGO I MET AN OLD MAN PASSING THROUGH ON HIS WAY NORTH, IN SEARCH OF A BETTER LIFE. HE'D LOST HIS FAMILY AND LOST HIS FAITH...

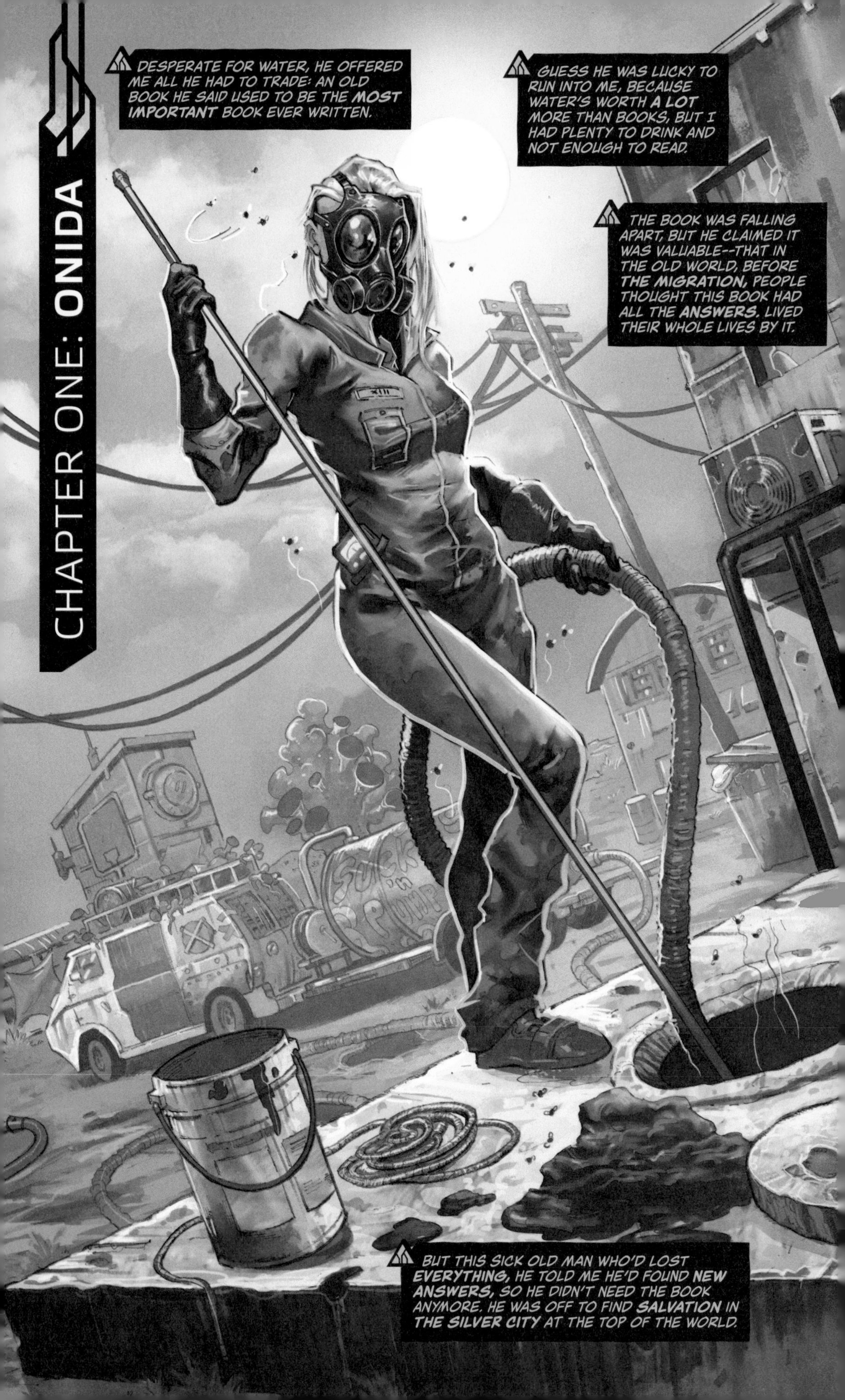
CHAPTER ONE: ONIDA
DESPERATE FOR WATER, HE OFFERED ME ALL HE HAD TO TRADE: AN OLD BOOK HE SAID USED TO BE THE **MOST IMPORTANT** BOOK EVER WRITTEN.
GUESS HE WAS LUCKY TO RUN INTO ME, BECAUSE WATER'S WORTH **A LOT** MORE THAN BOOKS, BUT I HAD PLENTY TO DRINK AND NOT ENOUGH TO READ.
THE BOOK WAS FALLING APART, BUT HE CLAIMED IT WAS VALUABLE--THAT IN THE OLD WORLD, BEFORE **THE MIGRATION,** PEOPLE THOUGHT THIS BOOK HAD ALL THE **ANSWERS.** LIVED THEIR WHOLE LIVES BY IT.
BUT THIS SICK OLD MAN WHO'D LOST **EVERYTHING,** HE TOLD ME HE'D FOUND **NEW ANSWERS,** SO HE DIDN'T NEED THE BOOK ANYMORE. HE WAS OFF TO FIND **SALVATION** IN **THE SILVER CITY** AT THE TOP OF THE WORLD.

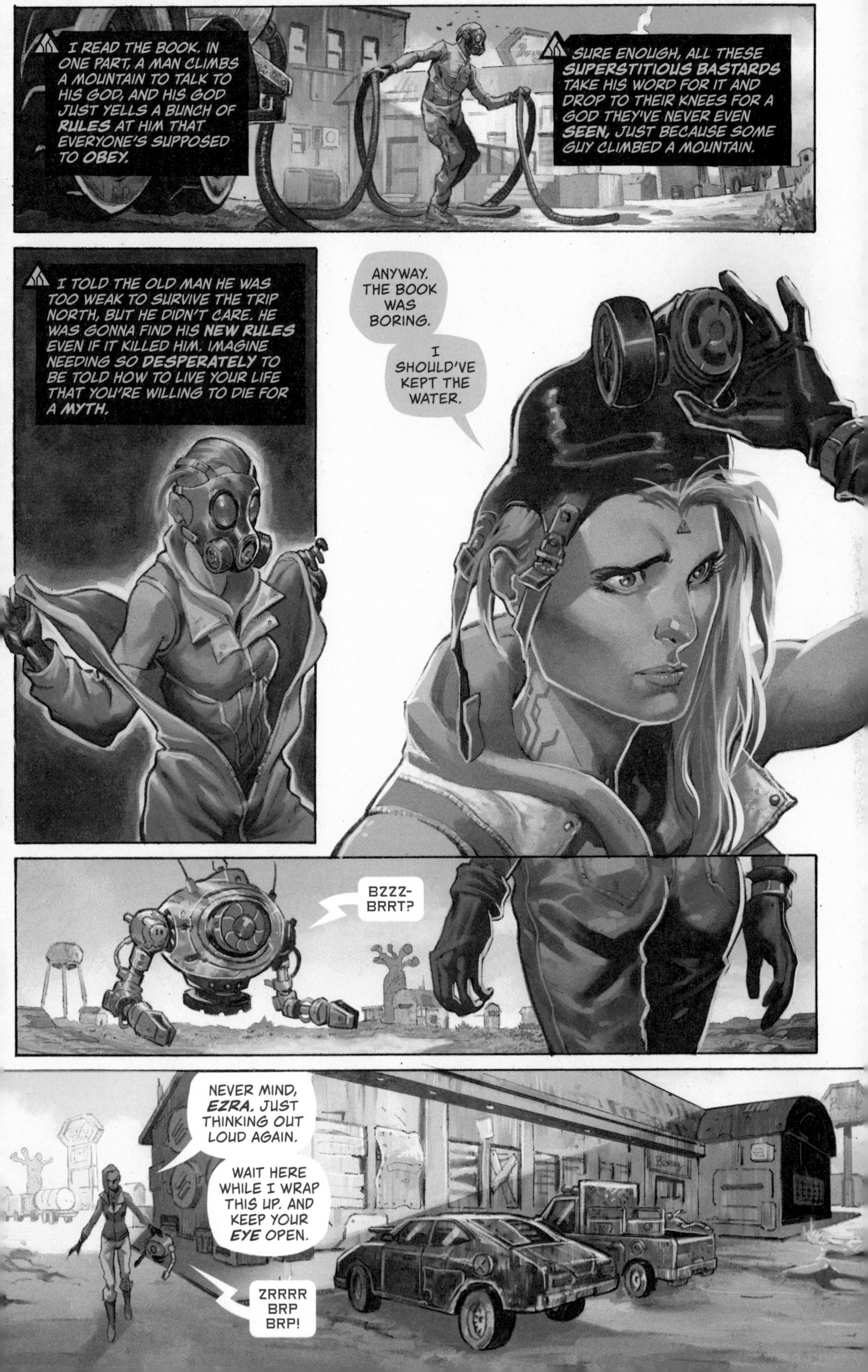
I READ THE BOOK. IN ONE PART, A MAN CLIMBS A MOUNTAIN TO TALK TO HIS GOD, AND HIS GOD JUST YELLS A BUNCH OF RULES AT HIM THAT EVERYONE'S SUPPOSED TO OBEY.
SURE ENOUGH, ALL THESE SUPERSTITIOUS BASTARDS TAKE HIS WORD FOR IT AND DROP TO THEIR KNEES FOR A GOD THEY'VE NEVER EVEN SEEN, JUST BECAUSE SOME GUY CLIMBED A MOUNTAIN.
I TOLD THE OLD MAN HE WAS TOO WEAK TO SURVIVE THE TRIP NORTH, BUT HE DIDN'T CARE. HE WAS GONNA FIND HIS NEW RULES EVEN IF IT KILLED HIM. IMAGINE NEEDING SO DESPERATELY TO BE TOLD HOW TO LIVE YOUR LIFE THAT YOU'RE WILLING TO DIE FOR A MYTH.
ANYWAY. THE BOOK WAS BORING.
I SHOULD'VE KEPT THE WATER.
BZZZ-BRRT?
NEVER MIND, EZRA. JUST THINKING OUT LOUD AGAIN.
WAIT HERE WHILE I WRAP THIS UP. AND KEEP YOUR EYE OPEN.
ZRRRR BRP BRP!

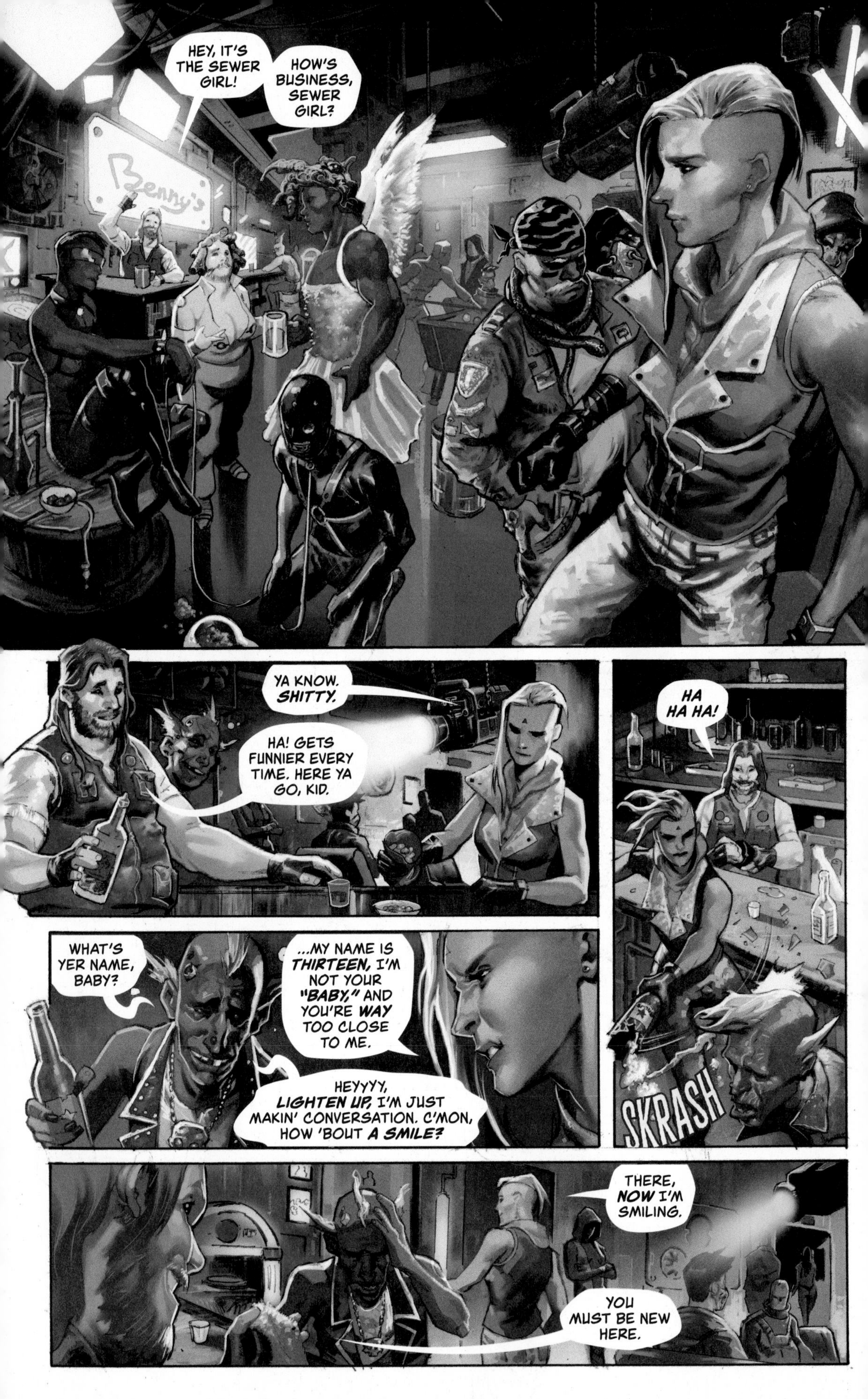

HEY, IT'S THE SEWER GIRL!
HOW'S BUSINESS, SEWER GIRL?
Benny's
YA KNOW. SHITTY.
HA! GETS FUNNIER EVERY TIME. HERE YA GO, KID.
HA HA HA!
WHAT'S YER NAME, BABY?
...MY NAME IS THIRTEEN, I'M NOT YOUR "BABY," AND YOU'RE WAY TOO CLOSE TO ME.
HEYYYY, LIGHTEN UP, I'M JUST MAKIN' CONVERSATION. C'MON, HOW 'BOUT A SMILE?
SKRASH
THERE, NOW I'M SMILING.
YOU MUST BE NEW HERE.

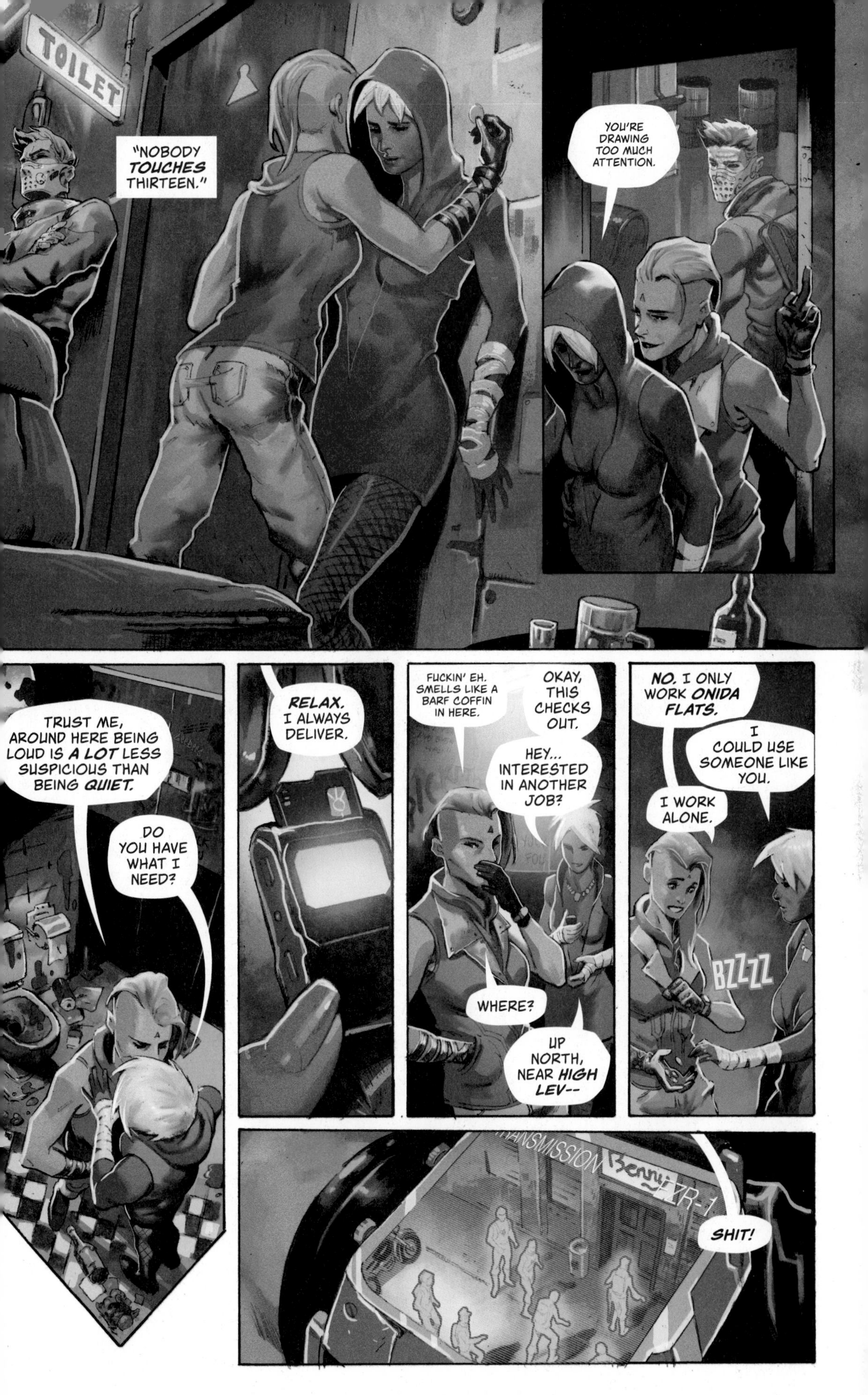
TOILET
"NOBODY TOUCHES THIRTEEN."
YOU'RE DRAWING TOO MUCH ATTENTION.
TRUST ME, AROUND HERE BEING LOUD IS A LOT LESS SUSPICIOUS THAN BEING QUIET.
DO YOU HAVE WHAT I NEED?
RELAX. I ALWAYS DELIVER.
FUCKIN' EH. SMELLS LIKE A BARF COFFIN IN HERE.
OKAY, THIS CHECKS OUT.
HEY... INTERESTED IN ANOTHER JOB?
WHERE?
UP NORTH, NEAR HIGH LEV--
NO. I ONLY WORK ONIDA FLATS.
I COULD USE SOMEONE LIKE YOU.
I WORK ALONE.
BZZZZ
TRANSMISSION
Benny
ZR-1
SHIT!

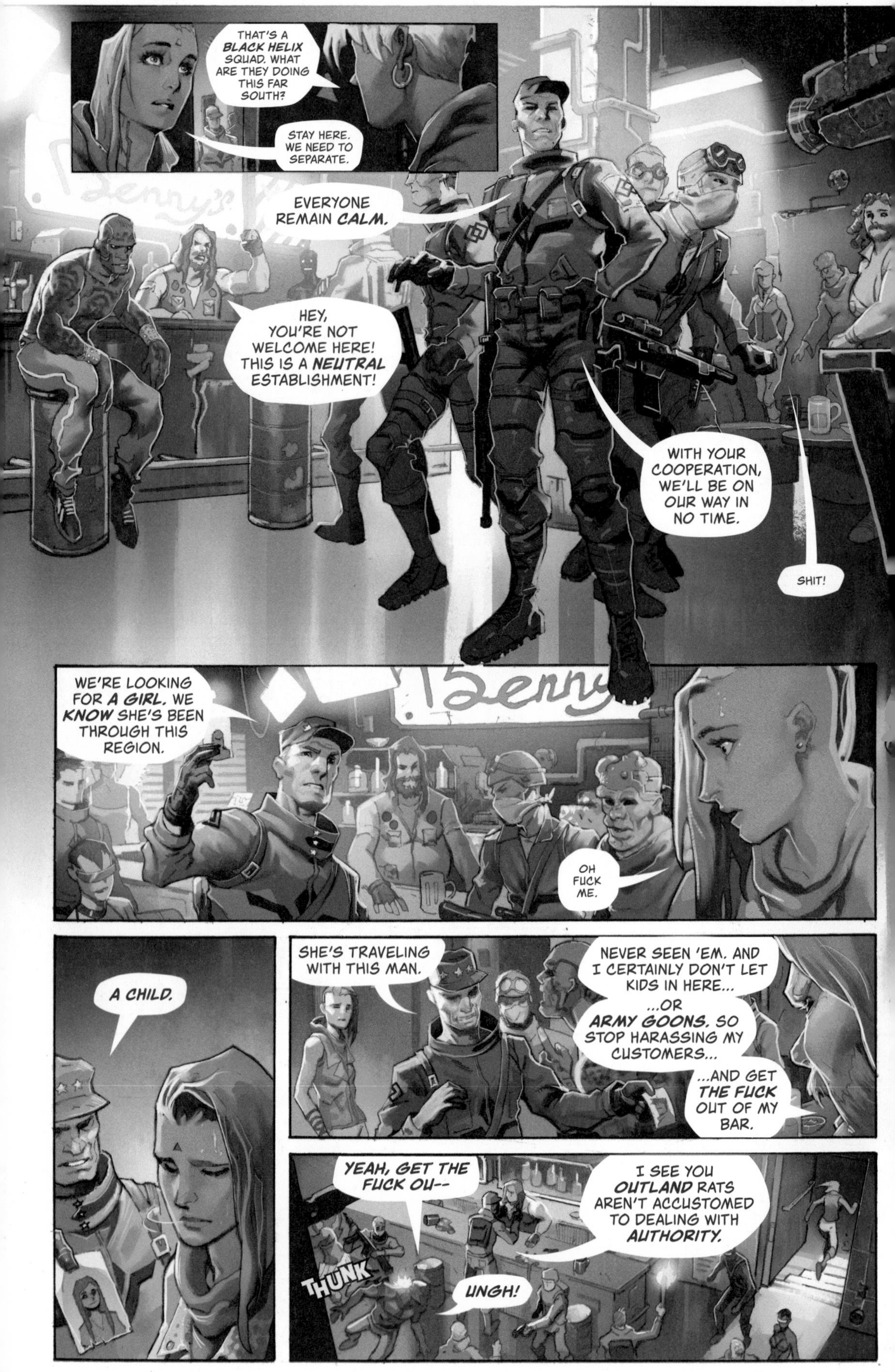
THAT'S A BLACK HELIX SQUAD. WHAT ARE THEY DOING THIS FAR SOUTH?
STAY HERE. WE NEED TO SEPARATE.
EVERYONE REMAIN CALM.
HEY, YOU'RE NOT WELCOME HERE! THIS IS A NEUTRAL ESTABLISHMENT!
WITH YOUR COOPERATION, WE'LL BE ON OUR WAY IN NO TIME.
SHIT!
WE'RE LOOKING FOR A GIRL. WE KNOW SHE'S BEEN THROUGH THIS REGION.
OH FUCK ME.
A CHILD.
SHE'S TRAVELING WITH THIS MAN.
NEVER SEEN 'EM. AND I CERTAINLY DON'T LET KIDS IN HERE...
...OR ARMY GOONS. SO STOP HARASSING MY CUSTOMERS...
...AND GET THE FUCK OUT OF MY BAR.
YEAH, GET THE FUCK OU--
THUNK
UNGH!
I SEE YOU OUTLAND RATS AREN'T ACCUSTOMED TO DEALING WITH AUTHORITY.

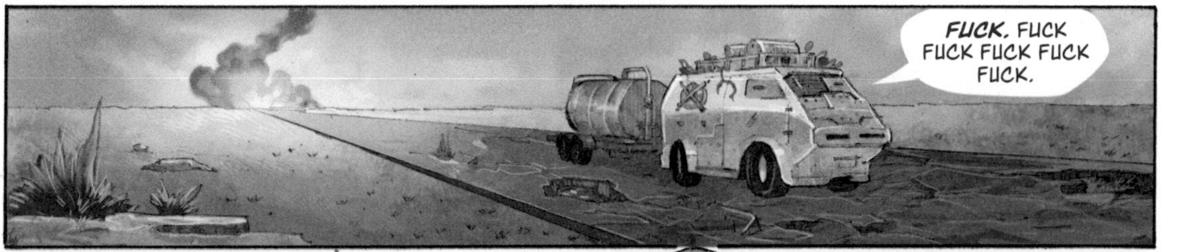
FUCK. FUCK FUCK FUCK FUCK FUCK.

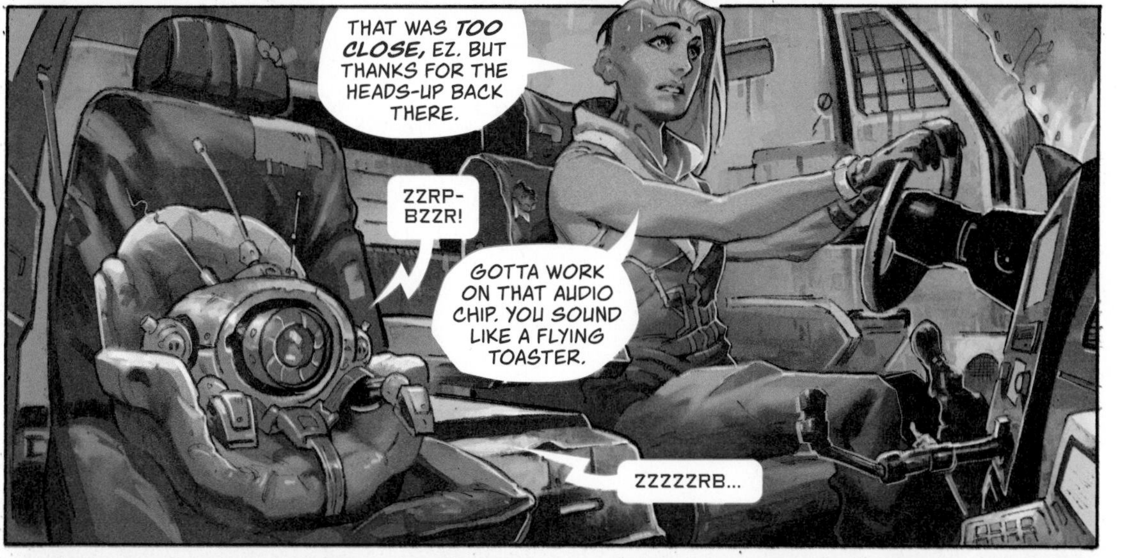
THAT WAS TOO CLOSE, EZ. BUT THANKS FOR THE HEADS-UP BACK THERE.
ZZRP-BZZR!
GOTTA WORK ON THAT AUDIO CHIP. YOU SOUND LIKE A FLYING TOASTER.
ZZZZZRB...

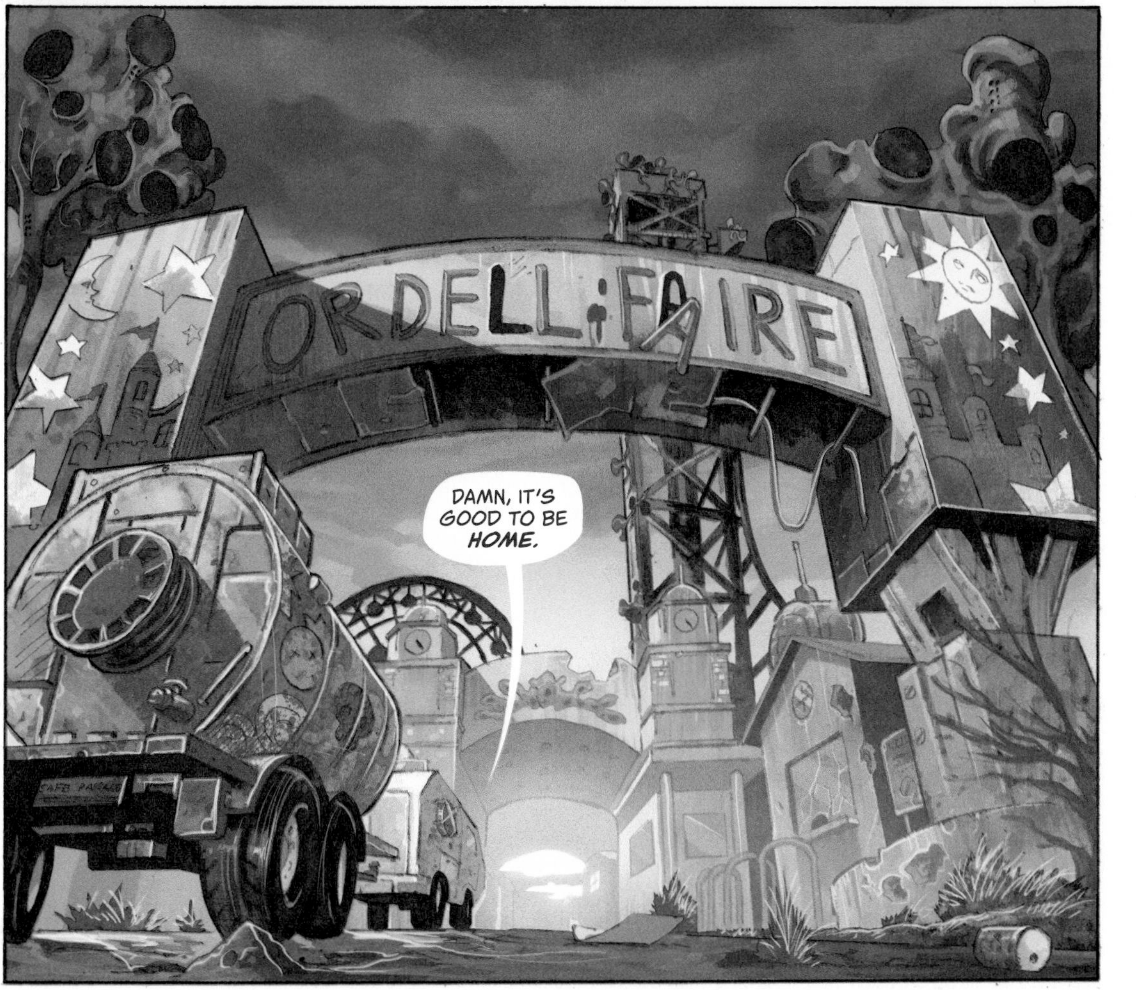
ORDELL FAIRE
DAMN, IT'S GOOD TO BE HOME.

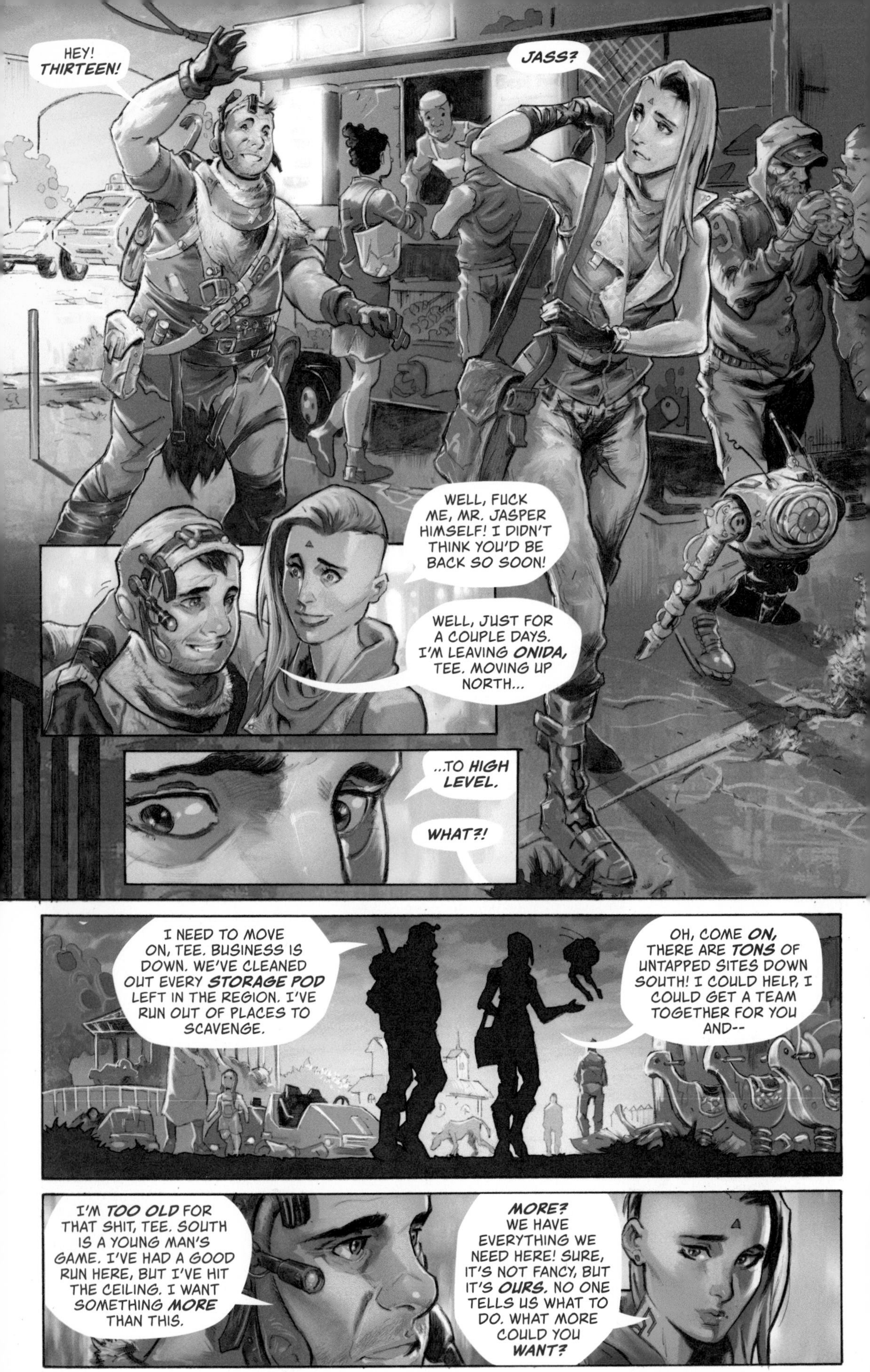
HEY! THIRTEEN!
JASS?
WELL, FUCK ME, MR. JASPER HIMSELF! I DIDN'T THINK YOU'D BE BACK SO SOON!
WELL, JUST FOR A COUPLE DAYS. I'M LEAVING ONIDA, TEE. MOVING UP NORTH...
...TO HIGH LEVEL.
WHAT?!
I NEED TO MOVE ON, TEE. BUSINESS IS DOWN. WE'VE CLEANED OUT EVERY STORAGE POD LEFT IN THE REGION. I'VE RUN OUT OF PLACES TO SCAVENGE.
OH, COME ON, THERE ARE TONS OF UNTAPPED SITES DOWN SOUTH! I COULD HELP, I COULD GET A TEAM TOGETHER FOR YOU AND--
I'M TOO OLD FOR THAT SHIT, TEE. SOUTH IS A YOUNG MAN'S GAME. I'VE HAD A GOOD RUN HERE, BUT I'VE HIT THE CEILING. I WANT SOMETHING MORE THAN THIS.
MORE? WE HAVE EVERYTHING WE NEED HERE! SURE, IT'S NOT FANCY, BUT IT'S OURS. NO ONE TELLS US WHAT TO DO. WHAT MORE COULD YOU WANT?

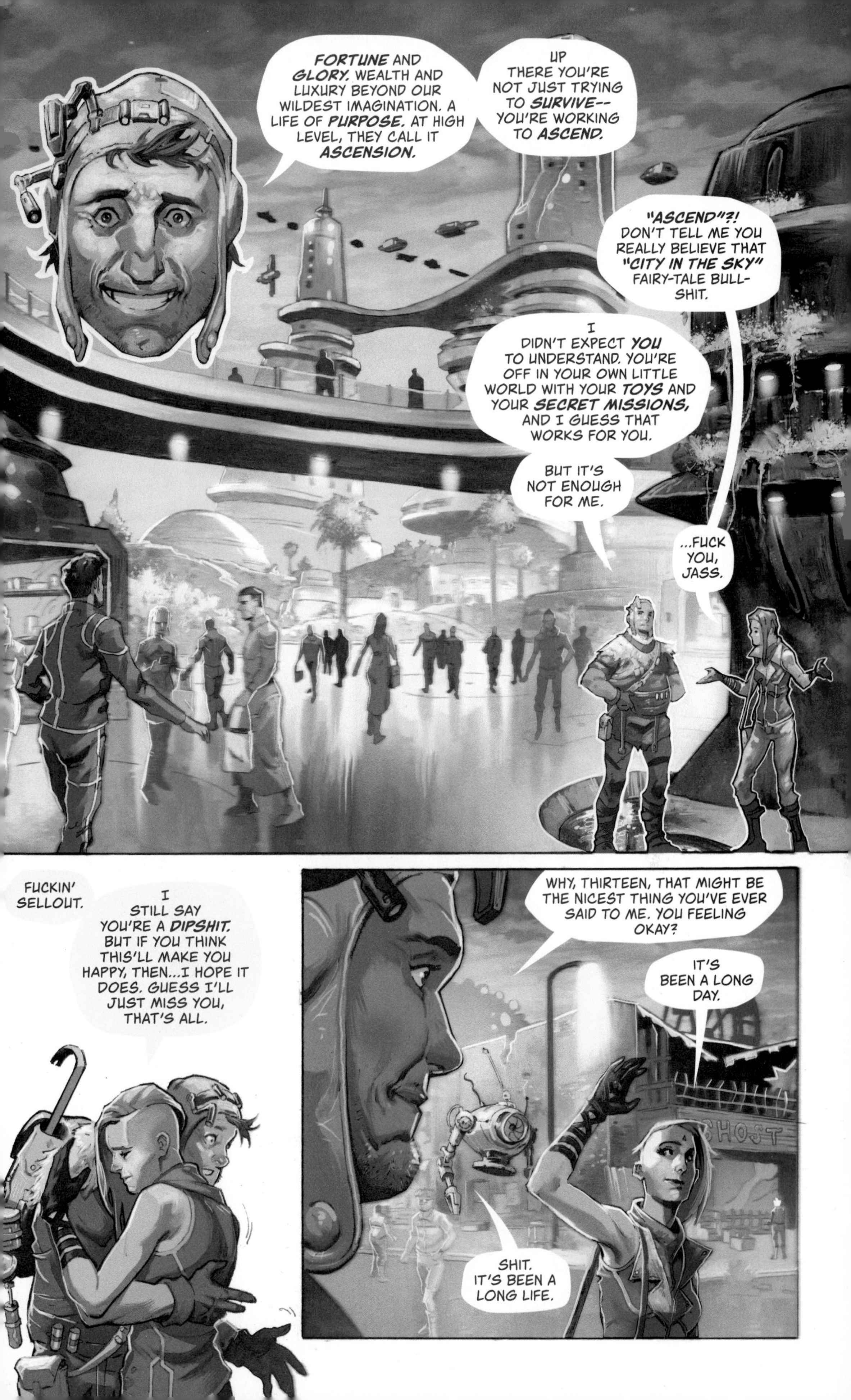
FORTUNE AND GLORY. WEALTH AND LUXURY BEYOND OUR WILDEST IMAGINATION. A LIFE OF PURPOSE. AT HIGH LEVEL, THEY CALL IT ASCENSION.
UP THERE YOU'RE NOT JUST TRYING TO SURVIVE-- YOU'RE WORKING TO ASCEND.
"ASCEND"?! DON'T TELL ME YOU REALLY BELIEVE THAT "CITY IN THE SKY" FAIRY-TALE BULL-SHIT.
I DIDN'T EXPECT YOU TO UNDERSTAND. YOU'RE OFF IN YOUR OWN LITTLE WORLD WITH YOUR TOYS AND YOUR SECRET MISSIONS, AND I GUESS THAT WORKS FOR YOU.
BUT IT'S NOT ENOUGH FOR ME.
...FUCK YOU, JASS.
FUCKIN' SELLOUT.
I STILL SAY YOU'RE A DIPSHIT. BUT IF YOU THINK THIS'LL MAKE YOU HAPPY, THEN...I HOPE IT DOES. GUESS I'LL JUST MISS YOU, THAT'S ALL.
WHY, THIRTEEN, THAT MIGHT BE THE NICEST THING YOU'VE EVER SAID TO ME. YOU FEELING OKAY?
IT'S BEEN A LONG DAY.
SHIT. IT'S BEEN A LONG LIFE.

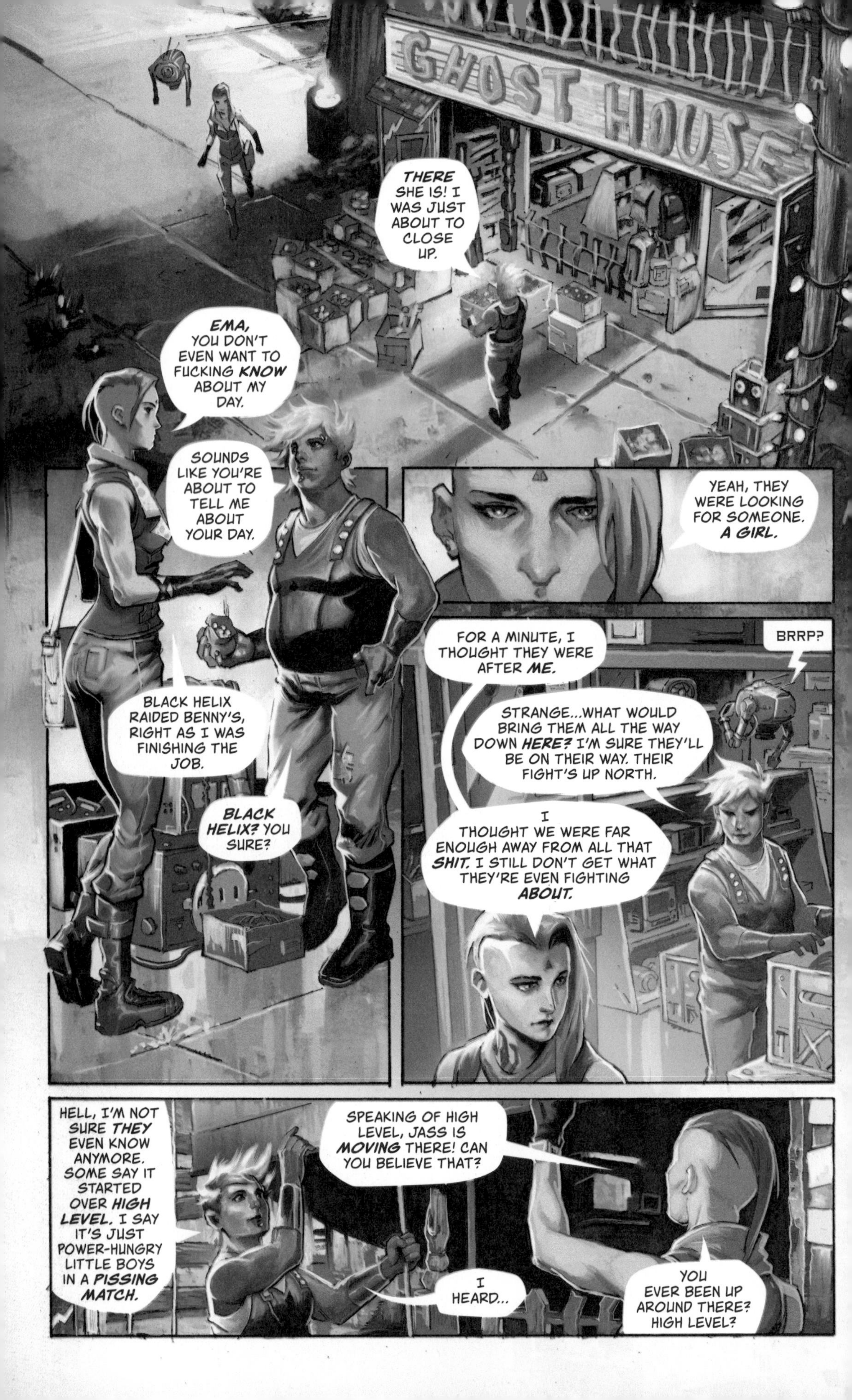
GHOST HOUSE
THERE SHE IS! I WAS JUST ABOUT TO CLOSE UP.
EMA, YOU DON'T EVEN WANT TO FUCKING KNOW ABOUT MY DAY.
SOUNDS LIKE YOU'RE ABOUT TO TELL ME ABOUT YOUR DAY.
BLACK HELIX RAIDED BENNY'S, RIGHT AS I WAS FINISHING THE JOB.
BLACK HELIX? YOU SURE?
YEAH, THEY WERE LOOKING FOR SOMEONE. A GIRL.
FOR A MINUTE, I THOUGHT THEY WERE AFTER ME.
BRRP?
STRANGE...WHAT WOULD BRING THEM ALL THE WAY DOWN HERE? I'M SURE THEY'LL BE ON THEIR WAY. THEIR FIGHT'S UP NORTH.
I THOUGHT WE WERE FAR ENOUGH AWAY FROM ALL THAT SHIT. I STILL DON'T GET WHAT THEY'RE EVEN FIGHTING ABOUT.
HELL, I'M NOT SURE THEY EVEN KNOW ANYMORE. SOME SAY IT STARTED OVER HIGH LEVEL. I SAY IT'S JUST POWER-HUNGRY LITTLE BOYS IN A PISSING MATCH.
SPEAKING OF HIGH LEVEL, JASS IS MOVING THERE! CAN YOU BELIEVE THAT?
I HEARD...
YOU EVER BEEN UP AROUND THERE? HIGH LEVEL?

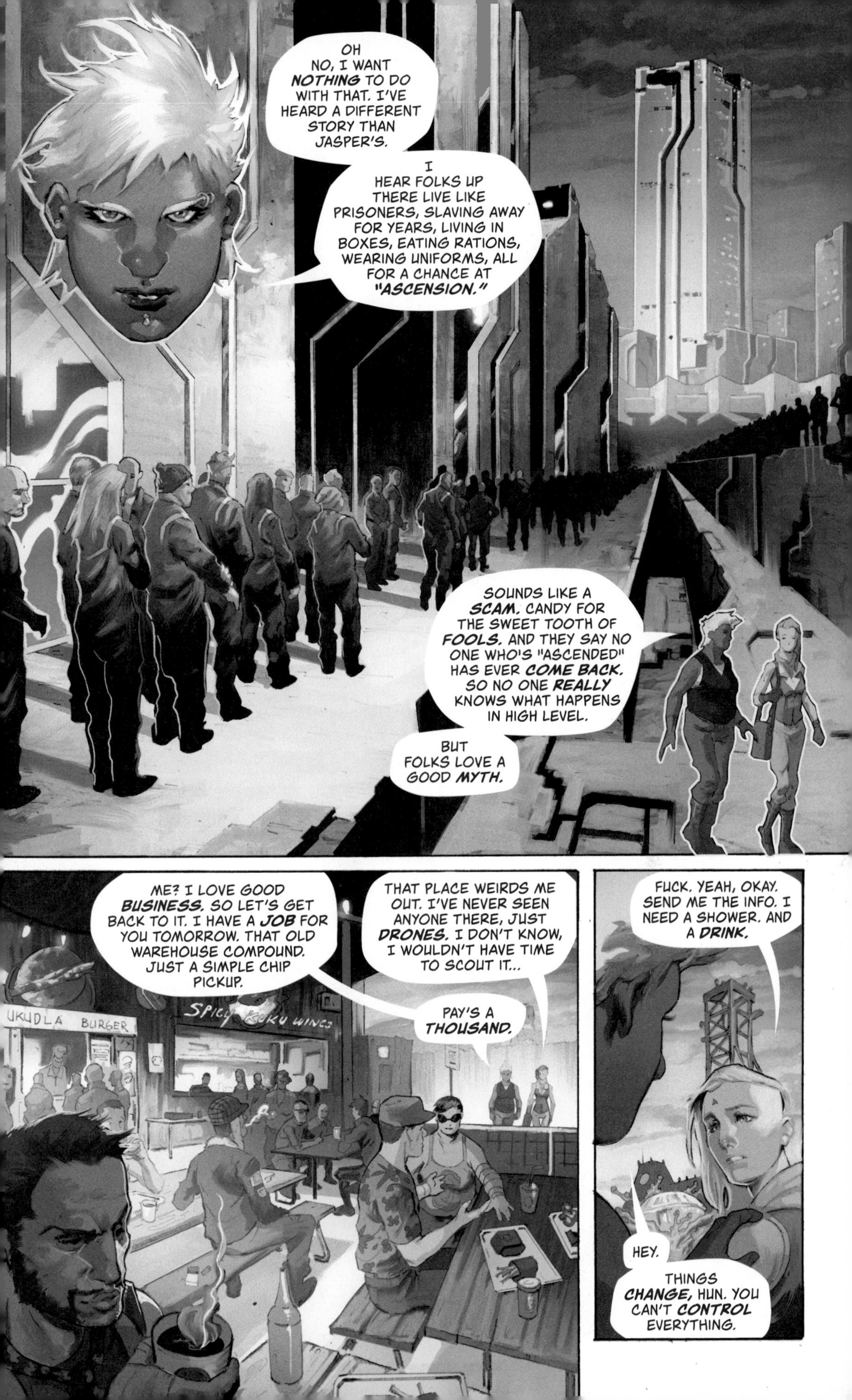
OH NO, I WANT NOTHING TO DO WITH THAT. I'VE HEARD A DIFFERENT STORY THAN JASPER'S.
I HEAR FOLKS UP THERE LIVE LIKE PRISONERS, SLAVING AWAY FOR YEARS, LIVING IN BOXES, EATING RATIONS, WEARING UNIFORMS, ALL FOR A CHANCE AT "ASCENSION."
SOUNDS LIKE A SCAM. CANDY FOR THE SWEET TOOTH OF FOOLS. AND THEY SAY NO ONE WHO'S "ASCENDED" HAS EVER COME BACK. SO NO ONE REALLY KNOWS WHAT HAPPENS IN HIGH LEVEL.
BUT FOLKS LOVE A GOOD MYTH.
ME? I LOVE GOOD BUSINESS. SO LET'S GET BACK TO IT. I HAVE A JOB FOR YOU TOMORROW. THAT OLD WAREHOUSE COMPOUND. JUST A SIMPLE CHIP PICKUP.
THAT PLACE WEIRDS ME OUT. I'VE NEVER SEEN ANYONE THERE, JUST DRONES. I DON'T KNOW, I WOULDN'T HAVE TIME TO SCOUT IT...
PAY'S A THOUSAND.
UKUDLA BURGER
SPICY KUKU WINGS
FUCK. YEAH, OKAY. SEND ME THE INFO. I NEED A SHOWER. AND A DRINK.
HEY.
THINGS CHANGE, HUN. YOU CAN'T CONTROL EVERYTHING.

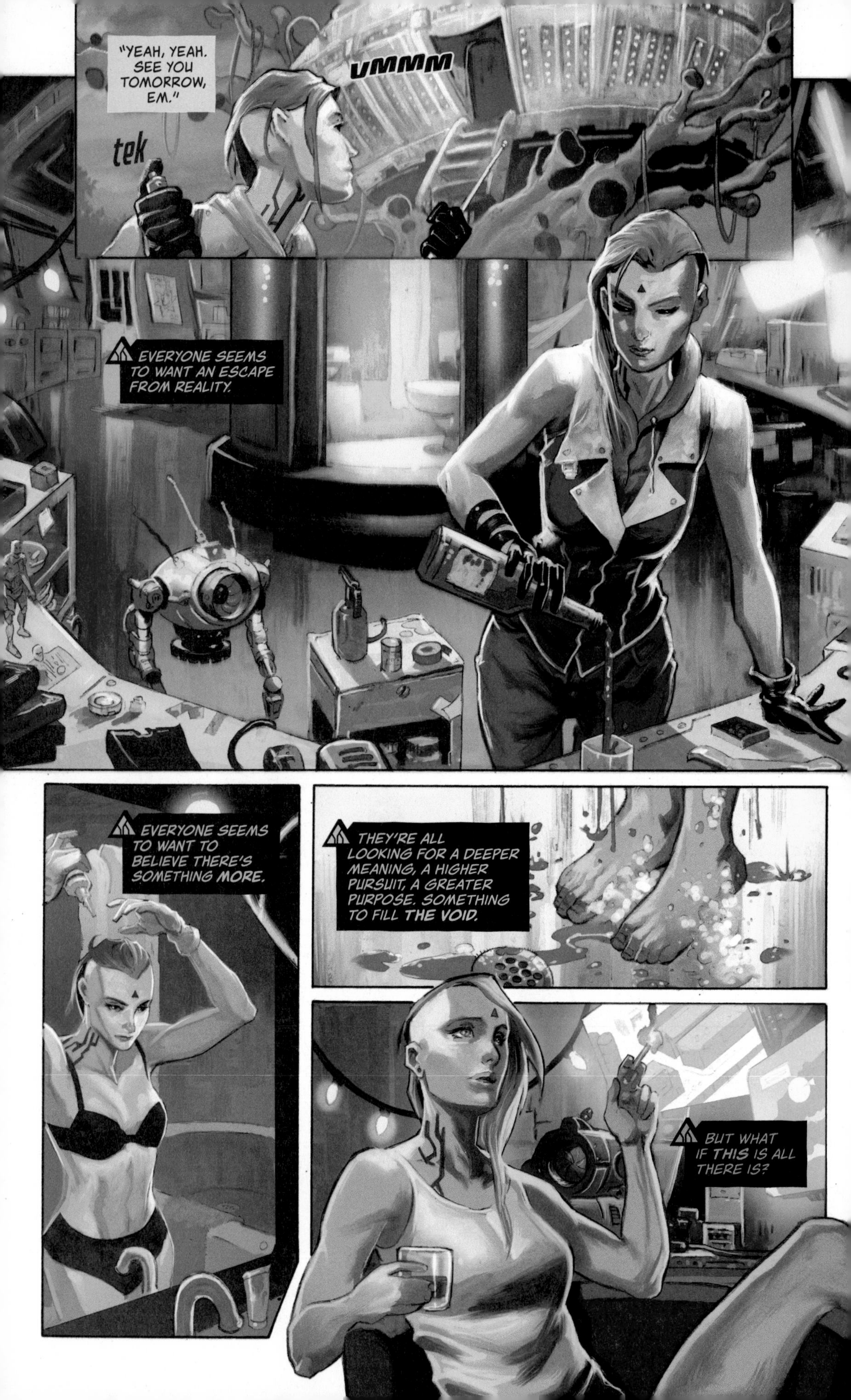
"YEAH, YEAH. SEE YOU TOMORROW, EM."
UMMM
tek
EVERYONE SEEMS TO WANT AN ESCAPE FROM REALITY.
EVERYONE SEEMS TO WANT TO BELIEVE THERE'S SOMETHING MORE.
THEY'RE ALL LOOKING FOR A DEEPER MEANING, A HIGHER PURSUIT, A GREATER PURPOSE. SOMETHING TO FILL THE VOID.
BUT WHAT IF THIS IS ALL THERE IS?

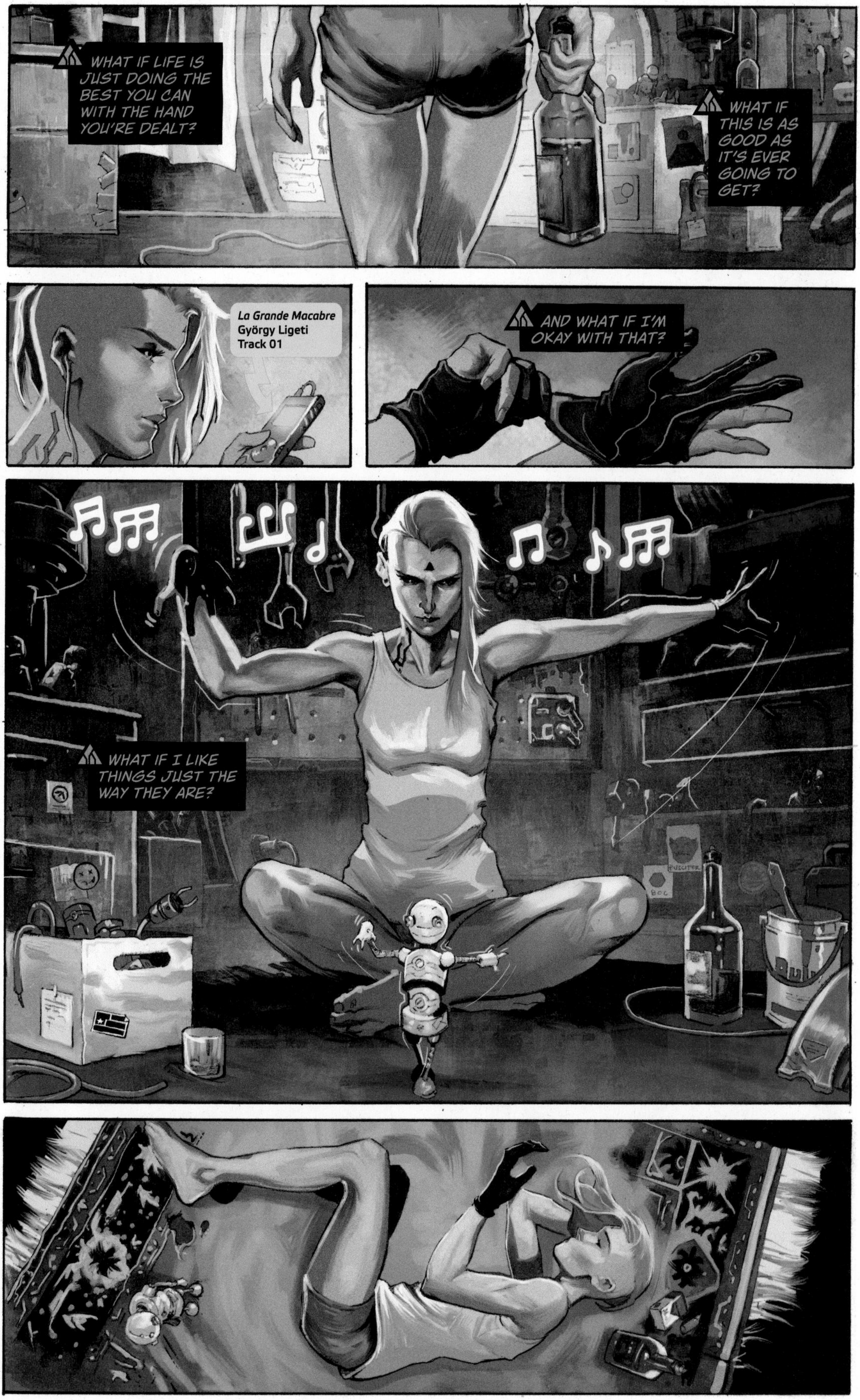
WHAT IF LIFE IS JUST DOING THE BEST YOU CAN WITH THE HAND YOU'RE DEALT?
WHAT IF THIS IS AS GOOD AS IT'S EVER GOING TO GET?
La Grande Macabre
György Ligeti
Track 01
AND WHAT IF I'M OKAY WITH THAT?
WHAT IF I LIKE THINGS JUST THE WAY THEY ARE?

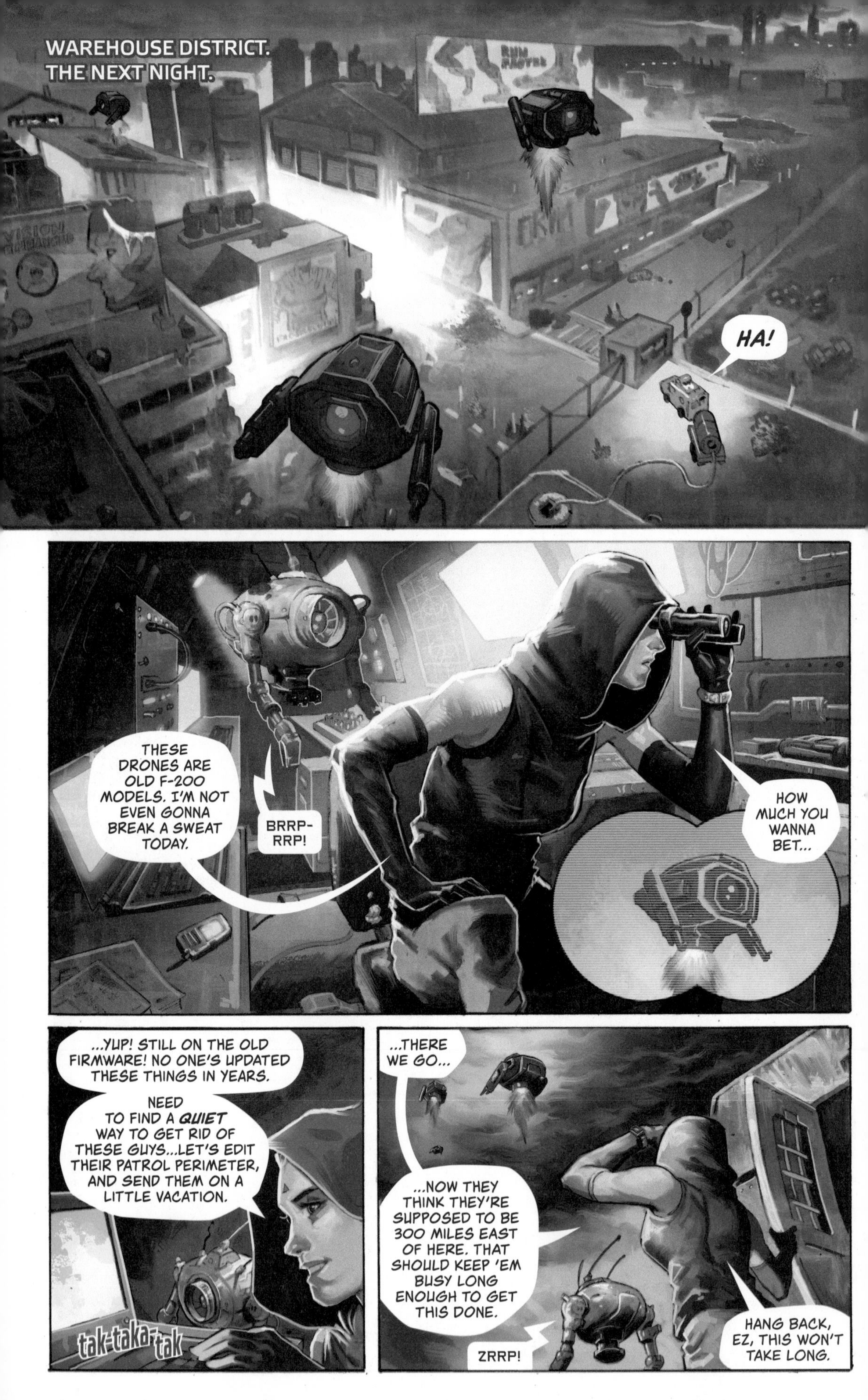
WAREHOUSE DISTRICT.
THE NEXT NIGHT.
HA!
THESE DRONES ARE OLD F-200 MODELS. I'M NOT EVEN GONNA BREAK A SWEAT TODAY.
BRRP-RRP!
HOW MUCH YOU WANNA BET...
...YUP! STILL ON THE OLD FIRMWARE! NO ONE'S UPDATED THESE THINGS IN YEARS.
NEED TO FIND A QUIET WAY TO GET RID OF THESE GUYS...LET'S EDIT THEIR PATROL PERIMETER, AND SEND THEM ON A LITTLE VACATION.
tak-taka-tak
...THERE WE GO...
...NOW THEY THINK THEY'RE SUPPOSED TO BE 300 MILES EAST OF HERE. THAT SHOULD KEEP 'EM BUSY LONG ENOUGH TO GET THIS DONE.
ZRRP!
HANG BACK, EZ, THIS WON'T TAKE LONG.

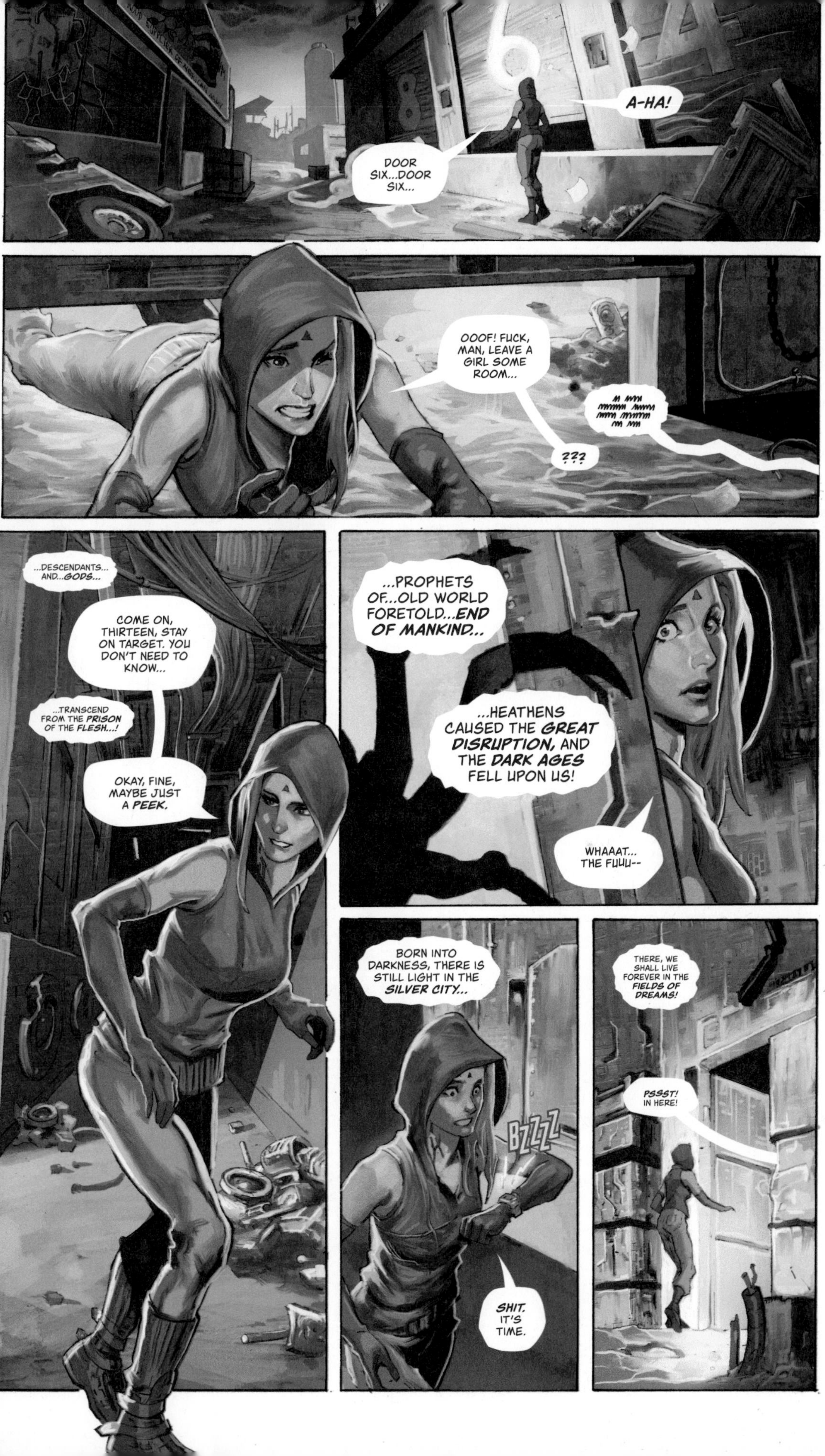
DOOR SIX...DOOR SIX...
A-HA!
OOOF! FUCK, MAN, LEAVE A GIRL SOME ROOM...
???
...DESCENDANTS... AND...GODS...
COME ON, THIRTEEN, STAY ON TARGET. YOU DON'T NEED TO KNOW...
...TRANSCEND FROM THE PRISON OF THE FLESH...!
OKAY, FINE, MAYBE JUST A PEEK.
...PROPHETS OF...OLD WORLD FORETOLD...END OF MANKIND...
...HEATHENS CAUSED THE GREAT DISRUPTION, AND THE DARK AGES FELL UPON US!
WHAAAT... THE FUUU--
BORN INTO DARKNESS, THERE IS STILL LIGHT IN THE SILVER CITY...
BZZZZ
SHIT. IT'S TIME.
THERE, WE SHALL LIVE FOREVER IN THE FIELDS OF DREAMS!
PSSST! IN HERE!

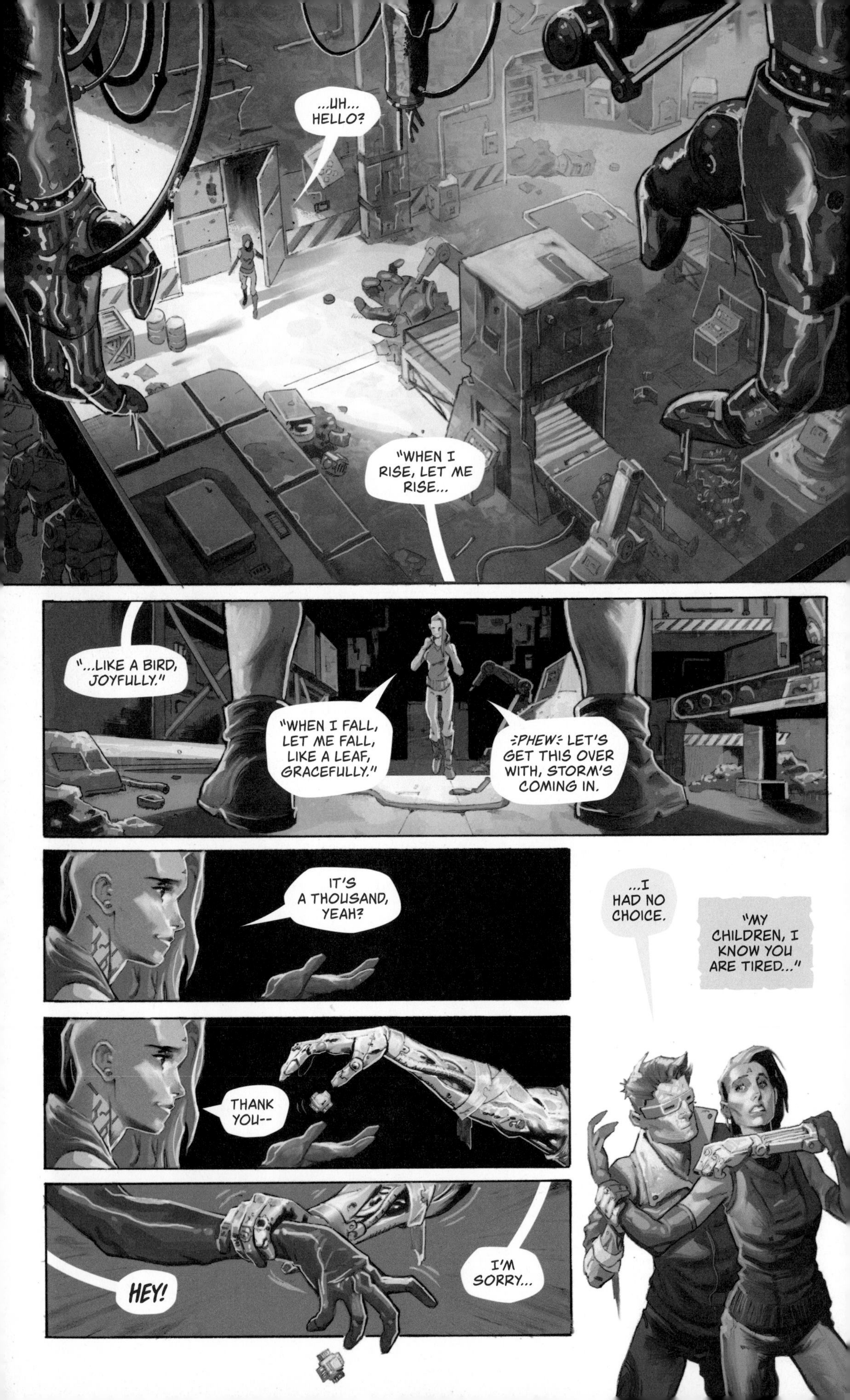
...UH... HELLO?
"WHEN I RISE, LET ME RISE...
"...LIKE A BIRD, JOYFULLY."
"WHEN I FALL, LET ME FALL, LIKE A LEAF, GRACEFULLY."
=PHEW= LET'S GET THIS OVER WITH, STORM'S COMING IN.
IT'S A THOUSAND, YEAH?
THANK YOU--
HEY!
I'M SORRY...
...I HAD NO CHOICE.
"MY CHILDREN, I KNOW YOU ARE TIRED..."

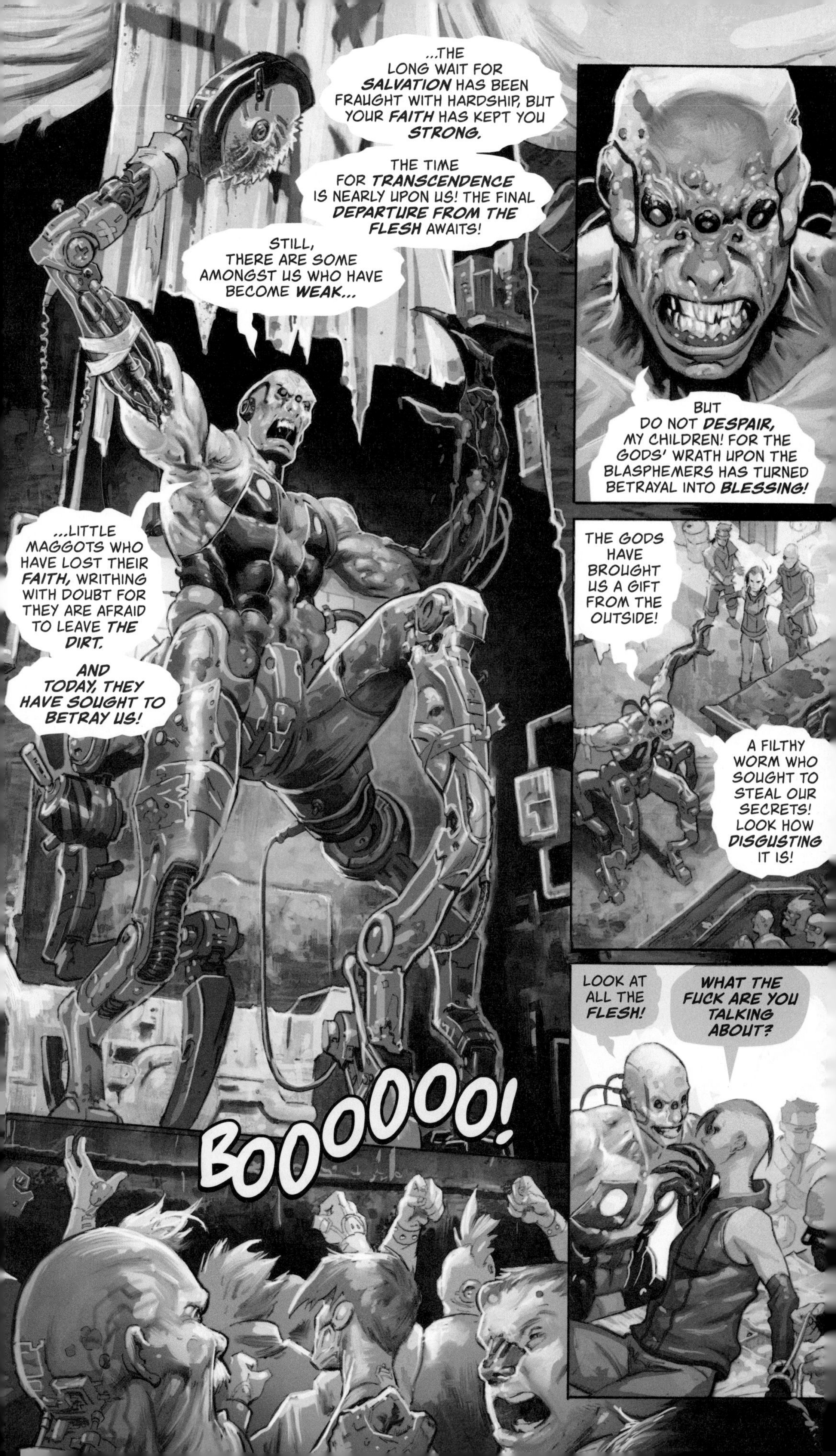
...THE LONG WAIT FOR SALVATION HAS BEEN FRAUGHT WITH HARDSHIP, BUT YOUR FAITH HAS KEPT YOU STRONG.
THE TIME FOR TRANSCENDENCE IS NEARLY UPON US! THE FINAL DEPARTURE FROM THE FLESH AWAITS!
STILL, THERE ARE SOME AMONGST US WHO HAVE BECOME WEAK...
...LITTLE MAGGOTS WHO HAVE LOST THEIR FAITH, WRITHING WITH DOUBT FOR THEY ARE AFRAID TO LEAVE THE DIRT.
AND TODAY, THEY HAVE SOUGHT TO BETRAY US!
BOOOOOO!
BUT DO NOT DESPAIR, MY CHILDREN! FOR THE GODS' WRATH UPON THE BLASPHEMERS HAS TURNED BETRAYAL INTO BLESSING!
THE GODS HAVE BROUGHT US A GIFT FROM THE OUTSIDE!
A FILTHY WORM WHO SOUGHT TO STEAL OUR SECRETS! LOOK HOW DISGUSTING IT IS!
LOOK AT ALL THE FLESH!
WHAT THE FUCK ARE YOU TALKING ABOUT?

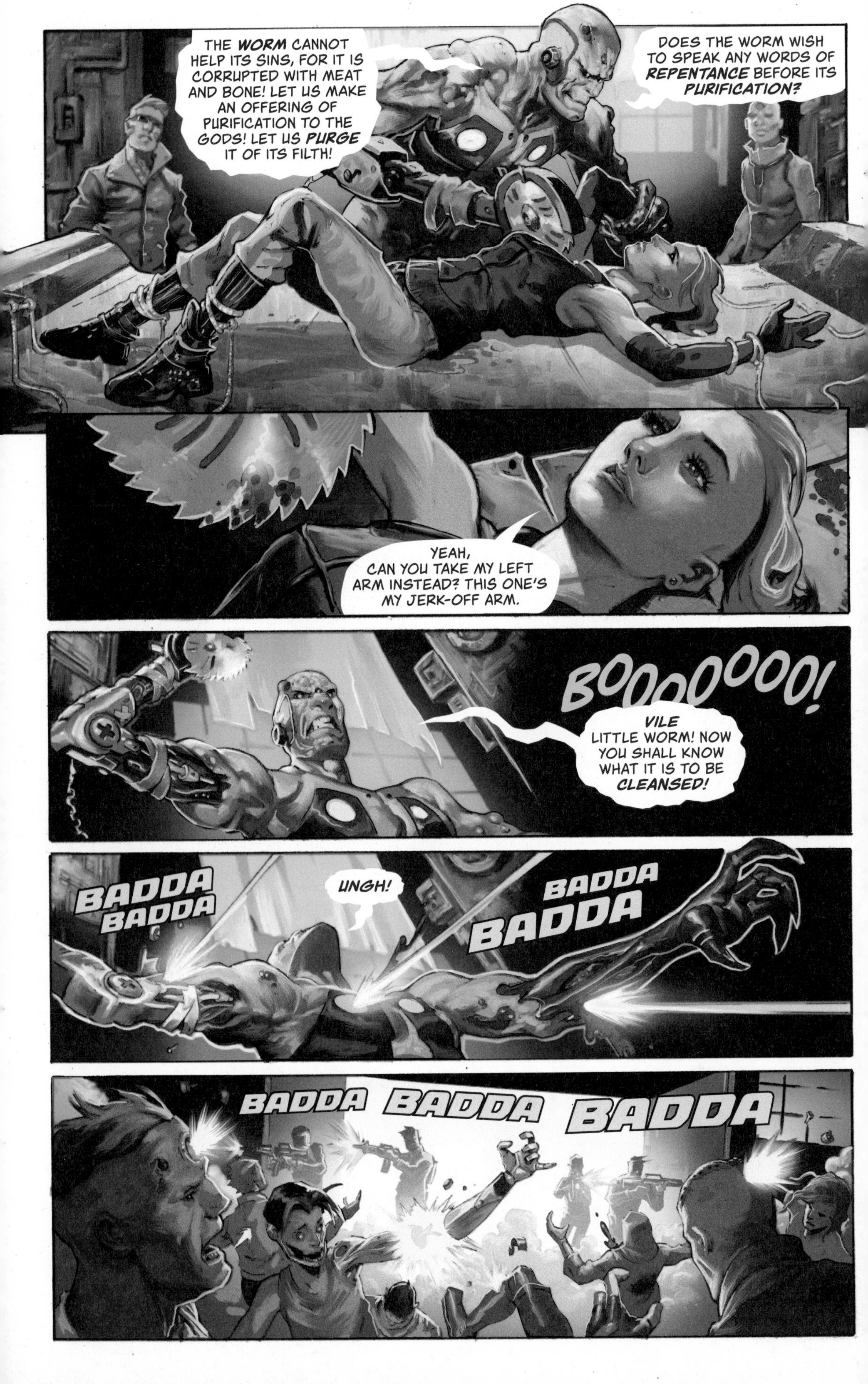
THE WORM CANNOT HELP ITS SINS, FOR IT IS CORRUPTED WITH MEAT AND BONE! LET US MAKE AN OFFERING OF PURIFICATION TO THE GODS! LET US PURGE IT OF ITS FILTH!
DOES THE WORM WISH TO SPEAK ANY WORDS OF REPENTANCE BEFORE ITS PURIFICATION?
YEAH, CAN YOU TAKE MY LEFT ARM INSTEAD? THIS ONE'S MY JERK-OFF ARM.
BOOOOOOO!
VILE LITTLE WORM! NOW YOU SHALL KNOW WHAT IT IS TO BE CLEANSED!
BADDA BADDA
UNGH!
BADDA BADDA
BADDA BADDA BADDA

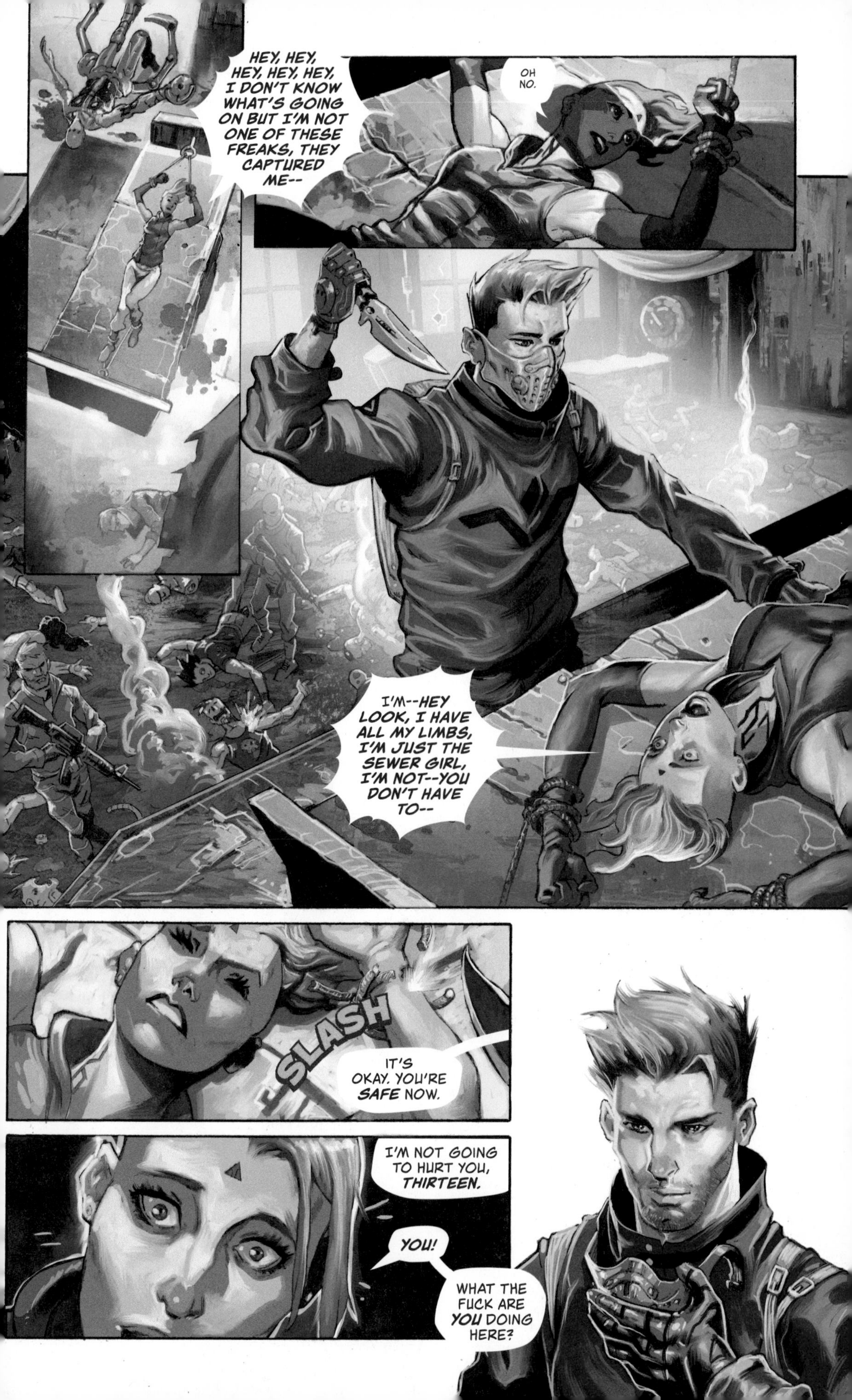
HEY, HEY, HEY, HEY, HEY, I DON'T KNOW WHAT'S GOING ON BUT I'M NOT ONE OF THESE FREAKS, THEY CAPTURED ME--
OH NO.
I'M--HEY LOOK, I HAVE ALL MY LIMBS, I'M JUST THE SEWER GIRL, I'M NOT--YOU DON'T HAVE TO--
SLASH
IT'S OKAY. YOU'RE SAFE NOW.
I'M NOT GOING TO HURT YOU, THIRTEEN.
YOU!
WHAT THE FUCK ARE YOU DOING HERE?

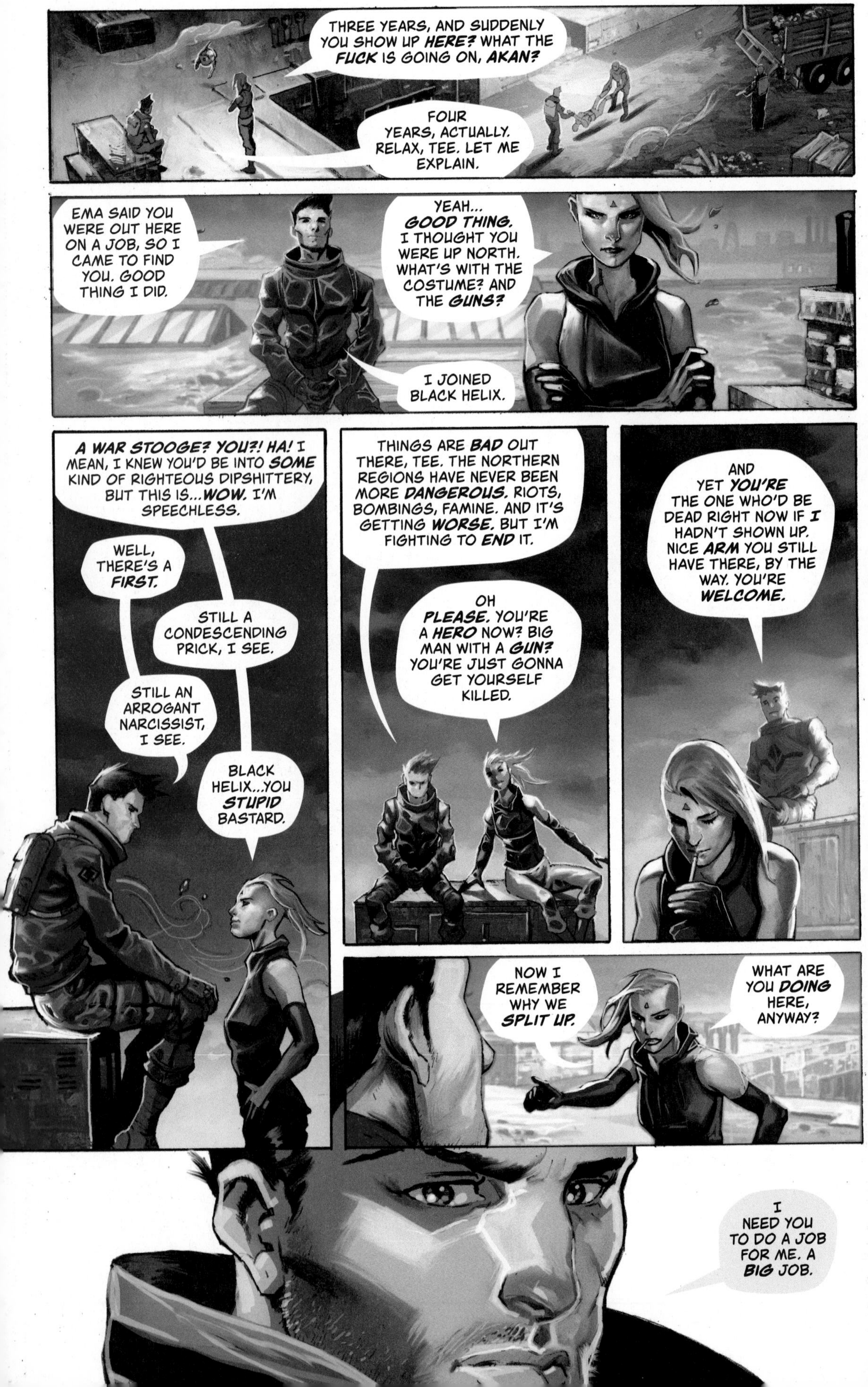
THREE YEARS, AND SUDDENLY YOU SHOW UP HERE? WHAT THE FUCK IS GOING ON, AKAN?
FOUR YEARS, ACTUALLY. RELAX, TEE. LET ME EXPLAIN.
EMA SAID YOU WERE OUT HERE ON A JOB, SO I CAME TO FIND YOU. GOOD THING I DID.
YEAH... GOOD THING. I THOUGHT YOU WERE UP NORTH. WHAT'S WITH THE COSTUME? AND THE GUNS?
I JOINED BLACK HELIX.
A WAR STOOGE? YOU?! HA! I MEAN, I KNEW YOU'D BE INTO SOME KIND OF RIGHTEOUS DIPSHITTERY, BUT THIS IS...WOW. I'M SPEECHLESS.
WELL, THERE'S A FIRST.
STILL A CONDESCENDING PRICK, I SEE.
STILL AN ARROGANT NARCISSIST, I SEE.
BLACK HELIX...YOU STUPID BASTARD.
THINGS ARE BAD OUT THERE, TEE. THE NORTHERN REGIONS HAVE NEVER BEEN MORE DANGEROUS. RIOTS, BOMBINGS, FAMINE. AND IT'S GETTING WORSE. BUT I'M FIGHTING TO END IT.
OH PLEASE. YOU'RE A HERO NOW? BIG MAN WITH A GUN? YOU'RE JUST GONNA GET YOURSELF KILLED.
AND YET YOU'RE THE ONE WHO'D BE DEAD RIGHT NOW IF I HADN'T SHOWN UP. NICE ARM YOU STILL HAVE THERE, BY THE WAY. YOU'RE WELCOME.
NOW I REMEMBER WHY WE SPLIT UP.
WHAT ARE YOU DOING HERE, ANYWAY?
I NEED YOU TO DO A JOB FOR ME. A BIG JOB.

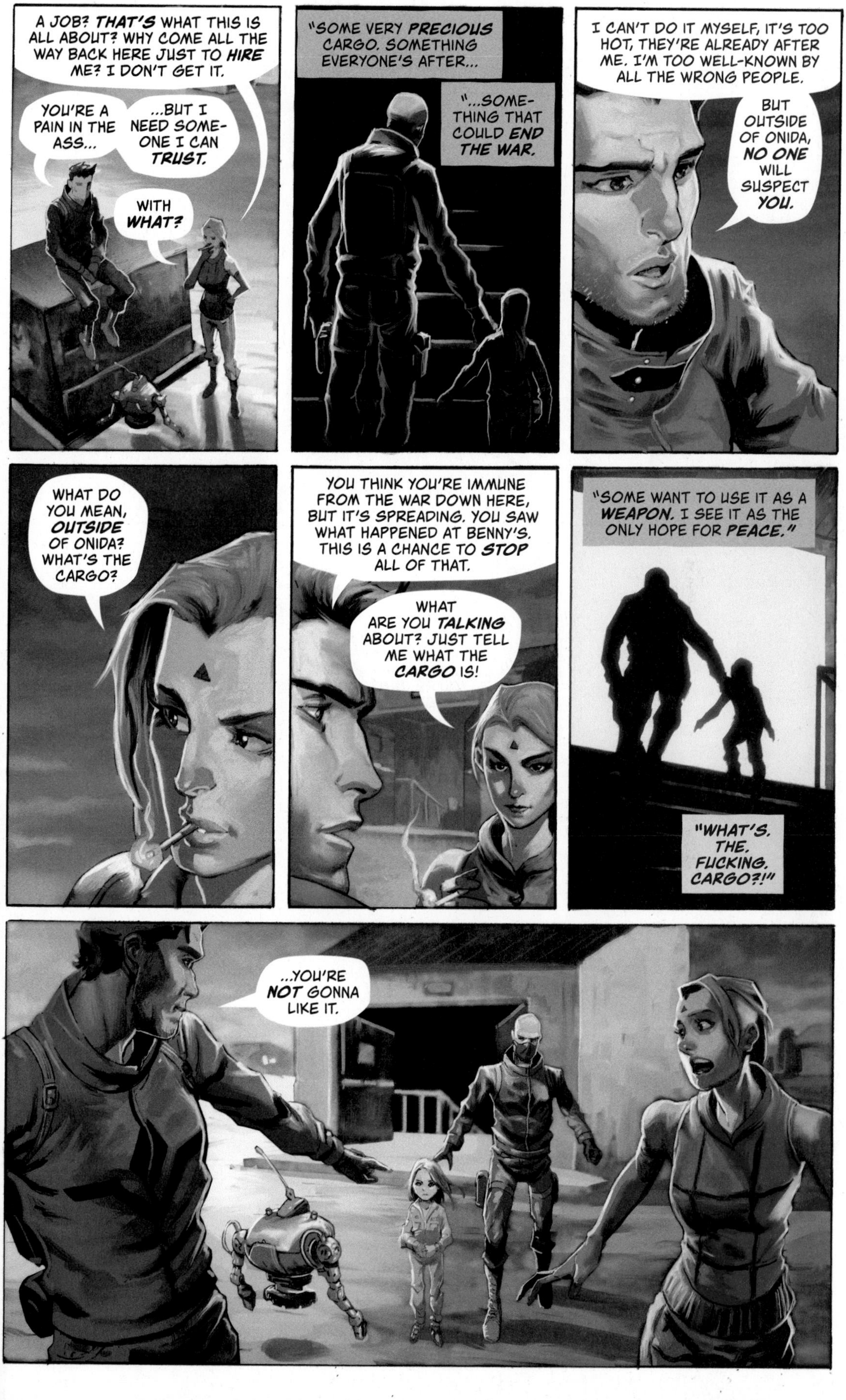
A JOB? THAT'S WHAT THIS IS ALL ABOUT? WHY COME ALL THE WAY BACK HERE JUST TO HIRE ME? I DON'T GET IT.
YOU'RE A PAIN IN THE ASS...
...BUT I NEED SOMEONE I CAN TRUST.
WITH WHAT?
"SOME VERY PRECIOUS CARGO. SOMETHING EVERYONE'S AFTER...
"...SOMETHING THAT COULD END THE WAR.
I CAN'T DO IT MYSELF, IT'S TOO HOT, THEY'RE ALREADY AFTER ME. I'M TOO WELL-KNOWN BY ALL THE WRONG PEOPLE.
BUT OUTSIDE OF ONIDA, NO ONE WILL SUSPECT YOU.
WHAT DO YOU MEAN, OUTSIDE OF ONIDA? WHAT'S THE CARGO?
YOU THINK YOU'RE IMMUNE FROM THE WAR DOWN HERE, BUT IT'S SPREADING. YOU SAW WHAT HAPPENED AT BENNY'S. THIS IS A CHANCE TO STOP ALL OF THAT.
WHAT ARE YOU TALKING ABOUT? JUST TELL ME WHAT THE CARGO IS!
"SOME WANT TO USE IT AS A WEAPON. I SEE IT AS THE ONLY HOPE FOR PEACE."
"WHAT'S. THE. FUCKING. CARGO?!"
...YOU'RE NOT GONNA LIKE IT.

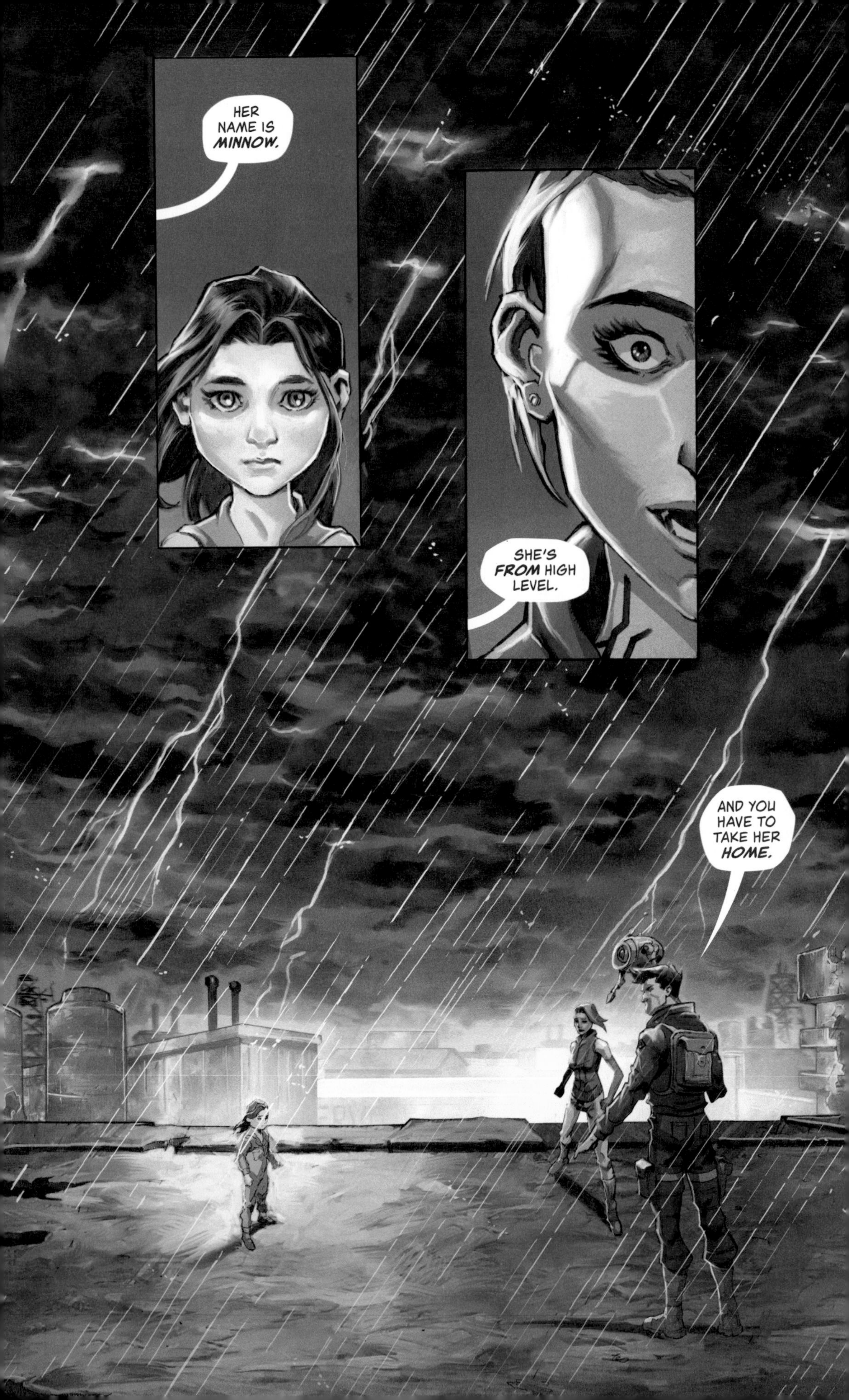
HER NAME IS MINNOW.
SHE'S FROM HIGH LEVEL.
AND YOU HAVE TO TAKE HER HOME.

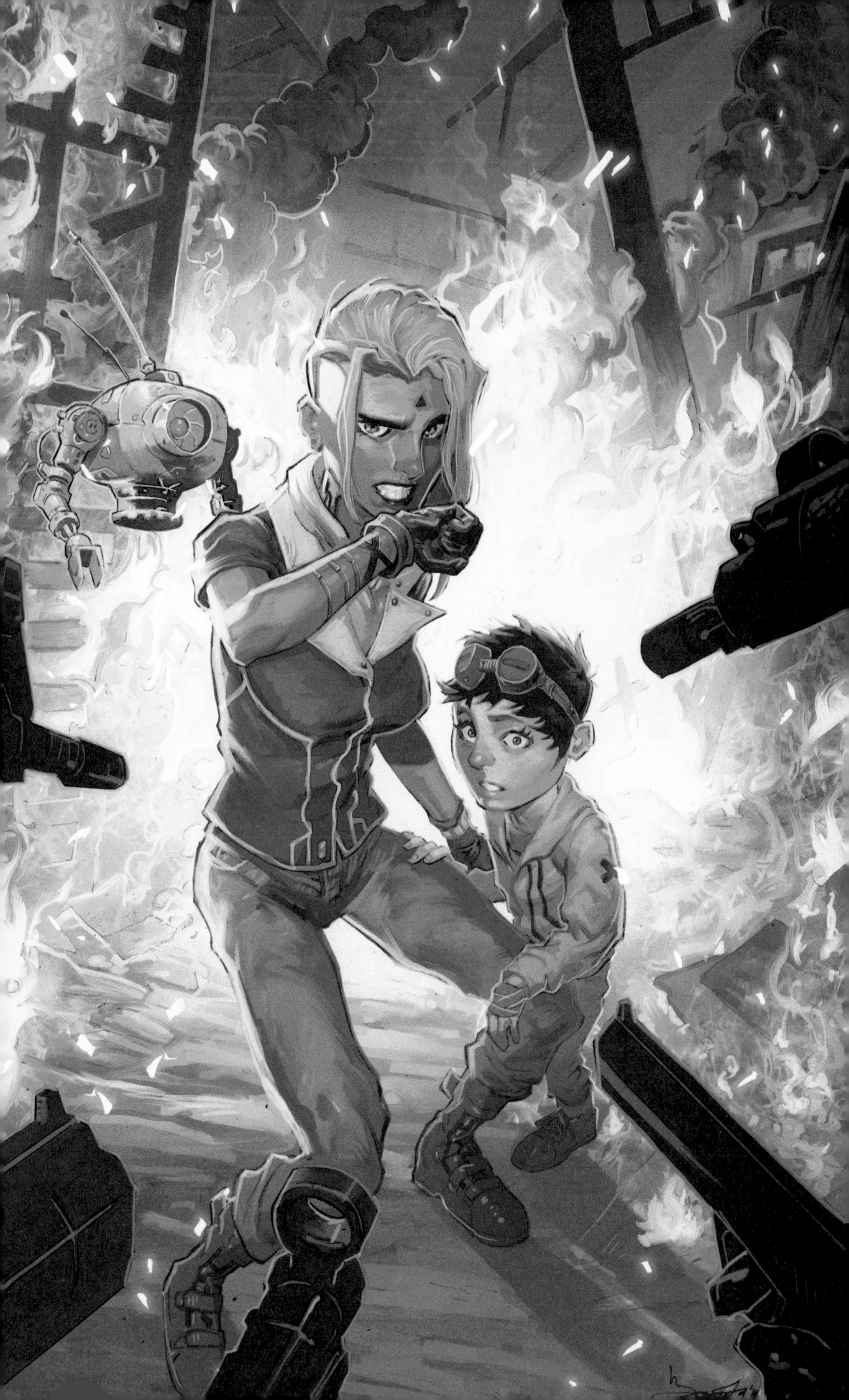

CHAPTER TWO
MINNOW

STORY
ROB SHERIDAN

ART
BARNABY BAGENDA

COLORS
ROMULO FAJARDO JR.

LETTERING
NATE PIEKOS OF BLAMBOT®

COVER
BARNABY BAGENDA AND ROMULO FAJARDO JR.

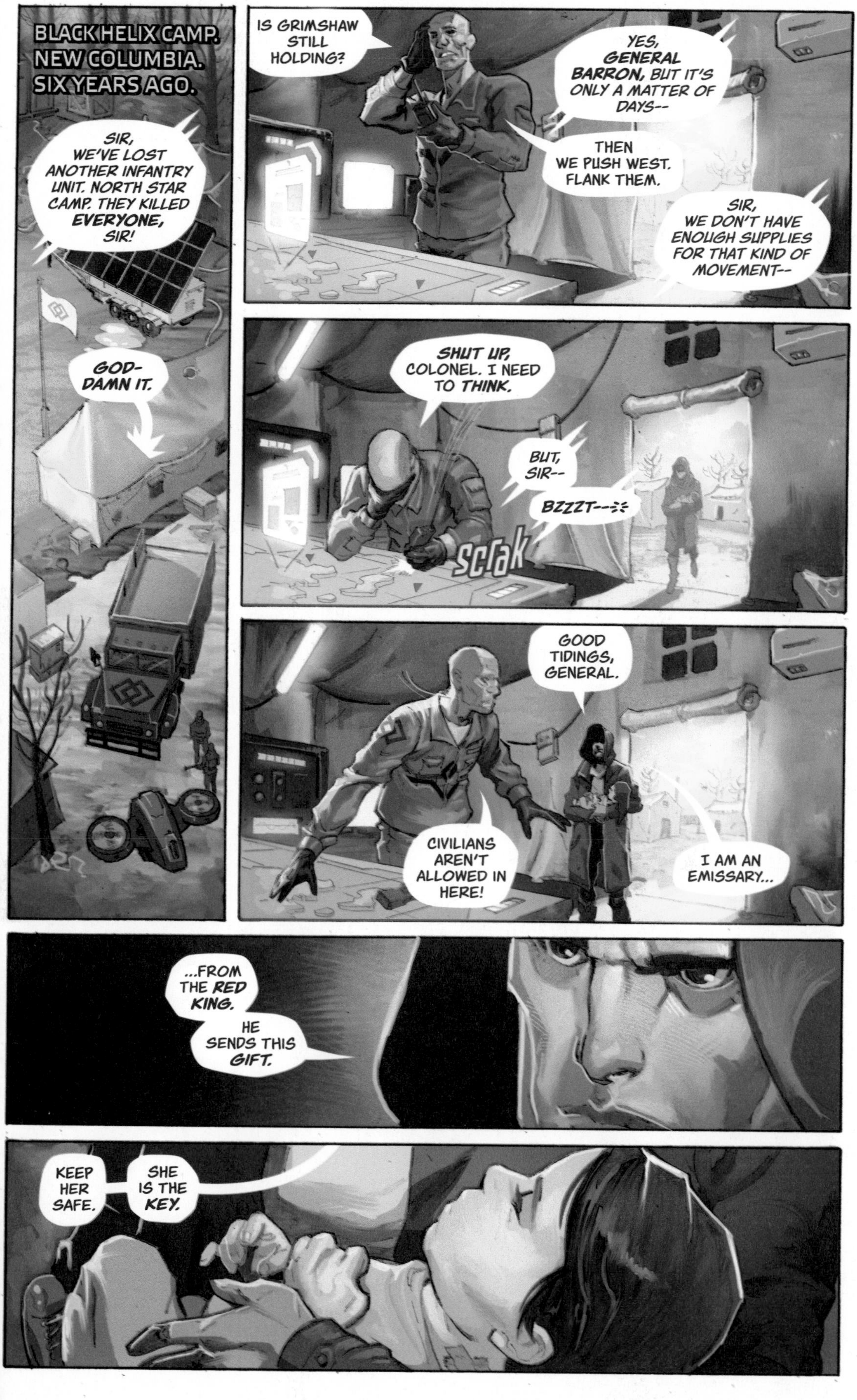
BLACK HELIX CAMP. NEW COLUMBIA. SIX YEARS AGO.
SIR, WE'VE LOST ANOTHER INFANTRY UNIT. NORTH STAR CAMP. THEY KILLED EVERYONE, SIR!
GOD-DAMN IT.
IS GRIMSHAW STILL HOLDING?
YES, GENERAL BARRON, BUT IT'S ONLY A MATTER OF DAYS--
THEN WE PUSH WEST. FLANK THEM.
SIR, WE DON'T HAVE ENOUGH SUPPLIES FOR THAT KIND OF MOVEMENT--
SHUT UP, COLONEL. I NEED TO THINK.
BUT, SIR--
BZZZT--
SCRAK
GOOD TIDINGS, GENERAL.
CIVILIANS AREN'T ALLOWED IN HERE!
I AM AN EMISSARY...
...FROM THE RED KING.
HE SENDS THIS GIFT.
KEEP HER SAFE.
SHE IS THE KEY.

CHAPTER TWO: **MINNOW**

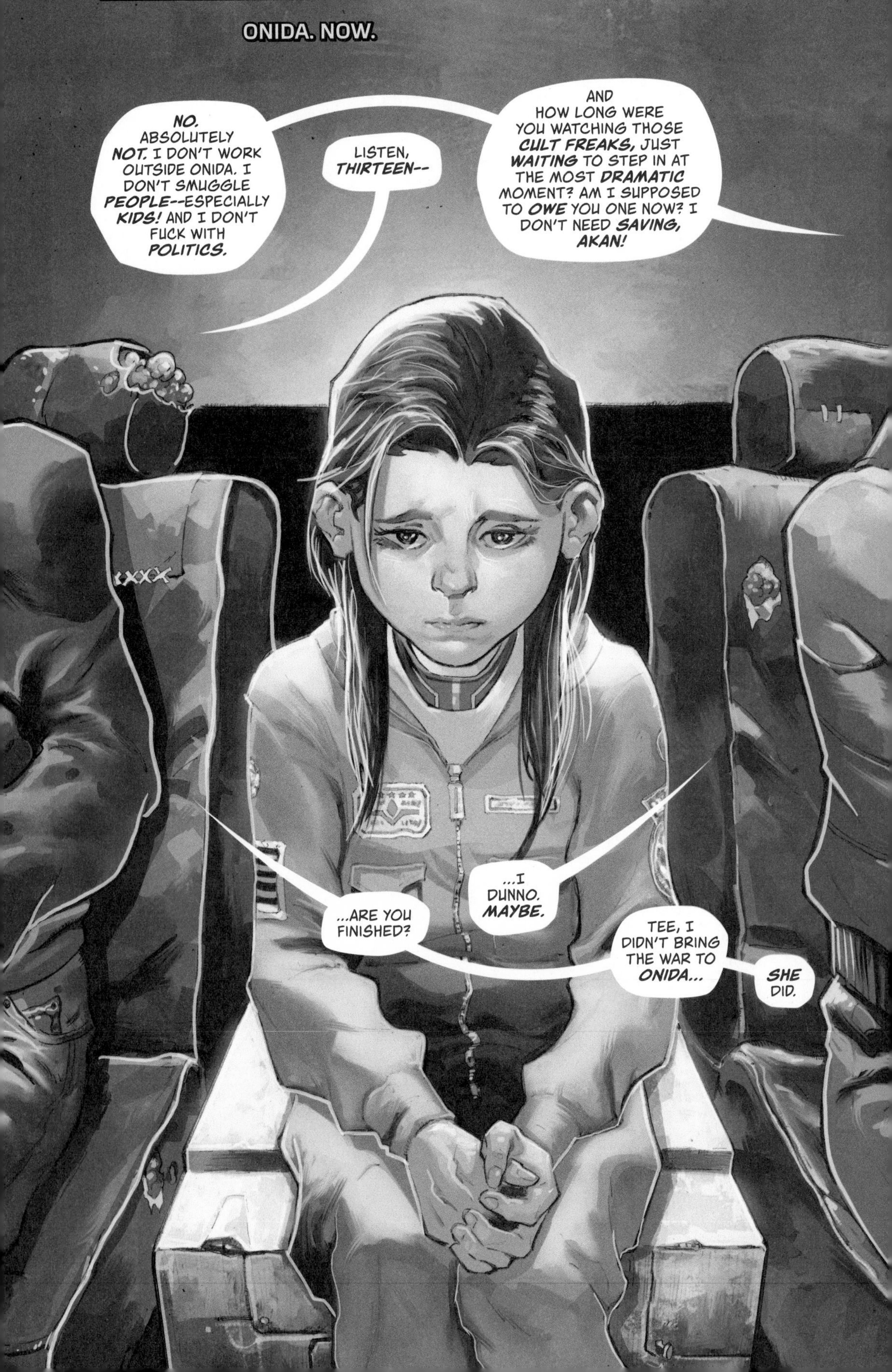
ONIDA. NOW.
NO. ABSOLUTELY NOT. I DON'T WORK OUTSIDE ONIDA. I DON'T SMUGGLE PEOPLE--ESPECIALLY KIDS! AND I DON'T FUCK WITH POLITICS.
AND HOW LONG WERE YOU WATCHING THOSE CULT FREAKS, JUST WAITING TO STEP IN AT THE MOST DRAMATIC MOMENT? AM I SUPPOSED TO OWE YOU ONE NOW? I DON'T NEED SAVING, AKAN!
LISTEN, THIRTEEN--
...ARE YOU FINISHED?
...I DUNNO. MAYBE.
TEE, I DIDN'T BRING THE WAR TO ONIDA...
SHE DID.

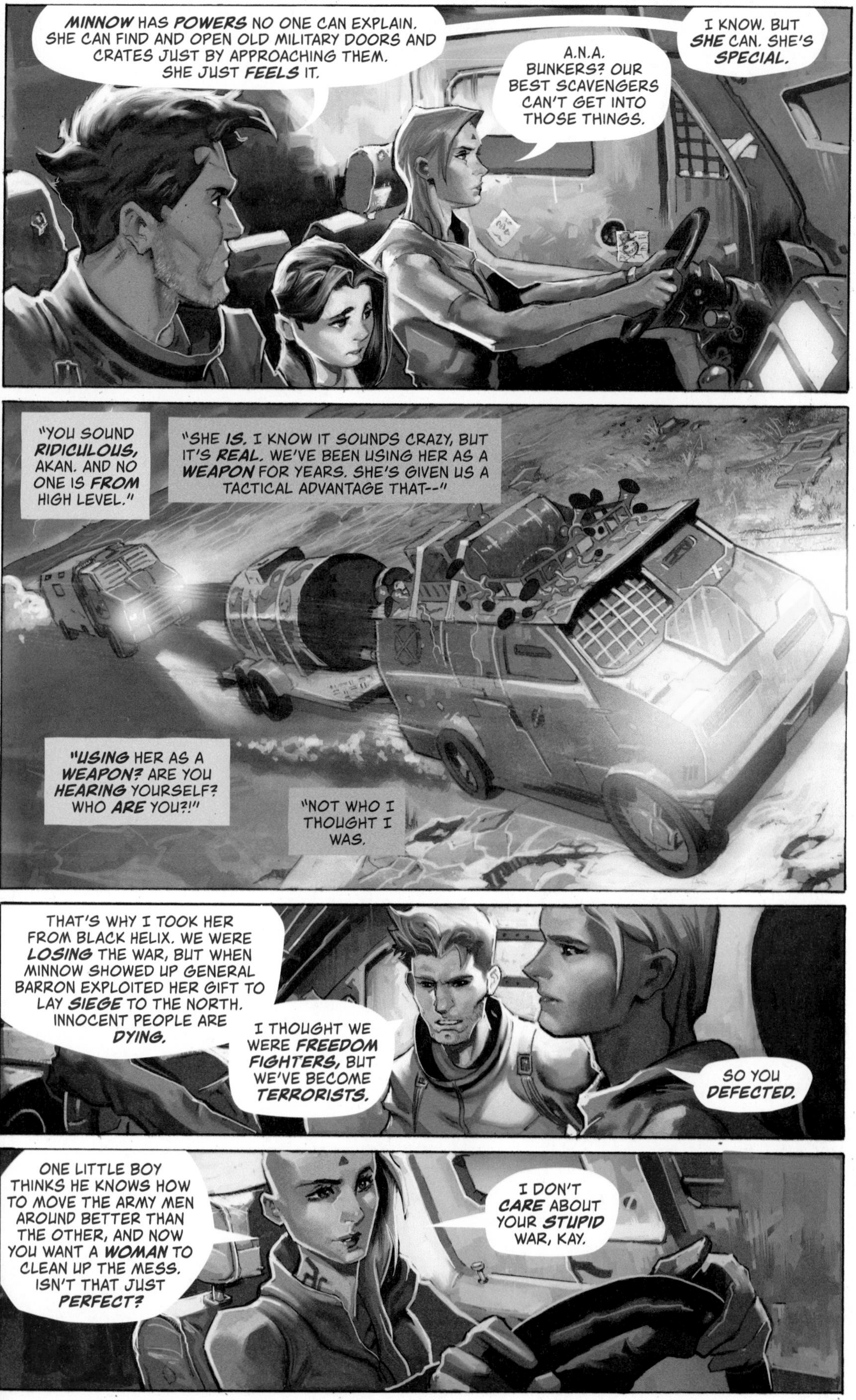
MINNOW HAS POWERS NO ONE CAN EXPLAIN. SHE CAN FIND AND OPEN OLD MILITARY DOORS AND CRATES JUST BY APPROACHING THEM. SHE JUST FEELS IT.
A.N.A. BUNKERS? OUR BEST SCAVENGERS CAN'T GET INTO THOSE THINGS.
I KNOW. BUT SHE CAN. SHE'S SPECIAL.
"YOU SOUND RIDICULOUS, AKAN. AND NO ONE IS FROM HIGH LEVEL."
"SHE IS. I KNOW IT SOUNDS CRAZY, BUT IT'S REAL. WE'VE BEEN USING HER AS A WEAPON FOR YEARS. SHE'S GIVEN US A TACTICAL ADVANTAGE THAT--"
"USING HER AS A WEAPON? ARE YOU HEARING YOURSELF? WHO ARE YOU?!"
"NOT WHO I THOUGHT I WAS.
THAT'S WHY I TOOK HER FROM BLACK HELIX. WE WERE LOSING THE WAR, BUT WHEN MINNOW SHOWED UP GENERAL BARRON EXPLOITED HER GIFT TO LAY SIEGE TO THE NORTH. INNOCENT PEOPLE ARE DYING.
I THOUGHT WE WERE FREEDOM FIGHTERS, BUT WE'VE BECOME TERRORISTS.
SO YOU DEFECTED.
ONE LITTLE BOY THINKS HE KNOWS HOW TO MOVE THE ARMY MEN AROUND BETTER THAN THE OTHER, AND NOW YOU WANT A WOMAN TO CLEAN UP THE MESS. ISN'T THAT JUST PERFECT?
I DON'T CARE ABOUT YOUR STUPID WAR, KAY.

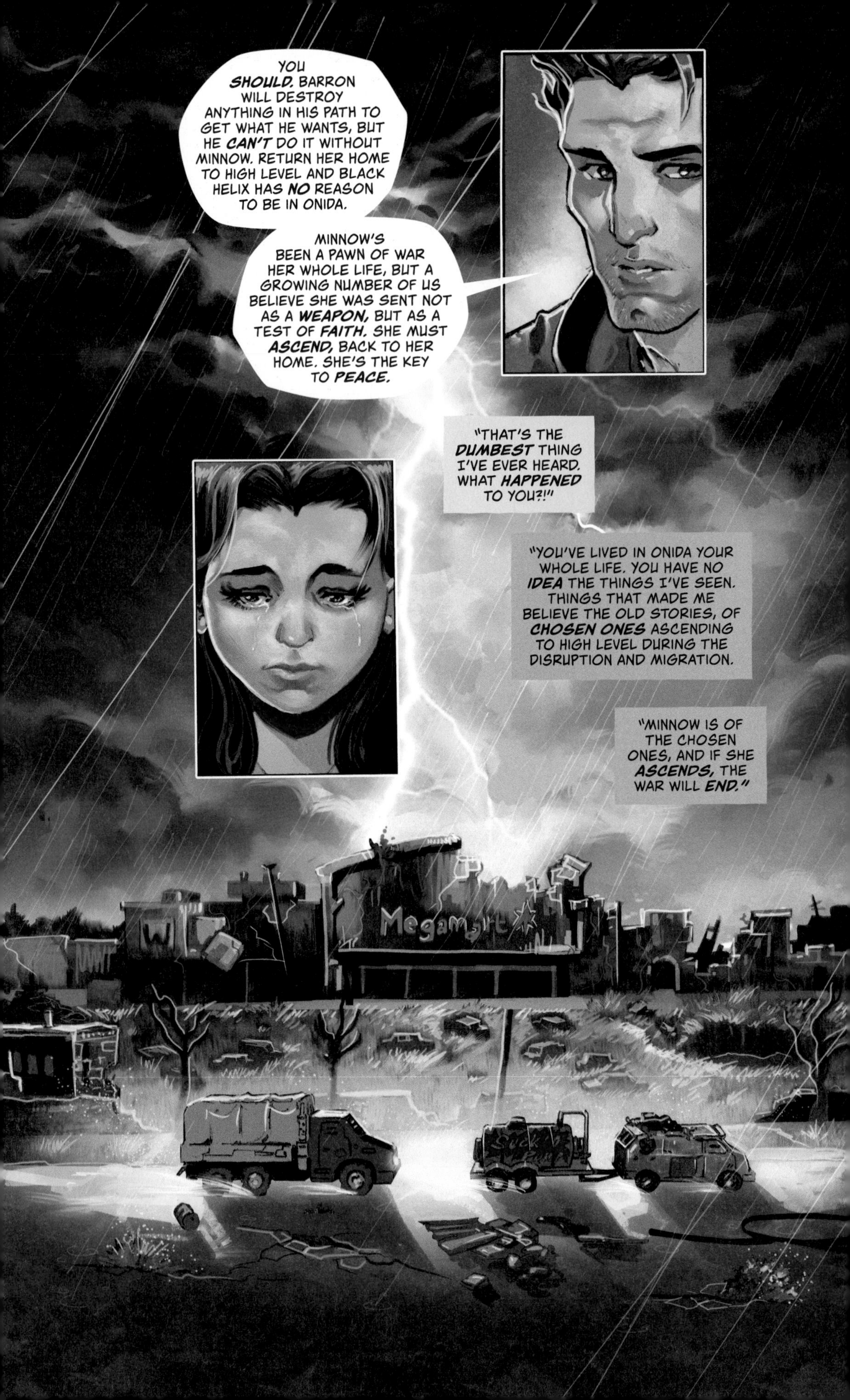
YOU SHOULD. BARRON WILL DESTROY ANYTHING IN HIS PATH TO GET WHAT HE WANTS, BUT HE CAN'T DO IT WITHOUT MINNOW. RETURN HER HOME TO HIGH LEVEL AND BLACK HELIX HAS NO REASON TO BE IN ONIDA.
MINNOW'S BEEN A PAWN OF WAR HER WHOLE LIFE, BUT A GROWING NUMBER OF US BELIEVE SHE WAS SENT NOT AS A WEAPON, BUT AS A TEST OF FAITH. SHE MUST ASCEND, BACK TO HER HOME. SHE'S THE KEY TO PEACE.
"THAT'S THE DUMBEST THING I'VE EVER HEARD. WHAT HAPPENED TO YOU?!"
"YOU'VE LIVED IN ONIDA YOUR WHOLE LIFE. YOU HAVE NO IDEA THE THINGS I'VE SEEN. THINGS THAT MADE ME BELIEVE THE OLD STORIES, OF CHOSEN ONES ASCENDING TO HIGH LEVEL DURING THE DISRUPTION AND MIGRATION.
"MINNOW IS OF THE CHOSEN ONES, AND IF SHE ASCENDS, THE WAR WILL END."
Megamart

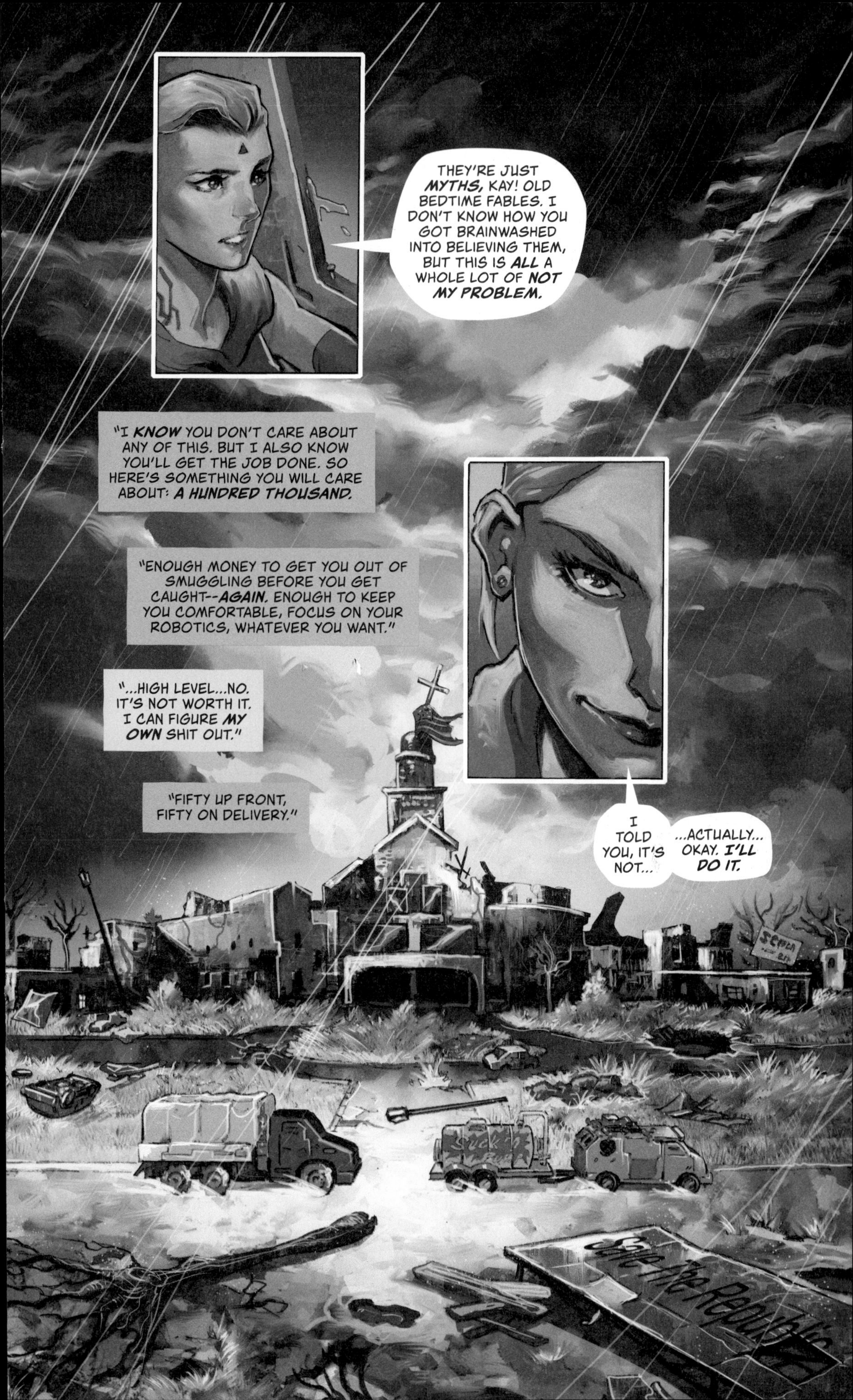
THEY'RE JUST MYTHS, KAY! OLD BEDTIME FABLES. I DON'T KNOW HOW YOU GOT BRAINWASHED INTO BELIEVING THEM, BUT THIS IS ALL A WHOLE LOT OF NOT MY PROBLEM.
"I KNOW YOU DON'T CARE ABOUT ANY OF THIS. BUT I ALSO KNOW YOU'LL GET THE JOB DONE. SO HERE'S SOMETHING YOU WILL CARE ABOUT: A HUNDRED THOUSAND.
"ENOUGH MONEY TO GET YOU OUT OF SMUGGLING BEFORE YOU GET CAUGHT--AGAIN. ENOUGH TO KEEP YOU COMFORTABLE, FOCUS ON YOUR ROBOTICS, WHATEVER YOU WANT."
"...HIGH LEVEL...NO. IT'S NOT WORTH IT. I CAN FIGURE MY OWN SHIT OUT."
"FIFTY UP FRONT, FIFTY ON DELIVERY."
I TOLD YOU, IT'S NOT...
...ACTUALLY... OKAY. I'LL DO IT.

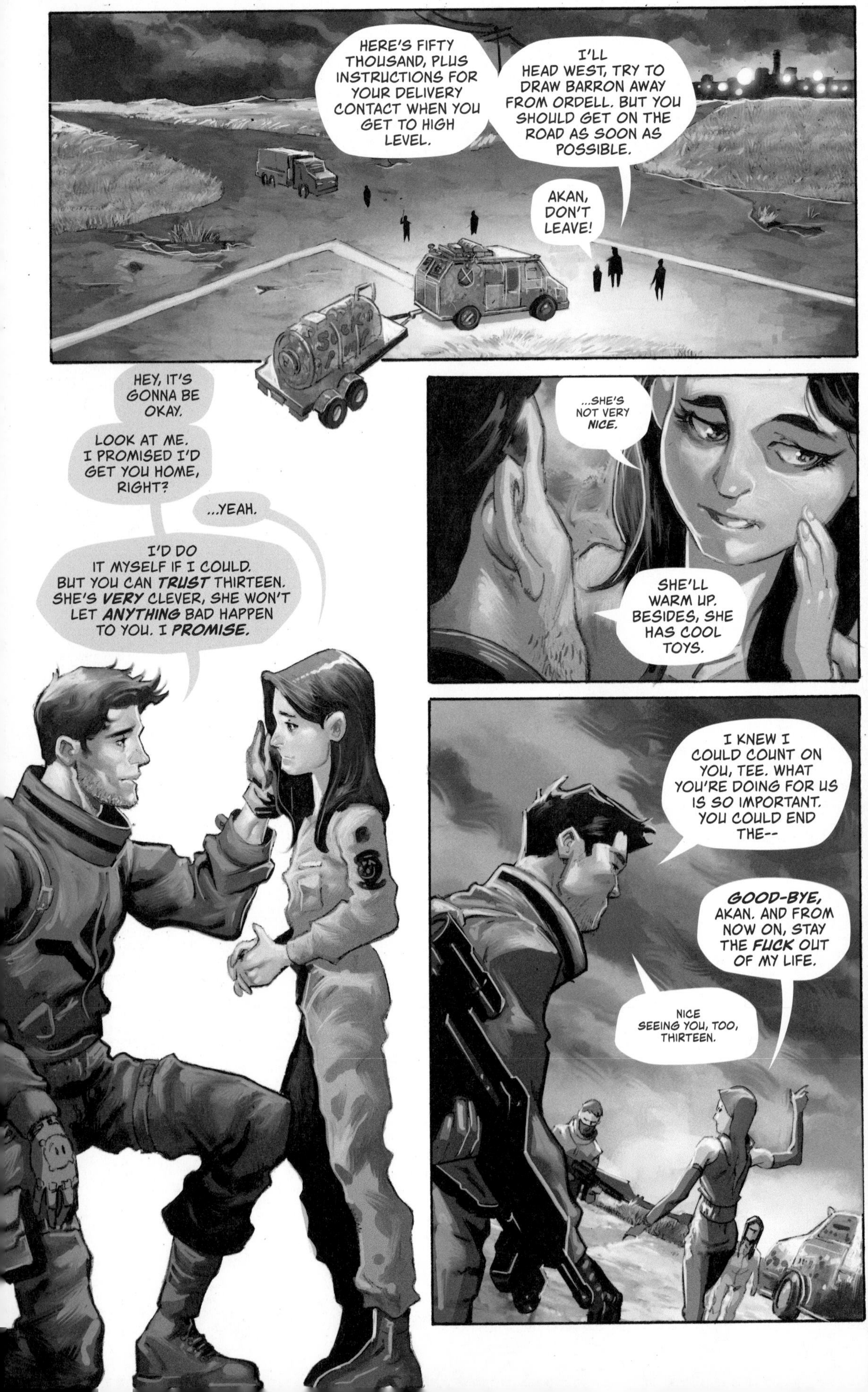
HERE'S FIFTY THOUSAND, PLUS INSTRUCTIONS FOR YOUR DELIVERY CONTACT WHEN YOU GET TO HIGH LEVEL.
I'LL HEAD WEST, TRY TO DRAW BARRON AWAY FROM ORDELL. BUT YOU SHOULD GET ON THE ROAD AS SOON AS POSSIBLE.
AKAN, DON'T LEAVE!
HEY, IT'S GONNA BE OKAY.
LOOK AT ME. I PROMISED I'D GET YOU HOME, RIGHT?
...YEAH.
I'D DO IT MYSELF IF I COULD. BUT YOU CAN TRUST THIRTEEN. SHE'S VERY CLEVER, SHE WON'T LET ANYTHING BAD HAPPEN TO YOU. I PROMISE.
...SHE'S NOT VERY NICE.
SHE'LL WARM UP. BESIDES, SHE HAS COOL TOYS.
I KNEW I COULD COUNT ON YOU, TEE. WHAT YOU'RE DOING FOR US IS SO IMPORTANT. YOU COULD END THE--
GOOD-BYE, AKAN. AND FROM NOW ON, STAY THE FUCK OUT OF MY LIFE.
NICE SEEING YOU, TOO, THIRTEEN.

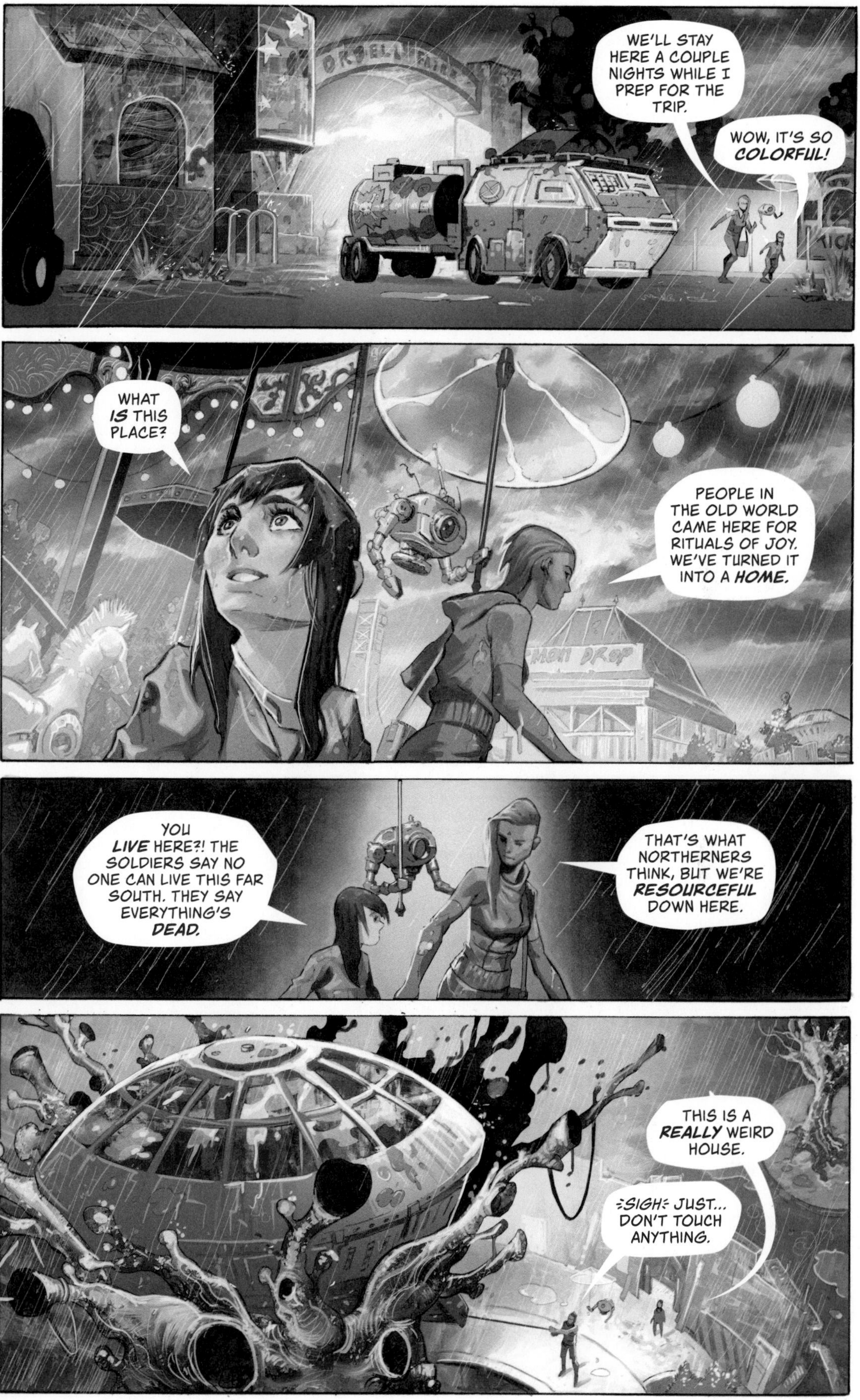
WE'LL STAY HERE A COUPLE NIGHTS WHILE I PREP FOR THE TRIP.
WOW, IT'S SO *COLORFUL!*
WHAT *IS* THIS PLACE?
PEOPLE IN THE OLD WORLD CAME HERE FOR RITUALS OF JOY. WE'VE TURNED IT INTO A *HOME.*
YOU *LIVE* HERE?! THE SOLDIERS SAY NO ONE CAN LIVE THIS FAR SOUTH. THEY SAY EVERYTHING'S *DEAD.*
THAT'S WHAT NORTHERNERS THINK, BUT WE'RE *RESOURCEFUL* DOWN HERE.
THIS IS A *REALLY* WEIRD HOUSE.
SIGH JUST... DON'T TOUCH ANYTHING.

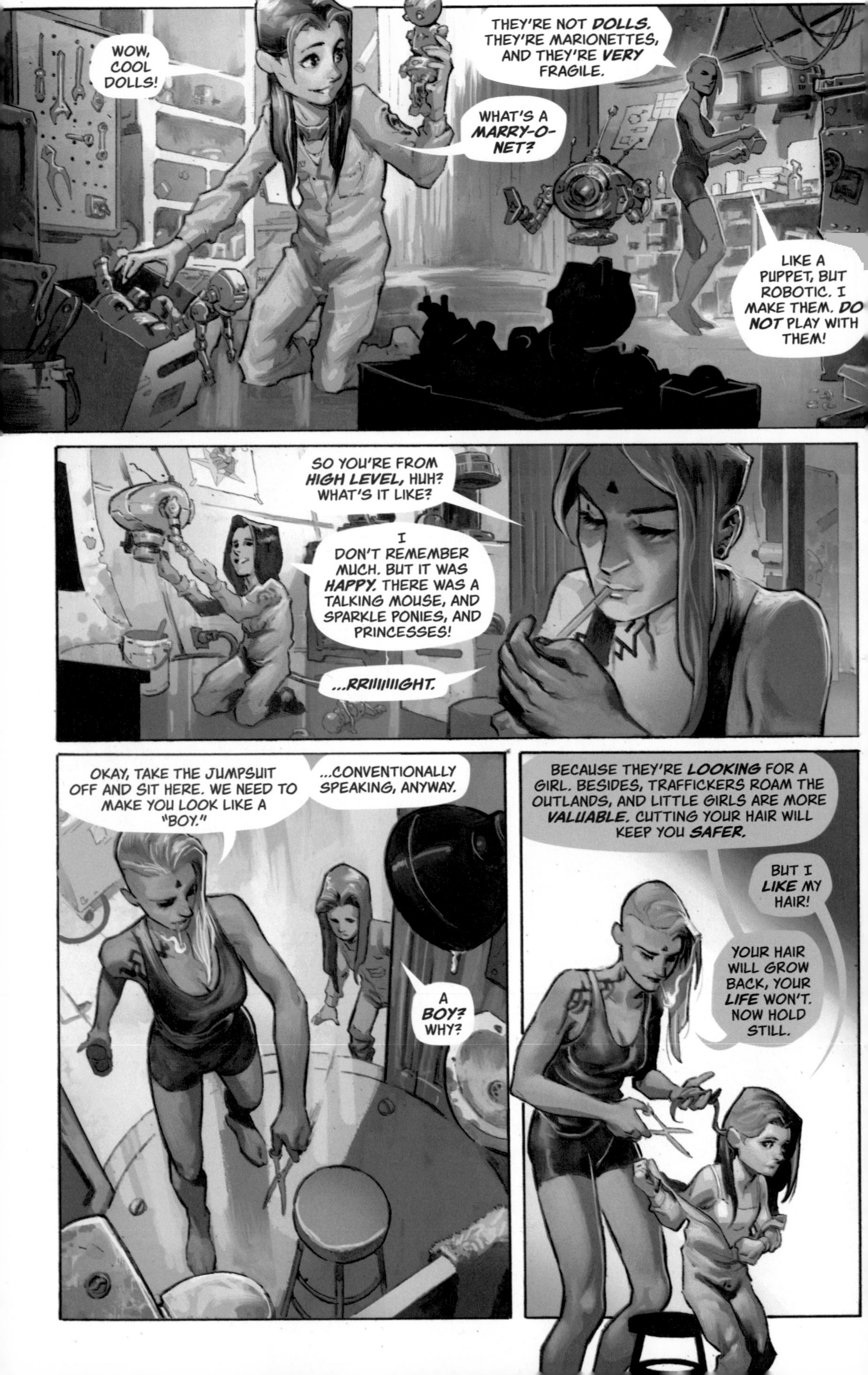
WOW, COOL DOLLS!
THEY'RE NOT DOLLS. THEY'RE MARIONETTES, AND THEY'RE VERY FRAGILE.
WHAT'S A MARRY-O-NET?
LIKE A PUPPET, BUT ROBOTIC. I MAKE THEM. DO NOT PLAY WITH THEM!
SO YOU'RE FROM HIGH LEVEL, HUH? WHAT'S IT LIKE?
I DON'T REMEMBER MUCH. BUT IT WAS HAPPY. THERE WAS A TALKING MOUSE, AND SPARKLE PONIES, AND PRINCESSES!
...RRIIIIIIIGHT.
OKAY, TAKE THE JUMPSUIT OFF AND SIT HERE. WE NEED TO MAKE YOU LOOK LIKE A "BOY."
...CONVENTIONALLY SPEAKING, ANYWAY.
A BOY? WHY?
BECAUSE THEY'RE LOOKING FOR A GIRL. BESIDES, TRAFFICKERS ROAM THE OUTLANDS, AND LITTLE GIRLS ARE MORE VALUABLE. CUTTING YOUR HAIR WILL KEEP YOU SAFER.
BUT I LIKE MY HAIR!
YOUR HAIR WILL GROW BACK, YOUR LIFE WON'T. NOW HOLD STILL.

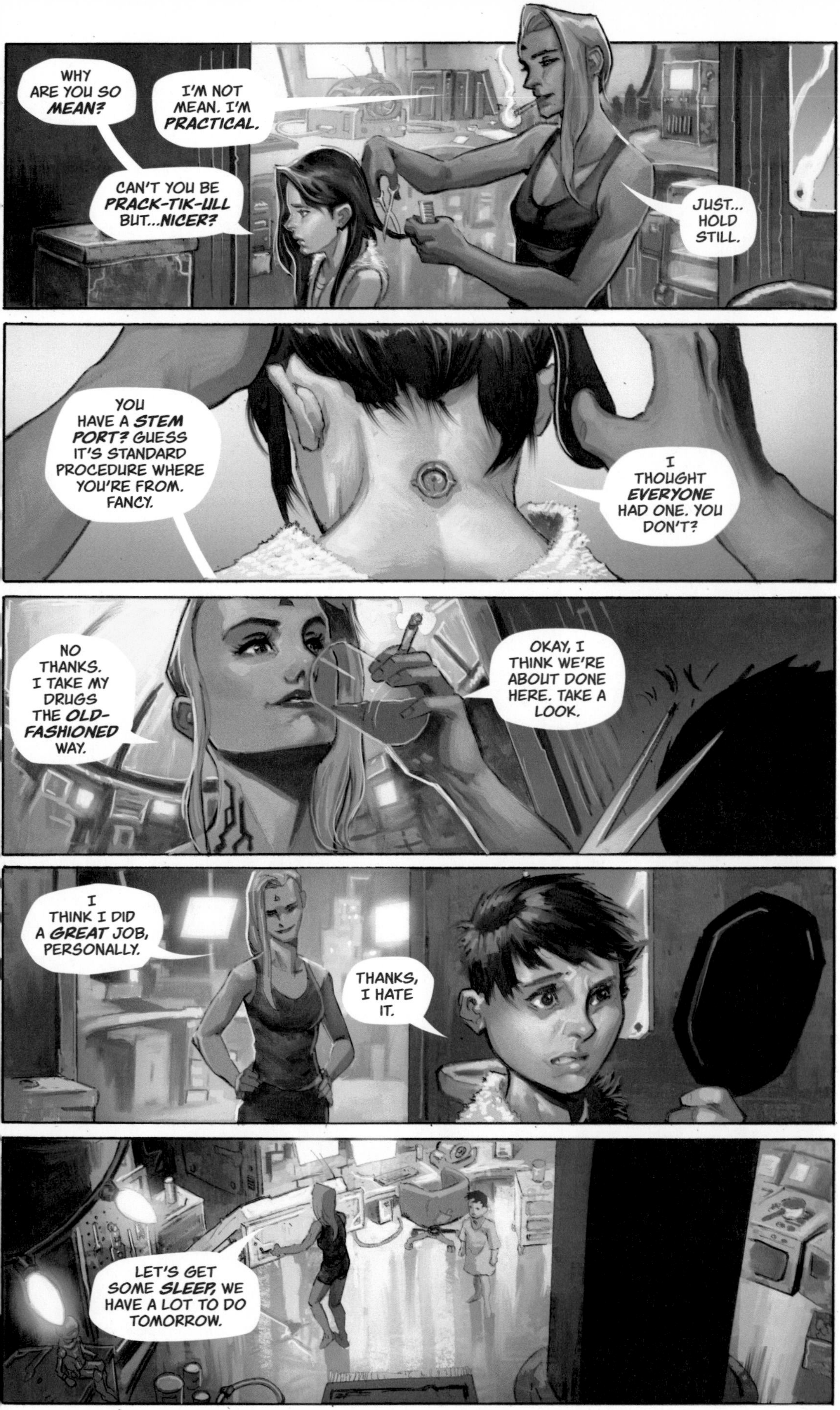
WHY ARE YOU SO MEAN?
I'M NOT MEAN. I'M PRACTICAL.
CAN'T YOU BE PRACK-TIK-ULL BUT...NICER?
JUST... HOLD STILL.
YOU HAVE A STEM PORT? GUESS IT'S STANDARD PROCEDURE WHERE YOU'RE FROM. FANCY.
I THOUGHT EVERYONE HAD ONE. YOU DON'T?
NO THANKS. I TAKE MY DRUGS THE OLD-FASHIONED WAY.
OKAY, I THINK WE'RE ABOUT DONE HERE. TAKE A LOOK.
I THINK I DID A GREAT JOB, PERSONALLY.
THANKS, I HATE IT.
LET'S GET SOME SLEEP, WE HAVE A LOT TO DO TOMORROW.

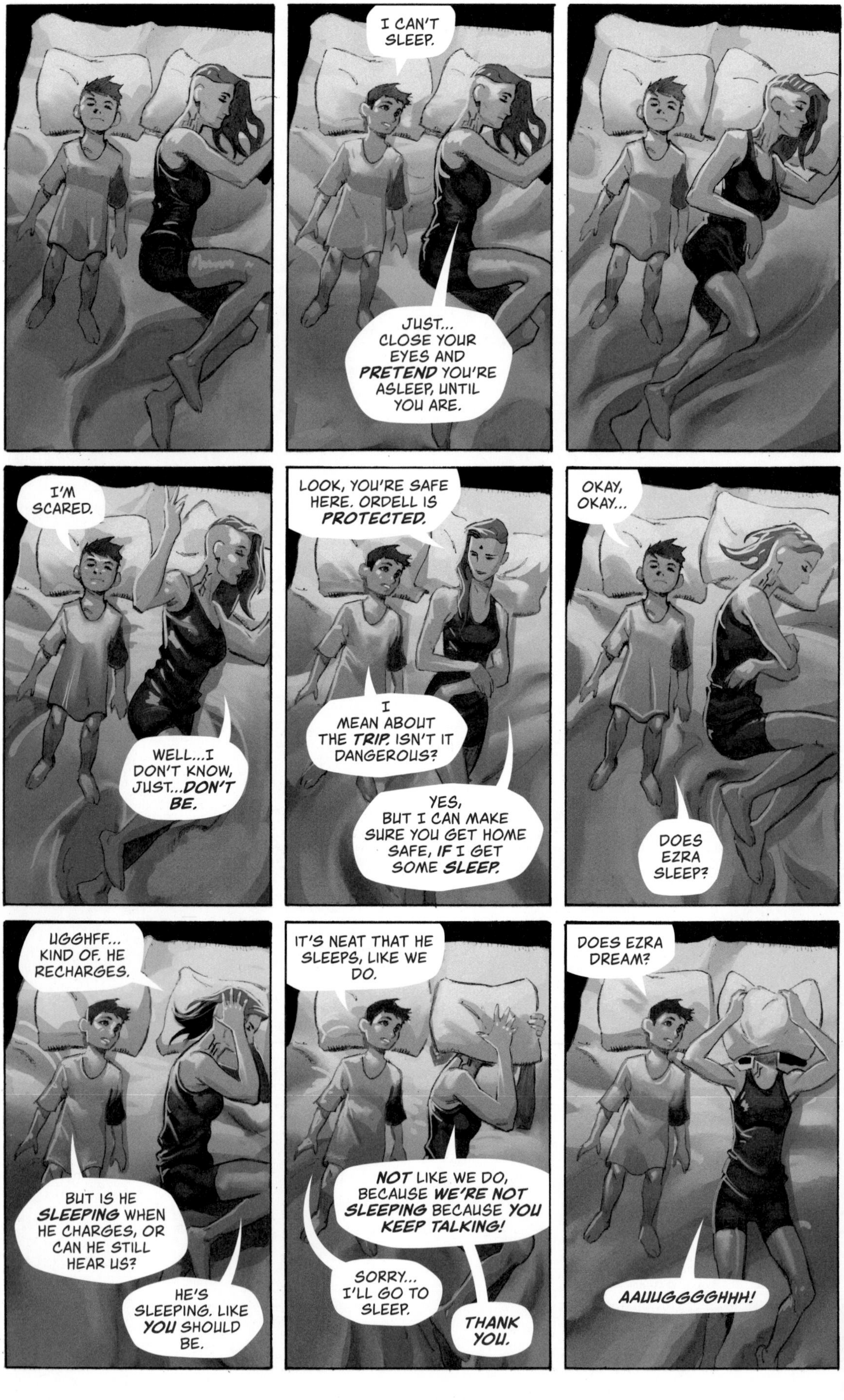
I CAN'T SLEEP.
JUST... CLOSE YOUR EYES AND PRETEND YOU'RE ASLEEP, UNTIL YOU ARE.
I'M SCARED.
WELL...I DON'T KNOW, JUST...DON'T BE.
LOOK, YOU'RE SAFE HERE. ORDELL IS PROTECTED.
I MEAN ABOUT THE TRIP. ISN'T IT DANGEROUS?
YES, BUT I CAN MAKE SURE YOU GET HOME SAFE, IF I GET SOME SLEEP.
OKAY, OKAY...
DOES EZRA SLEEP?
UGGHFF... KIND OF. HE RECHARGES.
BUT IS HE SLEEPING WHEN HE CHARGES, OR CAN HE STILL HEAR US?
HE'S SLEEPING. LIKE YOU SHOULD BE.
IT'S NEAT THAT HE SLEEPS, LIKE WE DO.
NOT LIKE WE DO, BECAUSE WE'RE NOT SLEEPING BECAUSE YOU KEEP TALKING!
SORRY... I'LL GO TO SLEEP.
THANK YOU.
DOES EZRA DREAM?
AAUUGGGGHHH!

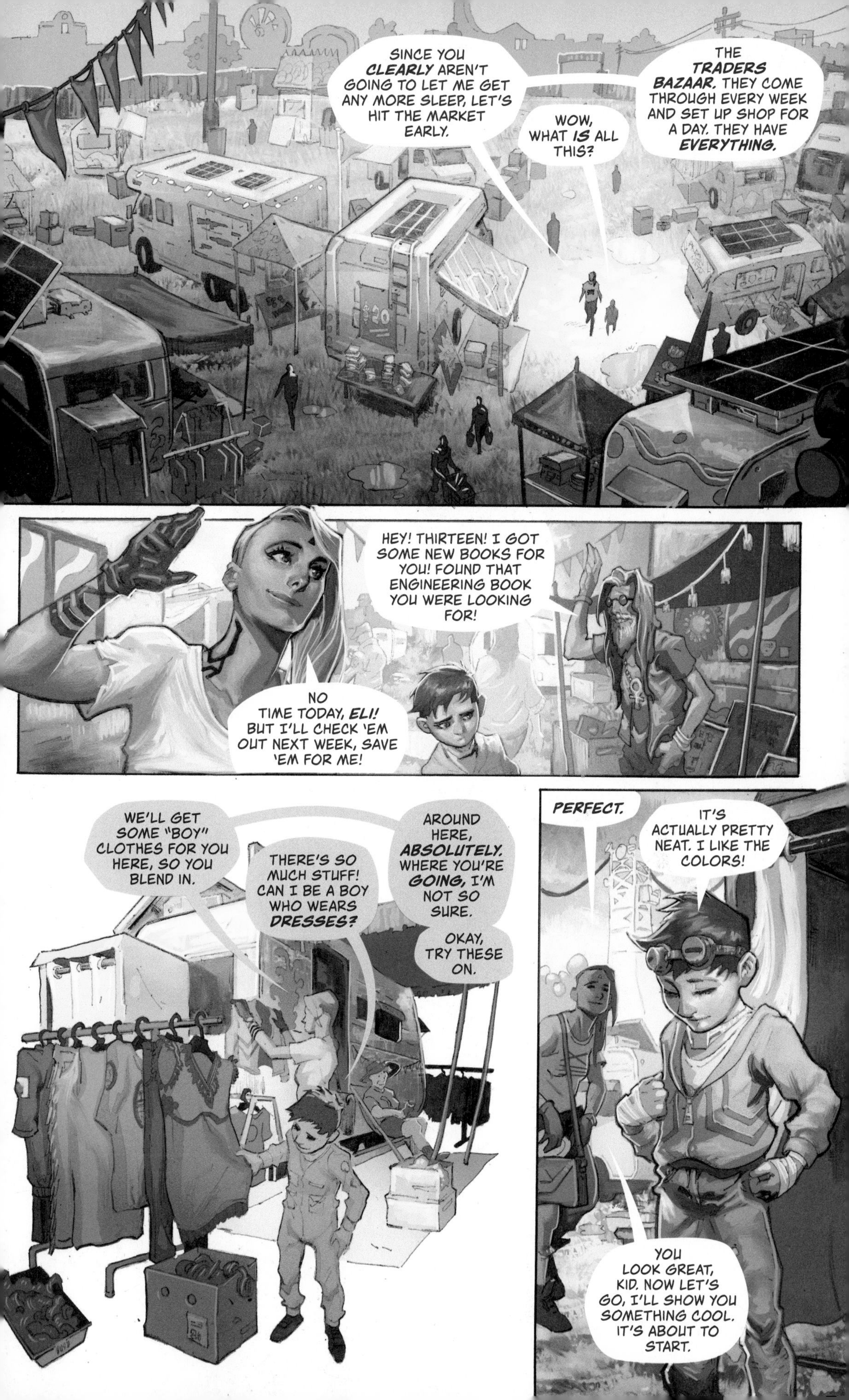
SINCE YOU CLEARLY AREN'T GOING TO LET ME GET ANY MORE SLEEP, LET'S HIT THE MARKET EARLY.
WOW, WHAT IS ALL THIS?
THE TRADERS BAZAAR. THEY COME THROUGH EVERY WEEK AND SET UP SHOP FOR A DAY. THEY HAVE EVERYTHING.
$20
HEY! THIRTEEN! I GOT SOME NEW BOOKS FOR YOU! FOUND THAT ENGINEERING BOOK YOU WERE LOOKING FOR!
NO TIME TODAY, ELI! BUT I'LL CHECK 'EM OUT NEXT WEEK, SAVE 'EM FOR ME!
WE'LL GET SOME "BOY" CLOTHES FOR YOU HERE, SO YOU BLEND IN.
THERE'S SO MUCH STUFF! CAN I BE A BOY WHO WEARS DRESSES?
AROUND HERE, ABSOLUTELY. WHERE YOU'RE GOING, I'M NOT SO SURE.
OKAY, TRY THESE ON.
PERFECT.
IT'S ACTUALLY PRETTY NEAT. I LIKE THE COLORS!
YOU LOOK GREAT, KID. NOW LET'S GO, I'LL SHOW YOU SOMETHING COOL. IT'S ABOUT TO START.

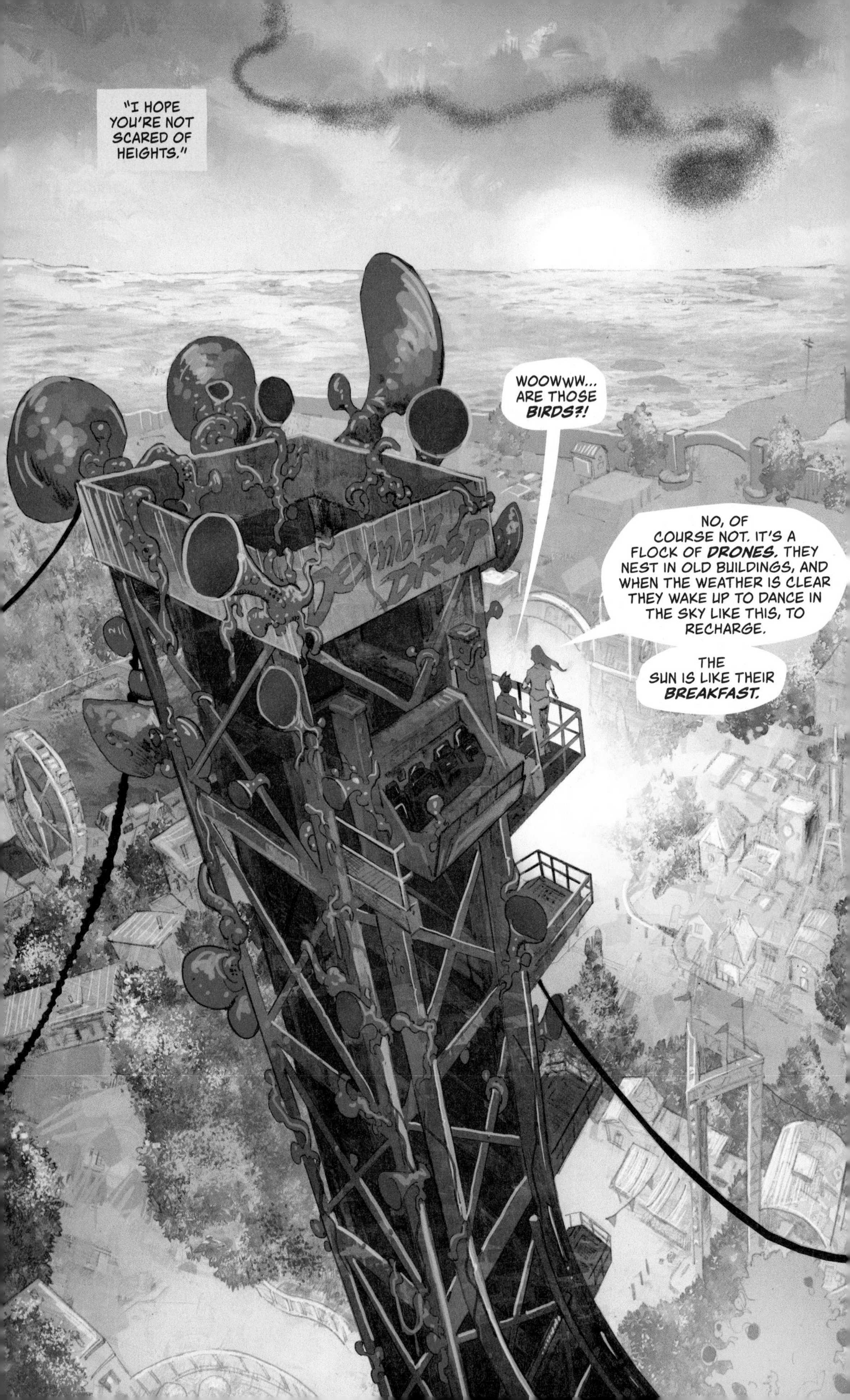
"I HOPE YOU'RE NOT SCARED OF HEIGHTS."
WOOWWW... ARE THOSE BIRDS?!
NO, OF COURSE NOT. IT'S A FLOCK OF DRONES. THEY NEST IN OLD BUILDINGS, AND WHEN THE WEATHER IS CLEAR THEY WAKE UP TO DANCE IN THE SKY LIKE THIS, TO RECHARGE.
THE SUN IS LIKE THEIR BREAKFAST.

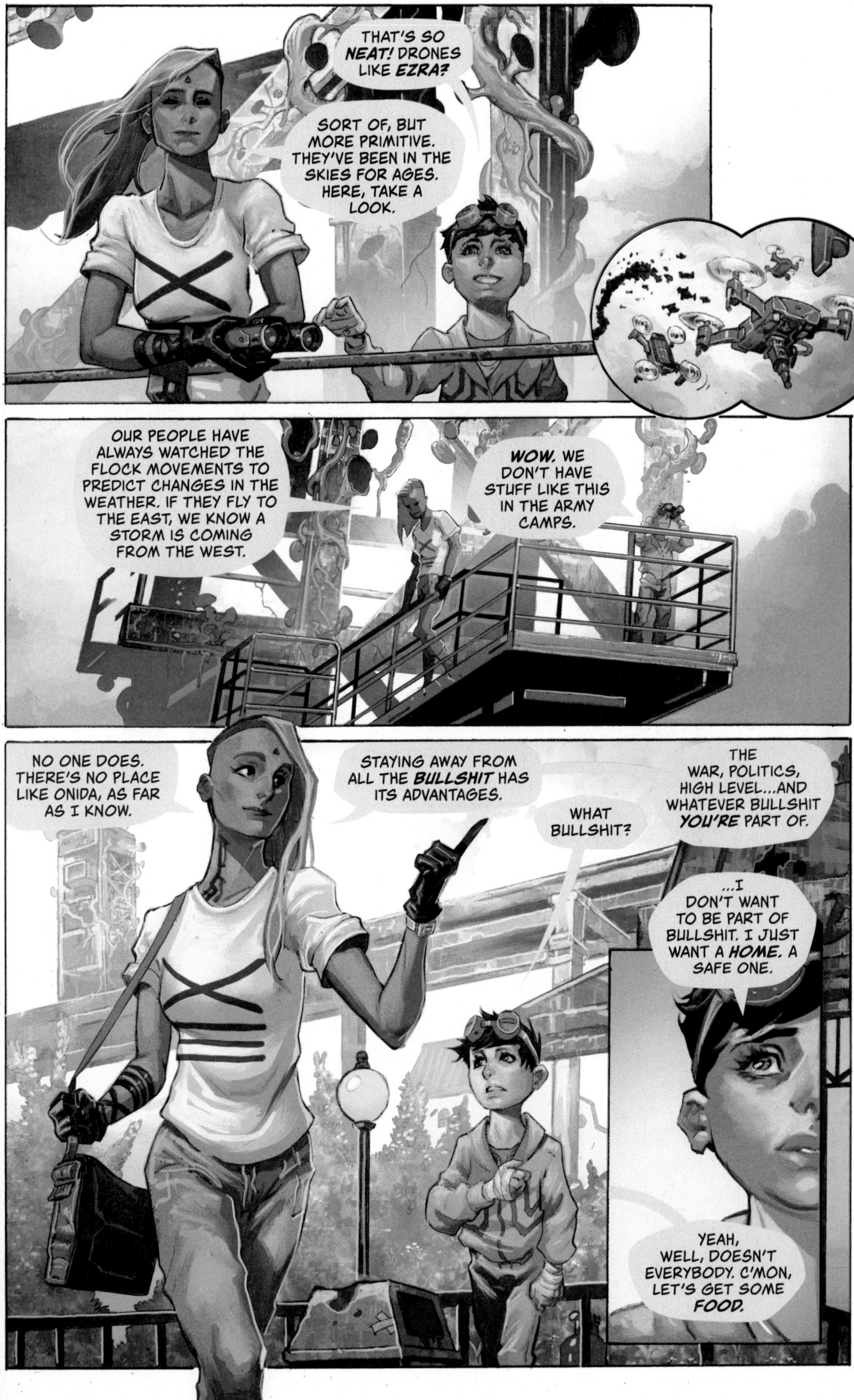
THAT'S SO **NEAT!** DRONES LIKE **EZRA?**
SORT OF, BUT MORE PRIMITIVE. THEY'VE BEEN IN THE SKIES FOR AGES. HERE, TAKE A LOOK.
OUR PEOPLE HAVE ALWAYS WATCHED THE FLOCK MOVEMENTS TO PREDICT CHANGES IN THE WEATHER. IF THEY FLY TO THE EAST, WE KNOW A STORM IS COMING FROM THE WEST.
WOW. WE DON'T HAVE STUFF LIKE THIS IN THE ARMY CAMPS.
NO ONE DOES. THERE'S NO PLACE LIKE ONIDA, AS FAR AS I KNOW.
STAYING AWAY FROM ALL THE **BULLSHIT** HAS ITS ADVANTAGES.
WHAT BULLSHIT?
THE WAR, POLITICS, HIGH LEVEL...AND WHATEVER BULLSHIT **YOU'RE** PART OF.
...I DON'T WANT TO BE PART OF BULLSHIT. I JUST WANT A **HOME.** A SAFE ONE.
YEAH, WELL, DOESN'T EVERYBODY. C'MON, LET'S GET SOME **FOOD.**

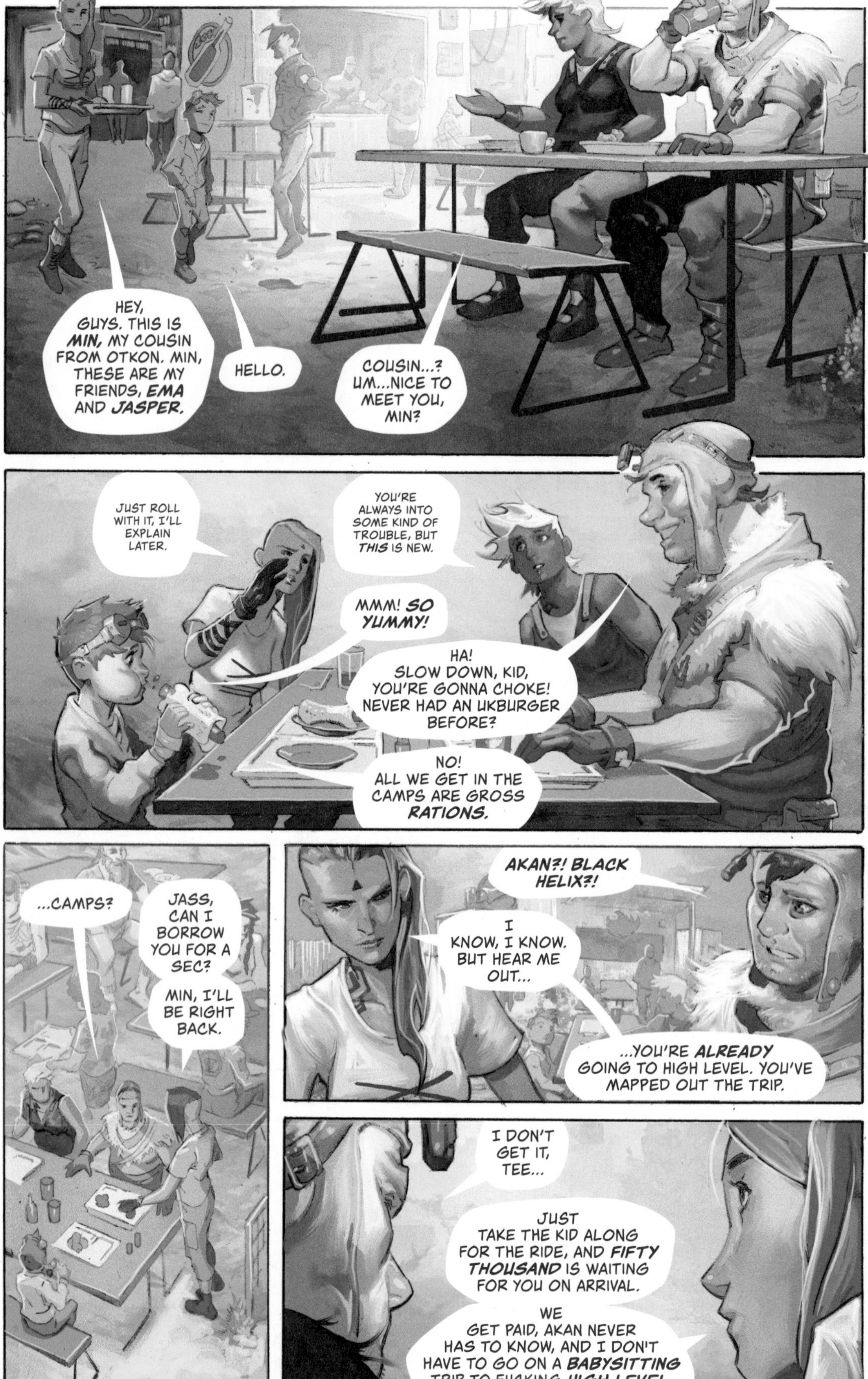
HEY, GUYS. THIS IS MIN, MY COUSIN FROM OTKON. MIN, THESE ARE MY FRIENDS, EMA AND JASPER.
HELLO.
COUSIN...? UM...NICE TO MEET YOU, MIN?
JUST ROLL WITH IT, I'LL EXPLAIN LATER.
YOU'RE ALWAYS INTO SOME KIND OF TROUBLE, BUT THIS IS NEW.
MMM! SO YUMMY!
HA! SLOW DOWN, KID, YOU'RE GONNA CHOKE! NEVER HAD AN UKBURGER BEFORE?
NO! ALL WE GET IN THE CAMPS ARE GROSS RATIONS.
...CAMPS?
JASS, CAN I BORROW YOU FOR A SEC?
MIN, I'LL BE RIGHT BACK.
AKAN?! BLACK HELIX?!
I KNOW, I KNOW. BUT HEAR ME OUT...
...YOU'RE ALREADY GOING TO HIGH LEVEL. YOU'VE MAPPED OUT THE TRIP.
I DON'T GET IT, TEE...
JUST TAKE THE KID ALONG FOR THE RIDE, AND FIFTY THOUSAND IS WAITING FOR YOU ON ARRIVAL.
WE GET PAID, AKAN NEVER HAS TO KNOW, AND I DON'T HAVE TO GO ON A BABYSITTING TRIP TO FUCKING HIGH LEVEL. EVERYONE WINS! ALSO--

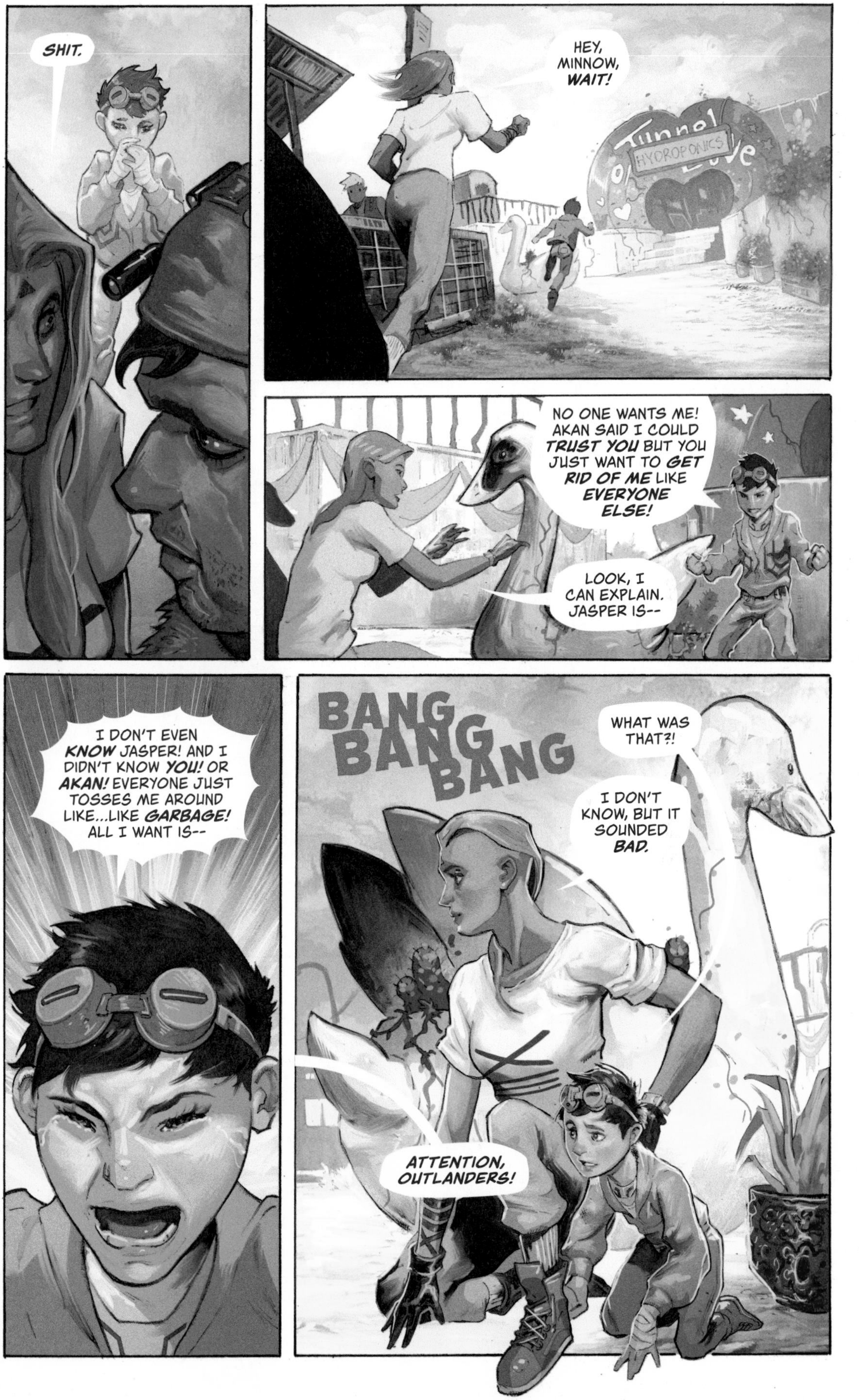
SHIT.
HEY, MINNOW, WAIT!
Tunnel of Love
HYDROPONICS
NO ONE WANTS ME! AKAN SAID I COULD TRUST YOU BUT YOU JUST WANT TO GET RID OF ME LIKE EVERYONE ELSE!
LOOK, I CAN EXPLAIN. JASPER IS--
I DON'T EVEN KNOW JASPER! AND I DIDN'T KNOW YOU! OR AKAN! EVERYONE JUST TOSSES ME AROUND LIKE...LIKE GARBAGE! ALL I WANT IS--
BANG BANG BANG
WHAT WAS THAT?!
I DON'T KNOW, BUT IT SOUNDED BAD.
ATTENTION, OUTLANDERS!

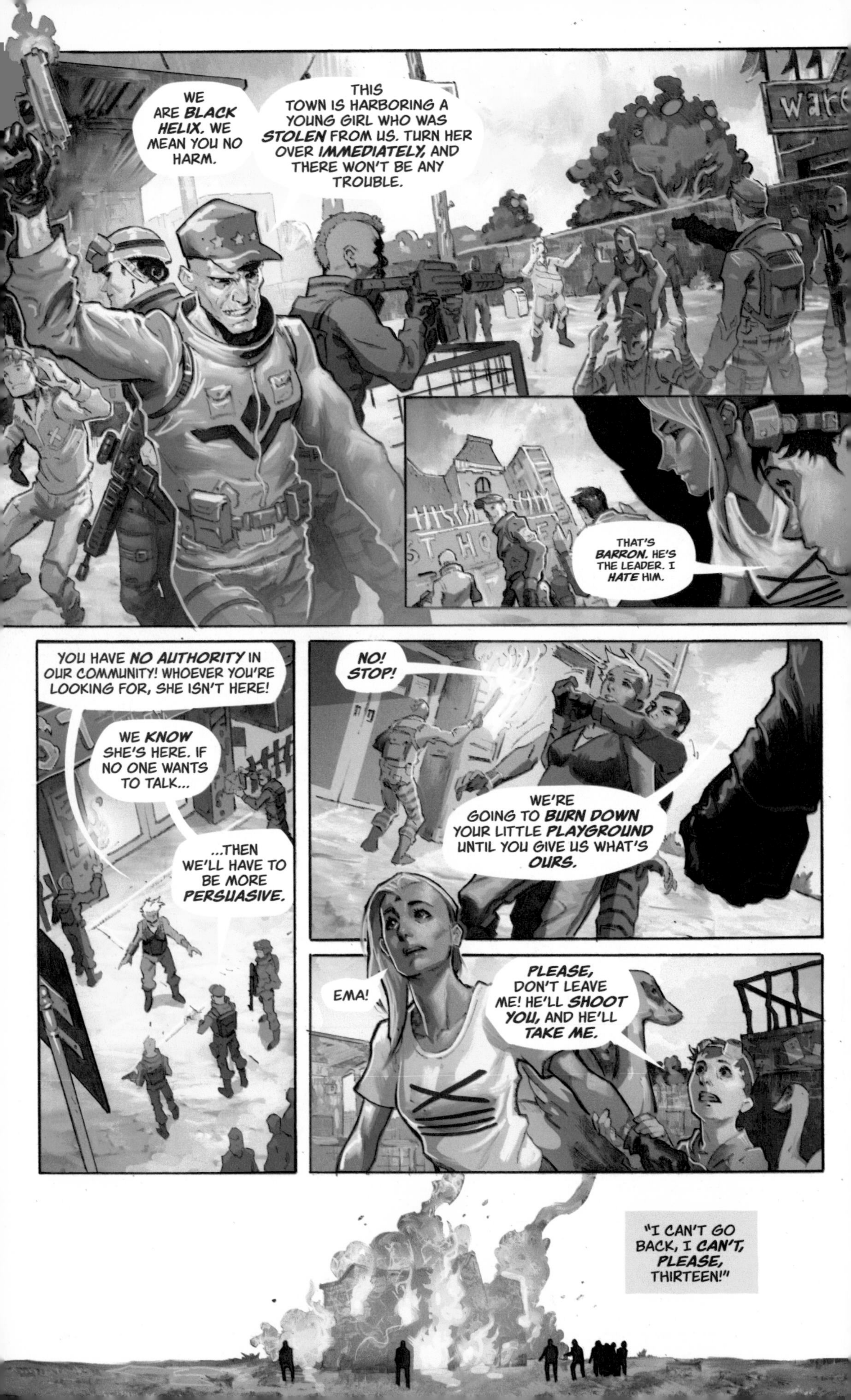
WE ARE BLACK HELIX. WE MEAN YOU NO HARM.
THIS TOWN IS HARBORING A YOUNG GIRL WHO WAS STOLEN FROM US. TURN HER OVER IMMEDIATELY, AND THERE WON'T BE ANY TROUBLE.
THAT'S BARRON. HE'S THE LEADER. I HATE HIM.
YOU HAVE NO AUTHORITY IN OUR COMMUNITY! WHOEVER YOU'RE LOOKING FOR, SHE ISN'T HERE!
WE KNOW SHE'S HERE. IF NO ONE WANTS TO TALK...
...THEN WE'LL HAVE TO BE MORE PERSUASIVE.
NO! STOP!
WE'RE GOING TO BURN DOWN YOUR LITTLE PLAYGROUND UNTIL YOU GIVE US WHAT'S OURS.
EMA!
PLEASE, DON'T LEAVE ME! HE'LL SHOOT YOU, AND HE'LL TAKE ME.
"I CAN'T GO BACK, I CAN'T, PLEASE, THIRTEEN!"

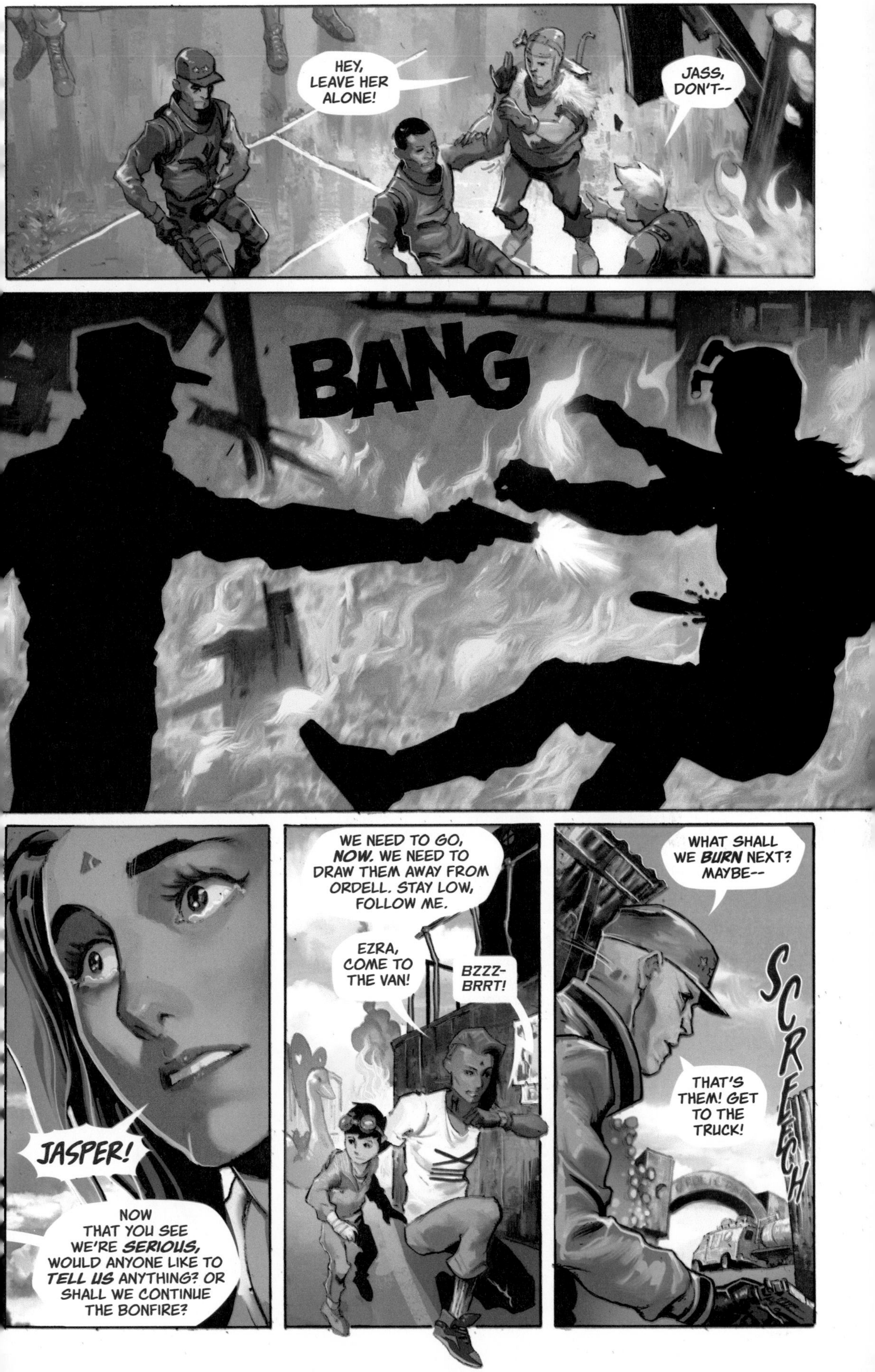
HEY, LEAVE HER ALONE!
JASS, DON'T--
BANG
JASPER!
NOW THAT YOU SEE WE'RE SERIOUS, WOULD ANYONE LIKE TO TELL US ANYTHING? OR SHALL WE CONTINUE THE BONFIRE?
WE NEED TO GO, NOW. WE NEED TO DRAW THEM AWAY FROM ORDELL. STAY LOW, FOLLOW ME.
EZRA, COME TO THE VAN!
BZZZ-BRRT!
WHAT SHALL WE BURN NEXT? MAYBE--
SCREECH
THAT'S THEM! GET TO THE TRUCK!

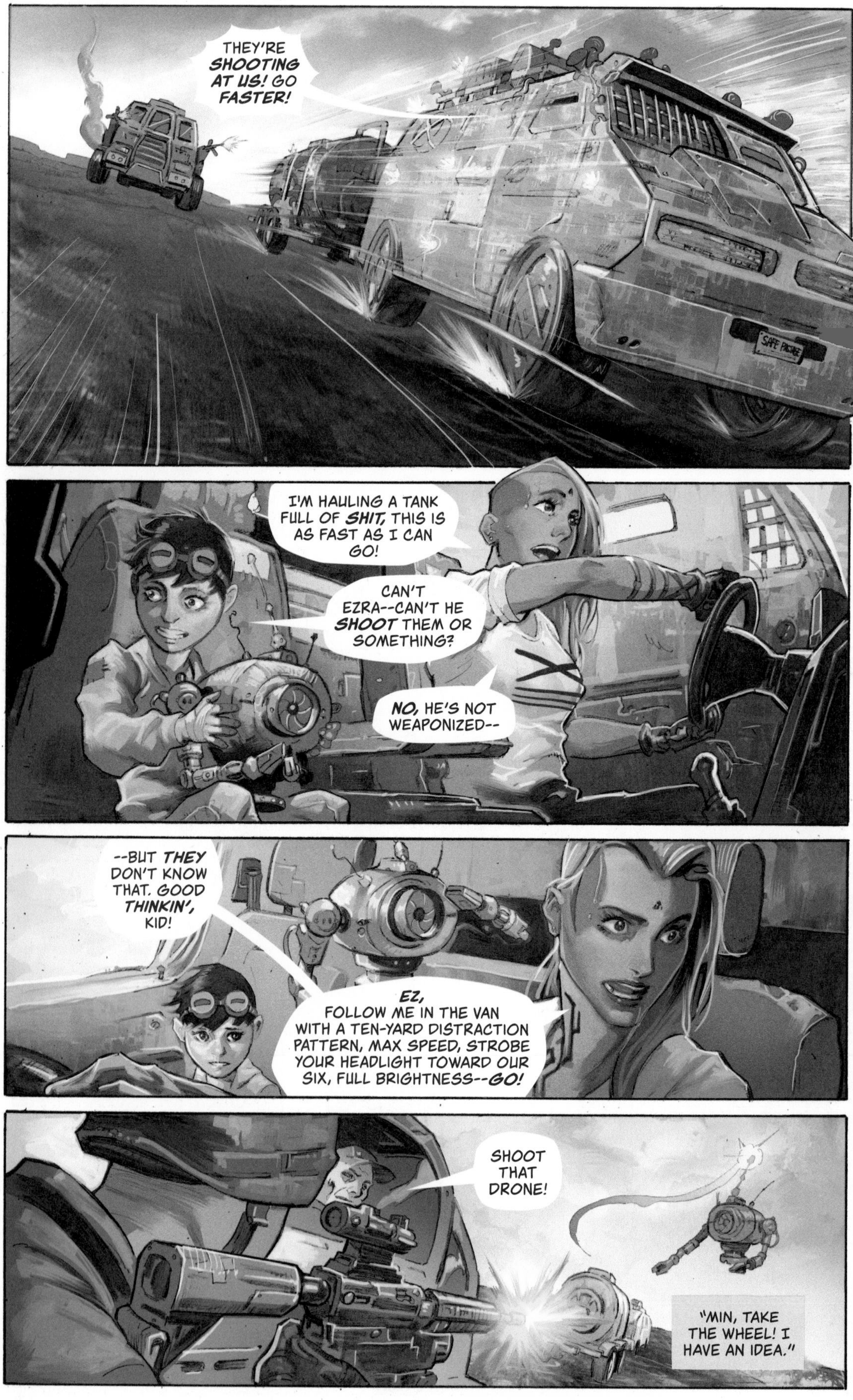
THEY'RE SHOOTING AT US! GO FASTER!
I'M HAULING A TANK FULL OF SHIT, THIS IS AS FAST AS I CAN GO!
CAN'T EZRA--CAN'T HE SHOOT THEM OR SOMETHING?
NO, HE'S NOT WEAPONIZED--
--BUT THEY DON'T KNOW THAT. GOOD THINKIN', KID!
EZ, FOLLOW ME IN THE VAN WITH A TEN-YARD DISTRACTION PATTERN, MAX SPEED, STROBE YOUR HEADLIGHT TOWARD OUR SIX, FULL BRIGHTNESS--GO!
SHOOT THAT DRONE!
"MIN, TAKE THE WHEEL! I HAVE AN IDEA."

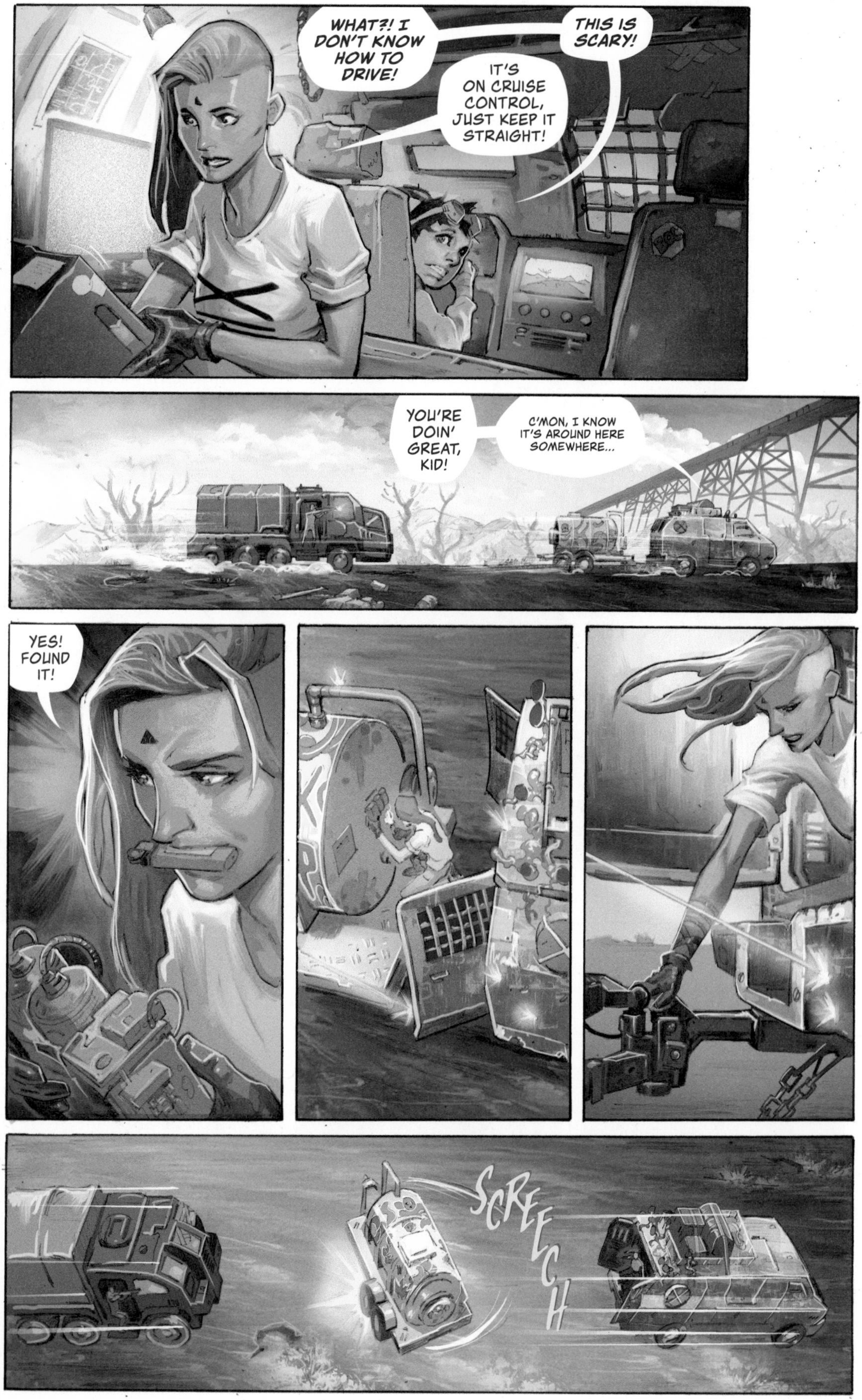
WHAT?! I DON'T KNOW HOW TO DRIVE!
THIS IS SCARY!
IT'S ON CRUISE CONTROL, JUST KEEP IT STRAIGHT!
YOU'RE DOIN' GREAT, KID!
C'MON, I KNOW IT'S AROUND HERE SOMEWHERE...
YES! FOUND IT!
SCREECH

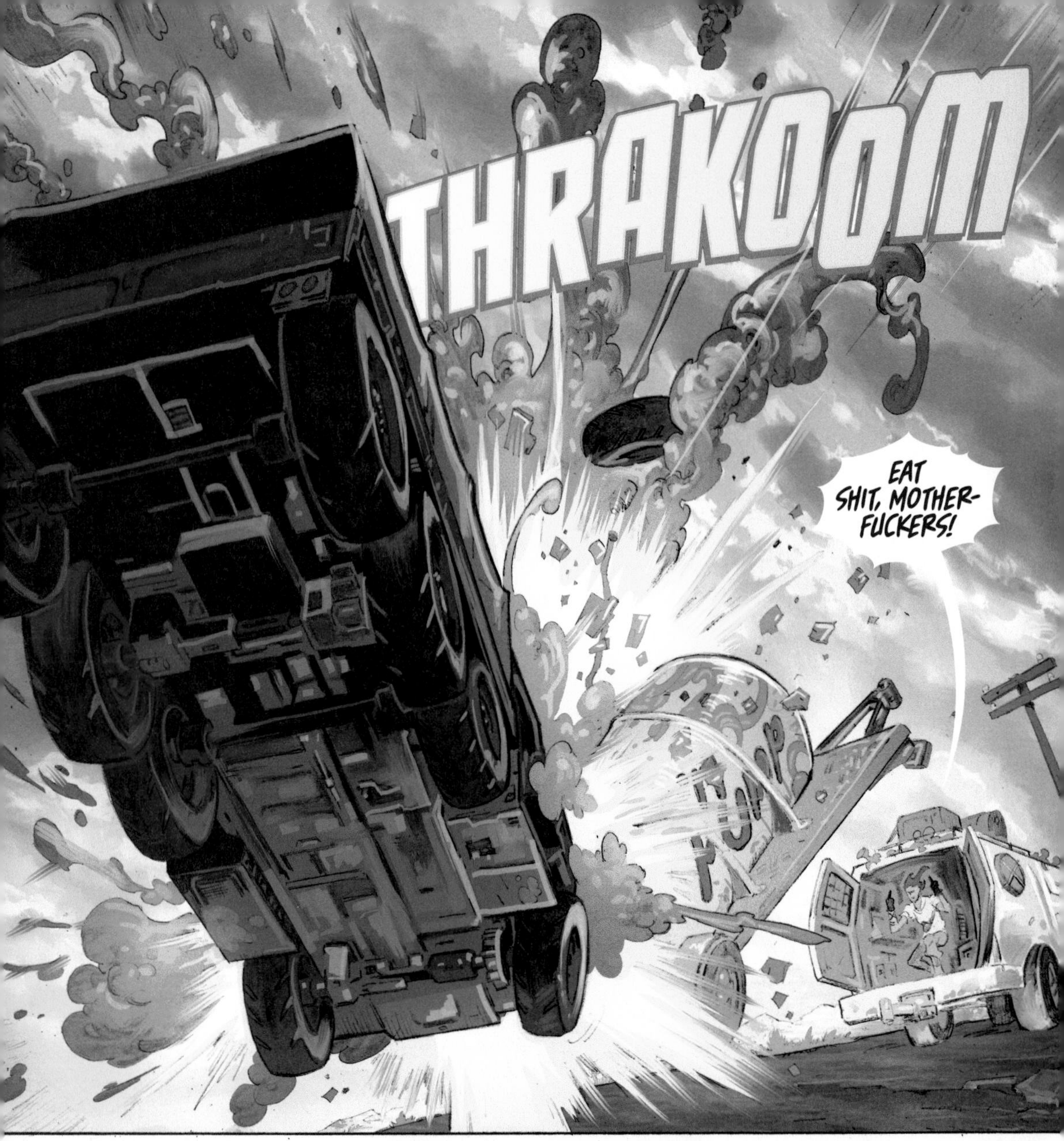
THRAKOOM
EAT SHIT, MOTHER-FUCKERS!

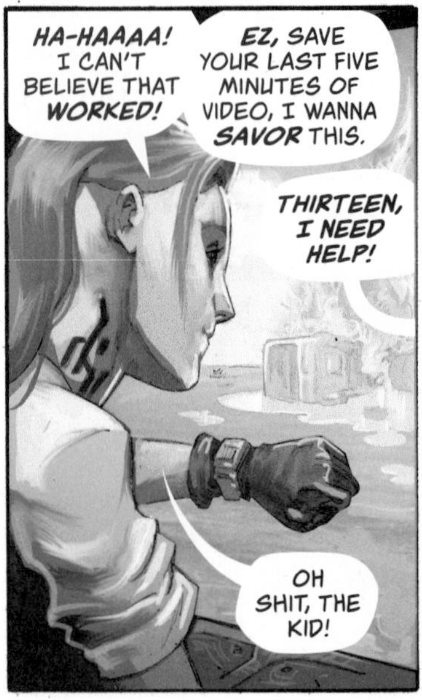
HA-HAAAA! I CAN'T BELIEVE THAT WORKED!
EZ, SAVE YOUR LAST FIVE MINUTES OF VIDEO, I WANNA SAVOR THIS.
THIRTEEN, I NEED HELP!
OH SHIT, THE KID!

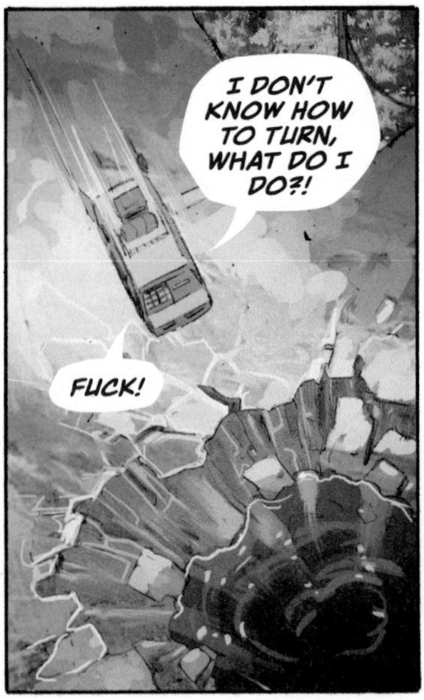
I DON'T KNOW HOW TO TURN, WHAT DO I DO?!
FUCK!

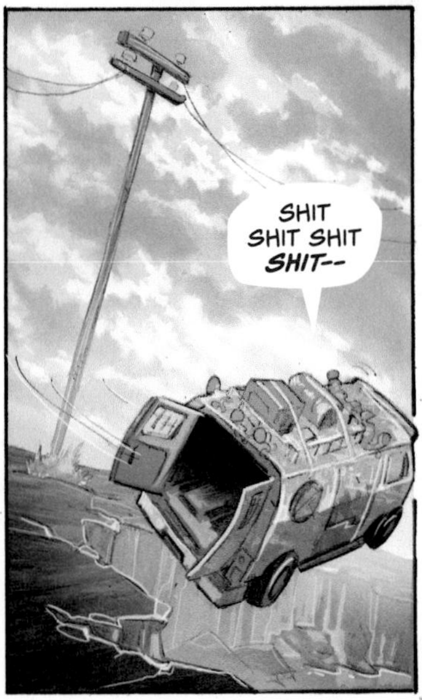
SHIT SHIT SHIT SHIT--

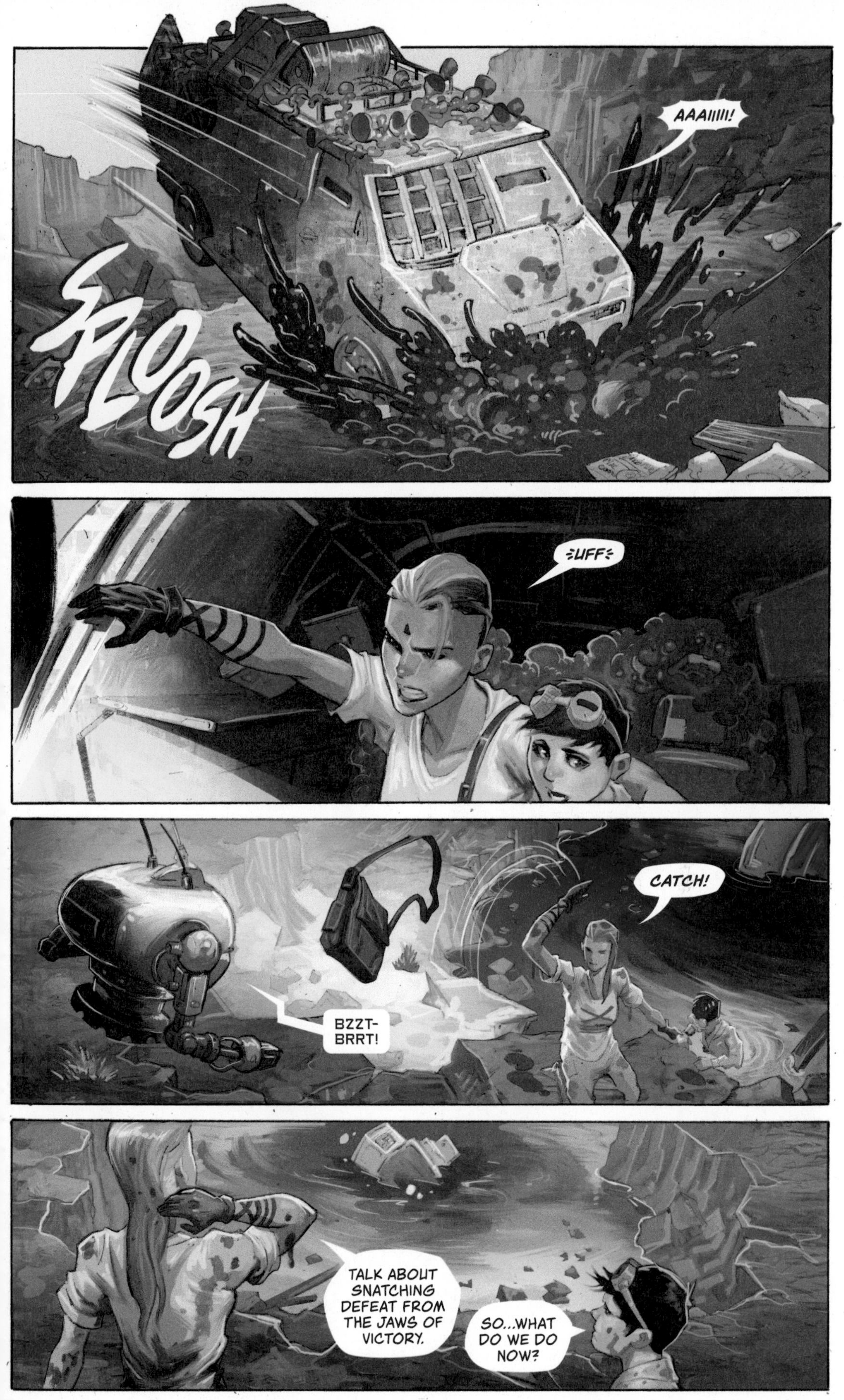
SPLOOSH
AAAIIIII!
UFF
CATCH!
BZZT-BRRT!
TALK ABOUT SNATCHING DEFEAT FROM THE JAWS OF VICTORY.
SO...WHAT DO WE DO NOW?

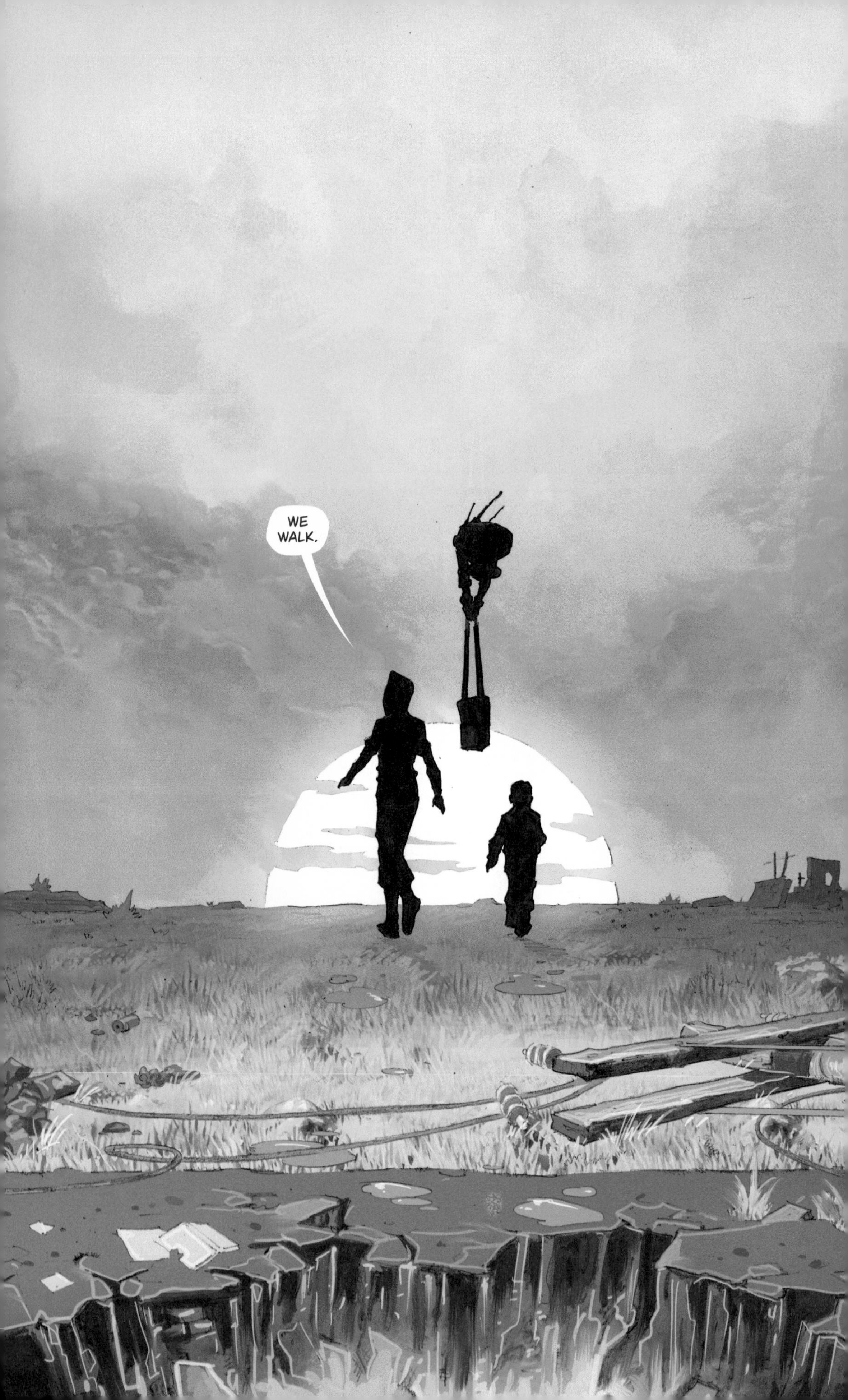
WE WALK.

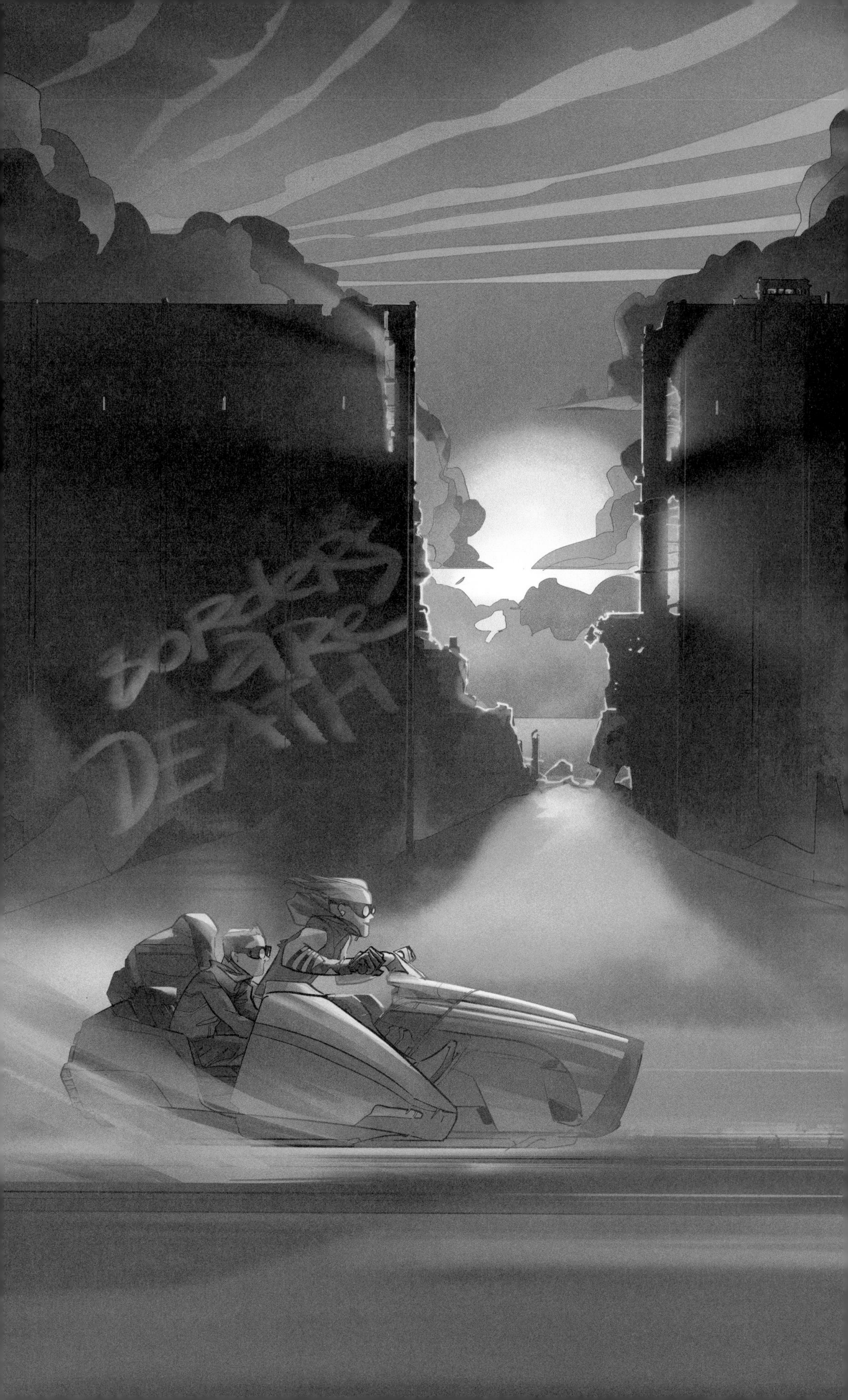
borders are
DEATH

CHAPTER THREE
THE OUTLANDS

STORY
ROB SHERIDAN

BREAKDOWNS
BARNABY BAGENDA

LINE ART
BARNABY BAGENDA AND AMANCAY NAHUELPAN

COLORS
ROMULO FAJARDO JR.

LETTERING
NATE PIEKOS OF BLAMBOT®

COVER
OTTO SCHMIDT

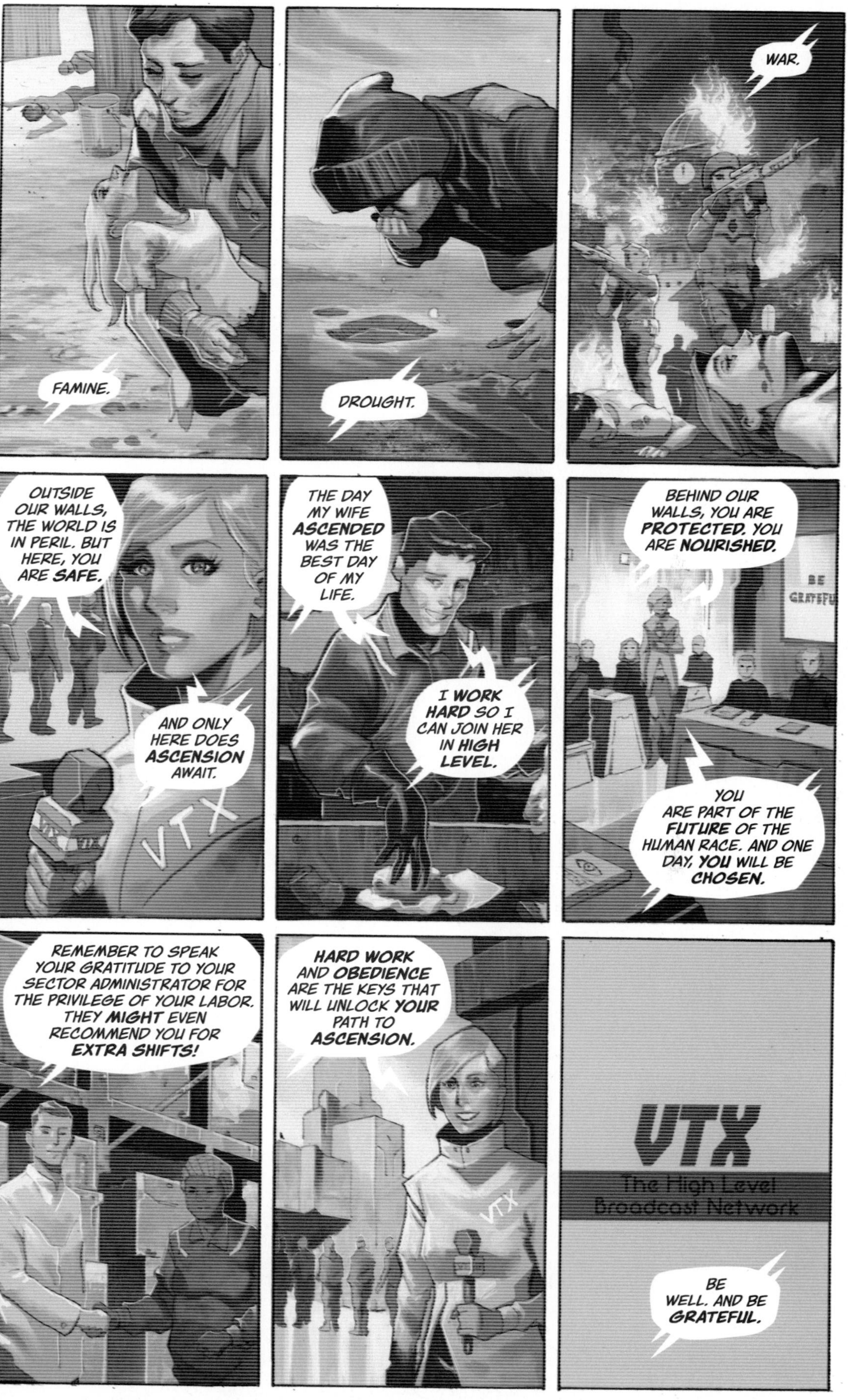
FAMINE.
DROUGHT.
WAR.
OUTSIDE OUR WALLS, THE WORLD IS IN PERIL. BUT HERE, YOU ARE **SAFE.**
AND ONLY HERE DOES **ASCENSION** AWAIT.
VTX
THE DAY MY WIFE **ASCENDED** WAS THE BEST DAY OF MY LIFE.
I **WORK HARD** SO I CAN JOIN HER IN **HIGH LEVEL.**
BEHIND OUR WALLS, YOU ARE **PROTECTED.** YOU ARE **NOURISHED.**
BE GRATEFU
YOU ARE PART OF THE **FUTURE** OF THE HUMAN RACE. AND ONE DAY, **YOU** WILL BE **CHOSEN.**
REMEMBER TO SPEAK YOUR GRATITUDE TO YOUR SECTOR ADMINISTRATOR FOR THE PRIVILEGE OF YOUR LABOR. THEY **MIGHT** EVEN RECOMMEND YOU FOR **EXTRA SHIFTS!**
HARD WORK AND **OBEDIENCE** ARE THE KEYS THAT WILL UNLOCK **YOUR** PATH TO **ASCENSION.**
VTX
VTX
The High Level Broadcast Network
BE WELL. AND BE **GRATEFUL.**

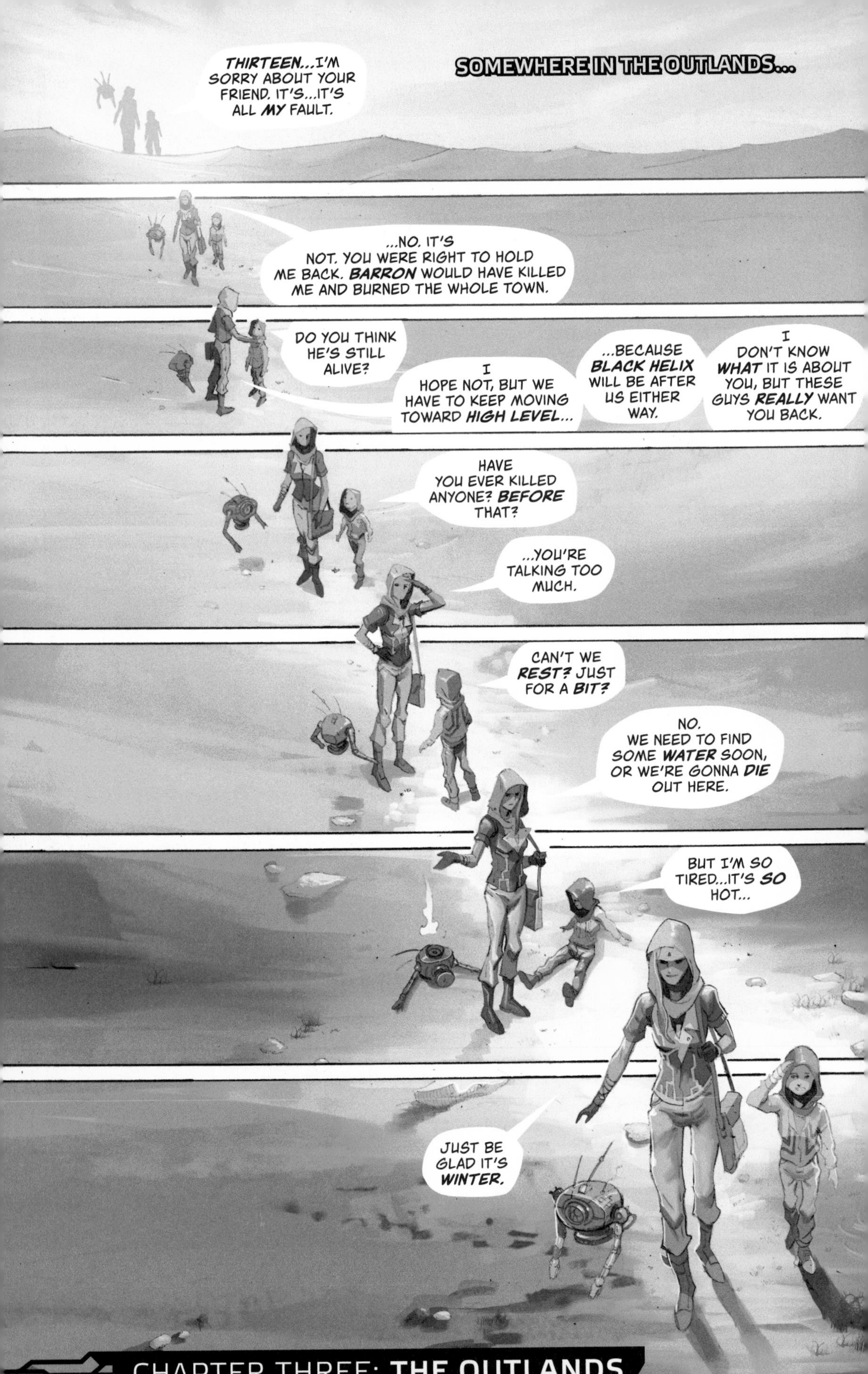
SOMEWHERE IN THE OUTLANDS...
THIRTEEN...I'M SORRY ABOUT YOUR FRIEND. IT'S...IT'S ALL MY FAULT.
...NO. IT'S NOT. YOU WERE RIGHT TO HOLD ME BACK. BARRON WOULD HAVE KILLED ME AND BURNED THE WHOLE TOWN.
DO YOU THINK HE'S STILL ALIVE?
I HOPE NOT, BUT WE HAVE TO KEEP MOVING TOWARD HIGH LEVEL...
...BECAUSE BLACK HELIX WILL BE AFTER US EITHER WAY.
I DON'T KNOW WHAT IT IS ABOUT YOU, BUT THESE GUYS REALLY WANT YOU BACK.
HAVE YOU EVER KILLED ANYONE? BEFORE THAT?
...YOU'RE TALKING TOO MUCH.
CAN'T WE REST? JUST FOR A BIT?
NO. WE NEED TO FIND SOME WATER SOON, OR WE'RE GONNA DIE OUT HERE.
BUT I'M SO TIRED...IT'S SO HOT...
JUST BE GLAD IT'S WINTER.

CHAPTER THREE: THE OUTLANDS

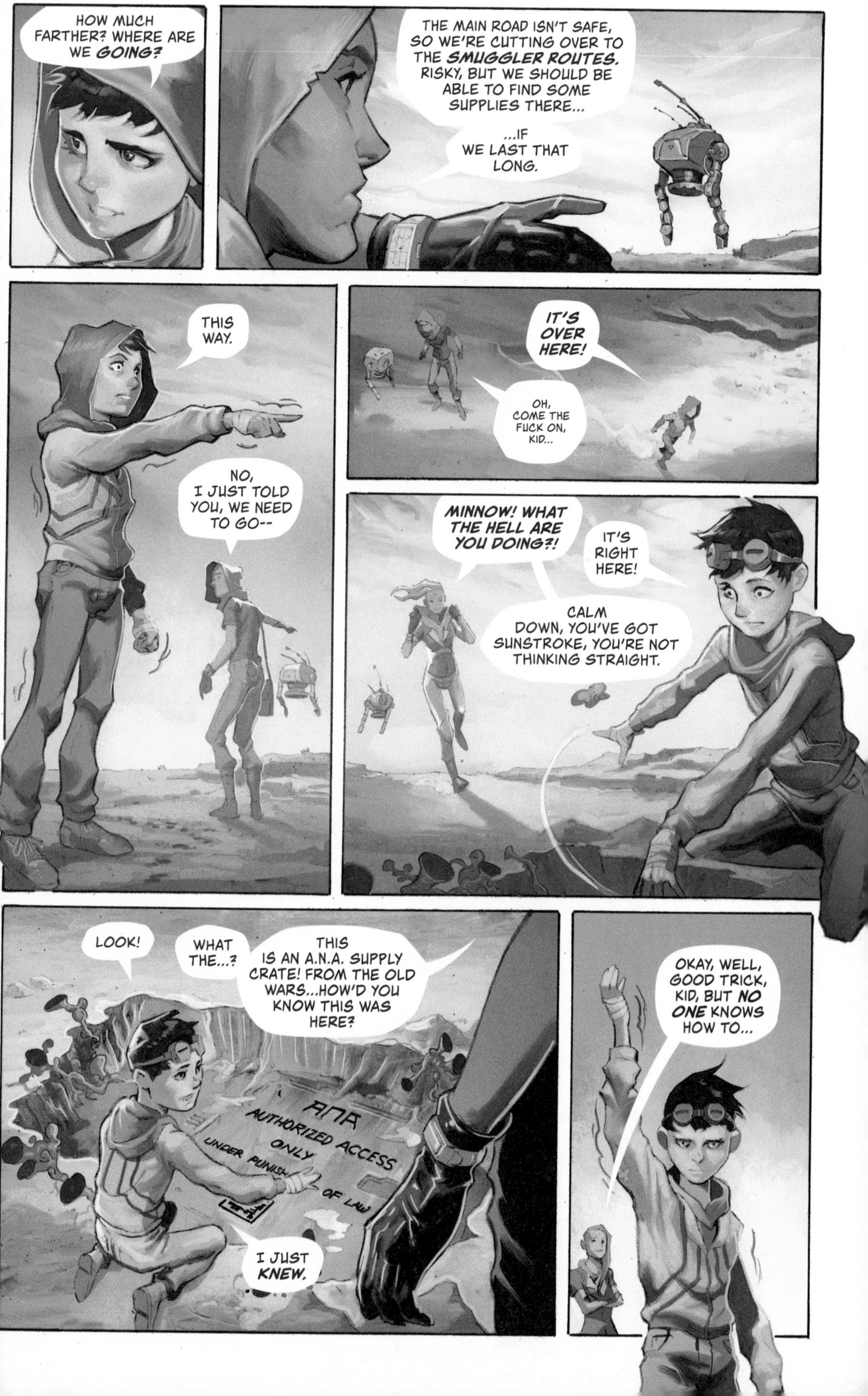
HOW MUCH FARTHER? WHERE ARE WE GOING?
THE MAIN ROAD ISN'T SAFE, SO WE'RE CUTTING OVER TO THE SMUGGLER ROUTES. RISKY, BUT WE SHOULD BE ABLE TO FIND SOME SUPPLIES THERE...
...IF WE LAST THAT LONG.
THIS WAY.
NO, I JUST TOLD YOU, WE NEED TO GO--
IT'S OVER HERE!
OH, COME THE FUCK ON, KID...
MINNOW! WHAT THE HELL ARE YOU DOING?!
IT'S RIGHT HERE!
CALM DOWN, YOU'VE GOT SUNSTROKE, YOU'RE NOT THINKING STRAIGHT.
LOOK!
WHAT THE...?
THIS IS AN A.N.A. SUPPLY CRATE! FROM THE OLD WARS...HOW'D YOU KNOW THIS WAS HERE?
AUTHORIZED ACCESS
ONLY
UNDER PUNISH
OF LAW
I JUST KNEW.
OKAY, WELL, GOOD TRICK, KID, BUT NO ONE KNOWS HOW TO...

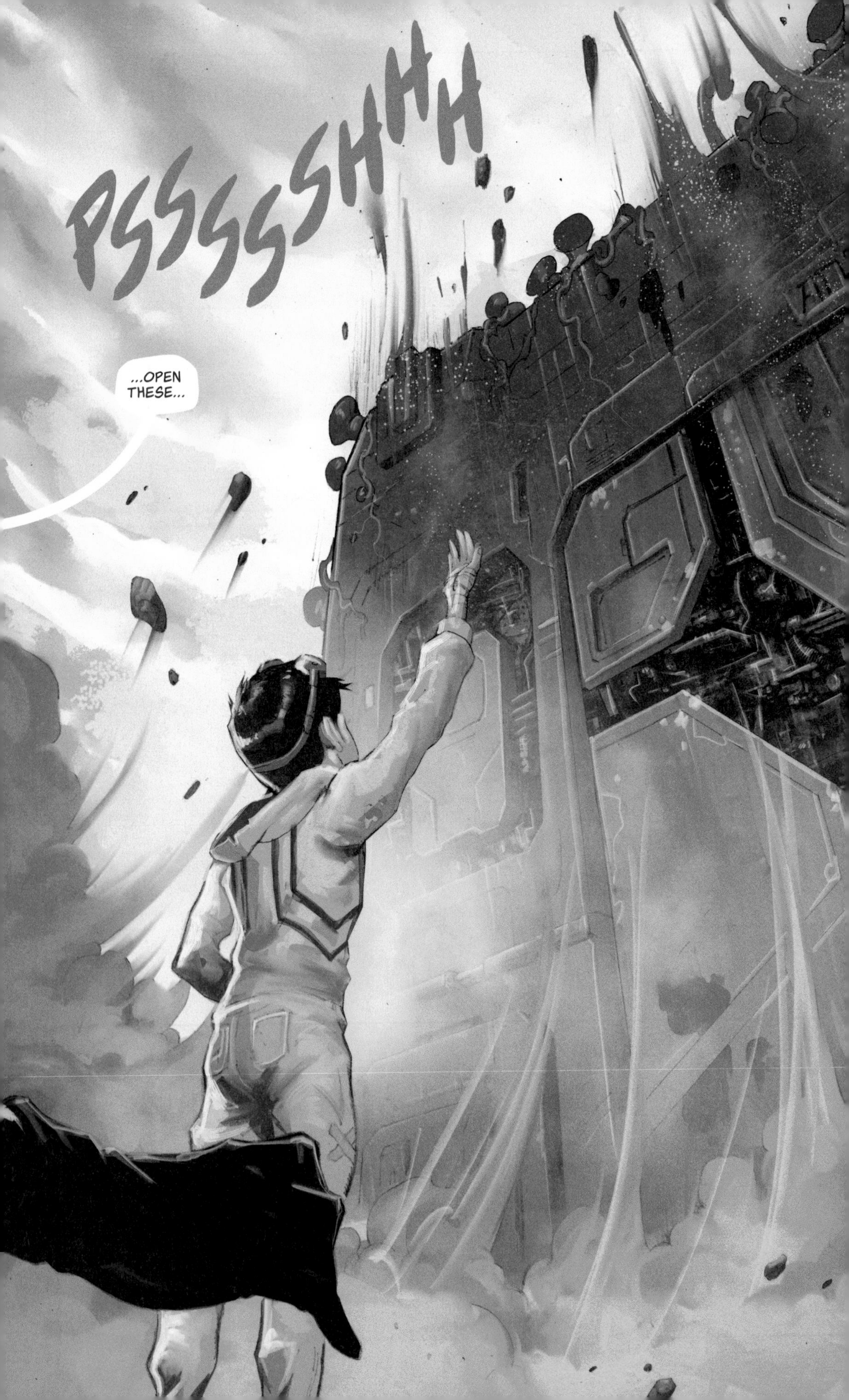
PSSSSSHHH
...OPEN THESE...

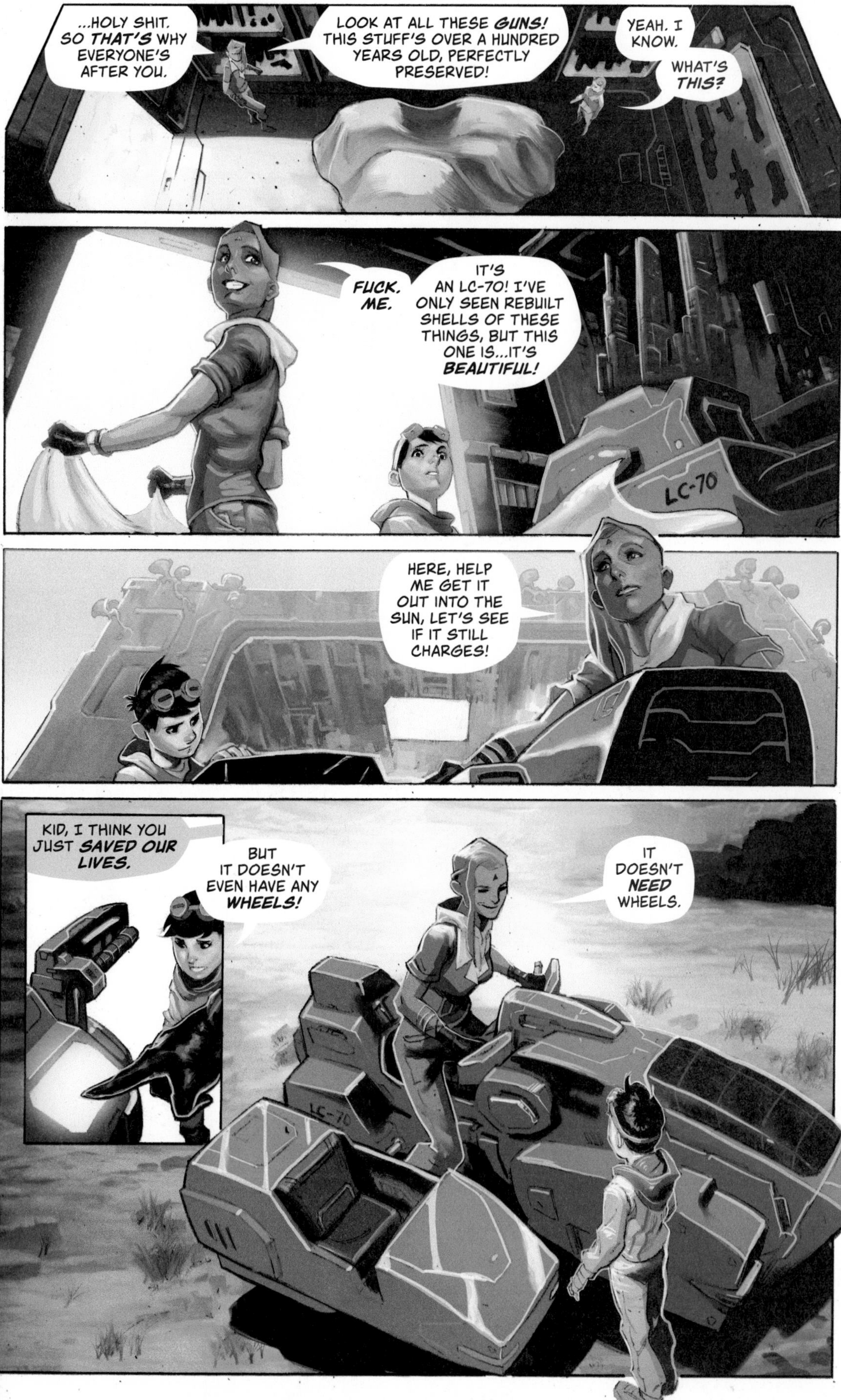
...HOLY SHIT. SO THAT'S WHY EVERYONE'S AFTER YOU.
LOOK AT ALL THESE GUNS! THIS STUFF'S OVER A HUNDRED YEARS OLD, PERFECTLY PRESERVED!
YEAH. I KNOW.
WHAT'S THIS?
FUCK. ME.
IT'S AN LC-70! I'VE ONLY SEEN REBUILT SHELLS OF THESE THINGS, BUT THIS ONE IS...IT'S BEAUTIFUL!
LC-70
HERE, HELP ME GET IT OUT INTO THE SUN, LET'S SEE IF IT STILL CHARGES!
KID, I THINK YOU JUST SAVED OUR LIVES.
BUT IT DOESN'T EVEN HAVE ANY WHEELS!
IT DOESN'T NEED WHEELS.
LC-70

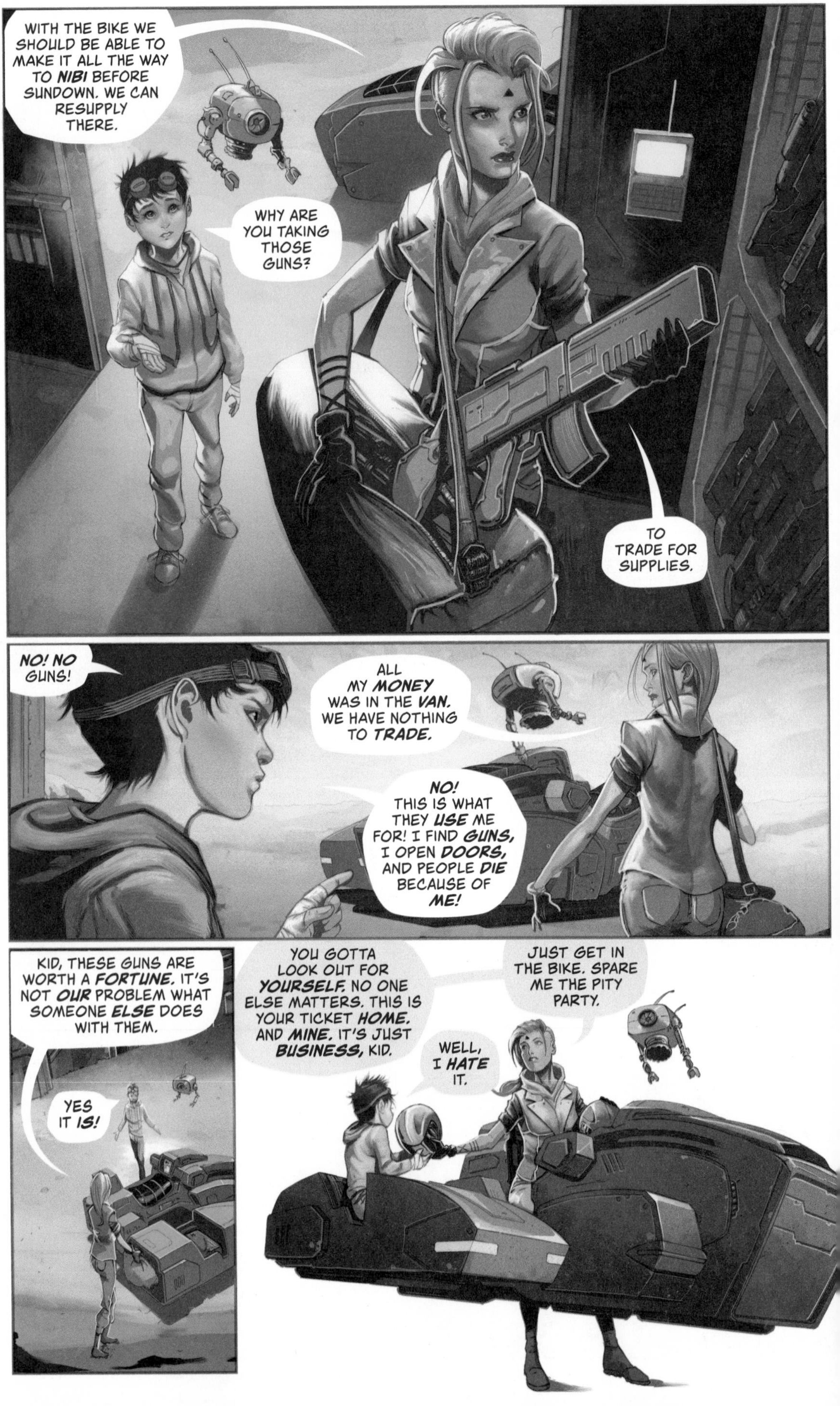
WITH THE BIKE WE SHOULD BE ABLE TO MAKE IT ALL THE WAY TO NIBI BEFORE SUNDOWN. WE CAN RESUPPLY THERE.
WHY ARE YOU TAKING THOSE GUNS?
TO TRADE FOR SUPPLIES.
NO! NO GUNS!
ALL MY MONEY WAS IN THE VAN. WE HAVE NOTHING TO TRADE.
NO! THIS IS WHAT THEY USE ME FOR! I FIND GUNS, I OPEN DOORS, AND PEOPLE DIE BECAUSE OF ME!
KID, THESE GUNS ARE WORTH A FORTUNE. IT'S NOT OUR PROBLEM WHAT SOMEONE ELSE DOES WITH THEM.
YES IT IS!
YOU GOTTA LOOK OUT FOR YOURSELF. NO ONE ELSE MATTERS. THIS IS YOUR TICKET HOME. AND MINE. IT'S JUST BUSINESS, KID.
WELL, I HATE IT.
JUST GET IN THE BIKE. SPARE ME THE PITY PARTY.

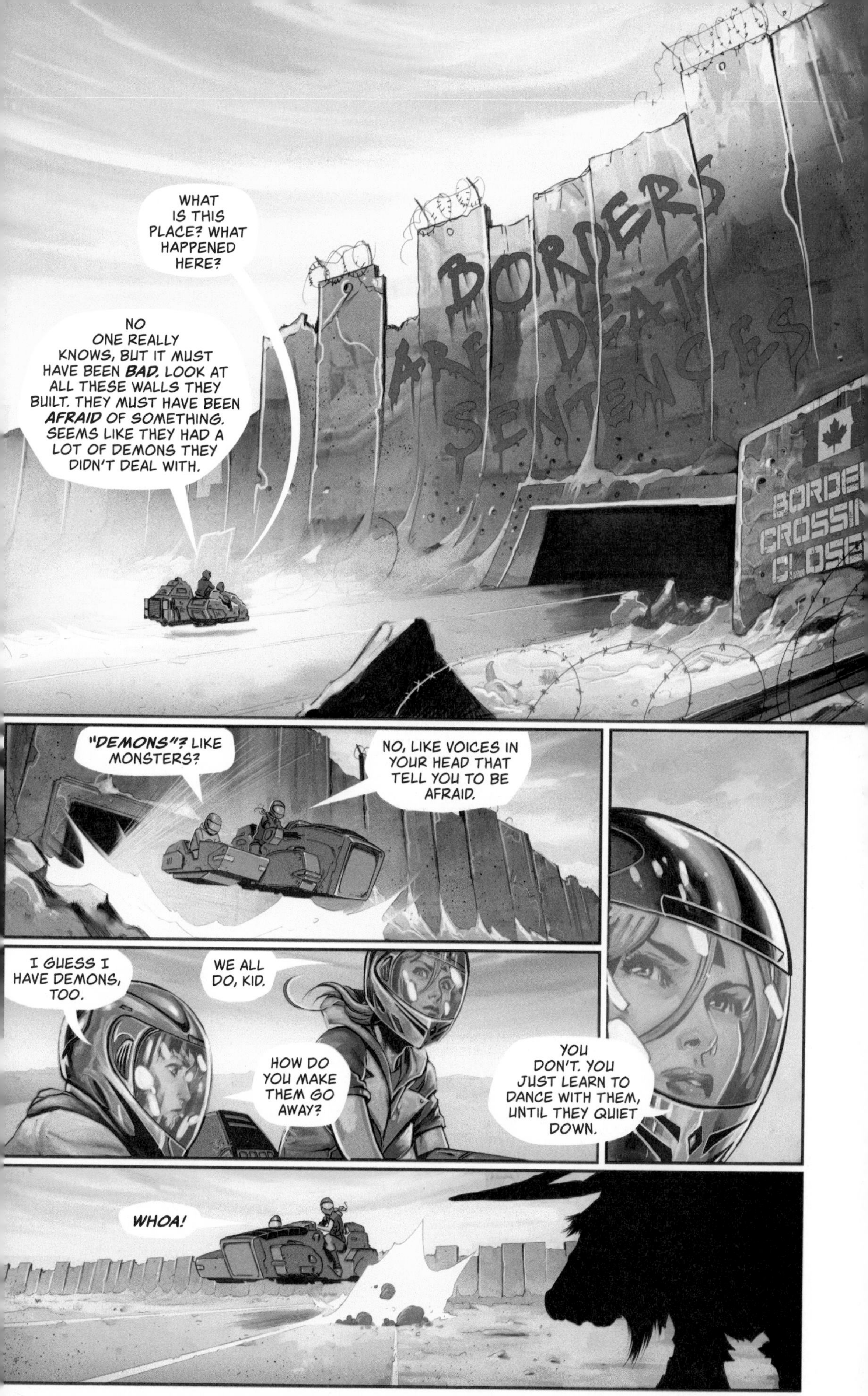

BORDERS ARE DEATH SENTENCES
BORDER CROSSING CLOSE
WHAT IS THIS PLACE? WHAT HAPPENED HERE?
NO ONE REALLY KNOWS, BUT IT MUST HAVE BEEN BAD. LOOK AT ALL THESE WALLS THEY BUILT. THEY MUST HAVE BEEN AFRAID OF SOMETHING. SEEMS LIKE THEY HAD A LOT OF DEMONS THEY DIDN'T DEAL WITH.
"DEMONS"? LIKE MONSTERS?
NO, LIKE VOICES IN YOUR HEAD THAT TELL YOU TO BE AFRAID.
I GUESS I HAVE DEMONS, TOO.
WE ALL DO, KID.
HOW DO YOU MAKE THEM GO AWAY?
YOU DON'T. YOU JUST LEARN TO DANCE WITH THEM, UNTIL THEY QUIET DOWN.
WHOA!

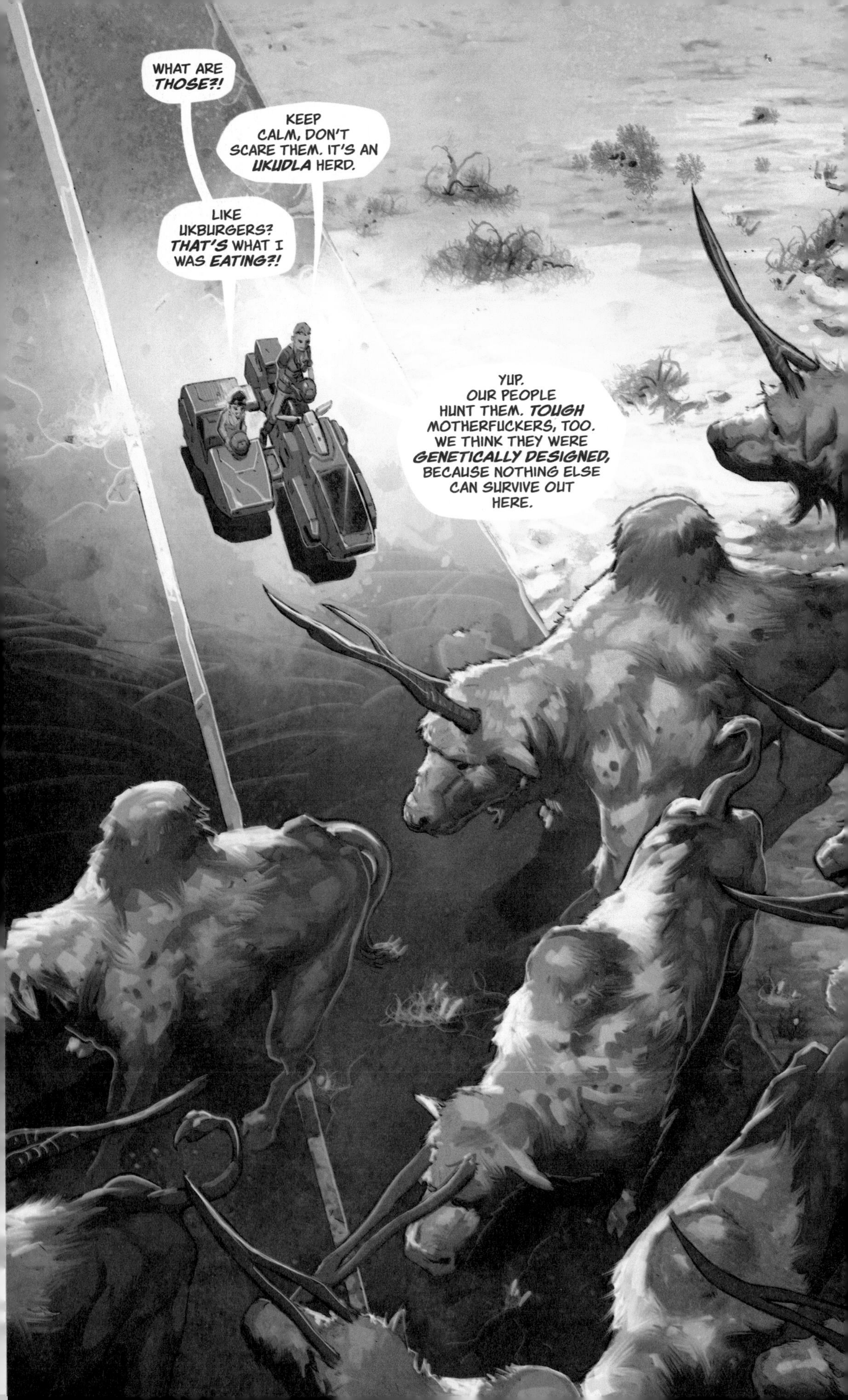
WHAT ARE THOSE?!
KEEP CALM, DON'T SCARE THEM. IT'S AN UKUDLA HERD.
LIKE UKBURGERS? THAT'S WHAT I WAS EATING?!
YUP. OUR PEOPLE HUNT THEM. TOUGH MOTHERFUCKERS, TOO. WE THINK THEY WERE GENETICALLY DESIGNED, BECAUSE NOTHING ELSE CAN SURVIVE OUT HERE.

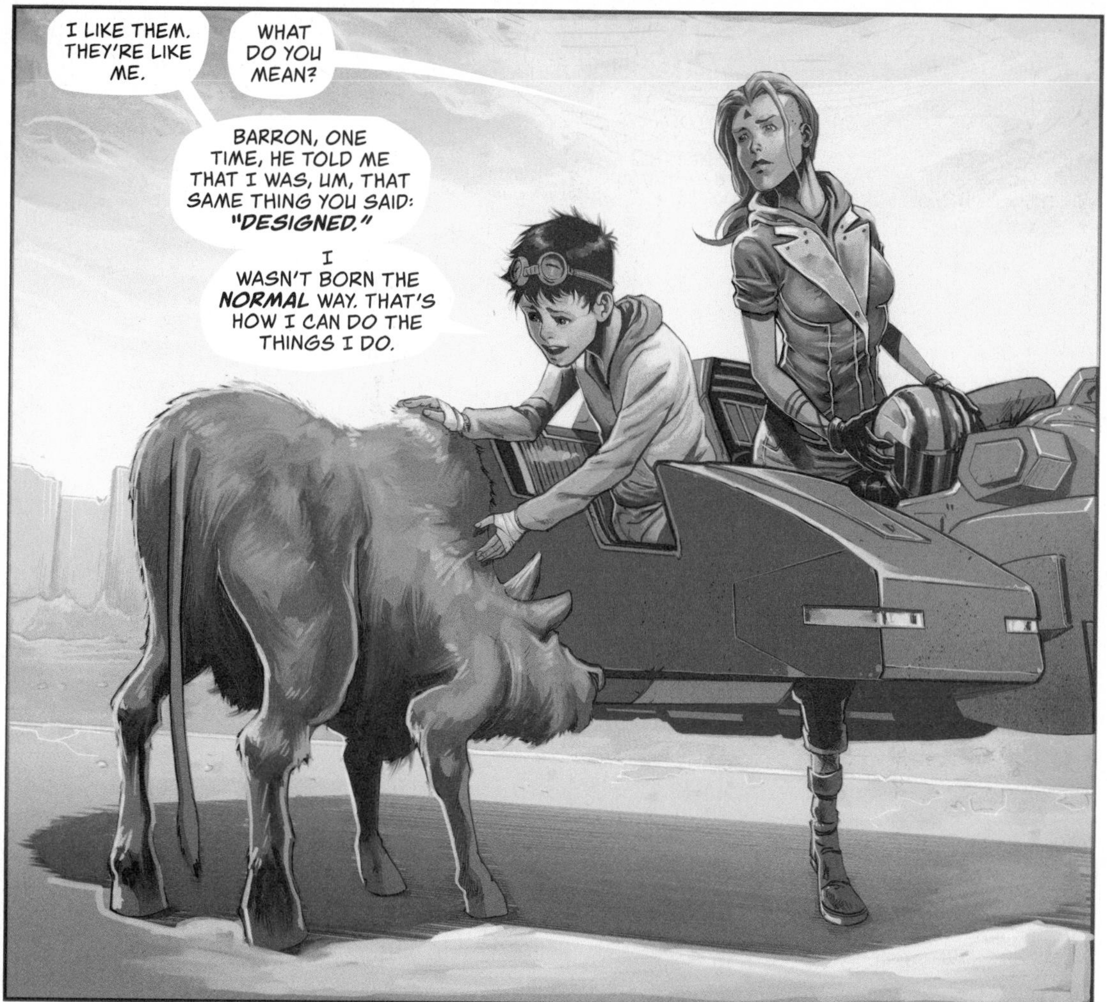
I LIKE THEM. THEY'RE LIKE ME.
WHAT DO YOU MEAN?
BARRON, ONE TIME, HE TOLD ME THAT I WAS, UM, THAT SAME THING YOU SAID: "DESIGNED."
I WASN'T BORN THE NORMAL WAY. THAT'S HOW I CAN DO THE THINGS I DO.

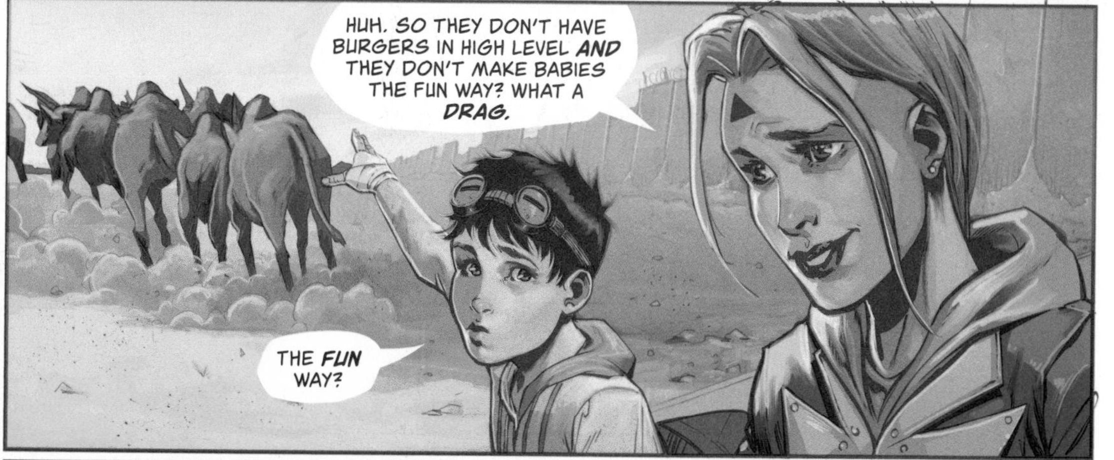
HUH. SO THEY DON'T HAVE BURGERS IN HIGH LEVEL AND THEY DON'T MAKE BABIES THE FUN WAY? WHAT A DRAG.
THE FUN WAY?

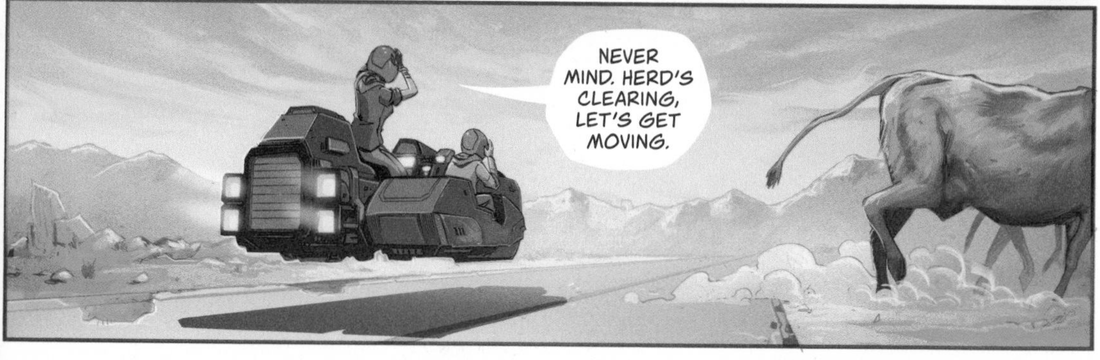
NEVER MIND. HERD'S CLEARING, LET'S GET MOVING.

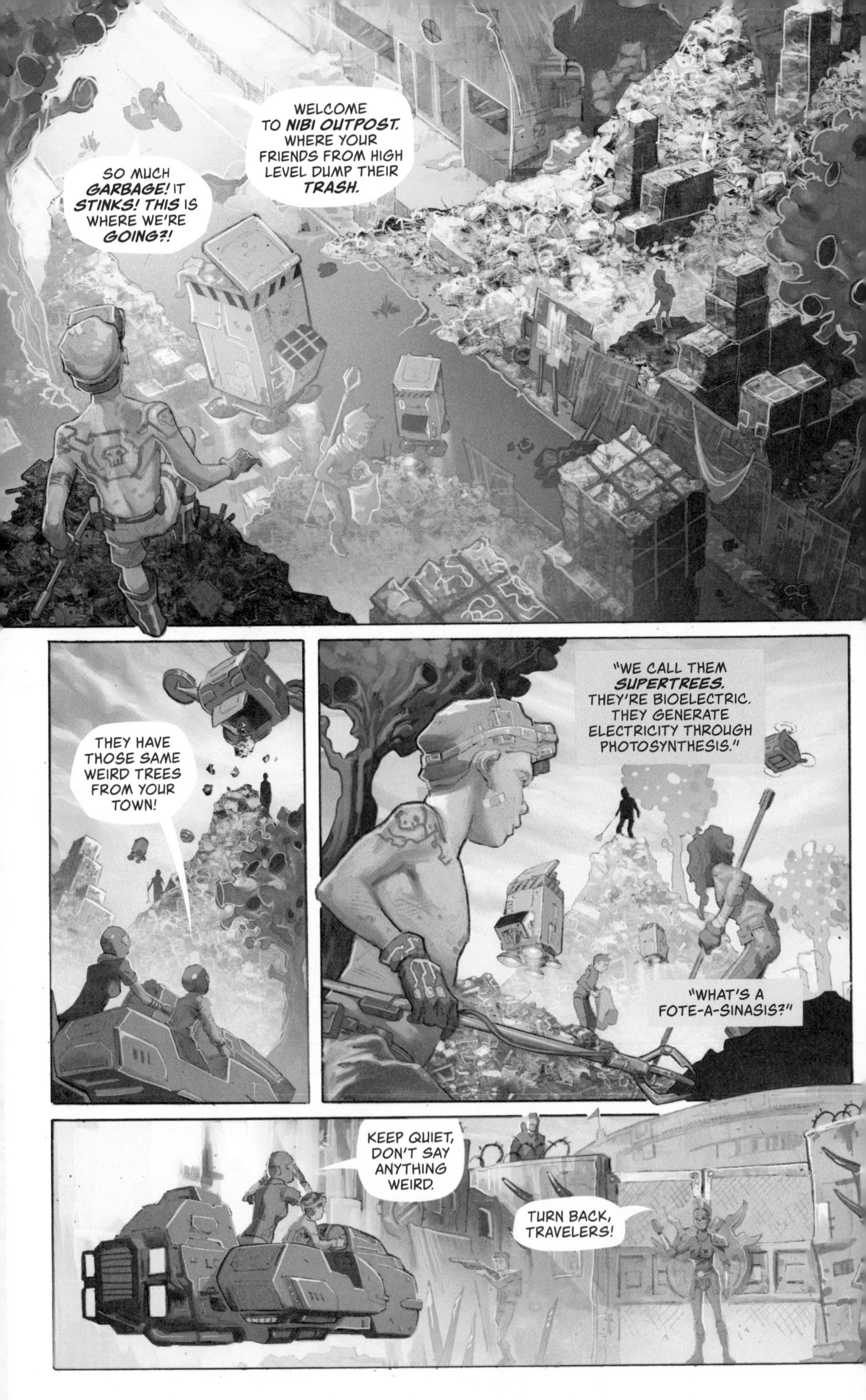
SO MUCH GARBAGE! IT STINKS! THIS IS WHERE WE'RE GOING?!
WELCOME TO NIBI OUTPOST. WHERE YOUR FRIENDS FROM HIGH LEVEL DUMP THEIR TRASH.
THEY HAVE THOSE SAME WEIRD TREES FROM YOUR TOWN!
"WE CALL THEM SUPERTREES. THEY'RE BIOELECTRIC. THEY GENERATE ELECTRICITY THROUGH PHOTOSYNTHESIS."
"WHAT'S A FOTE-A-SINASIS?"
KEEP QUIET, DON'T SAY ANYTHING WEIRD.
TURN BACK, TRAVELERS!

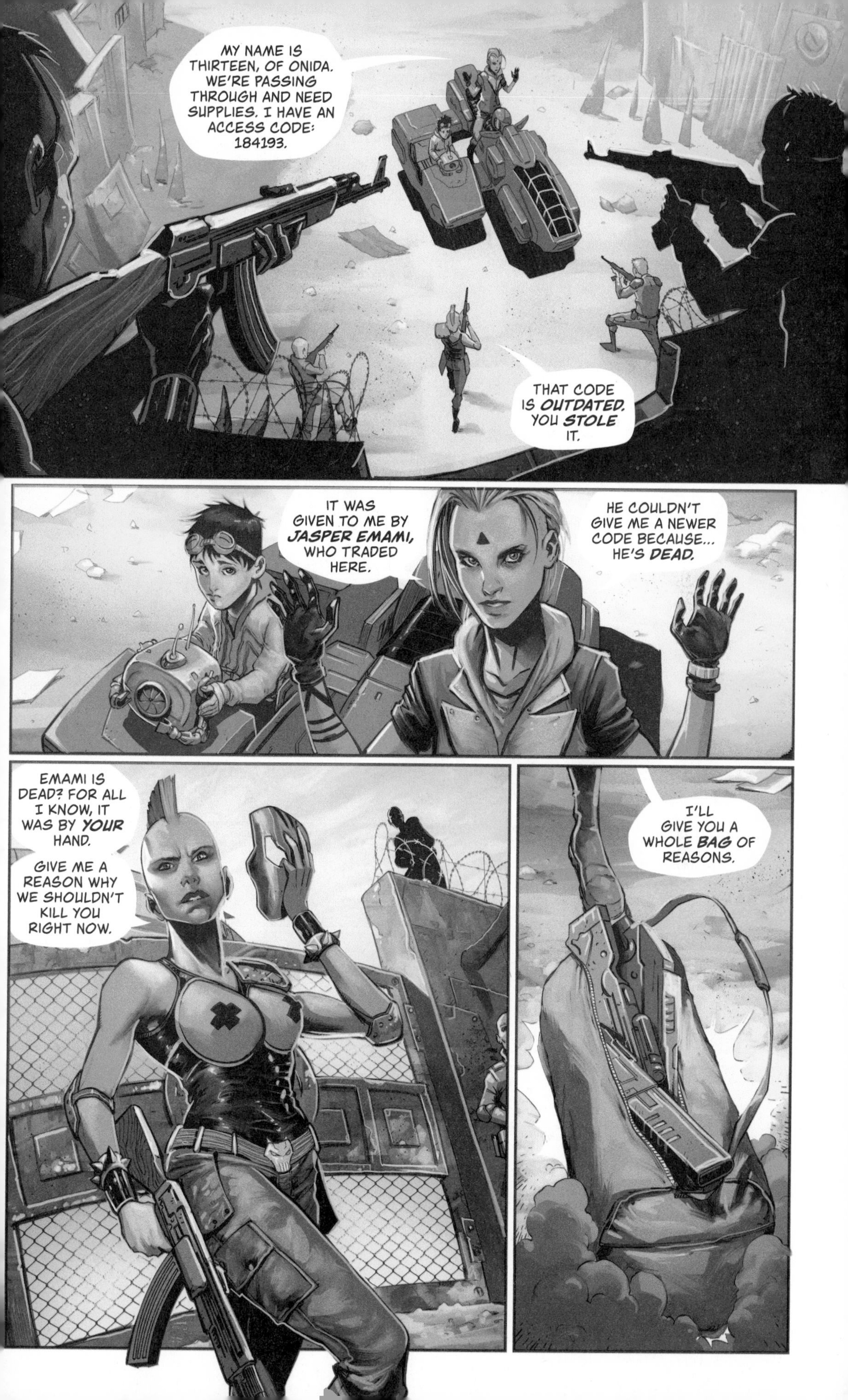
MY NAME IS THIRTEEN, OF ONIDA. WE'RE PASSING THROUGH AND NEED SUPPLIES. I HAVE AN ACCESS CODE: 184193.
THAT CODE IS OUTDATED. YOU STOLE IT.
IT WAS GIVEN TO ME BY JASPER EMAMI, WHO TRADED HERE.
HE COULDN'T GIVE ME A NEWER CODE BECAUSE... HE'S DEAD.
EMAMI IS DEAD? FOR ALL I KNOW, IT WAS BY YOUR HAND.
GIVE ME A REASON WHY WE SHOULDN'T KILL YOU RIGHT NOW.
I'LL GIVE YOU A WHOLE BAG OF REASONS.

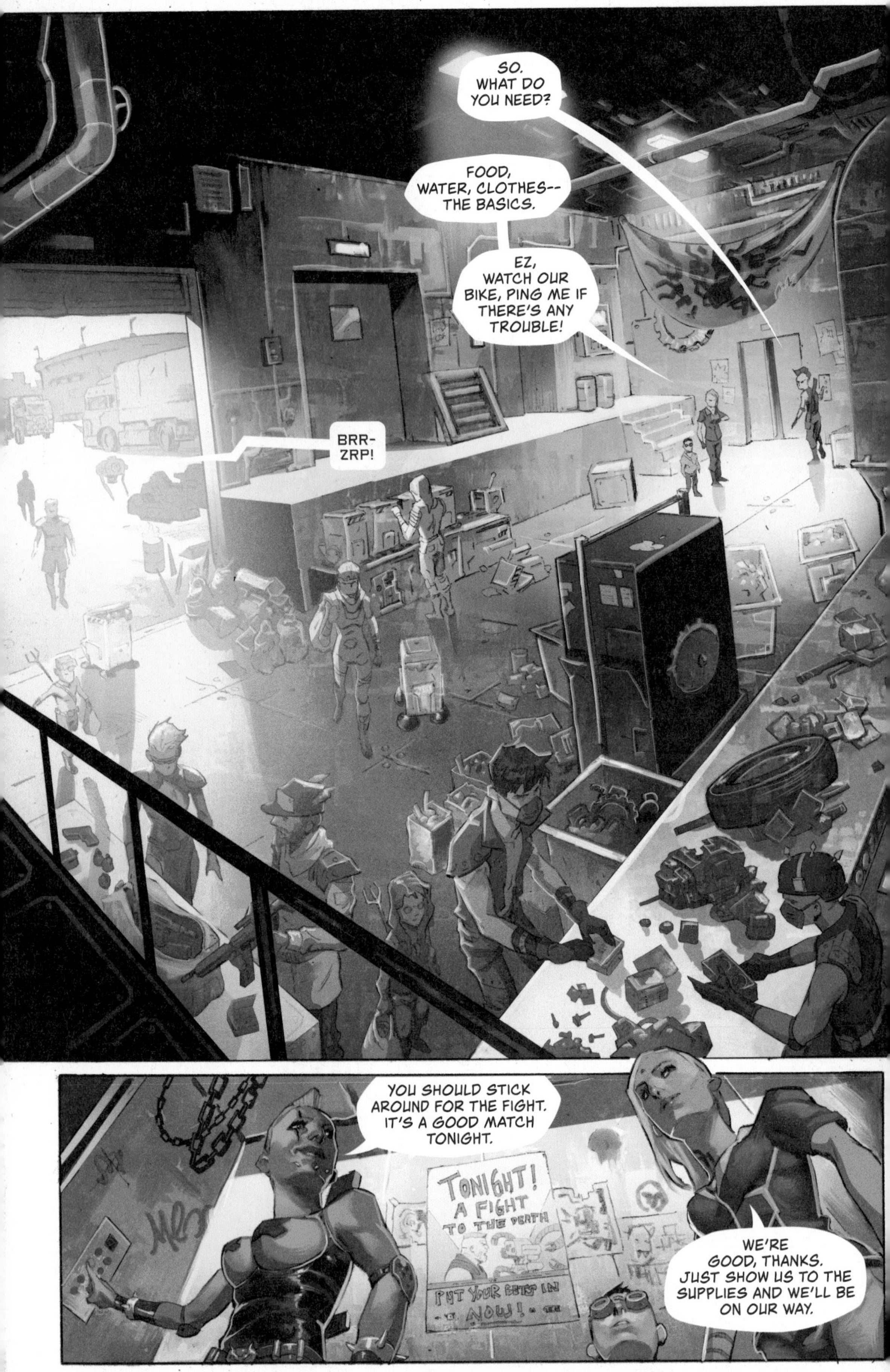
SO. WHAT DO YOU NEED?
FOOD, WATER, CLOTHES-- THE BASICS.
EZ, WATCH OUR BIKE, PING ME IF THERE'S ANY TROUBLE!
BRR- ZRP!
YOU SHOULD STICK AROUND FOR THE FIGHT. IT'S A GOOD MATCH TONIGHT.
TONIGHT! A FIGHT TO THE DEATH
PUT YOUR BETS IN NOW!
WE'RE GOOD, THANKS. JUST SHOW US TO THE SUPPLIES AND WE'LL BE ON OUR WAY.

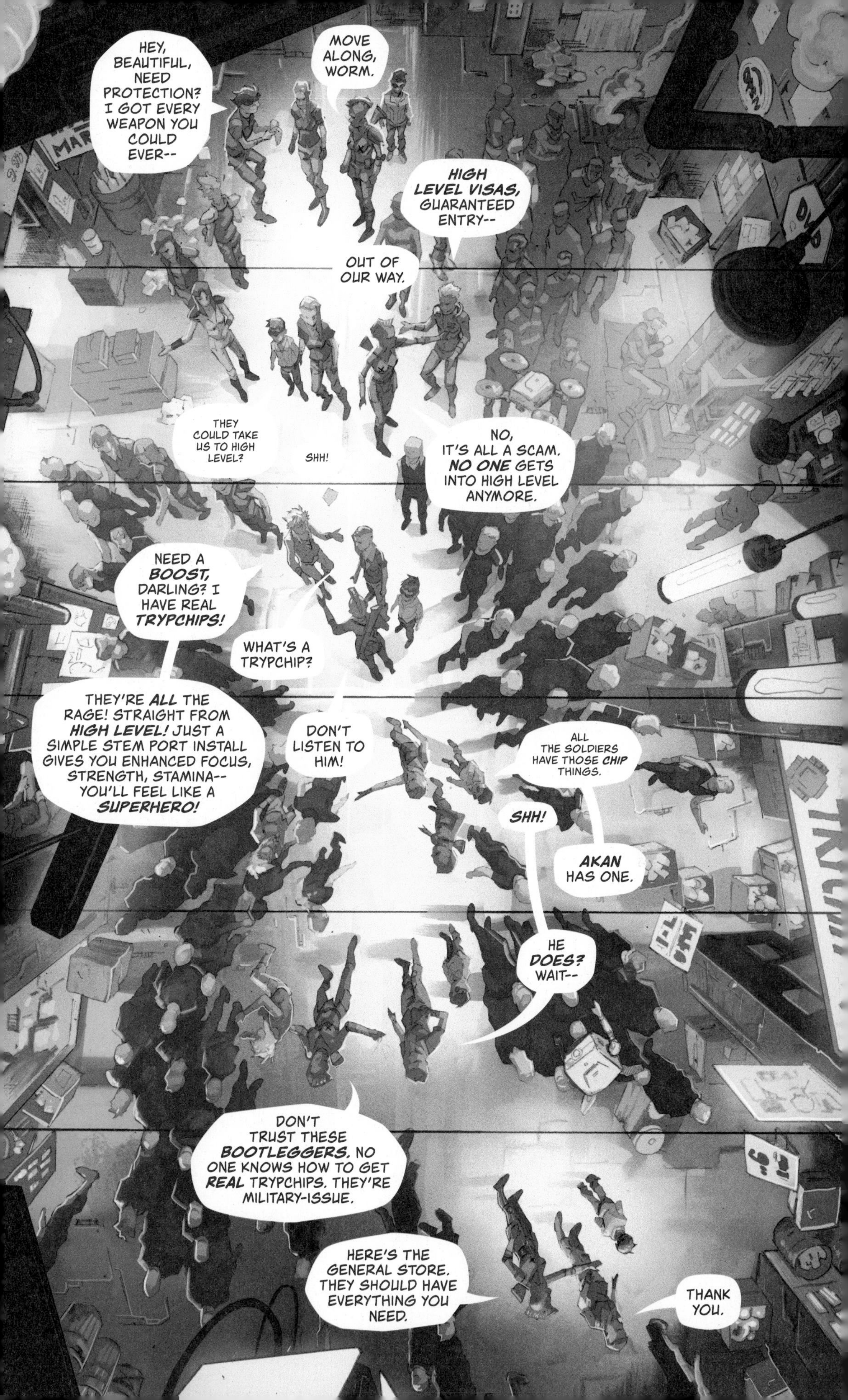

HEY, BEAUTIFUL, NEED PROTECTION? I GOT EVERY WEAPON YOU COULD EVER--
MOVE ALONG, WORM.
HIGH LEVEL VISAS, GUARANTEED ENTRY--
OUT OF OUR WAY.
THEY COULD TAKE US TO HIGH LEVEL?
SHH!
NO, IT'S ALL A SCAM. NO ONE GETS INTO HIGH LEVEL ANYMORE.
NEED A BOOST, DARLING? I HAVE REAL TRYPCHIPS!
WHAT'S A TRYPCHIP?
THEY'RE ALL THE RAGE! STRAIGHT FROM HIGH LEVEL! JUST A SIMPLE STEM PORT INSTALL GIVES YOU ENHANCED FOCUS, STRENGTH, STAMINA-- YOU'LL FEEL LIKE A SUPERHERO!
DON'T LISTEN TO HIM!
ALL THE SOLDIERS HAVE THOSE CHIP THINGS.
SHH!
AKAN HAS ONE.
HE DOES? WAIT--
DON'T TRUST THESE BOOTLEGGERS. NO ONE KNOWS HOW TO GET REAL TRYPCHIPS. THEY'RE MILITARY-ISSUE.
HERE'S THE GENERAL STORE. THEY SHOULD HAVE EVERYTHING YOU NEED.
THANK YOU.

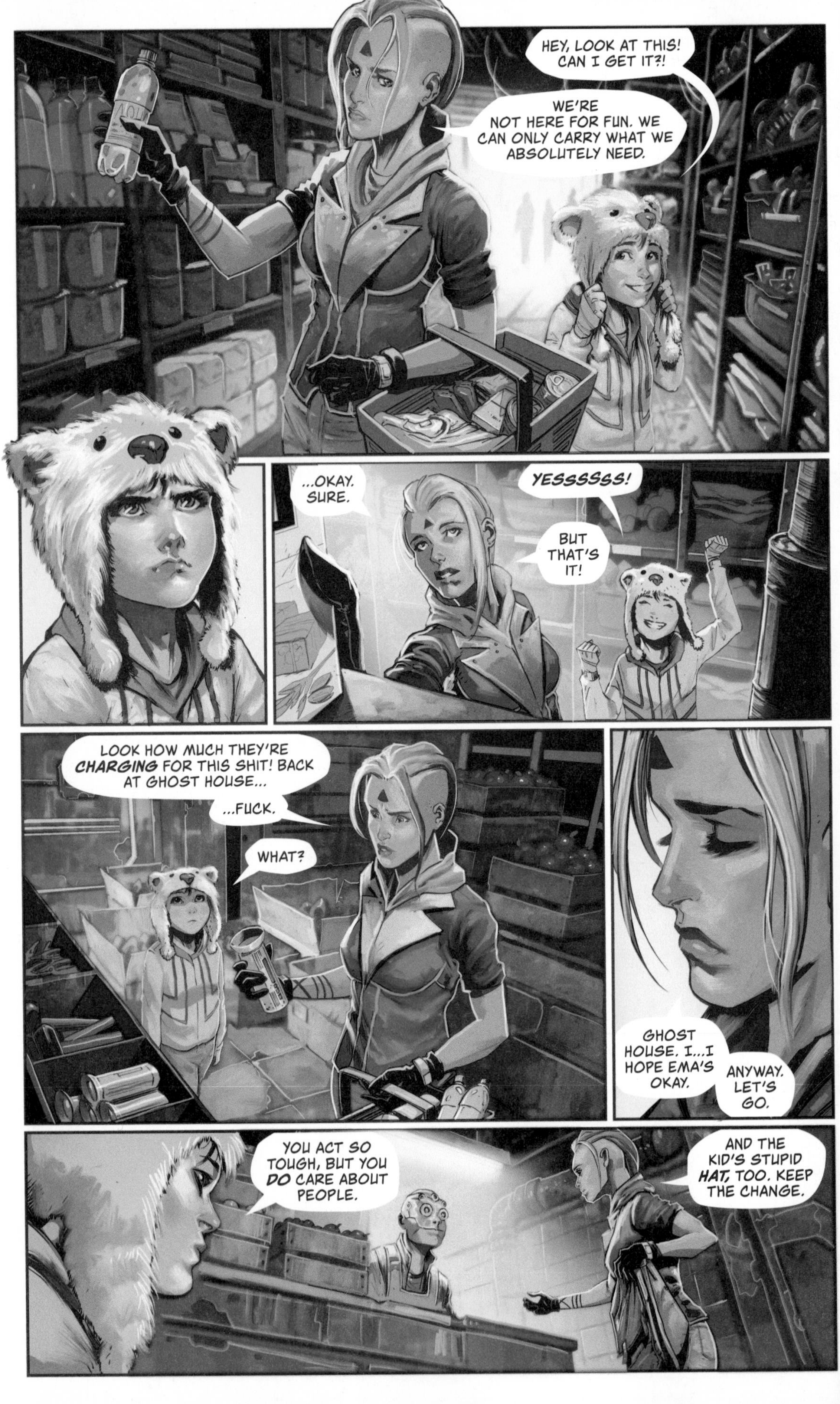
HEY, LOOK AT THIS! CAN I GET IT?!
WE'RE NOT HERE FOR FUN. WE CAN ONLY CARRY WHAT WE ABSOLUTELY NEED.
...OKAY. SURE.
YESSSSSS!
BUT THAT'S IT!
LOOK HOW MUCH THEY'RE CHARGING FOR THIS SHIT! BACK AT GHOST HOUSE...
...FUCK.
WHAT?
GHOST HOUSE. I...I HOPE EMA'S OKAY.
ANYWAY. LET'S GO.
YOU ACT SO TOUGH, BUT YOU DO CARE ABOUT PEOPLE.
AND THE KID'S STUPID HAT, TOO. KEEP THE CHANGE.

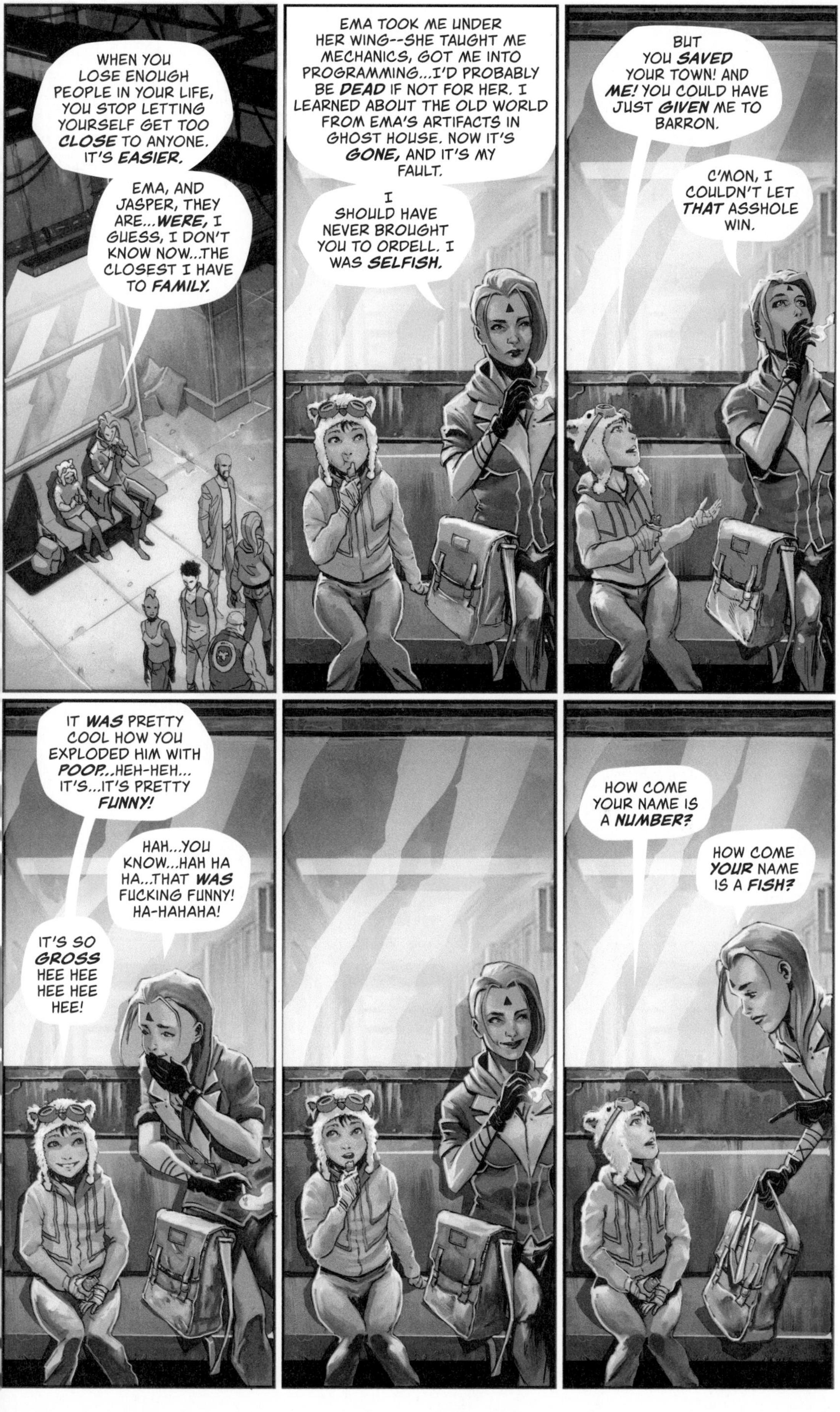
WHEN YOU LOSE ENOUGH PEOPLE IN YOUR LIFE, YOU STOP LETTING YOURSELF GET TOO CLOSE TO ANYONE. IT'S EASIER.
EMA, AND JASPER, THEY ARE...WERE, I GUESS, I DON'T KNOW NOW...THE CLOSEST I HAVE TO FAMILY.
EMA TOOK ME UNDER HER WING--SHE TAUGHT ME MECHANICS, GOT ME INTO PROGRAMMING...I'D PROBABLY BE DEAD IF NOT FOR HER. I LEARNED ABOUT THE OLD WORLD FROM EMA'S ARTIFACTS IN GHOST HOUSE. NOW IT'S GONE, AND IT'S MY FAULT.
I SHOULD HAVE NEVER BROUGHT YOU TO ORDELL. I WAS SELFISH.
BUT YOU SAVED YOUR TOWN! AND ME! YOU COULD HAVE JUST GIVEN ME TO BARRON.
C'MON, I COULDN'T LET THAT ASSHOLE WIN.
IT WAS PRETTY COOL HOW YOU EXPLODED HIM WITH POOP...HEH-HEH... IT'S...IT'S PRETTY FUNNY!
HAH...YOU KNOW...HAH HA HA...THAT WAS FUCKING FUNNY! HA-HAHAHA!
IT'S SO GROSS HEE HEE HEE HEE HEE!
HOW COME YOUR NAME IS A NUMBER?
HOW COME YOUR NAME IS A FISH?

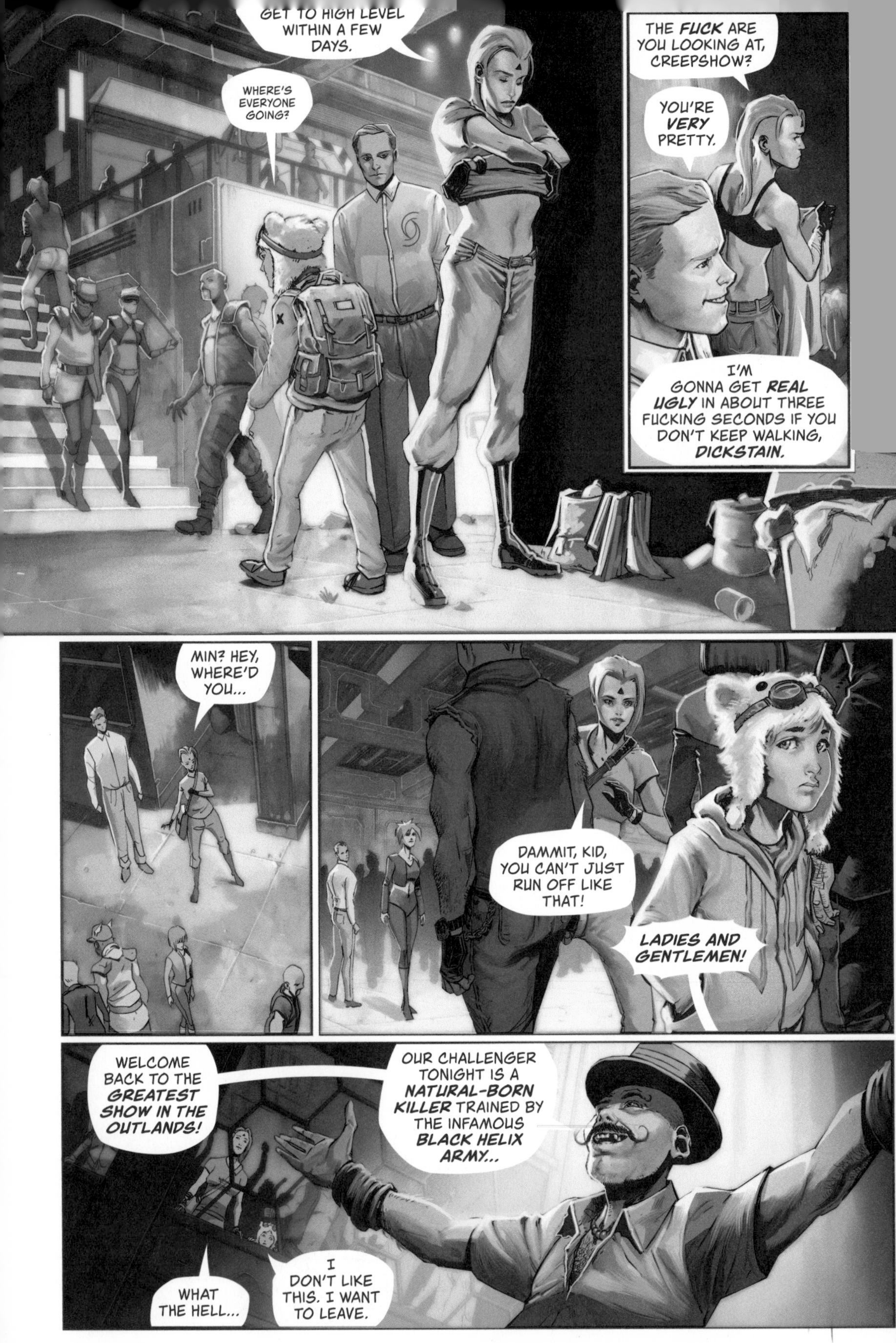
GET TO HIGH LEVEL WITHIN A FEW DAYS.
WHERE'S EVERYONE GOING?
THE FUCK ARE YOU LOOKING AT, CREEPSHOW?
YOU'RE VERY PRETTY.
I'M GONNA GET REAL UGLY IN ABOUT THREE FUCKING SECONDS IF YOU DON'T KEEP WALKING, DICKSTAIN.
MIN? HEY, WHERE'D YOU...
DAMMIT, KID, YOU CAN'T JUST RUN OFF LIKE THAT!
LADIES AND GENTLEMEN!
WELCOME BACK TO THE GREATEST SHOW IN THE OUTLANDS!
OUR CHALLENGER TONIGHT IS A NATURAL-BORN KILLER TRAINED BY THE INFAMOUS BLACK HELIX ARMY...
WHAT THE HELL...
I DON'T LIKE THIS. I WANT TO LEAVE.

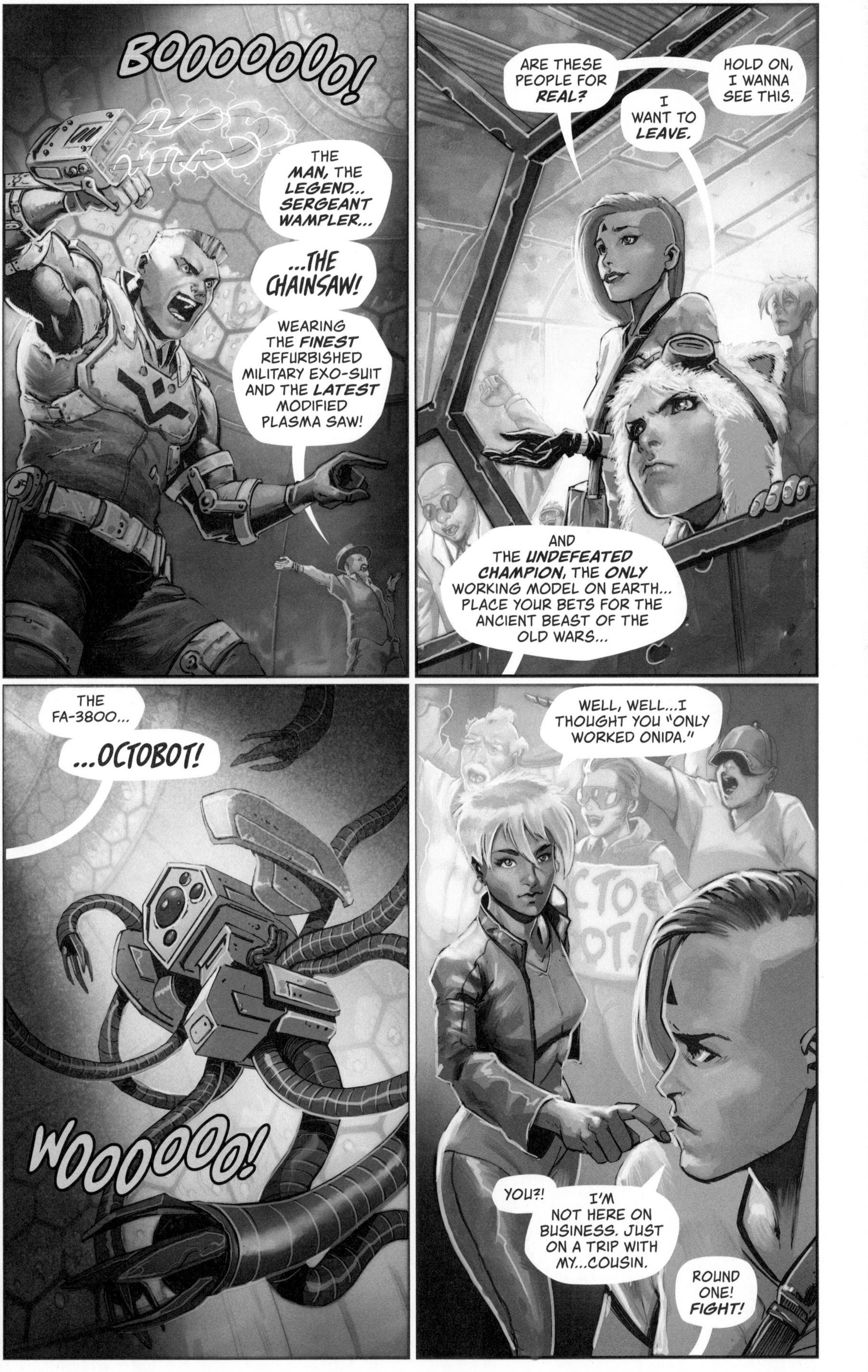
BOOOOOOO!
THE MAN, THE LEGEND... SERGEANT WAMPLER...
...THE CHAINSAW!
WEARING THE FINEST REFURBISHED MILITARY EXO-SUIT AND THE LATEST MODIFIED PLASMA SAW!
ARE THESE PEOPLE FOR REAL?
HOLD ON, I WANNA SEE THIS.
I WANT TO LEAVE.
AND THE UNDEFEATED CHAMPION, THE ONLY WORKING MODEL ON EARTH... PLACE YOUR BETS FOR THE ANCIENT BEAST OF THE OLD WARS...
THE FA-3800...
...OCTOBOT!
WOOOOOO!
WELL, WELL...I THOUGHT YOU "ONLY WORKED ONIDA."
YOU?!
I'M NOT HERE ON BUSINESS. JUST ON A TRIP WITH MY...COUSIN.
ROUND ONE! FIGHT!

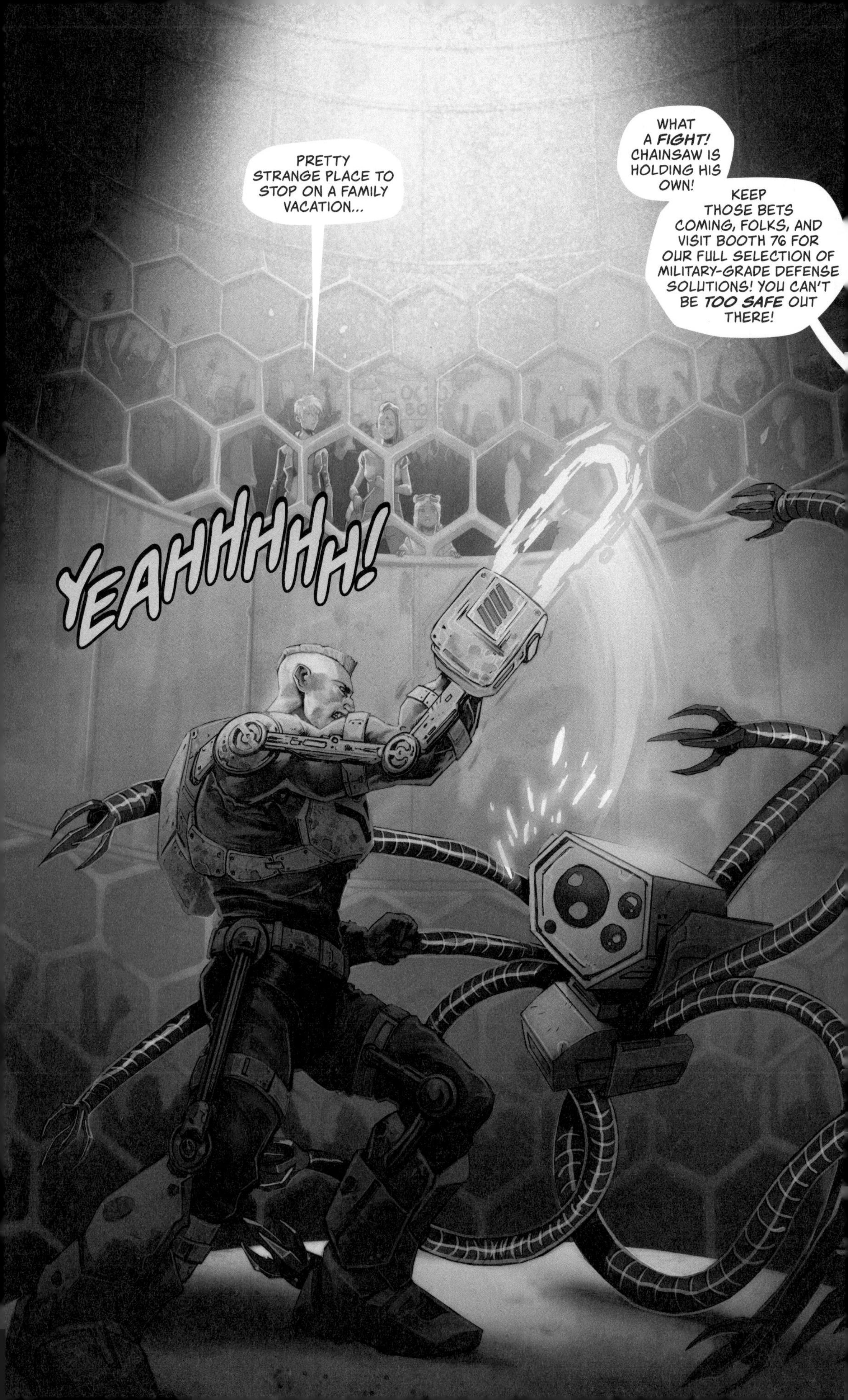
PRETTY STRANGE PLACE TO STOP ON A FAMILY VACATION...
WHAT A *FIGHT!* CHAINSAW IS HOLDING HIS OWN!
KEEP THOSE BETS COMING, FOLKS, AND VISIT BOOTH 76 FOR OUR FULL SELECTION OF MILITARY-GRADE DEFENSE SOLUTIONS! YOU CAN'T BE *TOO SAFE* OUT THERE!
YEAHHHHHH!

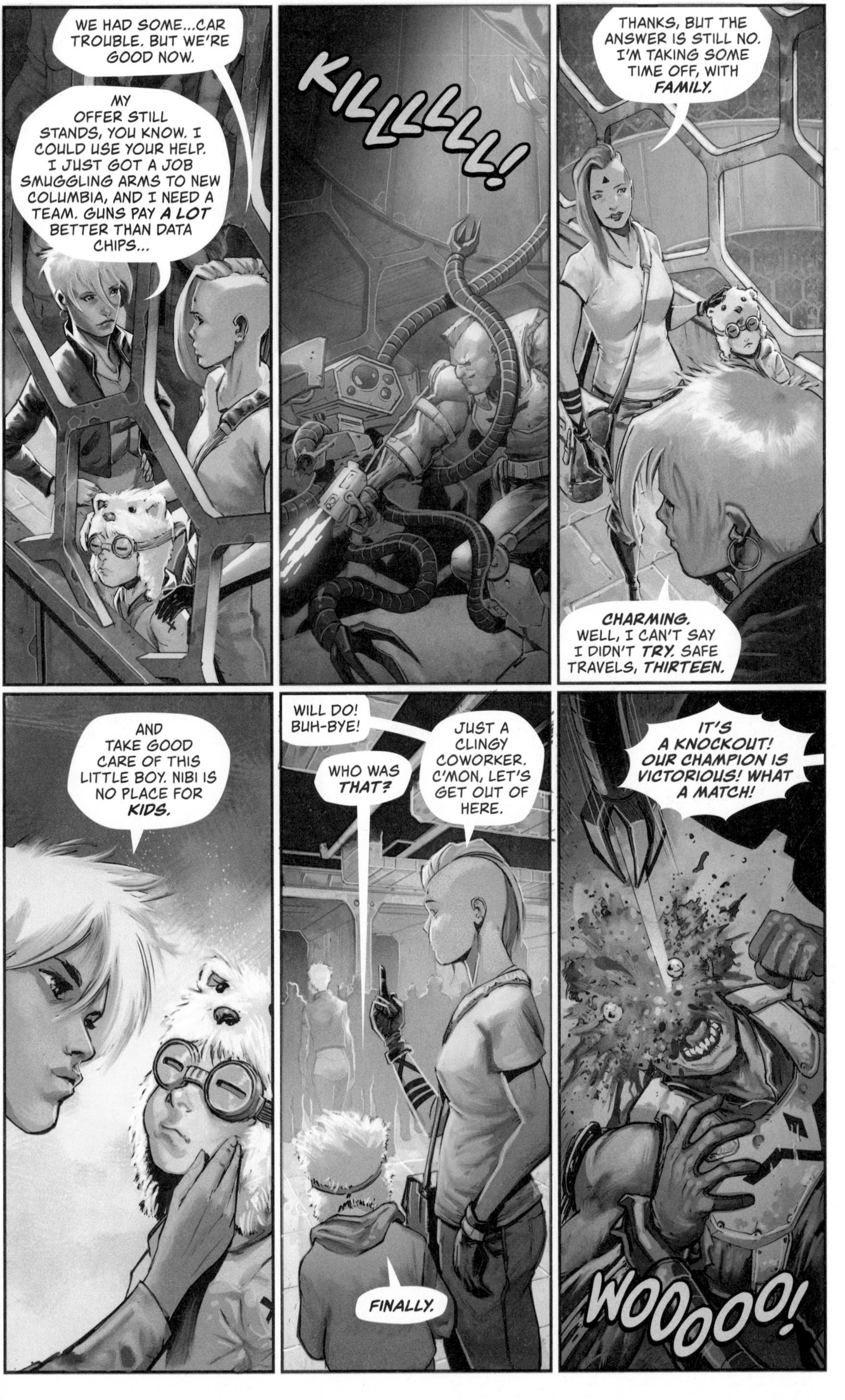
WE HAD SOME...CAR TROUBLE. BUT WE'RE GOOD NOW.
MY OFFER STILL STANDS, YOU KNOW. I COULD USE YOUR HELP. I JUST GOT A JOB SMUGGLING ARMS TO NEW COLUMBIA, AND I NEED A TEAM. GUNS PAY A LOT BETTER THAN DATA CHIPS...
KILLLLLL!
THANKS, BUT THE ANSWER IS STILL NO. I'M TAKING SOME TIME OFF, WITH FAMILY.
CHARMING. WELL, I CAN'T SAY I DIDN'T TRY. SAFE TRAVELS, THIRTEEN.
AND TAKE GOOD CARE OF THIS LITTLE BOY. NIBI IS NO PLACE FOR KIDS.
WILL DO! BUH-BYE!
WHO WAS THAT?
JUST A CLINGY COWORKER. C'MON, LET'S GET OUT OF HERE.
FINALLY.
IT'S A KNOCKOUT! OUR CHAMPION IS VICTORIOUS! WHAT A MATCH!
WOOOOOO!

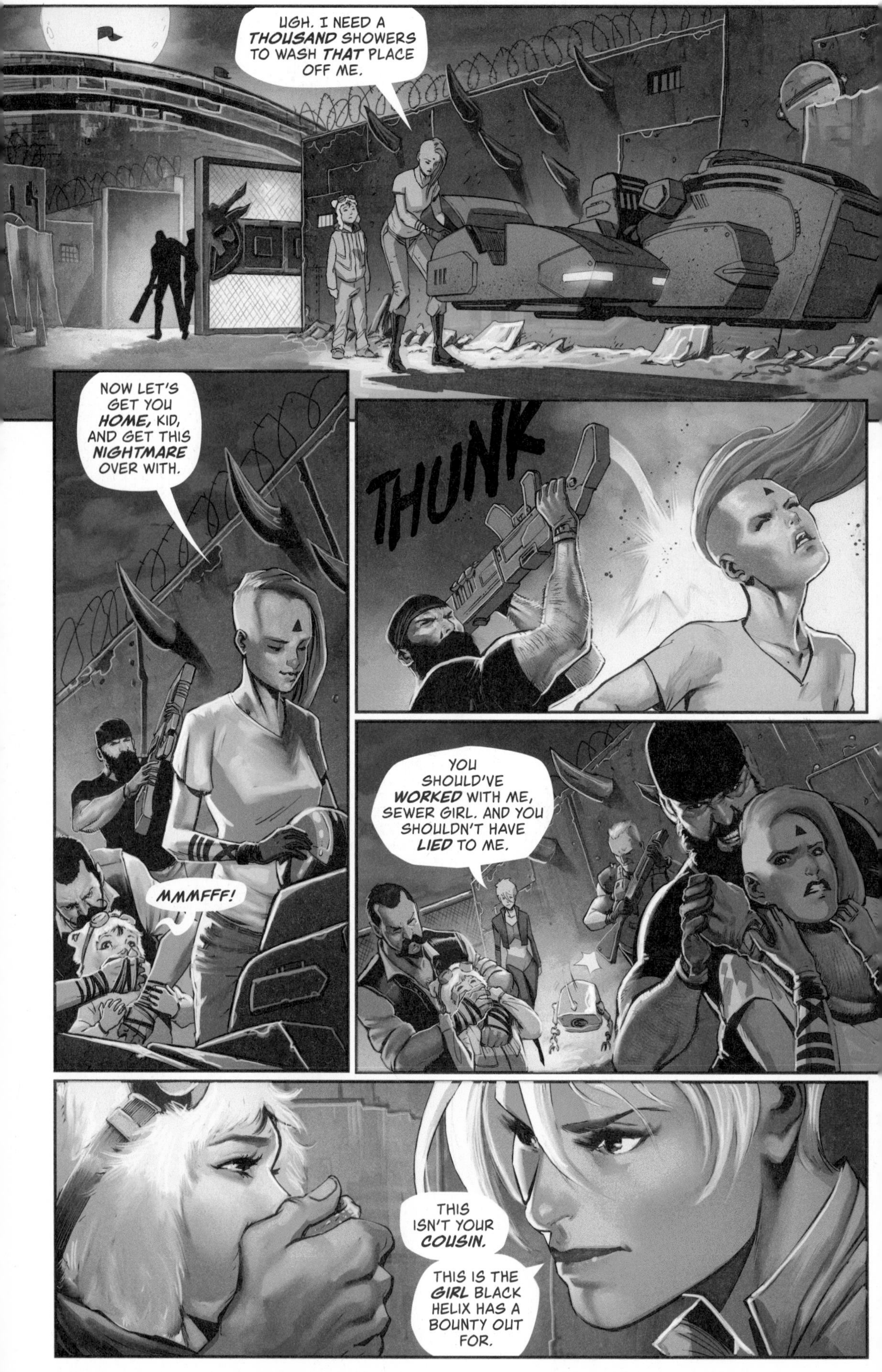
UGH. I NEED A THOUSAND SHOWERS TO WASH THAT PLACE OFF ME.
NOW LET'S GET YOU HOME, KID, AND GET THIS NIGHTMARE OVER WITH.
MMMFFF!
THUNK
YOU SHOULD'VE WORKED WITH ME, SEWER GIRL. AND YOU SHOULDN'T HAVE LIED TO ME.
THIS ISN'T YOUR COUSIN.
THIS IS THE GIRL BLACK HELIX HAS A BOUNTY OUT FOR.

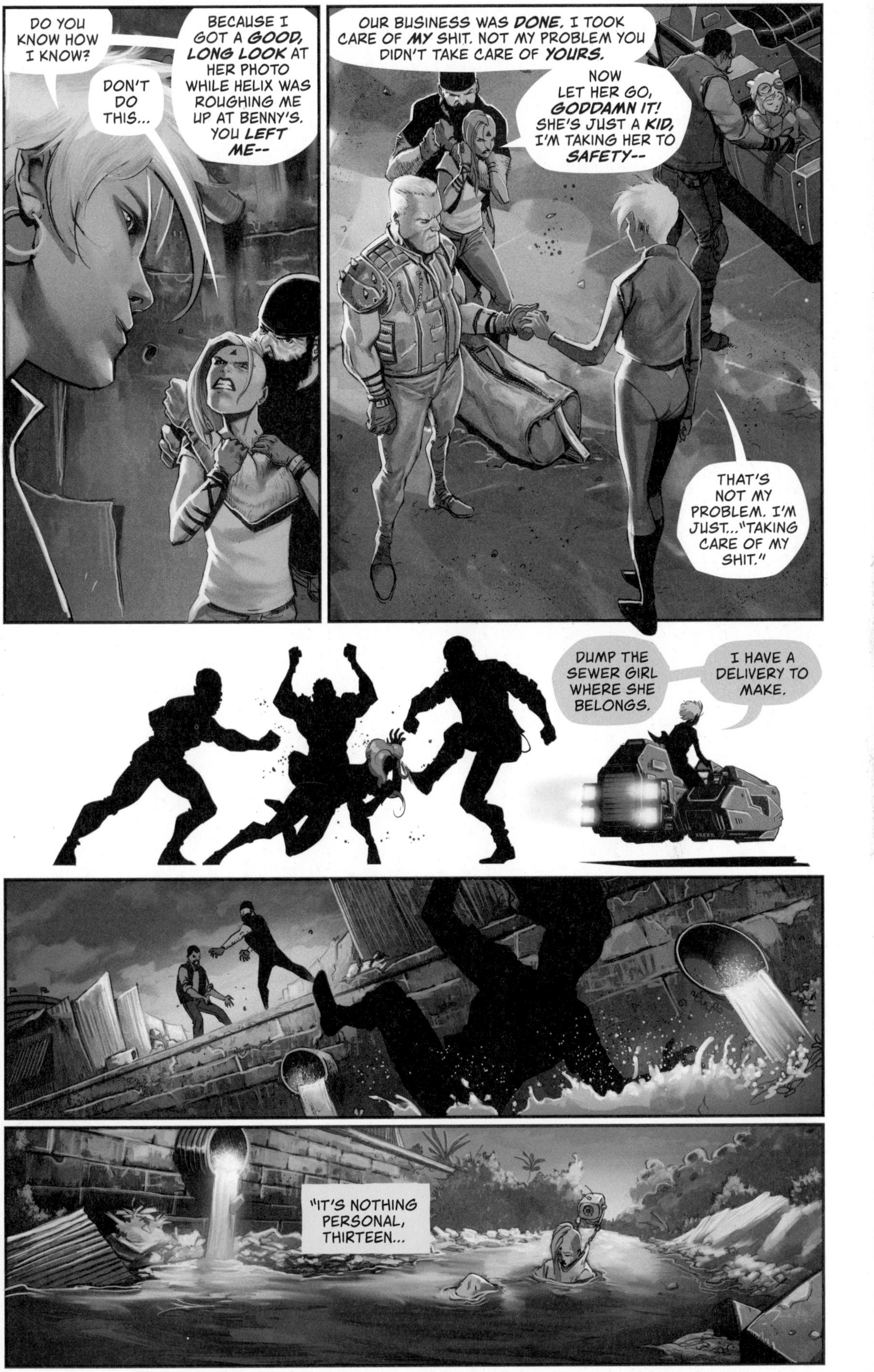
DO YOU KNOW HOW I KNOW?
DON'T DO THIS...
BECAUSE I GOT A GOOD, LONG LOOK AT HER PHOTO WHILE HELIX WAS ROUGHING ME UP AT BENNY'S. YOU LEFT ME--
OUR BUSINESS WAS DONE. I TOOK CARE OF MY SHIT. NOT MY PROBLEM YOU DIDN'T TAKE CARE OF YOURS.
NOW LET HER GO, GODDAMN IT! SHE'S JUST A KID, I'M TAKING HER TO SAFETY--
THAT'S NOT MY PROBLEM. I'M JUST..."TAKING CARE OF MY SHIT."
DUMP THE SEWER GIRL WHERE SHE BELONGS.
I HAVE A DELIVERY TO MAKE.
"IT'S NOTHING PERSONAL, THIRTEEN...

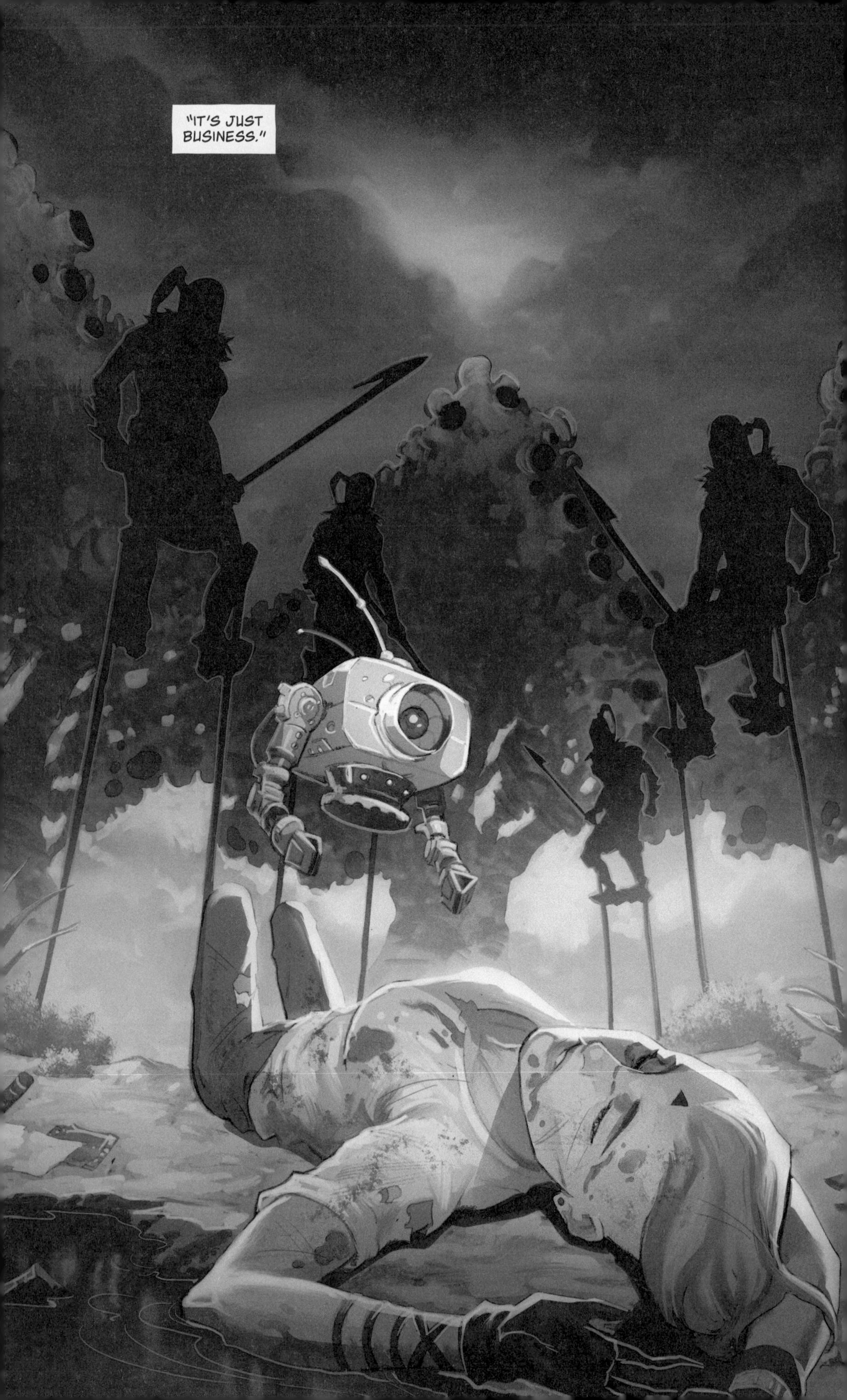
"IT'S JUST BUSINESS."

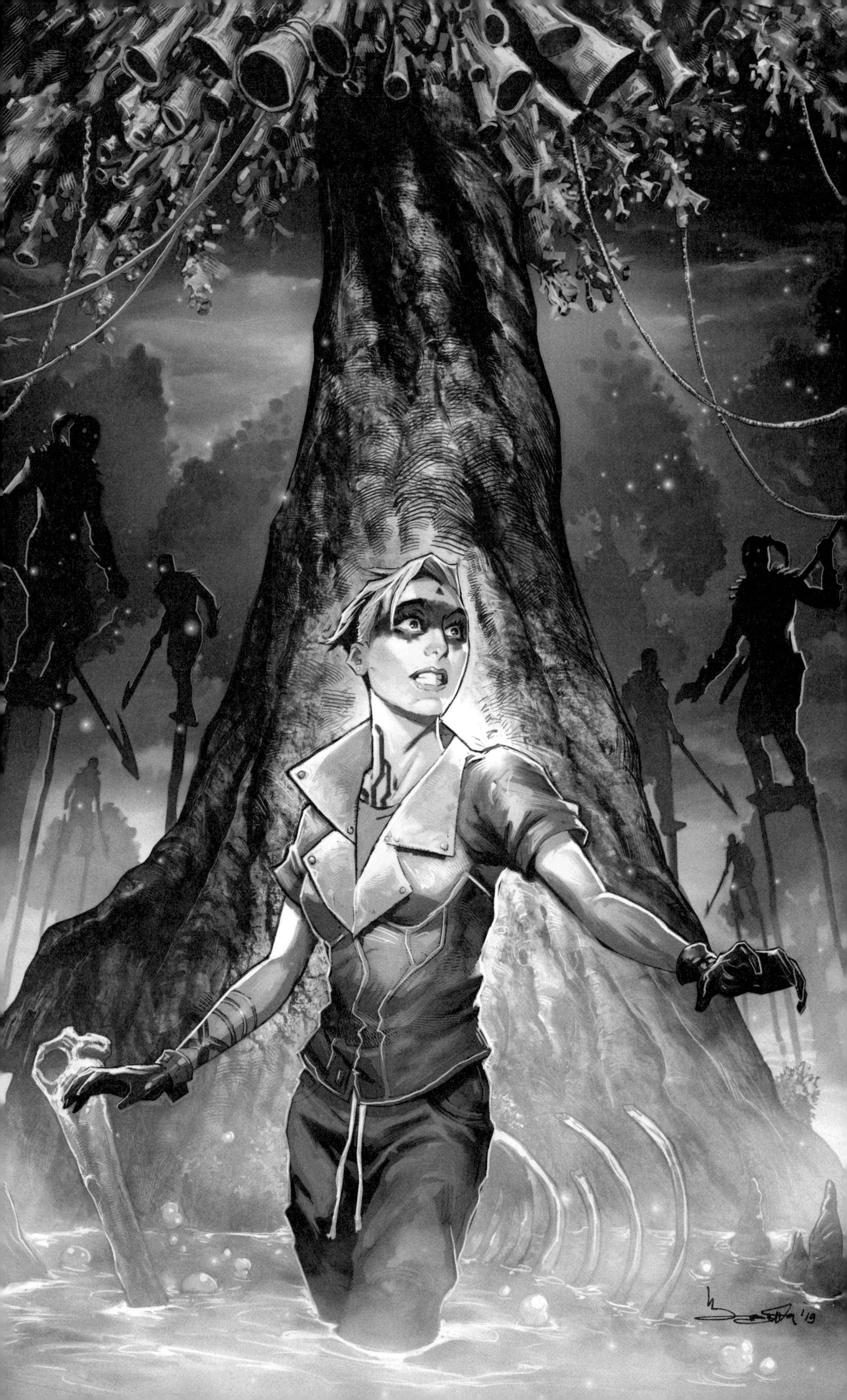

CHAPTER FOUR
PLEASURE ISLAND

STORY
ROB SHERIDAN

ART
BARNABY BAGENDA AND AMANCAY NAHUELPAN

COLORS
ROMULO FAJARDO JR.

LETTERING
NATE PIEKOS OF BLAMBOT®

COVER
BARNABY BAGENDA AND ROMULO FAJARDO JR.

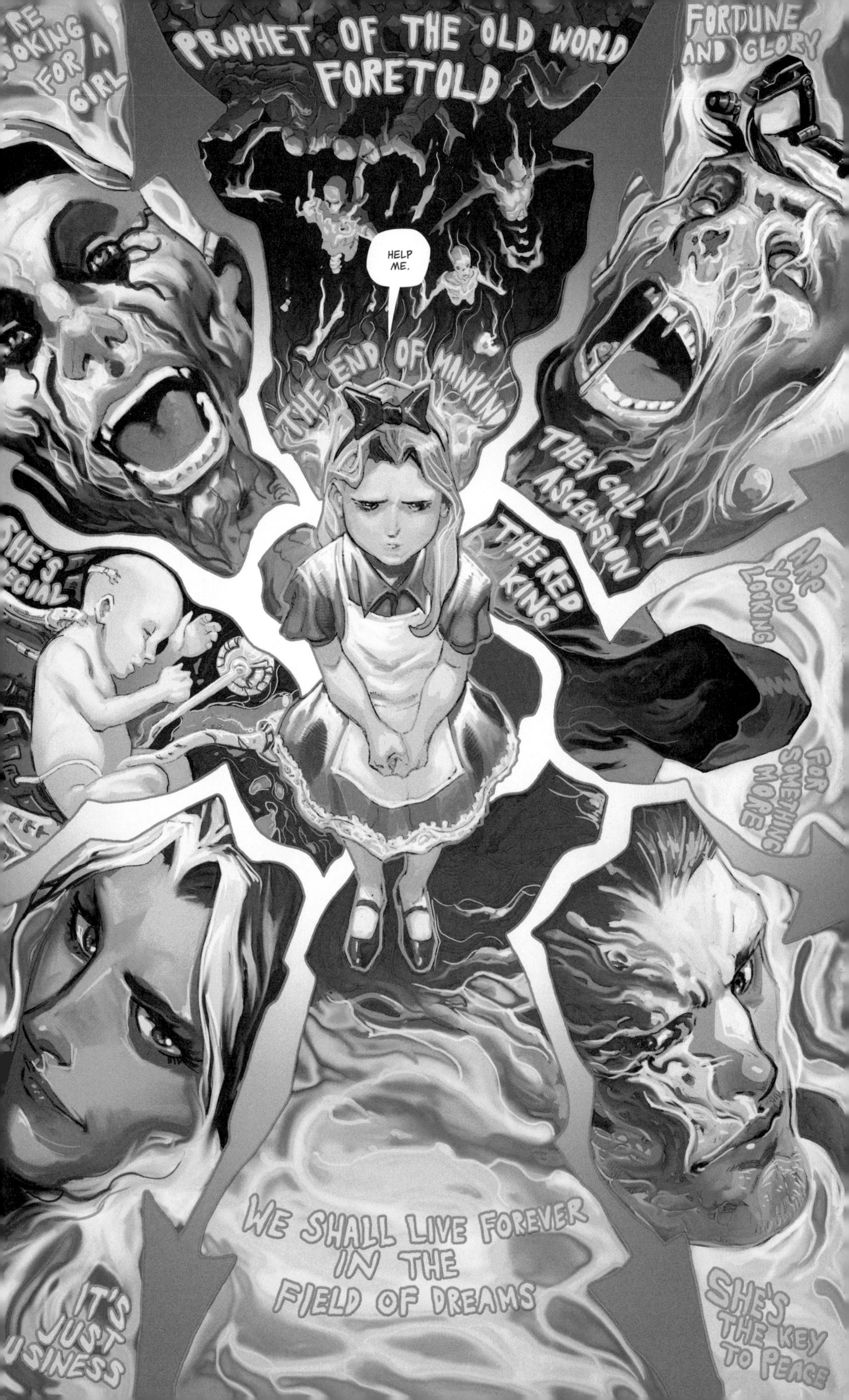

PROPHET OF THE OLD WORLD FORETOLD
FORTUNE AND GLORY
HELP ME.
THE END OF MANKIND
THEY CALL IT ASCENSION
THE RED KING
SHE'S ...ECIAL
ARE YOU LOOKING
FOR SOMETHING MORE
WE SHALL LIVE FOREVER IN THE FIELD OF DREAMS
IT'S JUST ...USINESS
SHE'S THE KEY TO PEACE

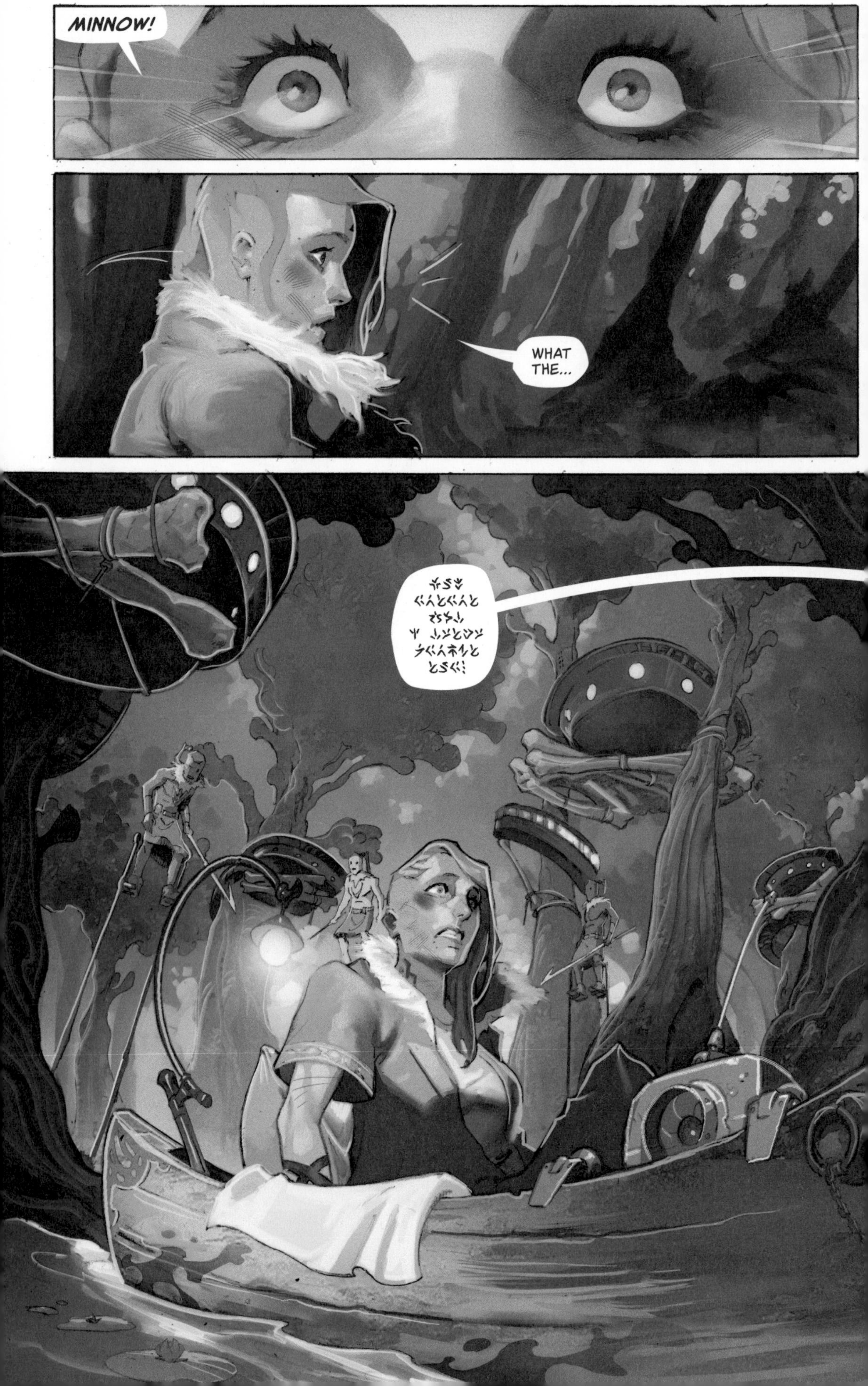
MINNOW!
WHAT THE...

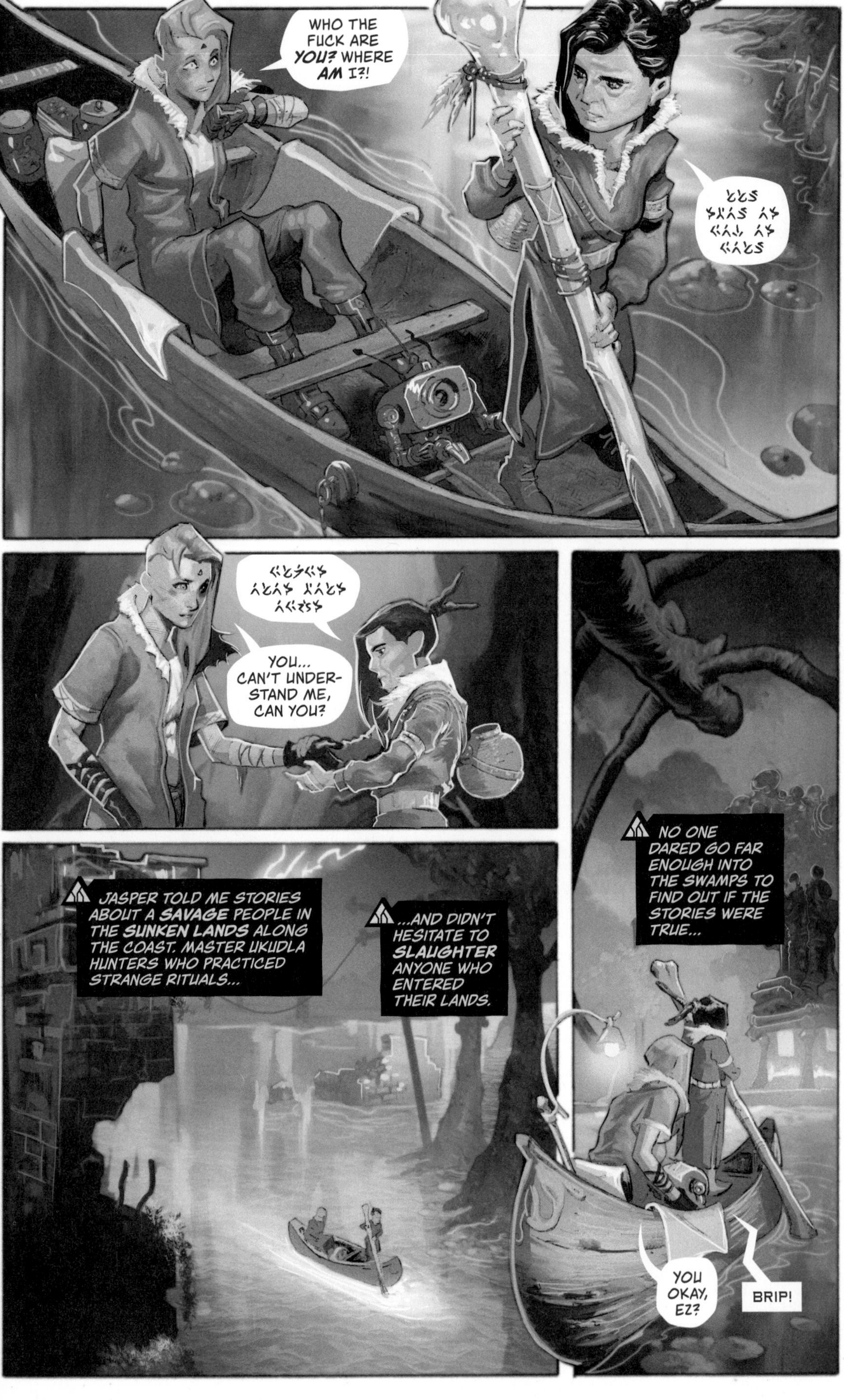
WHO THE FUCK ARE YOU? WHERE AM I?!
YOU... CAN'T UNDERSTAND ME, CAN YOU?
JASPER TOLD ME STORIES ABOUT A SAVAGE PEOPLE IN THE SUNKEN LANDS ALONG THE COAST. MASTER UKUDLA HUNTERS WHO PRACTICED STRANGE RITUALS...
...AND DIDN'T HESITATE TO SLAUGHTER ANYONE WHO ENTERED THEIR LANDS.
NO ONE DARED GO FAR ENOUGH INTO THE SWAMPS TO FIND OUT IF THE STORIES WERE TRUE...
YOU OKAY, EZ?
BRIP!

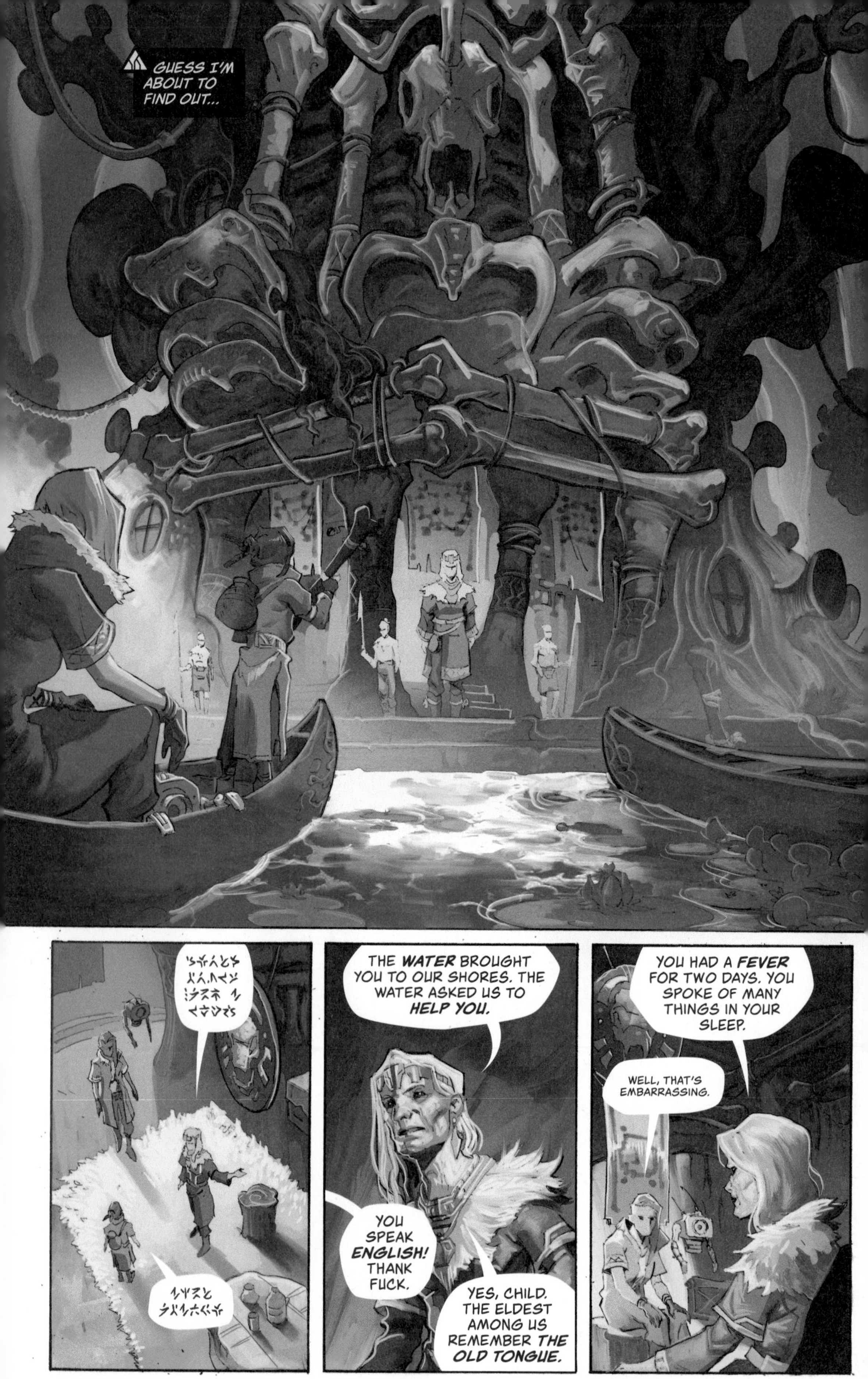
GUESS I'M ABOUT TO FIND OUT...
THE WATER BROUGHT YOU TO OUR SHORES. THE WATER ASKED US TO HELP YOU.
YOU SPEAK ENGLISH! THANK FUCK.
YES, CHILD. THE ELDEST AMONG US REMEMBER THE OLD TONGUE.
YOU HAD A FEVER FOR TWO DAYS. YOU SPOKE OF MANY THINGS IN YOUR SLEEP.
WELL, THAT'S EMBARRASSING.

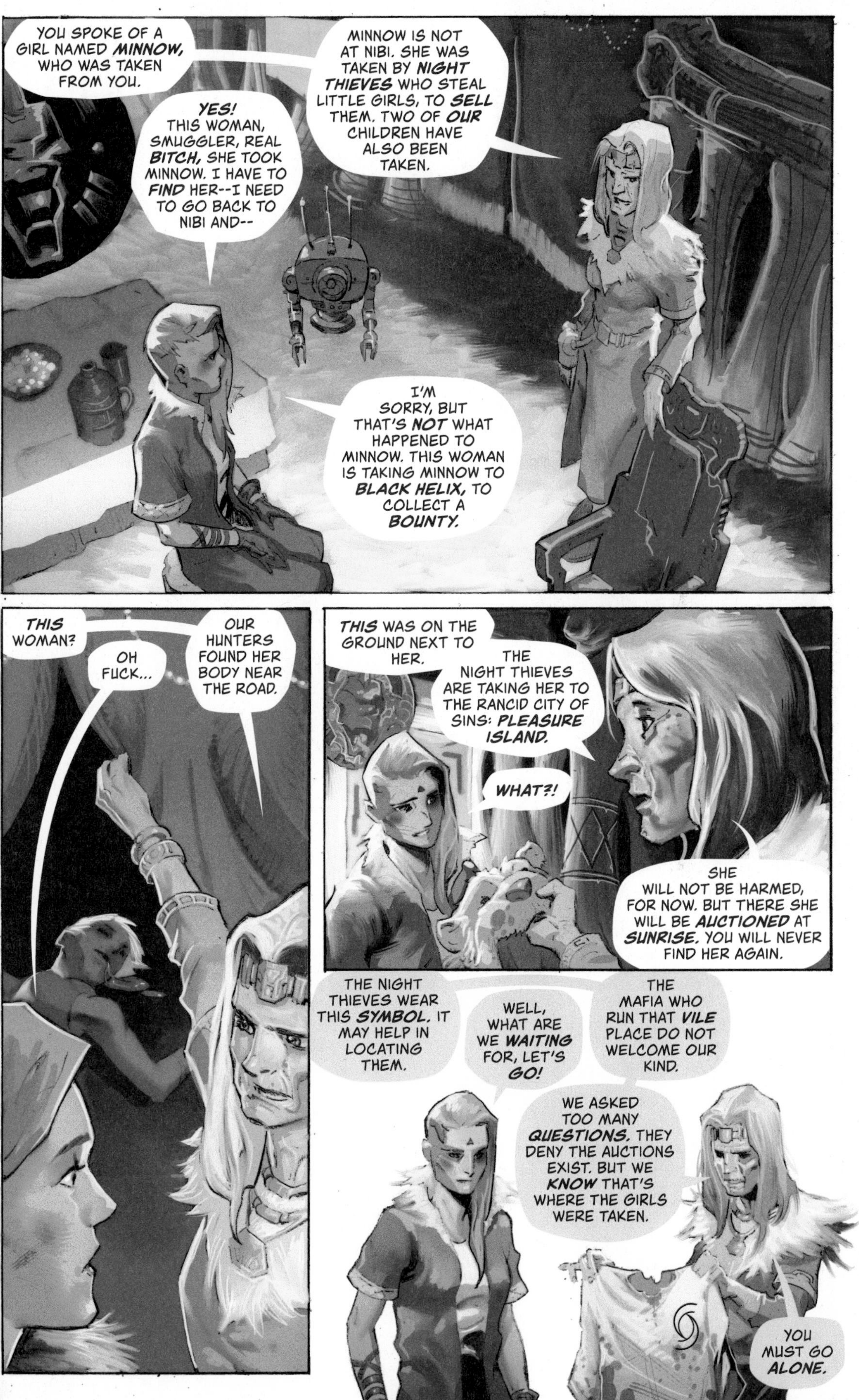
YOU SPOKE OF A GIRL NAMED MINNOW, WHO WAS TAKEN FROM YOU.
MINNOW IS NOT AT NIBI. SHE WAS TAKEN BY NIGHT THIEVES WHO STEAL LITTLE GIRLS, TO SELL THEM. TWO OF OUR CHILDREN HAVE ALSO BEEN TAKEN.
YES! THIS WOMAN, SMUGGLER, REAL BITCH, SHE TOOK MINNOW. I HAVE TO FIND HER--I NEED TO GO BACK TO NIBI AND--
I'M SORRY, BUT THAT'S NOT WHAT HAPPENED TO MINNOW. THIS WOMAN IS TAKING MINNOW TO BLACK HELIX, TO COLLECT A BOUNTY.
THIS WOMAN?
OUR HUNTERS FOUND HER BODY NEAR THE ROAD.
OH FUCK...
THIS WAS ON THE GROUND NEXT TO HER.
THE NIGHT THIEVES ARE TAKING HER TO THE RANCID CITY OF SINS: PLEASURE ISLAND.
WHAT?!
SHE WILL NOT BE HARMED, FOR NOW. BUT THERE SHE WILL BE AUCTIONED AT SUNRISE. YOU WILL NEVER FIND HER AGAIN.
THE NIGHT THIEVES WEAR THIS SYMBOL. IT MAY HELP IN LOCATING THEM.
WELL, WHAT ARE WE WAITING FOR, LET'S GO!
THE MAFIA WHO RUN THAT VILE PLACE DO NOT WELCOME OUR KIND.
WE ASKED TOO MANY QUESTIONS. THEY DENY THE AUCTIONS EXIST. BUT WE KNOW THAT'S WHERE THE GIRLS WERE TAKEN.
YOU MUST GO ALONE.

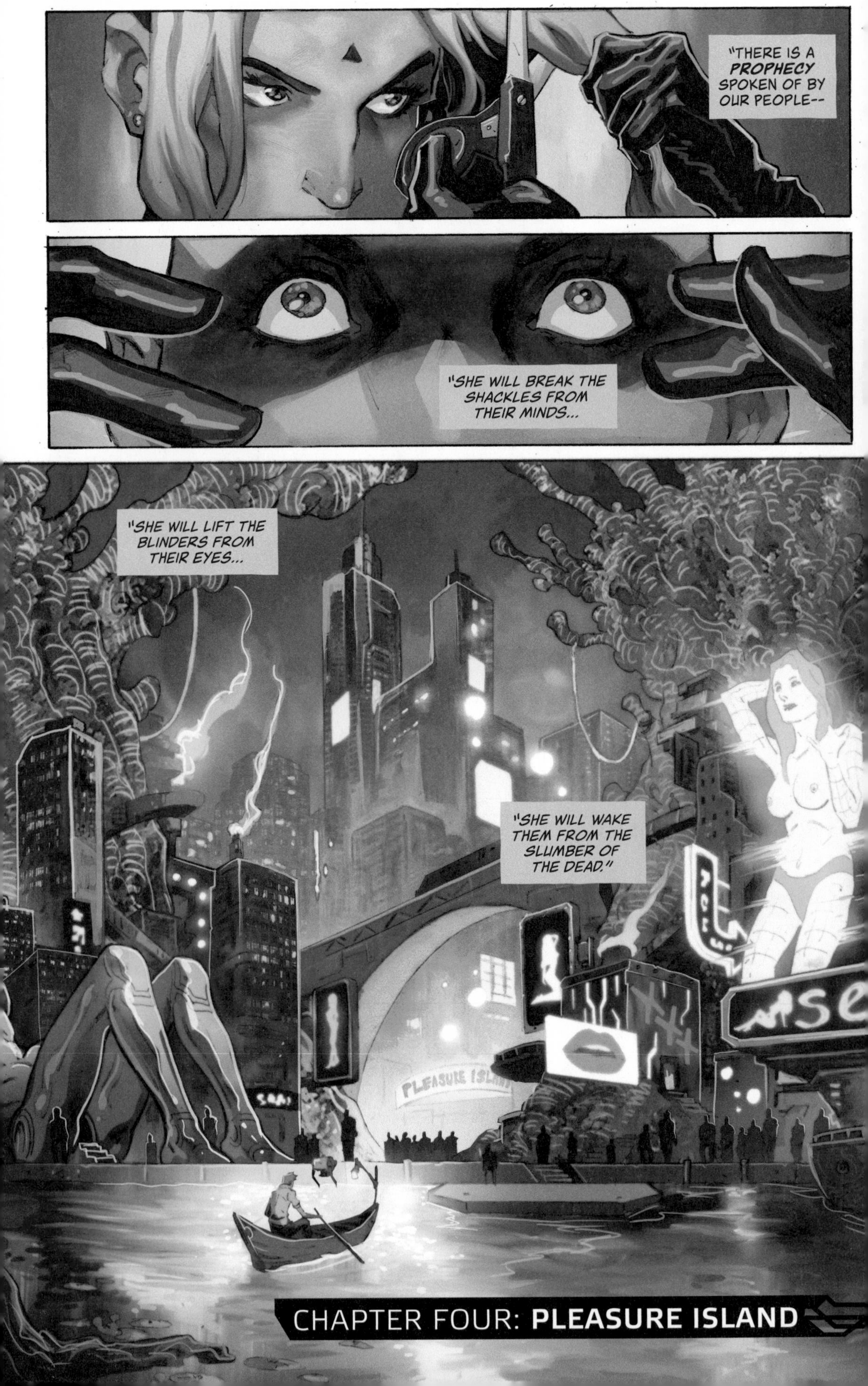
"THERE IS A **PROPHECY** SPOKEN OF BY OUR PEOPLE--
"SHE WILL BREAK THE SHACKLES FROM THEIR MINDS...
"SHE WILL LIFT THE BLINDERS FROM THEIR EYES...
"SHE WILL WAKE THEM FROM THE SLUMBER OF THE DEAD."
PLEASURE ISLAND
CHAPTER FOUR: **PLEASURE ISLAND**

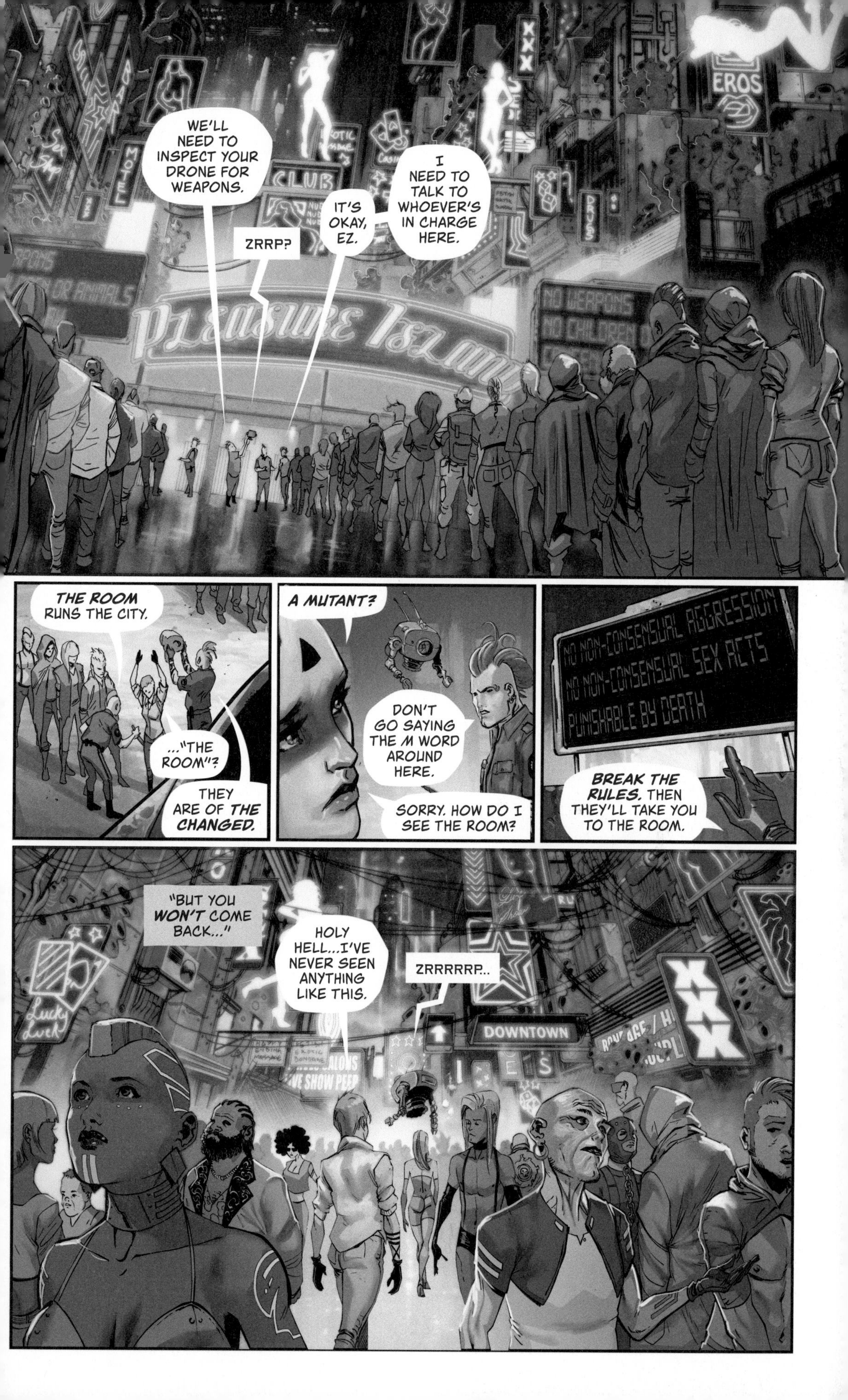
WE'LL NEED TO INSPECT YOUR DRONE FOR WEAPONS.
ZRRP?
IT'S OKAY, EZ.
I NEED TO TALK TO WHOEVER'S IN CHARGE HERE.
PLEASURE ISLAND
EROS
XXX
CLUB
MOTEL
DRUGS
NO WEAPONS
NO CHILDREN
THE ROOM RUNS THE CITY.
..."THE ROOM"?
THEY ARE OF THE CHANGED.
A MUTANT?
DON'T GO SAYING THE M WORD AROUND HERE.
SORRY. HOW DO I SEE THE ROOM?
NO NON-CONSENSUAL AGGRESSION
NO NON-CONSENSUAL SEX ACTS
PUNISHABLE BY DEATH
BREAK THE RULES. THEN THEY'LL TAKE YOU TO THE ROOM.
"BUT YOU WON'T COME BACK..."
HOLY HELL...I'VE NEVER SEEN ANYTHING LIKE THIS.
ZRRRRRP...
DOWNTOWN
XXX
Lucky Luck

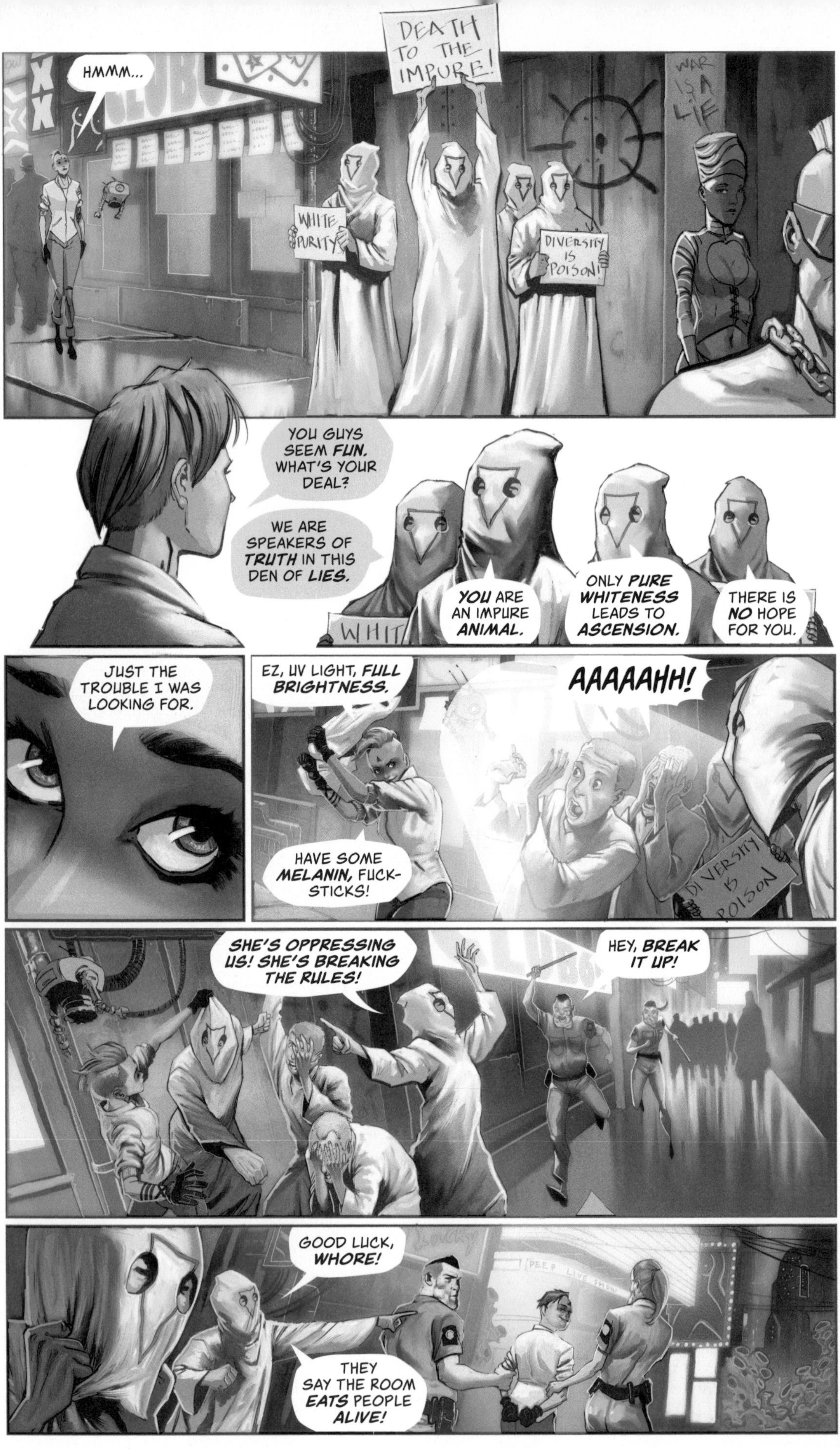
HMMM...
DEATH TO THE IMPURE!
WHITE PURITY
DIVERSITY IS POISON!
WAR IS A LIE
YOU GUYS SEEM FUN. WHAT'S YOUR DEAL?
WE ARE SPEAKERS OF TRUTH IN THIS DEN OF LIES.
YOU ARE AN IMPURE ANIMAL.
ONLY PURE WHITENESS LEADS TO ASCENSION.
THERE IS NO HOPE FOR YOU.
JUST THE TROUBLE I WAS LOOKING FOR.
EZ, UV LIGHT, FULL BRIGHTNESS.
AAAAAHH!
HAVE SOME MELANIN, FUCK-STICKS!
DIVERSITY IS POISON
SHE'S OPPRESSING US! SHE'S BREAKING THE RULES!
HEY, BREAK IT UP!
GOOD LUCK, WHORE!
THEY SAY THE ROOM EATS PEOPLE ALIVE!

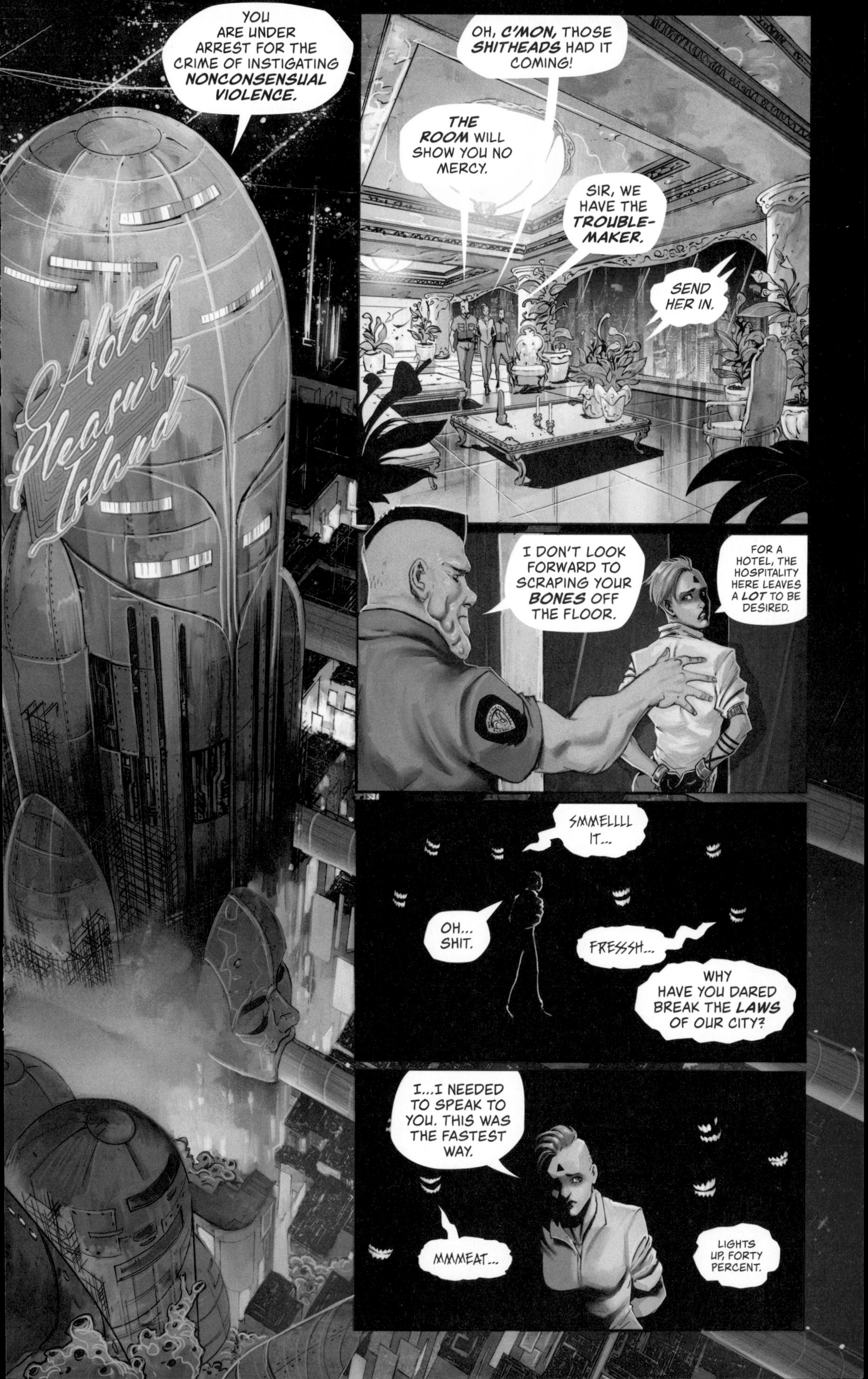

YOU ARE UNDER ARREST FOR THE CRIME OF INSTIGATING **NONCONSENSUAL VIOLENCE.**
Hotel Pleasure Island
OH, ***C'MON,*** THOSE ***SHITHEADS*** HAD IT COMING!
THE ROOM WILL SHOW YOU NO MERCY.
SIR, WE HAVE THE ***TROUBLE-MAKER.***
SEND HER IN.
I DON'T LOOK FORWARD TO SCRAPING YOUR ***BONES*** OFF THE FLOOR.
FOR A HOTEL, THE HOSPITALITY HERE LEAVES A ***LOT*** TO BE DESIRED.
SMMELLLL IT...
OH... SHIT.
FRESSSH...
WHY HAVE YOU DARED BREAK THE ***LAWS*** OF OUR CITY?
I...I NEEDED TO SPEAK TO YOU. THIS WAS THE FASTEST WAY.
MMMEAT...
LIGHTS UP, FORTY PERCENT.

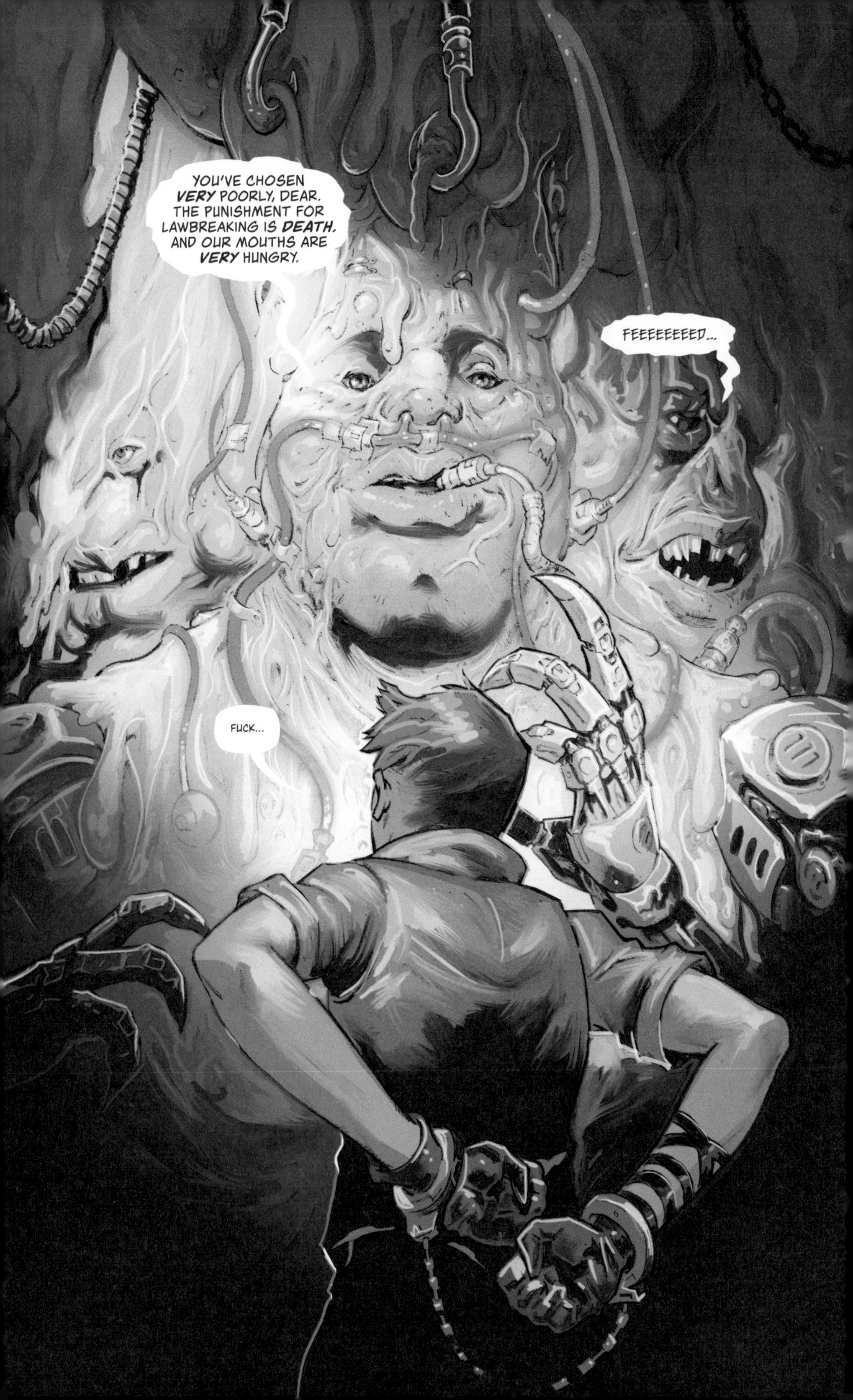
YOU'VE CHOSEN **VERY** POORLY, DEAR. THE PUNISHMENT FOR LAWBREAKING IS **DEATH.** AND OUR MOUTHS ARE **VERY** HUNGRY.
FEEEEEEEED...
FUCK...

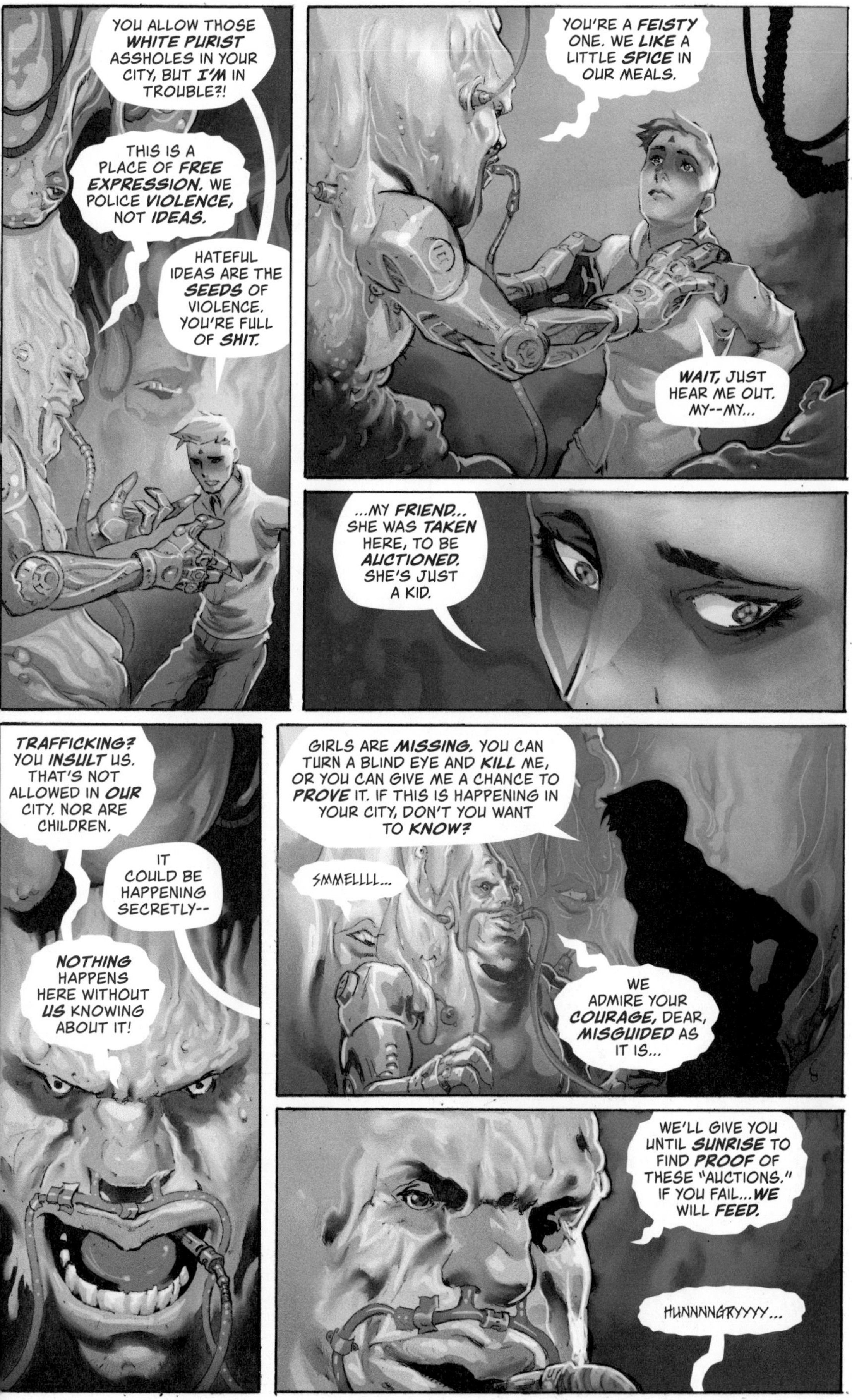
YOU ALLOW THOSE WHITE PURIST ASSHOLES IN YOUR CITY, BUT I'M IN TROUBLE?!
THIS IS A PLACE OF FREE EXPRESSION. WE POLICE VIOLENCE, NOT IDEAS.
HATEFUL IDEAS ARE THE SEEDS OF VIOLENCE. YOU'RE FULL OF SHIT.
YOU'RE A FEISTY ONE. WE LIKE A LITTLE SPICE IN OUR MEALS.
WAIT, JUST HEAR ME OUT. MY--MY...
...MY FRIEND... SHE WAS TAKEN HERE, TO BE AUCTIONED. SHE'S JUST A KID.
TRAFFICKING? YOU INSULT US. THAT'S NOT ALLOWED IN OUR CITY. NOR ARE CHILDREN.
IT COULD BE HAPPENING SECRETLY--
NOTHING HAPPENS HERE WITHOUT US KNOWING ABOUT IT!
GIRLS ARE MISSING. YOU CAN TURN A BLIND EYE AND KILL ME, OR YOU CAN GIVE ME A CHANCE TO PROVE IT. IF THIS IS HAPPENING IN YOUR CITY, DON'T YOU WANT TO KNOW?
SMMELLLL...
WE ADMIRE YOUR COURAGE, DEAR, MISGUIDED AS IT IS...
WE'LL GIVE YOU UNTIL SUNRISE TO FIND PROOF OF THESE "AUCTIONS." IF YOU FAIL...WE WILL FEED.
HUNNNNGRYYYY...

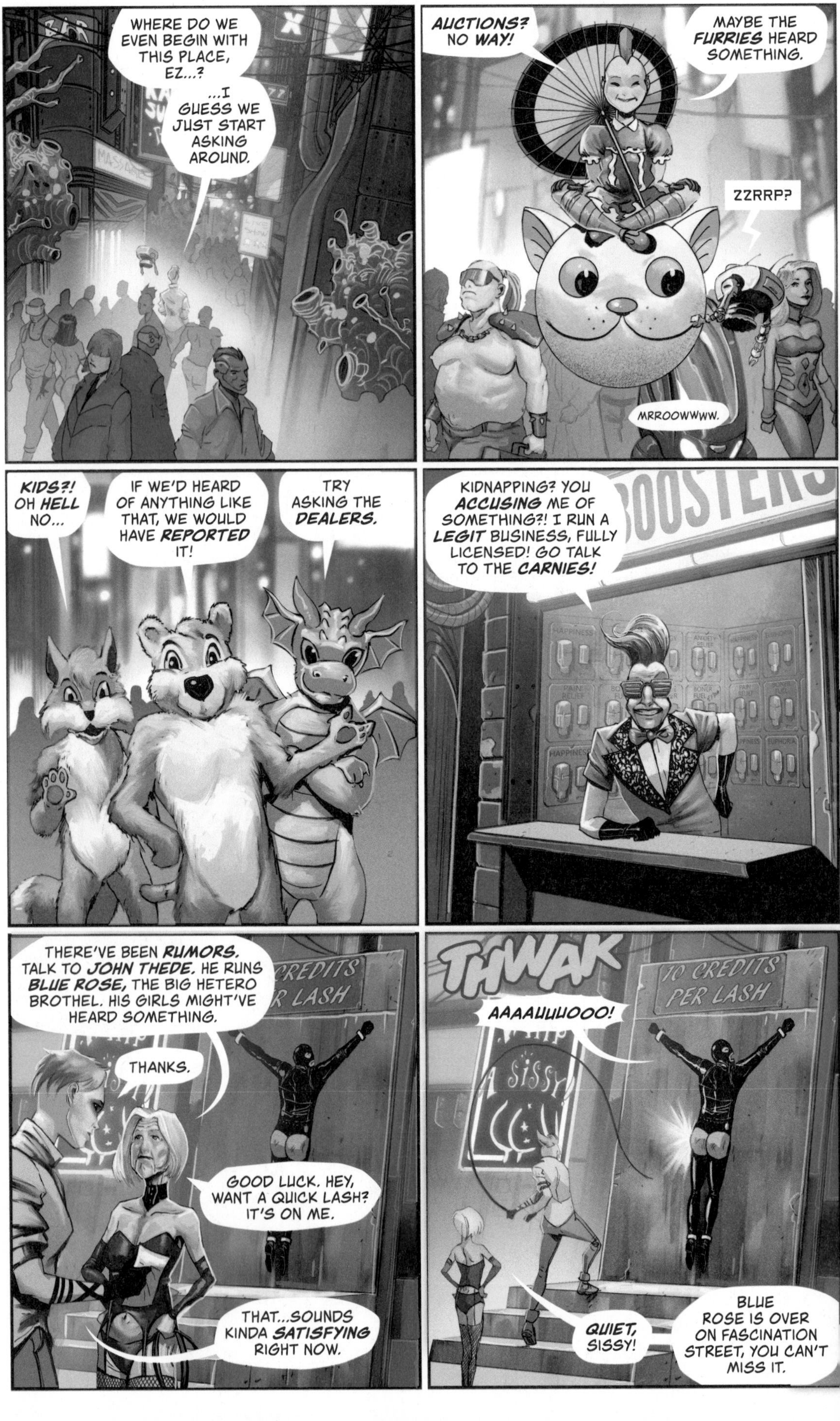
WHERE DO WE EVEN BEGIN WITH THIS PLACE, EZ...?
...I GUESS WE JUST START ASKING AROUND.
AUCTIONS? NO WAY!
MAYBE THE FURRIES HEARD SOMETHING.
ZZRRP?
MRROOWWWW.
KIDS?! OH HELL NO...
IF WE'D HEARD OF ANYTHING LIKE THAT, WE WOULD HAVE REPORTED IT!
TRY ASKING THE DEALERS.
BOOSTERS
KIDNAPPING? YOU ACCUSING ME OF SOMETHING?! I RUN A LEGIT BUSINESS, FULLY LICENSED! GO TALK TO THE CARNIES!
THERE'VE BEEN RUMORS. TALK TO JOHN THEDE. HE RUNS BLUE ROSE, THE BIG HETERO BROTHEL. HIS GIRLS MIGHT'VE HEARD SOMETHING.
THANKS.
GOOD LUCK. HEY, WANT A QUICK LASH? IT'S ON ME.
THAT...SOUNDS KINDA SATISFYING RIGHT NOW.
THWAK
10 CREDITS PER LASH
AAAAUUUOOO!
QUIET, SISSY!
BLUE ROSE IS OVER ON FASCINATION STREET, YOU CAN'T MISS IT.

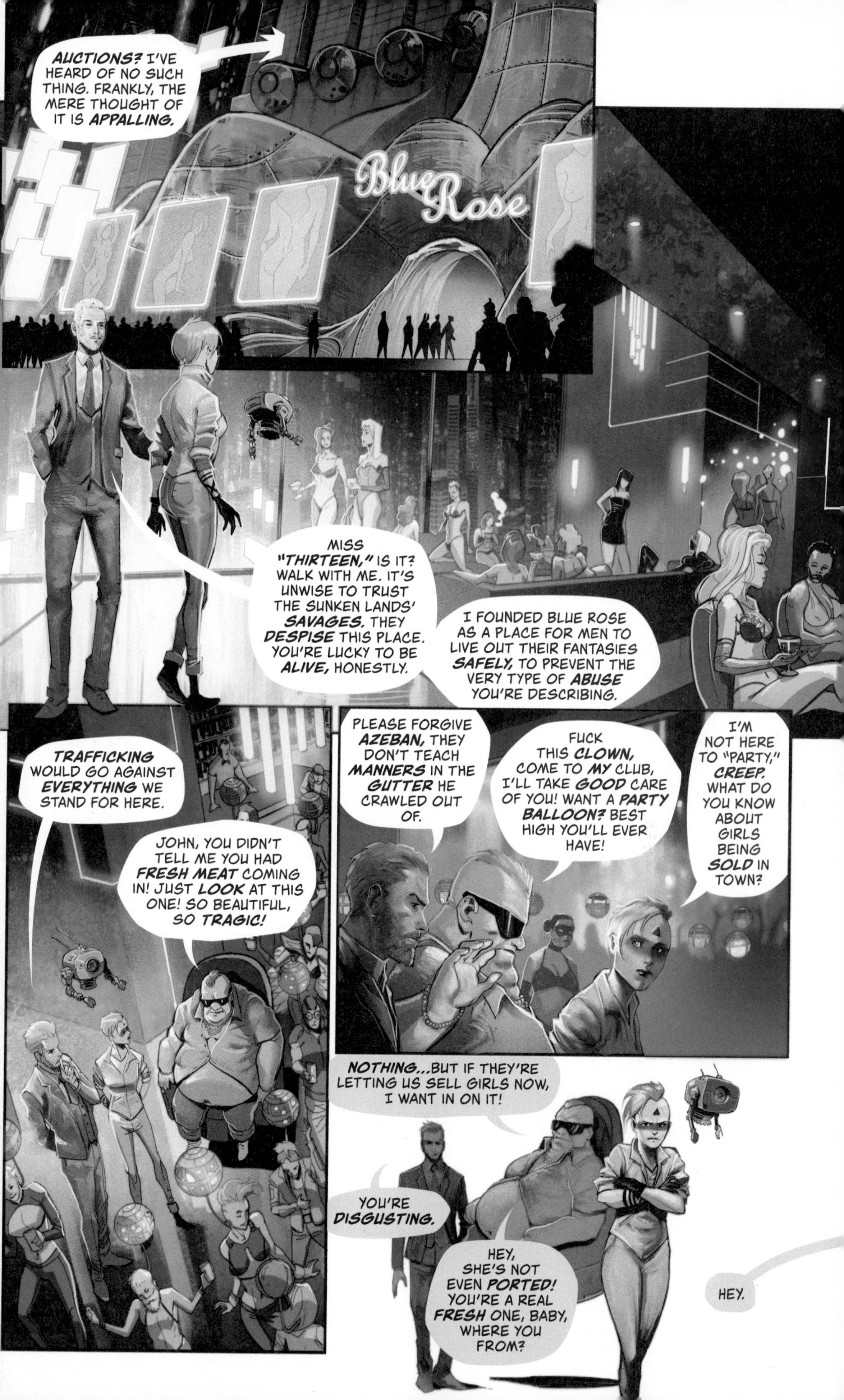
AUCTIONS? I'VE HEARD OF NO SUCH THING. FRANKLY, THE MERE THOUGHT OF IT IS APPALLING.
Blue Rose
MISS "THIRTEEN," IS IT? WALK WITH ME. IT'S UNWISE TO TRUST THE SUNKEN LANDS' SAVAGES. THEY DESPISE THIS PLACE. YOU'RE LUCKY TO BE ALIVE, HONESTLY.
I FOUNDED BLUE ROSE AS A PLACE FOR MEN TO LIVE OUT THEIR FANTASIES SAFELY, TO PREVENT THE VERY TYPE OF ABUSE YOU'RE DESCRIBING.
TRAFFICKING WOULD GO AGAINST EVERYTHING WE STAND FOR HERE.
JOHN, YOU DIDN'T TELL ME YOU HAD FRESH MEAT COMING IN! JUST LOOK AT THIS ONE! SO BEAUTIFUL, SO TRAGIC!
PLEASE FORGIVE AZEBAN, THEY DON'T TEACH MANNERS IN THE GUTTER HE CRAWLED OUT OF.
FUCK THIS CLOWN, COME TO MY CLUB, I'LL TAKE GOOD CARE OF YOU! WANT A PARTY BALLOON? BEST HIGH YOU'LL EVER HAVE!
I'M NOT HERE TO "PARTY," CREEP. WHAT DO YOU KNOW ABOUT GIRLS BEING SOLD IN TOWN?
NOTHING...BUT IF THEY'RE LETTING US SELL GIRLS NOW, I WANT IN ON IT!
YOU'RE DISGUSTING.
HEY, SHE'S NOT EVEN PORTED! YOU'RE A REAL FRESH ONE, BABY, WHERE YOU FROM?
HEY.

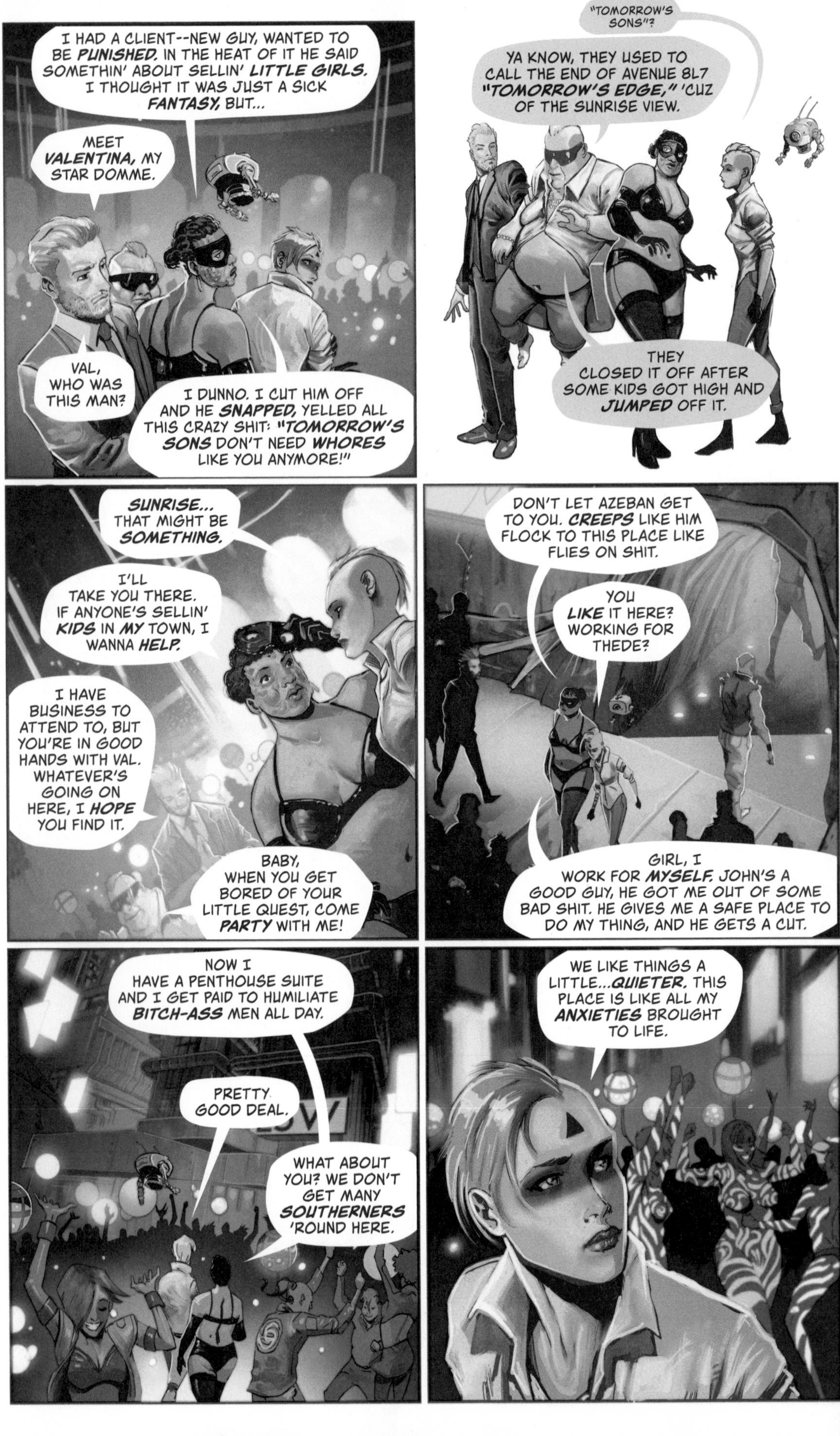

I HAD A CLIENT--NEW GUY, WANTED TO BE PUNISHED. IN THE HEAT OF IT HE SAID SOMETHIN' ABOUT SELLIN' LITTLE GIRLS. I THOUGHT IT WAS JUST A SICK FANTASY, BUT...
MEET VALENTINA, MY STAR DOMME.
VAL, WHO WAS THIS MAN?
I DUNNO. I CUT HIM OFF AND HE SNAPPED, YELLED ALL THIS CRAZY SHIT: "TOMORROW'S SONS DON'T NEED WHORES LIKE YOU ANYMORE!"
"TOMORROW'S SONS"?
YA KNOW, THEY USED TO CALL THE END OF AVENUE 8L7 "TOMORROW'S EDGE," 'CUZ OF THE SUNRISE VIEW.
THEY CLOSED IT OFF AFTER SOME KIDS GOT HIGH AND JUMPED OFF IT.
SUNRISE... THAT MIGHT BE SOMETHING.
I'LL TAKE YOU THERE. IF ANYONE'S SELLIN' KIDS IN MY TOWN, I WANNA HELP.
I HAVE BUSINESS TO ATTEND TO, BUT YOU'RE IN GOOD HANDS WITH VAL. WHATEVER'S GOING ON HERE, I HOPE YOU FIND IT.
BABY, WHEN YOU GET BORED OF YOUR LITTLE QUEST, COME PARTY WITH ME!
DON'T LET AZEBAN GET TO YOU. CREEPS LIKE HIM FLOCK TO THIS PLACE LIKE FLIES ON SHIT.
YOU LIKE IT HERE? WORKING FOR THEDE?
GIRL, I WORK FOR MYSELF. JOHN'S A GOOD GUY, HE GOT ME OUT OF SOME BAD SHIT. HE GIVES ME A SAFE PLACE TO DO MY THING, AND HE GETS A CUT.
NOW I HAVE A PENTHOUSE SUITE AND I GET PAID TO HUMILIATE BITCH-ASS MEN ALL DAY.
PRETTY GOOD DEAL.
WHAT ABOUT YOU? WE DON'T GET MANY SOUTHERNERS 'ROUND HERE.
WE LIKE THINGS A LITTLE...QUIETER. THIS PLACE IS LIKE ALL MY ANXIETIES BROUGHT TO LIFE.

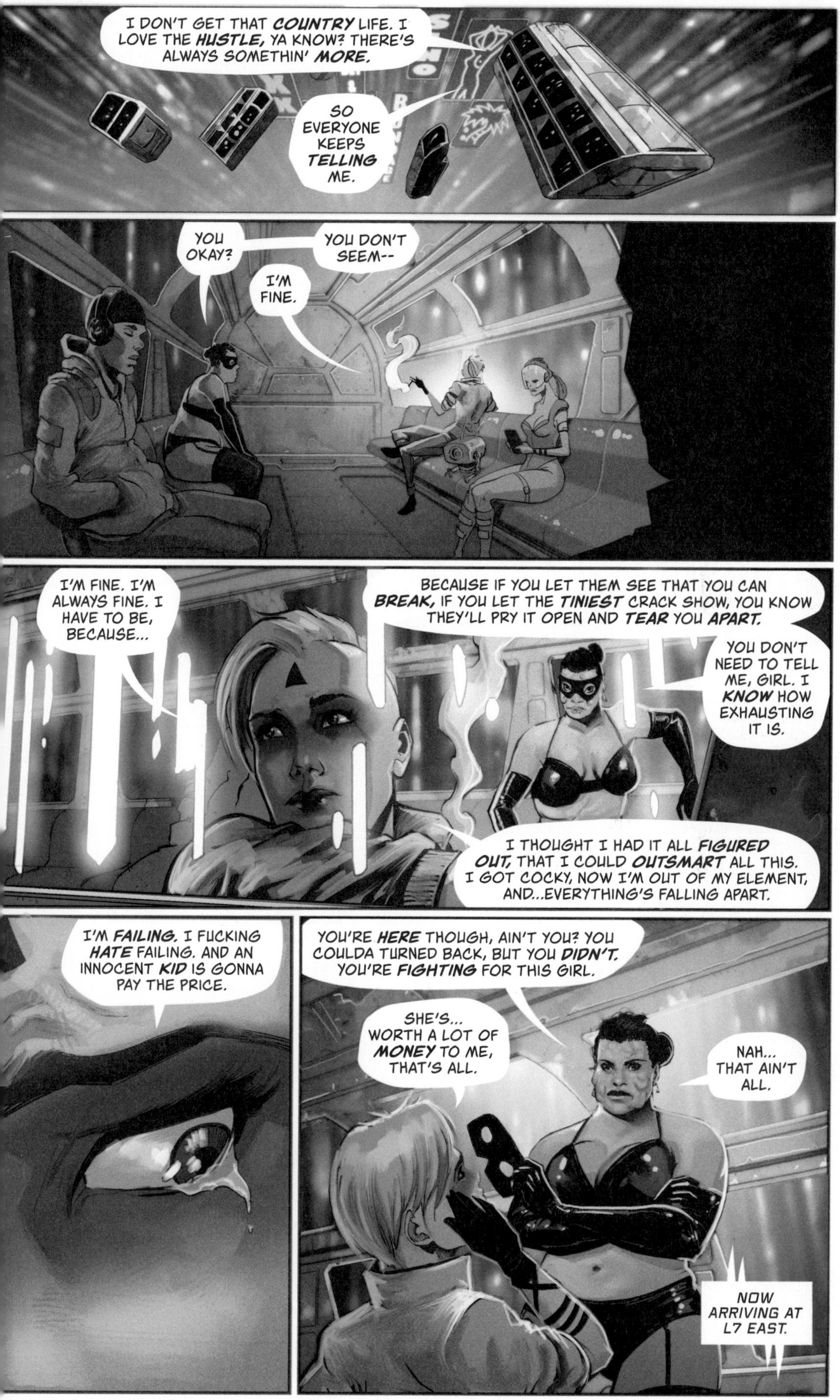

I DON'T GET THAT COUNTRY LIFE. I LOVE THE HUSTLE, YA KNOW? THERE'S ALWAYS SOMETHIN' MORE.
SO EVERYONE KEEPS TELLING ME.
YOU OKAY?
YOU DON'T SEEM--
I'M FINE.
I'M FINE. I'M ALWAYS FINE. I HAVE TO BE, BECAUSE...
BECAUSE IF YOU LET THEM SEE THAT YOU CAN BREAK, IF YOU LET THE TINIEST CRACK SHOW, YOU KNOW THEY'LL PRY IT OPEN AND TEAR YOU APART.
YOU DON'T NEED TO TELL ME, GIRL. I KNOW HOW EXHAUSTING IT IS.
I THOUGHT I HAD IT ALL FIGURED OUT, THAT I COULD OUTSMART ALL THIS. I GOT COCKY, NOW I'M OUT OF MY ELEMENT, AND...EVERYTHING'S FALLING APART.
I'M FAILING. I FUCKING HATE FAILING. AND AN INNOCENT KID IS GONNA PAY THE PRICE.
YOU'RE HERE THOUGH, AIN'T YOU? YOU COULDA TURNED BACK, BUT YOU DIDN'T. YOU'RE FIGHTING FOR THIS GIRL.
SHE'S... WORTH A LOT OF MONEY TO ME, THAT'S ALL.
NAH... THAT AIN'T ALL.
NOW ARRIVING AT L7 EAST.

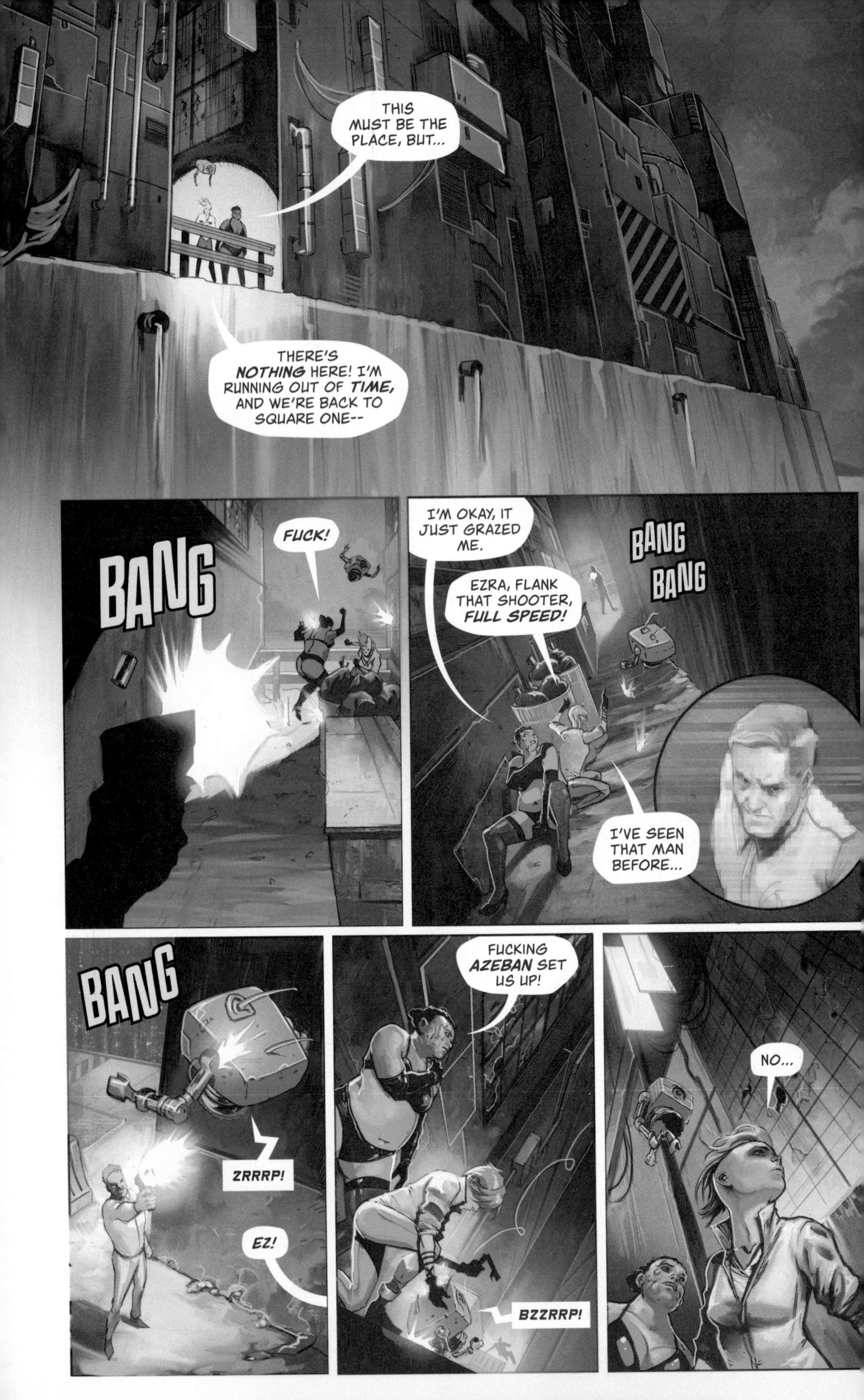
THIS MUST BE THE PLACE, BUT...
THERE'S NOTHING HERE! I'M RUNNING OUT OF TIME, AND WE'RE BACK TO SQUARE ONE--
BANG
FUCK!
I'M OKAY, IT JUST GRAZED ME.
BANG
BANG
EZRA, FLANK THAT SHOOTER, FULL SPEED!
I'VE SEEN THAT MAN BEFORE...
BANG
ZRRRP!
EZ!
FUCKING AZEBAN SET US UP!
BZZRRP!
NO...

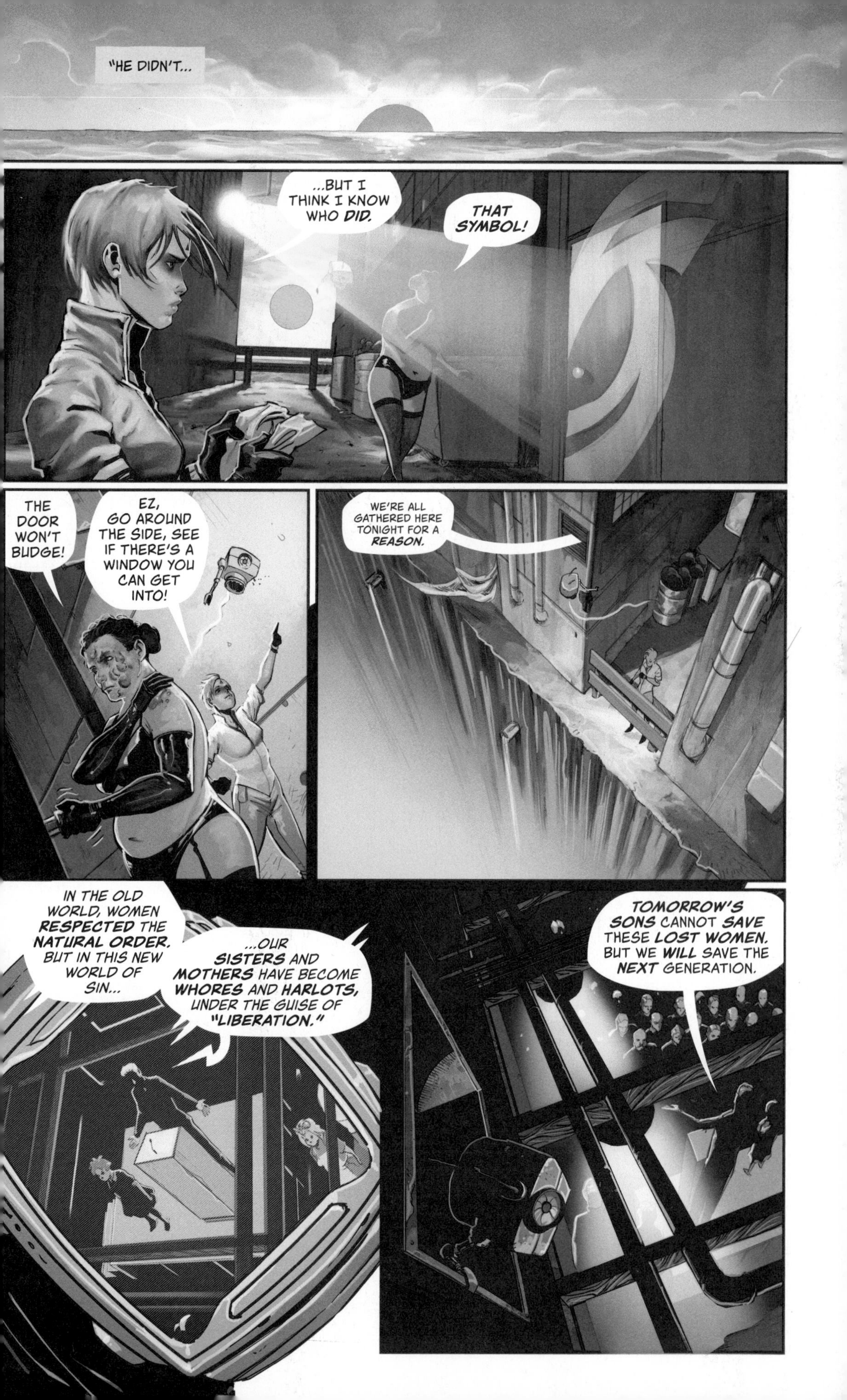
"HE DIDN'T...
...BUT I THINK I KNOW WHO DID.
THAT SYMBOL!
THE DOOR WON'T BUDGE!
EZ, GO AROUND THE SIDE, SEE IF THERE'S A WINDOW YOU CAN GET INTO!
WE'RE ALL GATHERED HERE TONIGHT FOR A REASON.
IN THE OLD WORLD, WOMEN RESPECTED THE NATURAL ORDER. BUT IN THIS NEW WORLD OF SIN...
...OUR SISTERS AND MOTHERS HAVE BECOME WHORES AND HARLOTS, UNDER THE GUISE OF "LIBERATION."
TOMORROW'S SONS CANNOT SAVE THESE LOST WOMEN. BUT WE WILL SAVE THE NEXT GENERATION.

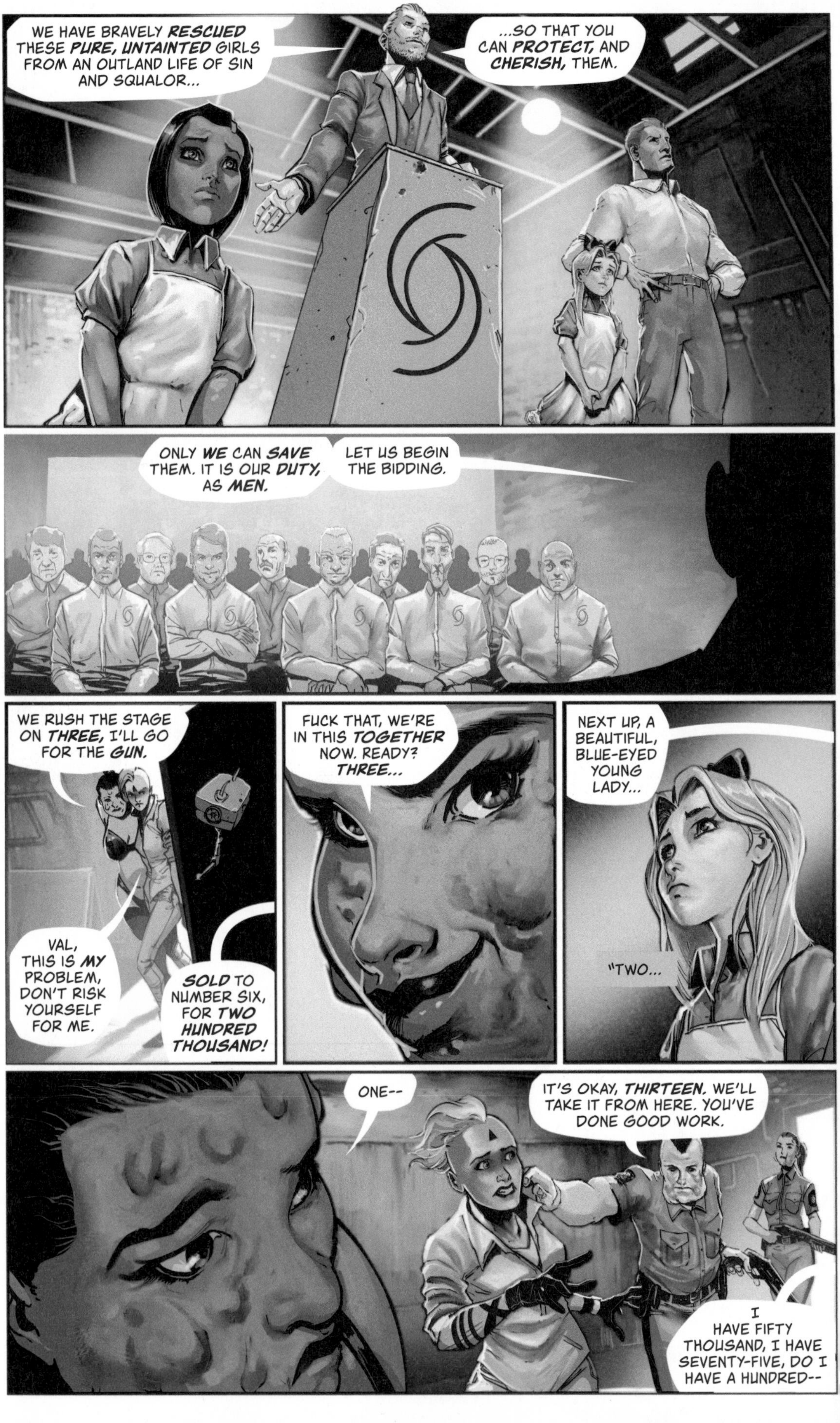
WE HAVE BRAVELY RESCUED THESE PURE, UNTAINTED GIRLS FROM AN OUTLAND LIFE OF SIN AND SQUALOR...
...SO THAT YOU CAN PROTECT, AND CHERISH, THEM.
ONLY WE CAN SAVE THEM. IT IS OUR DUTY, AS MEN.
LET US BEGIN THE BIDDING.
WE RUSH THE STAGE ON THREE, I'LL GO FOR THE GUN.
VAL, THIS IS MY PROBLEM, DON'T RISK YOURSELF FOR ME.
SOLD TO NUMBER SIX, FOR TWO HUNDRED THOUSAND!
FUCK THAT, WE'RE IN THIS TOGETHER NOW. READY? THREE...
NEXT UP, A BEAUTIFUL, BLUE-EYED YOUNG LADY...
"TWO...
ONE--
IT'S OKAY, THIRTEEN. WE'LL TAKE IT FROM HERE. YOU'VE DONE GOOD WORK.
I HAVE FIFTY THOUSAND, I HAVE SEVENTY-FIVE, DO I HAVE A HUNDRED--

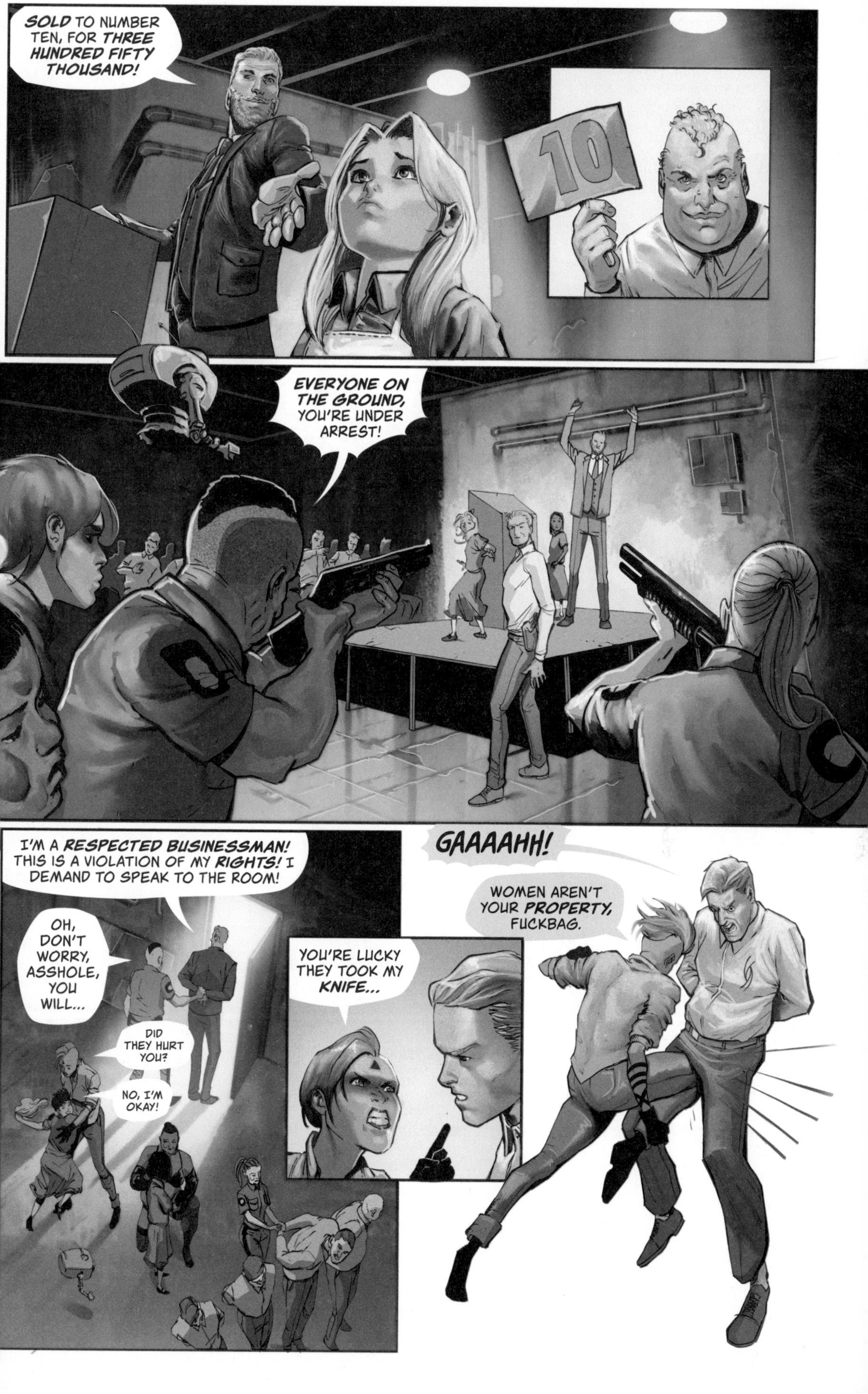
SOLD TO NUMBER TEN, FOR THREE HUNDRED FIFTY THOUSAND!
10
EVERYONE ON THE GROUND, YOU'RE UNDER ARREST!
I'M A RESPECTED BUSINESSMAN! THIS IS A VIOLATION OF MY RIGHTS! I DEMAND TO SPEAK TO THE ROOM!
OH, DON'T WORRY, ASSHOLE, YOU WILL...
DID THEY HURT YOU?
NO, I'M OKAY!
YOU'RE LUCKY THEY TOOK MY KNIFE...
GAAAAHH!
WOMEN AREN'T YOUR PROPERTY, FUCKBAG.

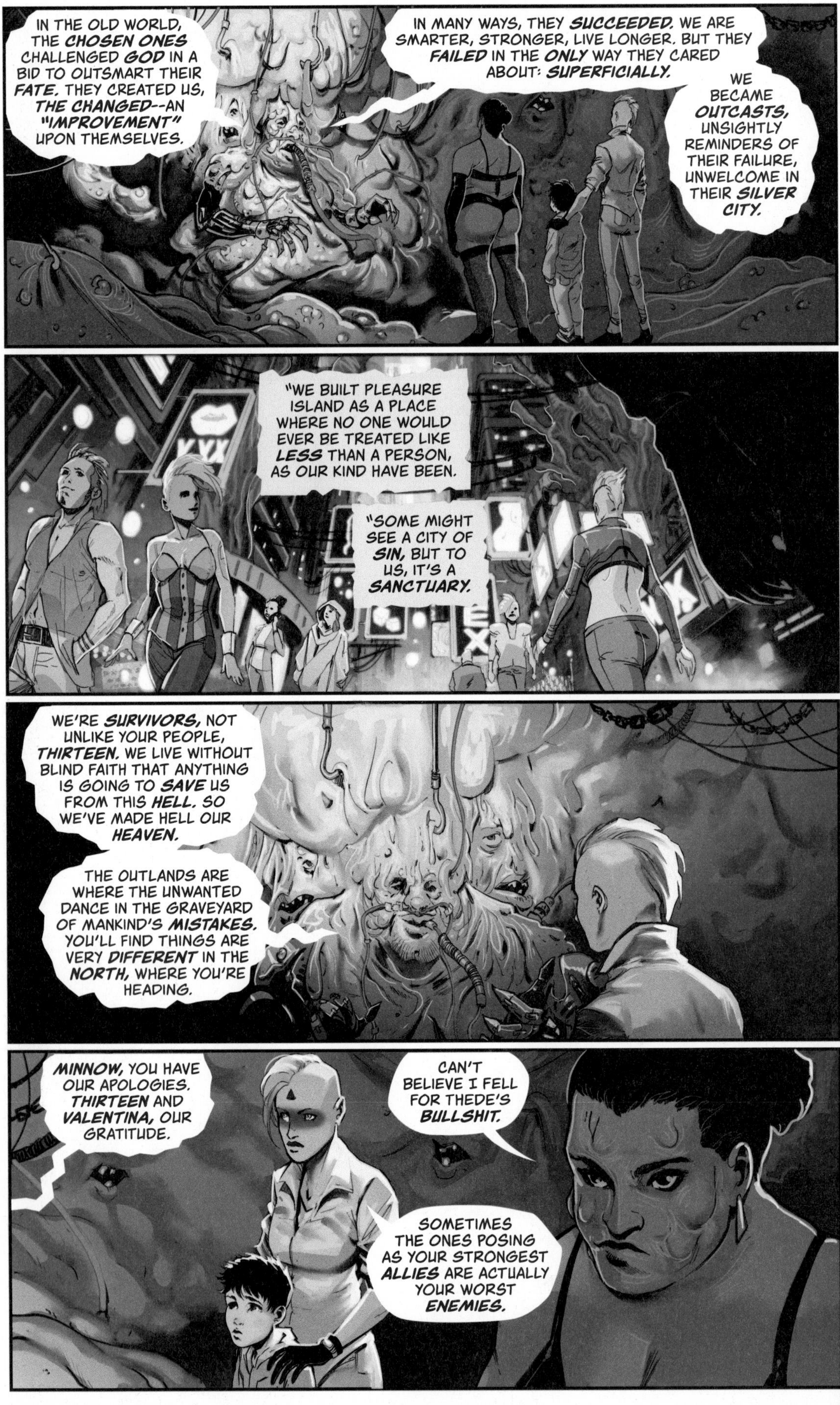
IN THE OLD WORLD, THE CHOSEN ONES CHALLENGED GOD IN A BID TO OUTSMART THEIR FATE. THEY CREATED US, THE CHANGED--AN "IMPROVEMENT" UPON THEMSELVES.
IN MANY WAYS, THEY SUCCEEDED. WE ARE SMARTER, STRONGER, LIVE LONGER. BUT THEY FAILED IN THE ONLY WAY THEY CARED ABOUT: SUPERFICIALLY.
WE BECAME OUTCASTS, UNSIGHTLY REMINDERS OF THEIR FAILURE, UNWELCOME IN THEIR SILVER CITY.
"WE BUILT PLEASURE ISLAND AS A PLACE WHERE NO ONE WOULD EVER BE TREATED LIKE LESS THAN A PERSON, AS OUR KIND HAVE BEEN.
"SOME MIGHT SEE A CITY OF SIN, BUT TO US, IT'S A SANCTUARY.
WE'RE SURVIVORS, NOT UNLIKE YOUR PEOPLE, THIRTEEN. WE LIVE WITHOUT BLIND FAITH THAT ANYTHING IS GOING TO SAVE US FROM THIS HELL. SO WE'VE MADE HELL OUR HEAVEN.
THE OUTLANDS ARE WHERE THE UNWANTED DANCE IN THE GRAVEYARD OF MANKIND'S MISTAKES. YOU'LL FIND THINGS ARE VERY DIFFERENT IN THE NORTH, WHERE YOU'RE HEADING.
MINNOW, YOU HAVE OUR APOLOGIES. THIRTEEN AND VALENTINA, OUR GRATITUDE.
CAN'T BELIEVE I FELL FOR THEDE'S BULLSHIT.
SOMETIMES THE ONES POSING AS YOUR STRONGEST ALLIES ARE ACTUALLY YOUR WORST ENEMIES.

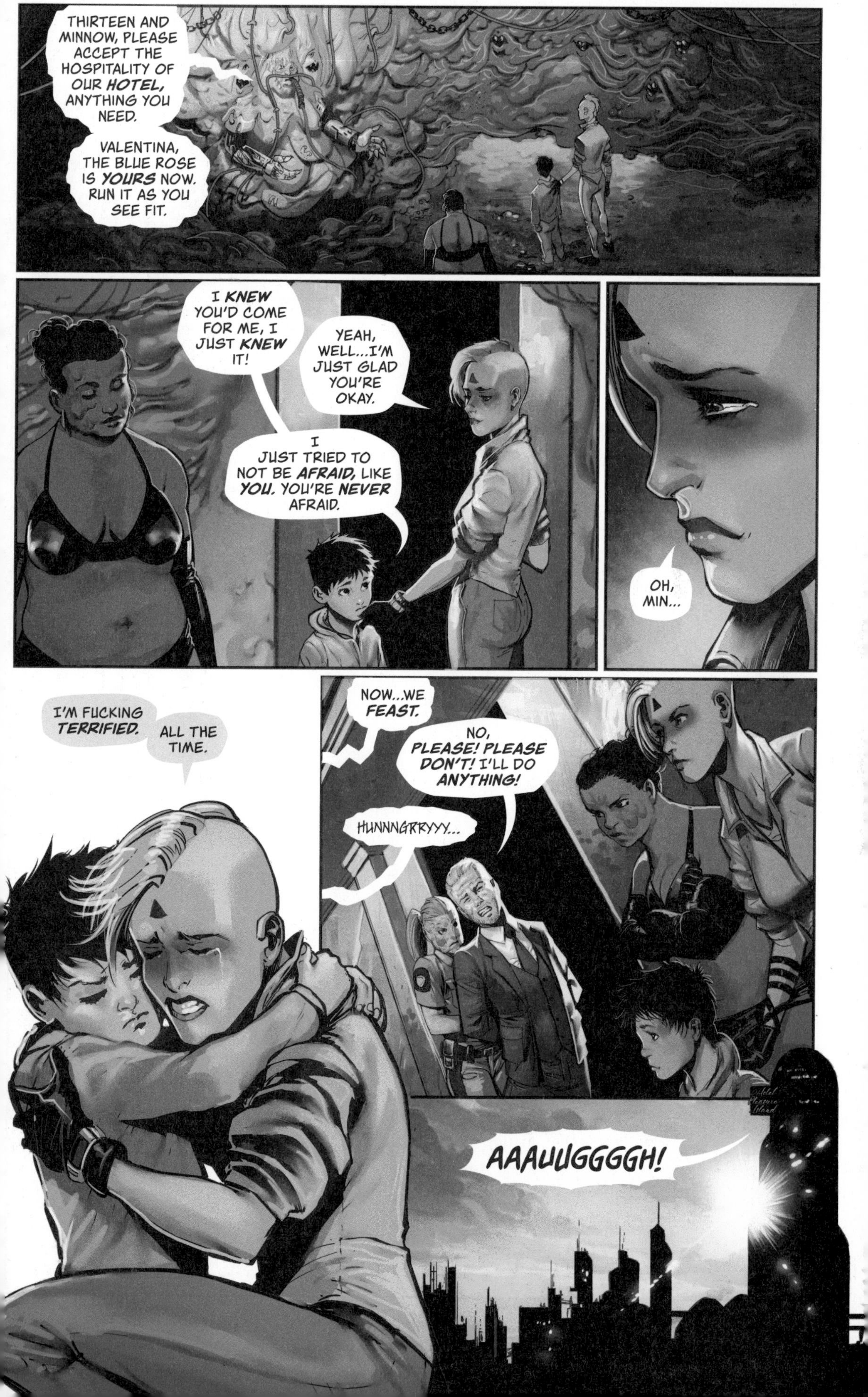
THIRTEEN AND MINNOW, PLEASE ACCEPT THE HOSPITALITY OF OUR HOTEL, ANYTHING YOU NEED.
VALENTINA, THE BLUE ROSE IS YOURS NOW. RUN IT AS YOU SEE FIT.
I KNEW YOU'D COME FOR ME, I JUST KNEW IT!
YEAH, WELL...I'M JUST GLAD YOU'RE OKAY.
I JUST TRIED TO NOT BE AFRAID, LIKE YOU. YOU'RE NEVER AFRAID.
OH, MIN...
I'M FUCKING TERRIFIED.
ALL THE TIME.
NOW...WE FEAST.
NO, PLEASE! PLEASE DON'T! I'LL DO ANYTHING!
HUNNNGRRYYY...
AAAUUGGGGH!

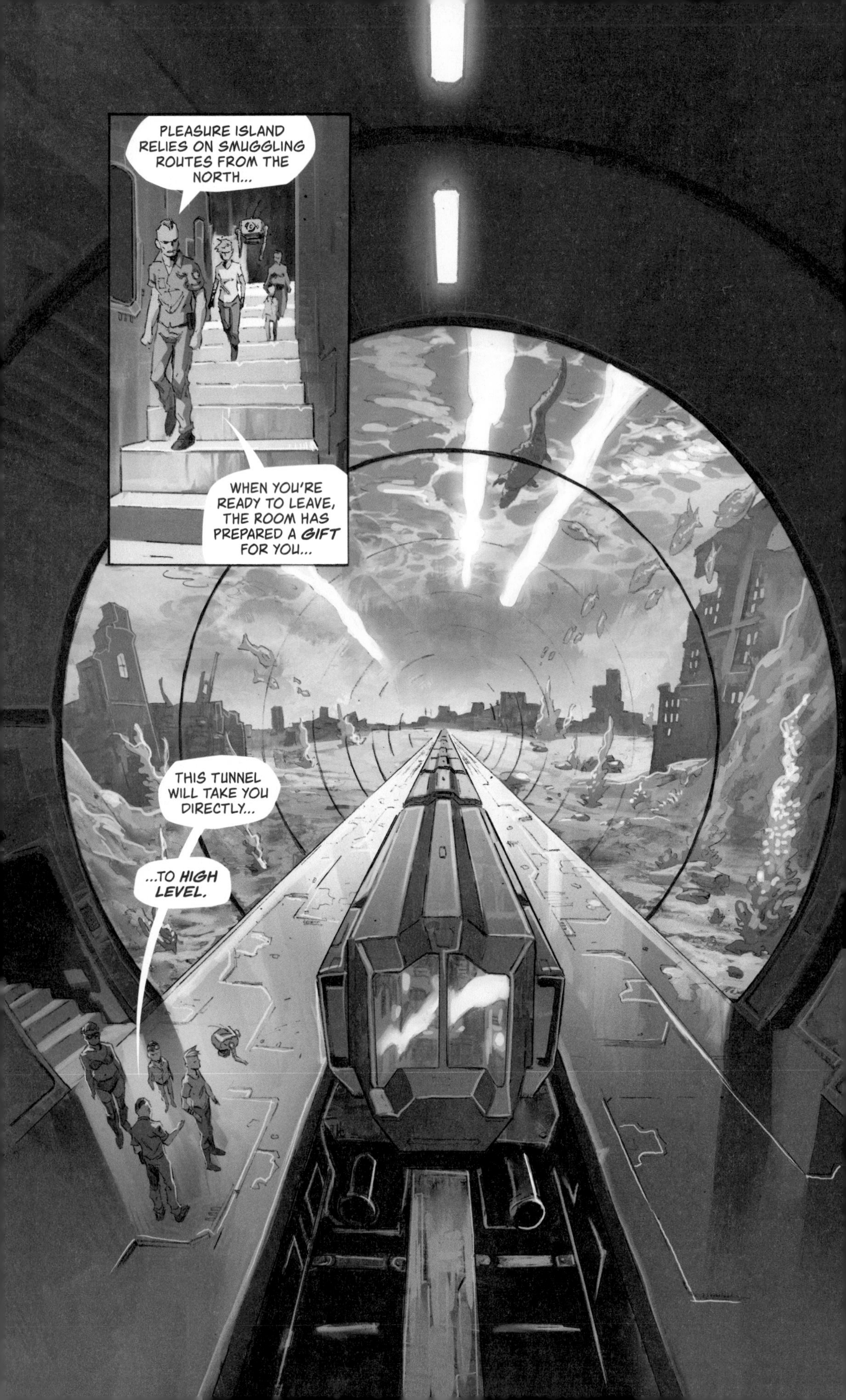
PLEASURE ISLAND RELIES ON SMUGGLING ROUTES FROM THE NORTH...
WHEN YOU'RE READY TO LEAVE, THE ROOM HAS PREPARED A *GIFT* FOR YOU...
THIS TUNNEL WILL TAKE YOU DIRECTLY...
...TO *HIGH LEVEL.*

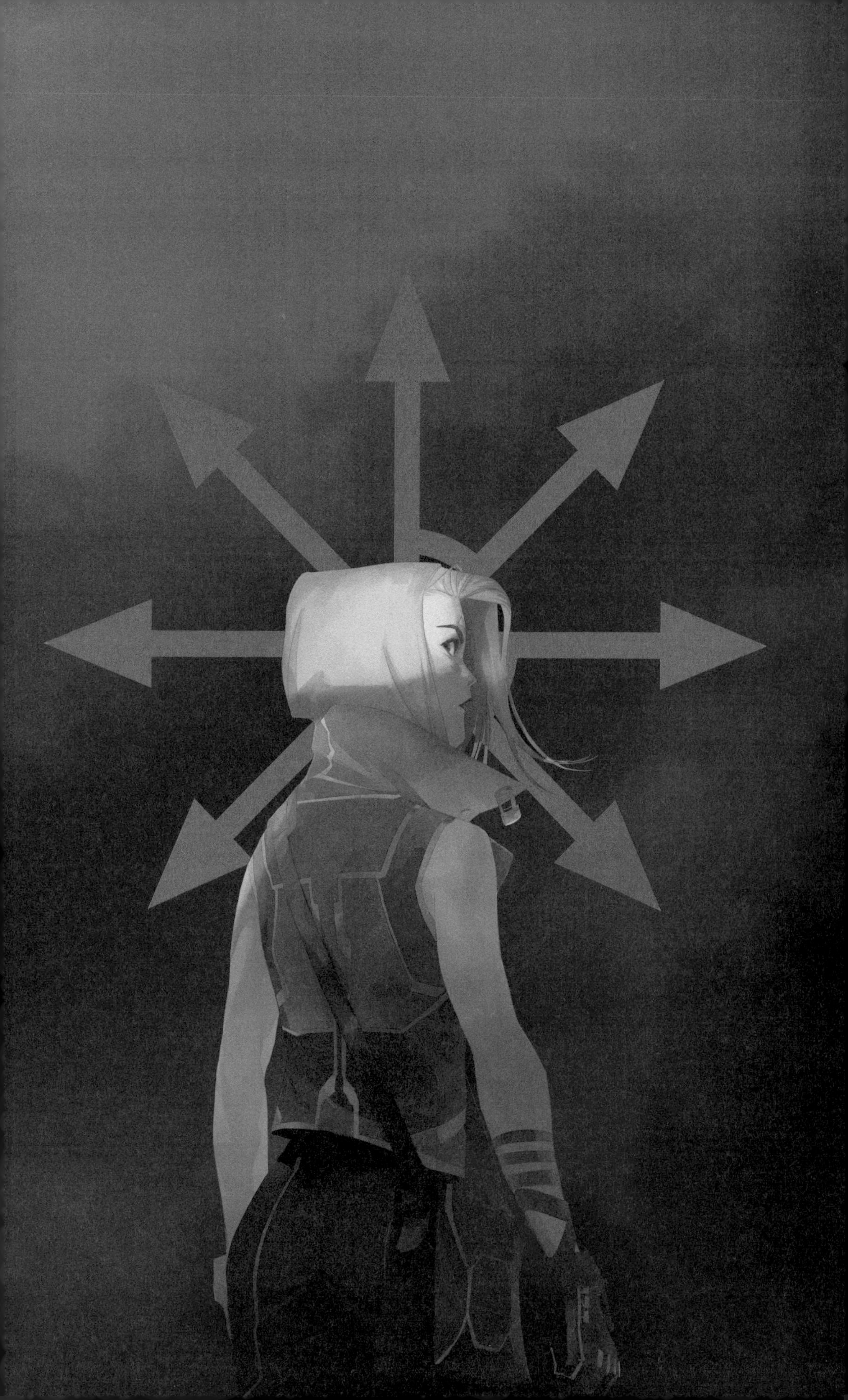

CHAPTER FIVE
LOW LEVEL

STORY
ROB SHERIDAN

ART
BARNABY BAGENDA AND OMAR FRANCIA

COLORS
ROMULO FAJARDO JR.

LETTERING
NATE PIEKOS OF BLAMBOT®

COVER
OTTO SCHMIDT

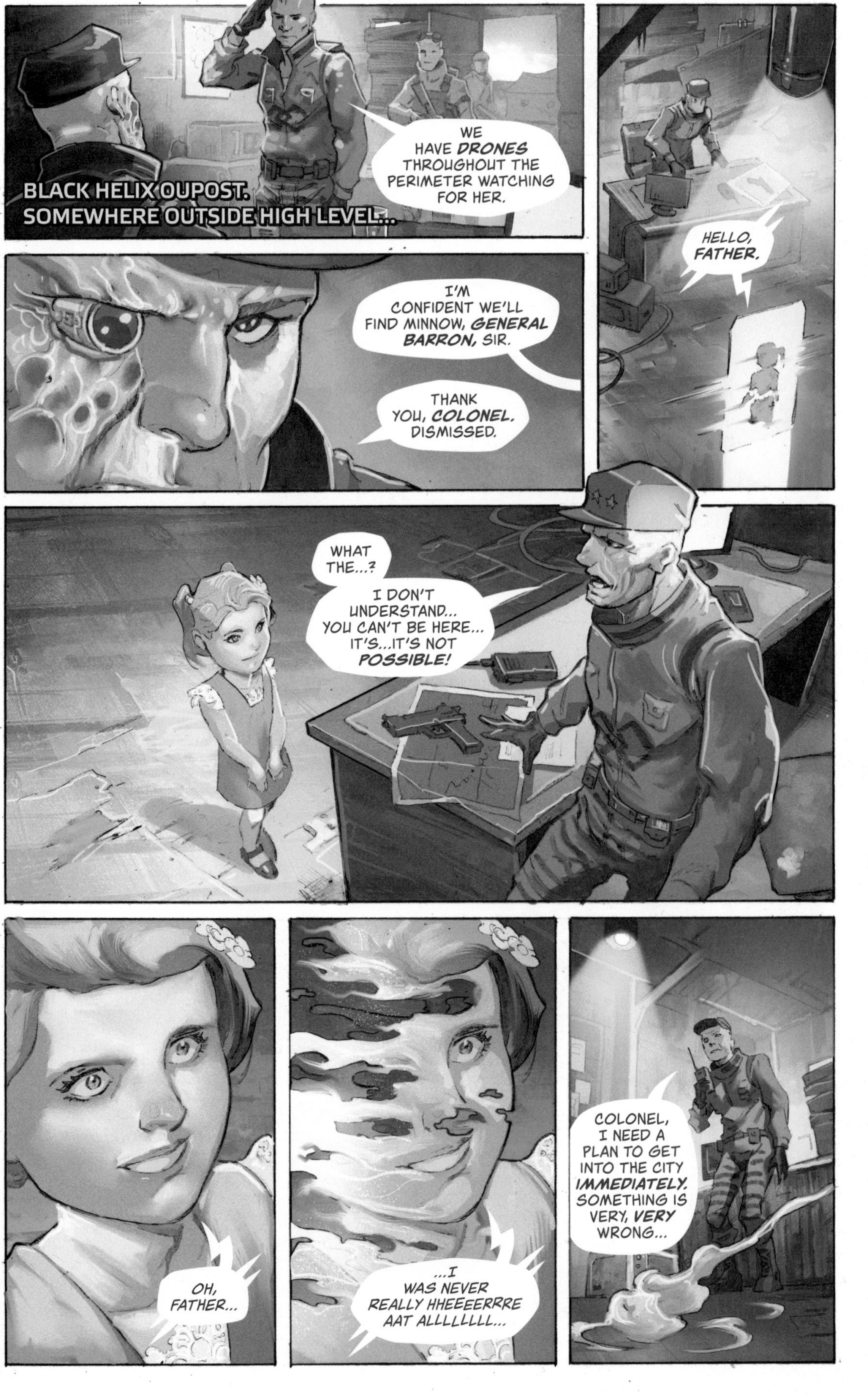
BLACK HELIX OUPOST.
SOMEWHERE OUTSIDE HIGH LEVEL...
WE HAVE DRONES THROUGHOUT THE PERIMETER WATCHING FOR HER.
I'M CONFIDENT WE'LL FIND MINNOW, GENERAL BARRON, SIR.
THANK YOU, COLONEL. DISMISSED.
HELLO, FATHER.
WHAT THE...?
I DON'T UNDERSTAND... YOU CAN'T BE HERE... IT'S...IT'S NOT POSSIBLE!
OH, FATHER...
...I WAS NEVER REALLY HHEEEERRRE AAT ALLLLLLLL...
COLONEL, I NEED A PLAN TO GET INTO THE CITY IMMEDIATELY. SOMETHING IS VERY, VERY WRONG...

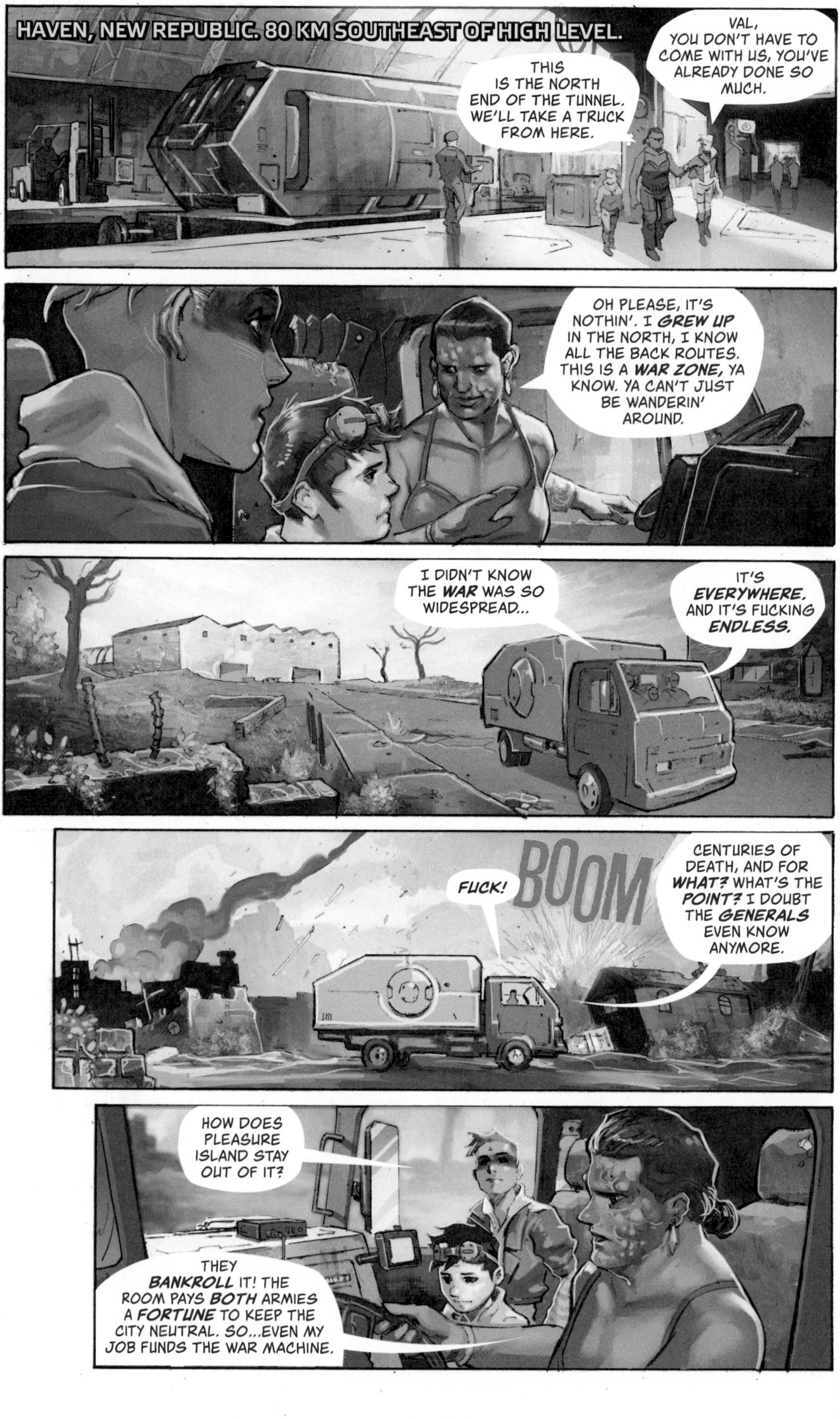
HAVEN, NEW REPUBLIC. 80 KM SOUTHEAST OF HIGH LEVEL.
THIS IS THE NORTH END OF THE TUNNEL. WE'LL TAKE A TRUCK FROM HERE.
VAL, YOU DON'T HAVE TO COME WITH US, YOU'VE ALREADY DONE SO MUCH.
OH PLEASE, IT'S NOTHIN'. I GREW UP IN THE NORTH, I KNOW ALL THE BACK ROUTES. THIS IS A WAR ZONE, YA KNOW. YA CAN'T JUST BE WANDERIN' AROUND.
I DIDN'T KNOW THE WAR WAS SO WIDESPREAD...
IT'S EVERYWHERE. AND IT'S FUCKING ENDLESS.
BOOM
FUCK!
CENTURIES OF DEATH, AND FOR WHAT? WHAT'S THE POINT? I DOUBT THE GENERALS EVEN KNOW ANYMORE.
HOW DOES PLEASURE ISLAND STAY OUT OF IT?
THEY BANKROLL IT! THE ROOM PAYS BOTH ARMIES A FORTUNE TO KEEP THE CITY NEUTRAL. SO...EVEN MY JOB FUNDS THE WAR MACHINE.

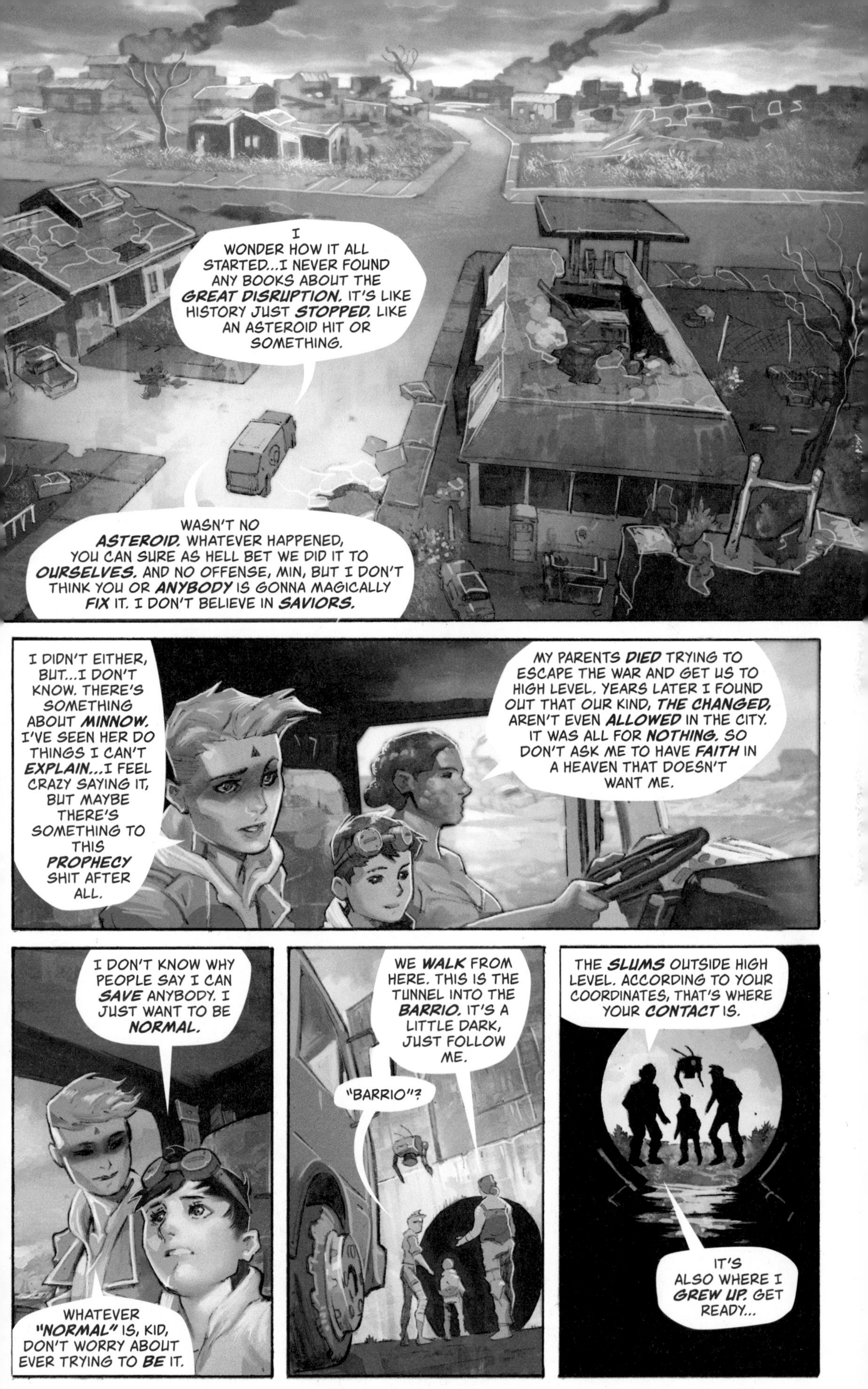
I WONDER HOW IT ALL STARTED...I NEVER FOUND ANY BOOKS ABOUT THE GREAT DISRUPTION. IT'S LIKE HISTORY JUST STOPPED. LIKE AN ASTEROID HIT OR SOMETHING.
WASN'T NO ASTEROID. WHATEVER HAPPENED, YOU CAN SURE AS HELL BET WE DID IT TO OURSELVES. AND NO OFFENSE, MIN, BUT I DON'T THINK YOU OR ANYBODY IS GONNA MAGICALLY FIX IT. I DON'T BELIEVE IN SAVIORS.
I DIDN'T EITHER, BUT...I DON'T KNOW. THERE'S SOMETHING ABOUT MINNOW. I'VE SEEN HER DO THINGS I CAN'T EXPLAIN...I FEEL CRAZY SAYING IT, BUT MAYBE THERE'S SOMETHING TO THIS PROPHECY SHIT AFTER ALL.
MY PARENTS DIED TRYING TO ESCAPE THE WAR AND GET US TO HIGH LEVEL. YEARS LATER I FOUND OUT THAT OUR KIND, THE CHANGED, AREN'T EVEN ALLOWED IN THE CITY. IT WAS ALL FOR NOTHING. SO DON'T ASK ME TO HAVE FAITH IN A HEAVEN THAT DOESN'T WANT ME.
I DON'T KNOW WHY PEOPLE SAY I CAN SAVE ANYBODY. I JUST WANT TO BE NORMAL.
WHATEVER "NORMAL" IS, KID, DON'T WORRY ABOUT EVER TRYING TO BE IT.
WE WALK FROM HERE. THIS IS THE TUNNEL INTO THE BARRIO. IT'S A LITTLE DARK, JUST FOLLOW ME.
"BARRIO"?
THE SLUMS OUTSIDE HIGH LEVEL. ACCORDING TO YOUR COORDINATES, THAT'S WHERE YOUR CONTACT IS.
IT'S ALSO WHERE I GREW UP. GET READY...

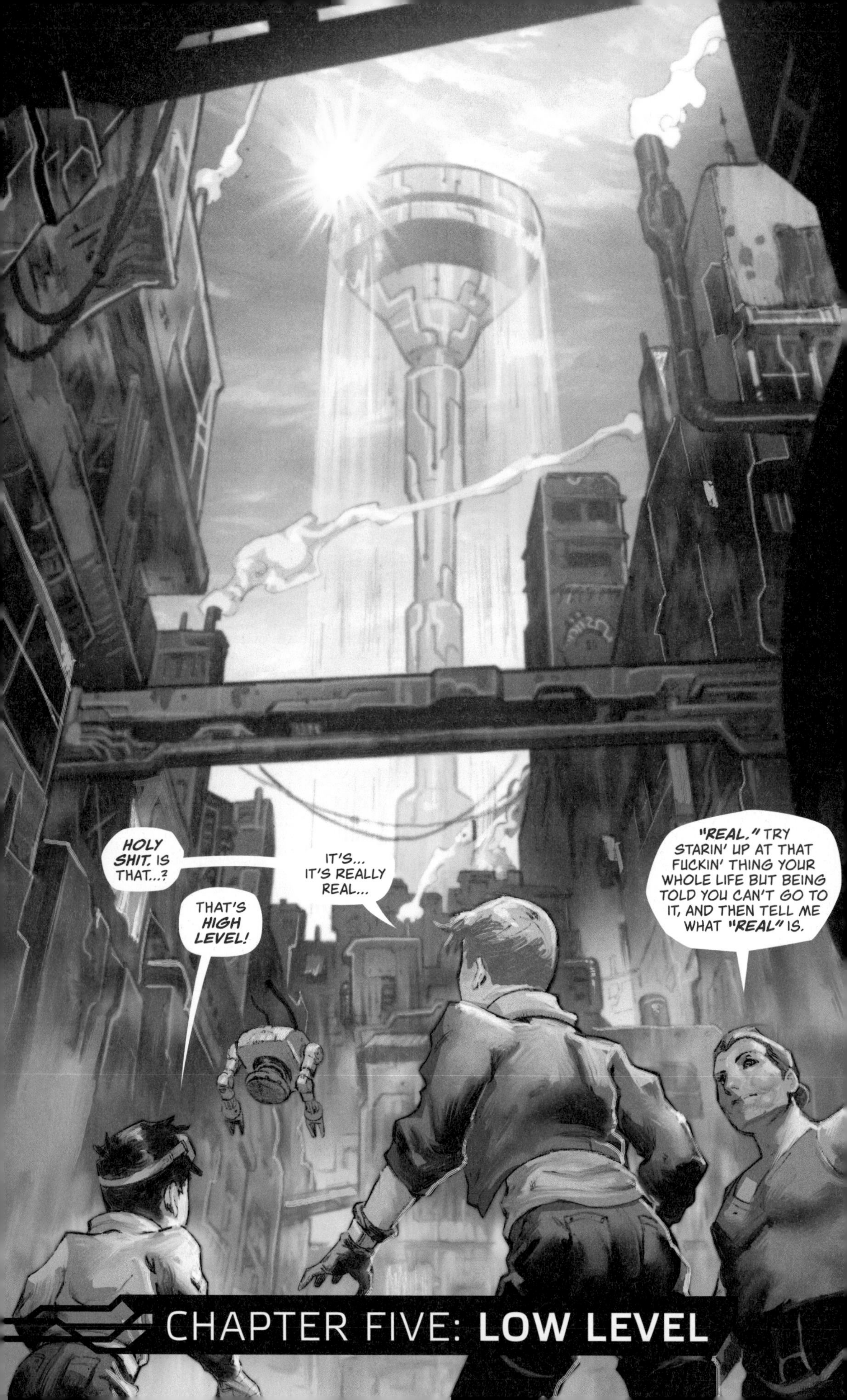
HOLY SHIT. IS THAT...?
IT'S... IT'S REALLY REAL...
THAT'S HIGH LEVEL!
"REAL." TRY STARIN' UP AT THAT FUCKIN' THING YOUR WHOLE LIFE BUT BEING TOLD YOU CAN'T GO TO IT, AND THEN TELL ME WHAT "REAL" IS.

CHAPTER FIVE: LOW LEVEL

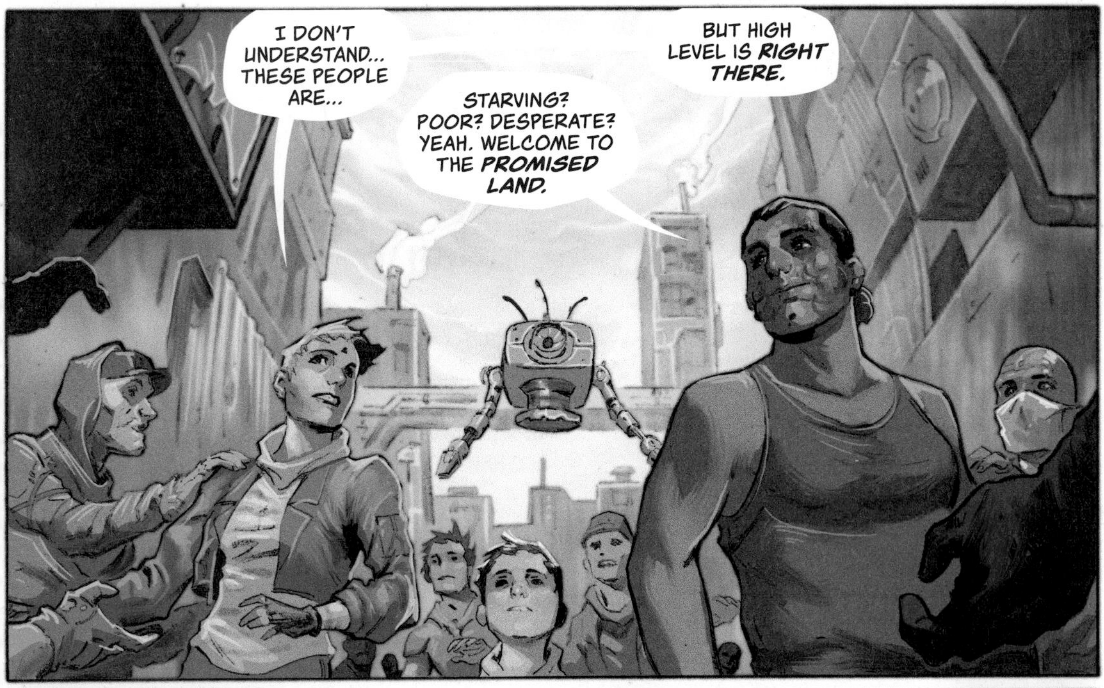
I DON'T UNDERSTAND... THESE PEOPLE ARE...
STARVING? POOR? DESPERATE? YEAH. WELCOME TO THE PROMISED LAND.
BUT HIGH LEVEL IS RIGHT THERE.

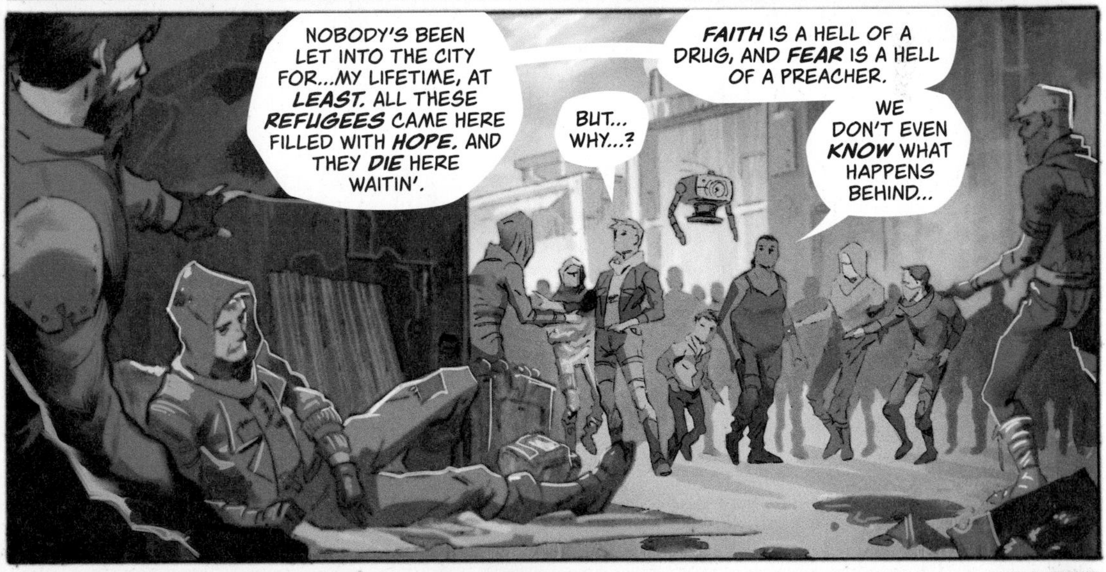
NOBODY'S BEEN LET INTO THE CITY FOR...MY LIFETIME, AT LEAST. ALL THESE REFUGEES CAME HERE FILLED WITH HOPE. AND THEY DIE HERE WAITIN'.
FAITH IS A HELL OF A DRUG, AND FEAR IS A HELL OF A PREACHER.
BUT... WHY...?
WE DON'T EVEN KNOW WHAT HAPPENS BEHIND...

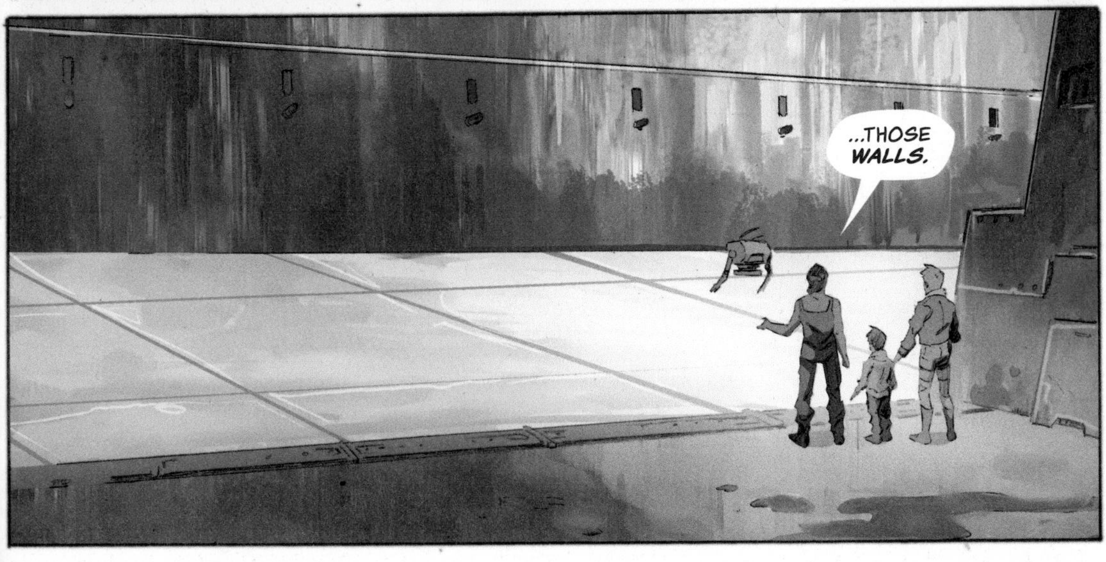
...THOSE WALLS.

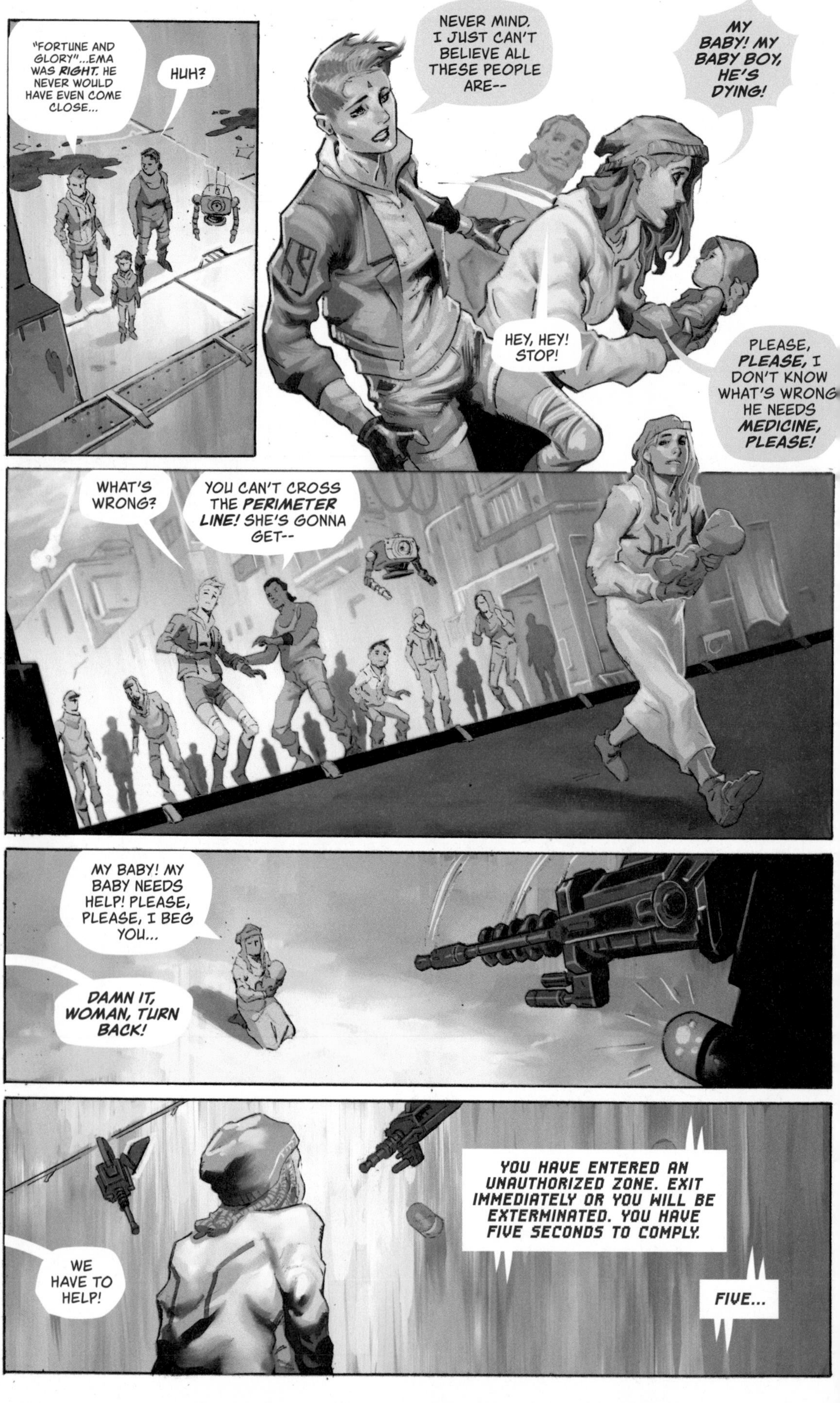
"FORTUNE AND GLORY"...EMA WAS RIGHT. HE NEVER WOULD HAVE EVEN COME CLOSE...
HUH?
NEVER MIND. I JUST CAN'T BELIEVE ALL THESE PEOPLE ARE--
MY BABY! MY BABY BOY, HE'S DYING!
HEY, HEY! STOP!
PLEASE, PLEASE, I DON'T KNOW WHAT'S WRONG HE NEEDS MEDICINE, PLEASE!
WHAT'S WRONG?
YOU CAN'T CROSS THE PERIMETER LINE! SHE'S GONNA GET--
MY BABY! MY BABY NEEDS HELP! PLEASE, PLEASE, I BEG YOU...
DAMN IT, WOMAN, TURN BACK!
WE HAVE TO HELP!
YOU HAVE ENTERED AN UNAUTHORIZED ZONE. EXIT IMMEDIATELY OR YOU WILL BE EXTERMINATED. YOU HAVE FIVE SECONDS TO COMPLY.
FIVE...

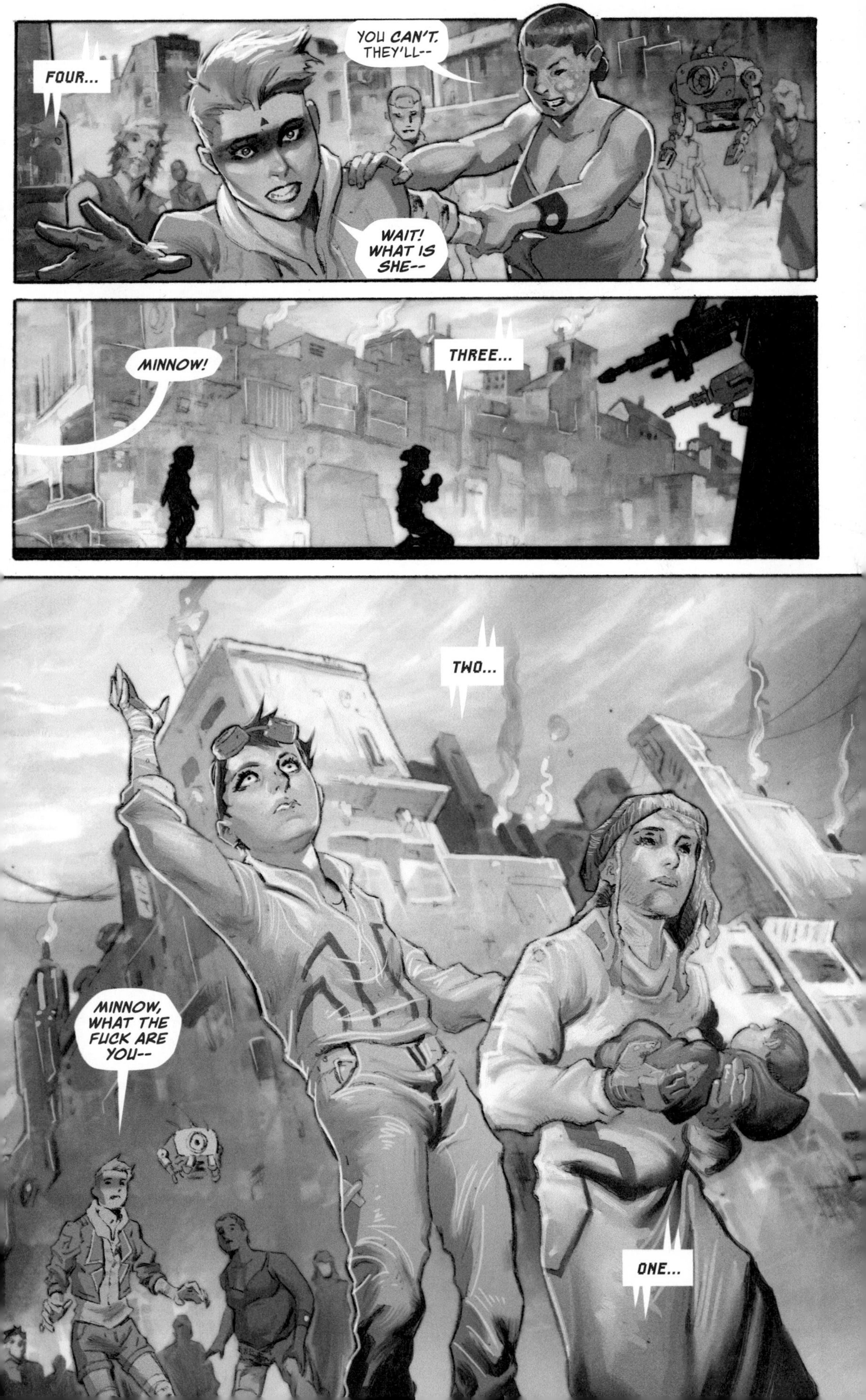
FOUR...
YOU CAN'T. THEY'LL--
WAIT! WHAT IS SHE--
MINNOW!
THREE...
TWO...
MINNOW, WHAT THE FUCK ARE YOU--
ONE...

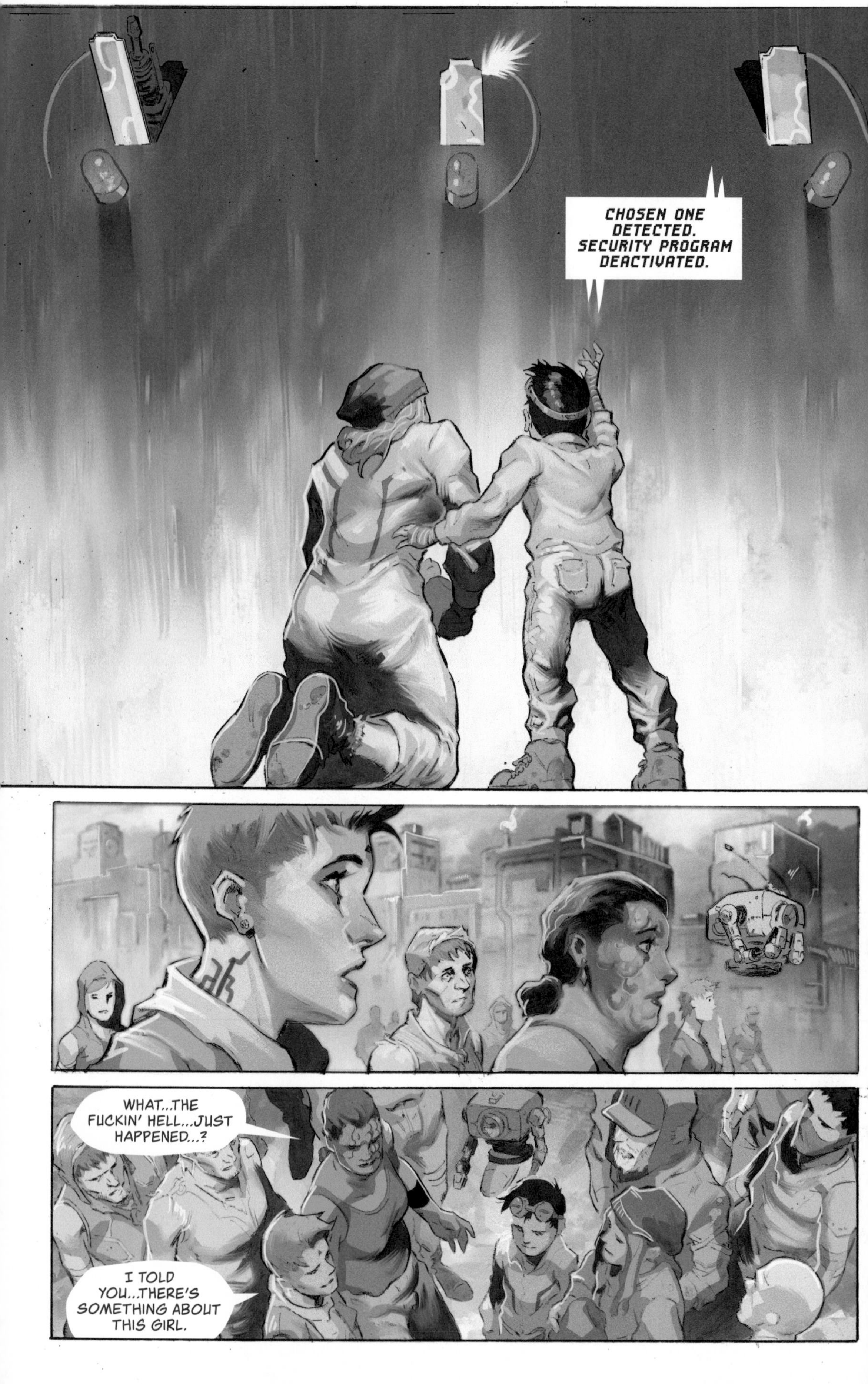
CHOSEN ONE DETECTED. SECURITY PROGRAM DEACTIVATED.
WHAT...THE FUCKIN' HELL...JUST HAPPENED...?
I TOLD YOU...THERE'S SOMETHING ABOUT THIS GIRL.

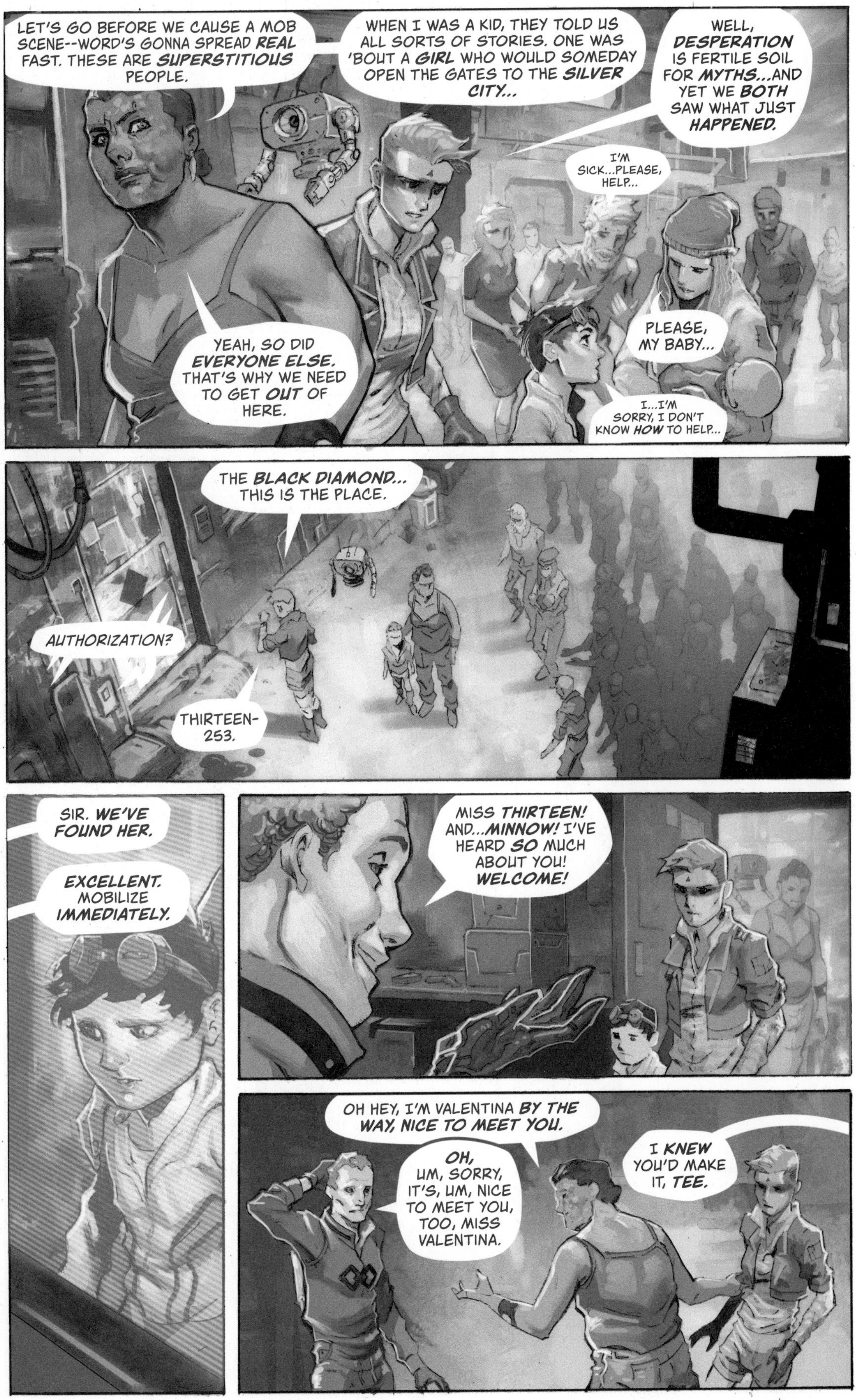
LET'S GO BEFORE WE CAUSE A MOB SCENE--WORD'S GONNA SPREAD REAL FAST. THESE ARE SUPERSTITIOUS PEOPLE.
WHEN I WAS A KID, THEY TOLD US ALL SORTS OF STORIES. ONE WAS 'BOUT A GIRL WHO WOULD SOMEDAY OPEN THE GATES TO THE SILVER CITY...
WELL, DESPERATION IS FERTILE SOIL FOR MYTHS...AND YET WE BOTH SAW WHAT JUST HAPPENED.
I'M SICK...PLEASE, HELP...
YEAH, SO DID EVERYONE ELSE. THAT'S WHY WE NEED TO GET OUT OF HERE.
PLEASE, MY BABY...
I...I'M SORRY, I DON'T KNOW HOW TO HELP...
THE BLACK DIAMOND... THIS IS THE PLACE.
AUTHORIZATION?
THIRTEEN-253.
SIR. WE'VE FOUND HER.
EXCELLENT. MOBILIZE IMMEDIATELY.
MISS THIRTEEN! AND...MINNOW! I'VE HEARD SO MUCH ABOUT YOU! WELCOME!
OH HEY, I'M VALENTINA BY THE WAY, NICE TO MEET YOU.
OH, UM, SORRY, IT'S, UM, NICE TO MEET YOU, TOO, MISS VALENTINA.
I KNEW YOU'D MAKE IT, TEE.

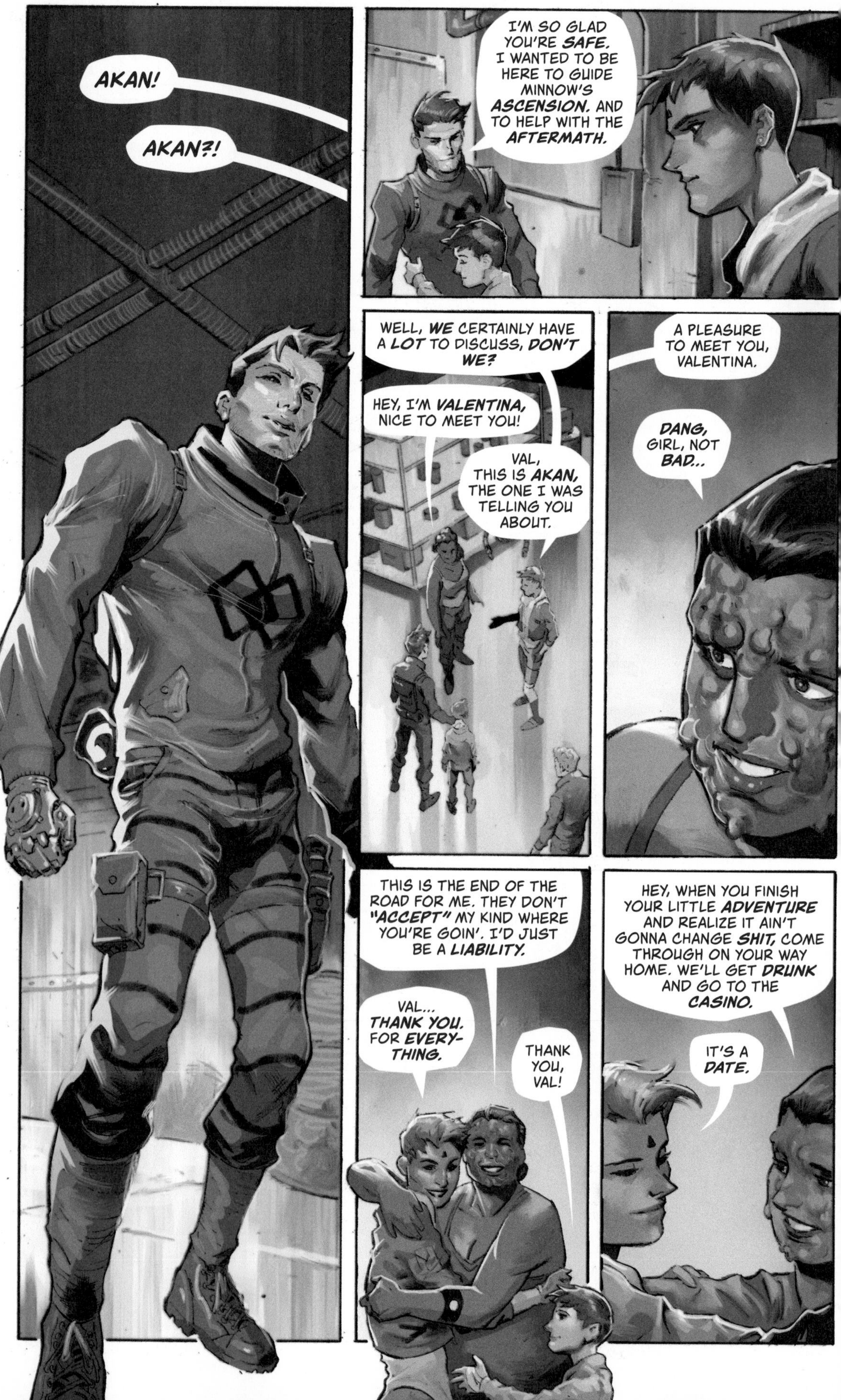
AKAN!
AKAN?!
I'M SO GLAD YOU'RE SAFE. I WANTED TO BE HERE TO GUIDE MINNOW'S ASCENSION. AND TO HELP WITH THE AFTERMATH.
WELL, WE CERTAINLY HAVE A LOT TO DISCUSS, DON'T WE?
HEY, I'M VALENTINA, NICE TO MEET YOU!
VAL, THIS IS AKAN, THE ONE I WAS TELLING YOU ABOUT.
A PLEASURE TO MEET YOU, VALENTINA.
DANG, GIRL, NOT BAD...
THIS IS THE END OF THE ROAD FOR ME. THEY DON'T "ACCEPT" MY KIND WHERE YOU'RE GOIN'. I'D JUST BE A LIABILITY.
VAL... THANK YOU. FOR EVERY-THING.
THANK YOU, VAL!
HEY, WHEN YOU FINISH YOUR LITTLE ADVENTURE AND REALIZE IT AIN'T GONNA CHANGE SHIT, COME THROUGH ON YOUR WAY HOME. WE'LL GET DRUNK AND GO TO THE CASINO.
IT'S A DATE.

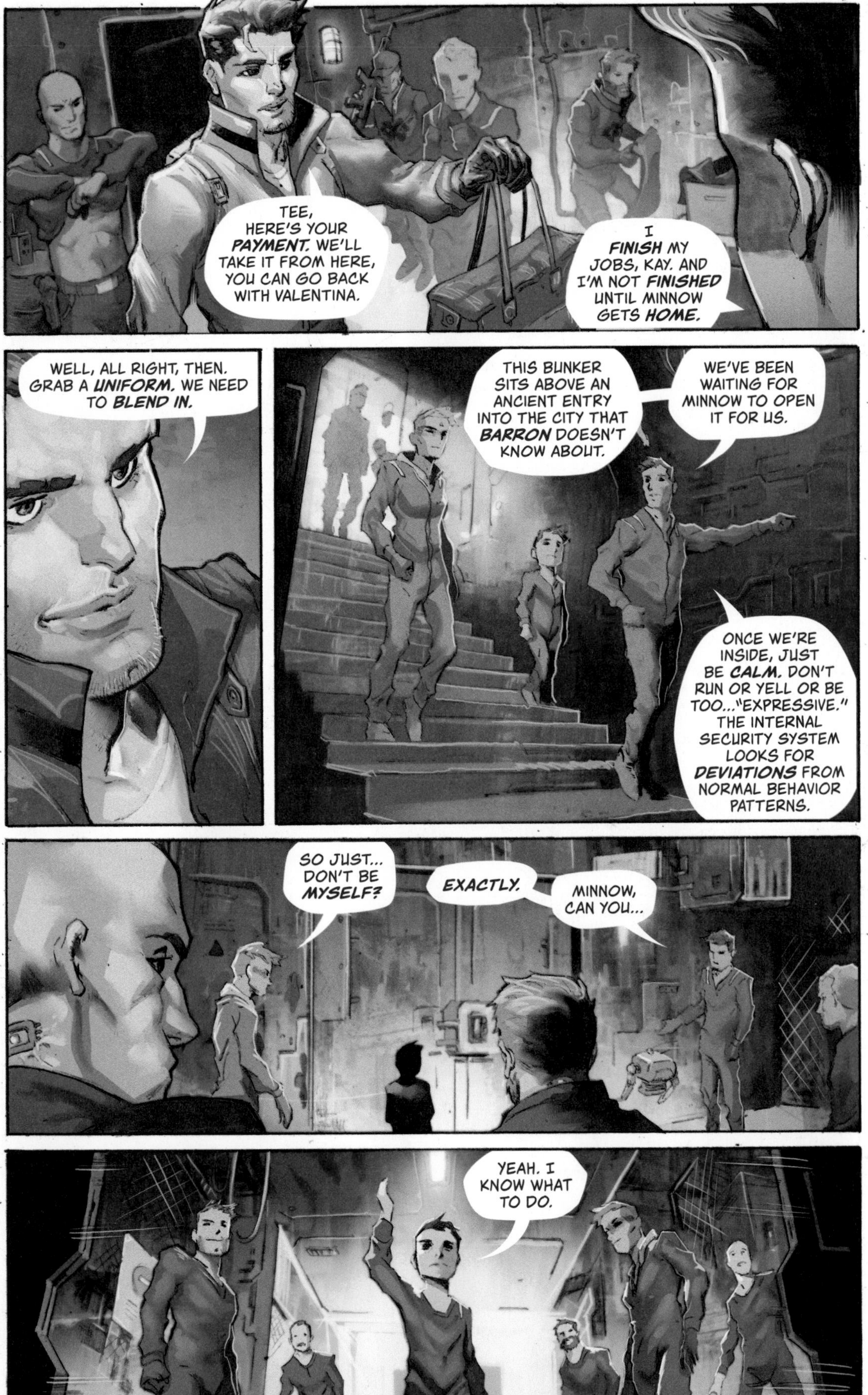
TEE, HERE'S YOUR PAYMENT. WE'LL TAKE IT FROM HERE, YOU CAN GO BACK WITH VALENTINA.
I FINISH MY JOBS, KAY. AND I'M NOT FINISHED UNTIL MINNOW GETS HOME.
WELL, ALL RIGHT, THEN. GRAB A UNIFORM. WE NEED TO BLEND IN.
THIS BUNKER SITS ABOVE AN ANCIENT ENTRY INTO THE CITY THAT BARRON DOESN'T KNOW ABOUT.
WE'VE BEEN WAITING FOR MINNOW TO OPEN IT FOR US.
ONCE WE'RE INSIDE, JUST BE CALM. DON'T RUN OR YELL OR BE TOO..."EXPRESSIVE." THE INTERNAL SECURITY SYSTEM LOOKS FOR DEVIATIONS FROM NORMAL BEHAVIOR PATTERNS.
SO JUST... DON'T BE MYSELF?
EXACTLY.
MINNOW, CAN YOU...
YEAH. I KNOW WHAT TO DO.

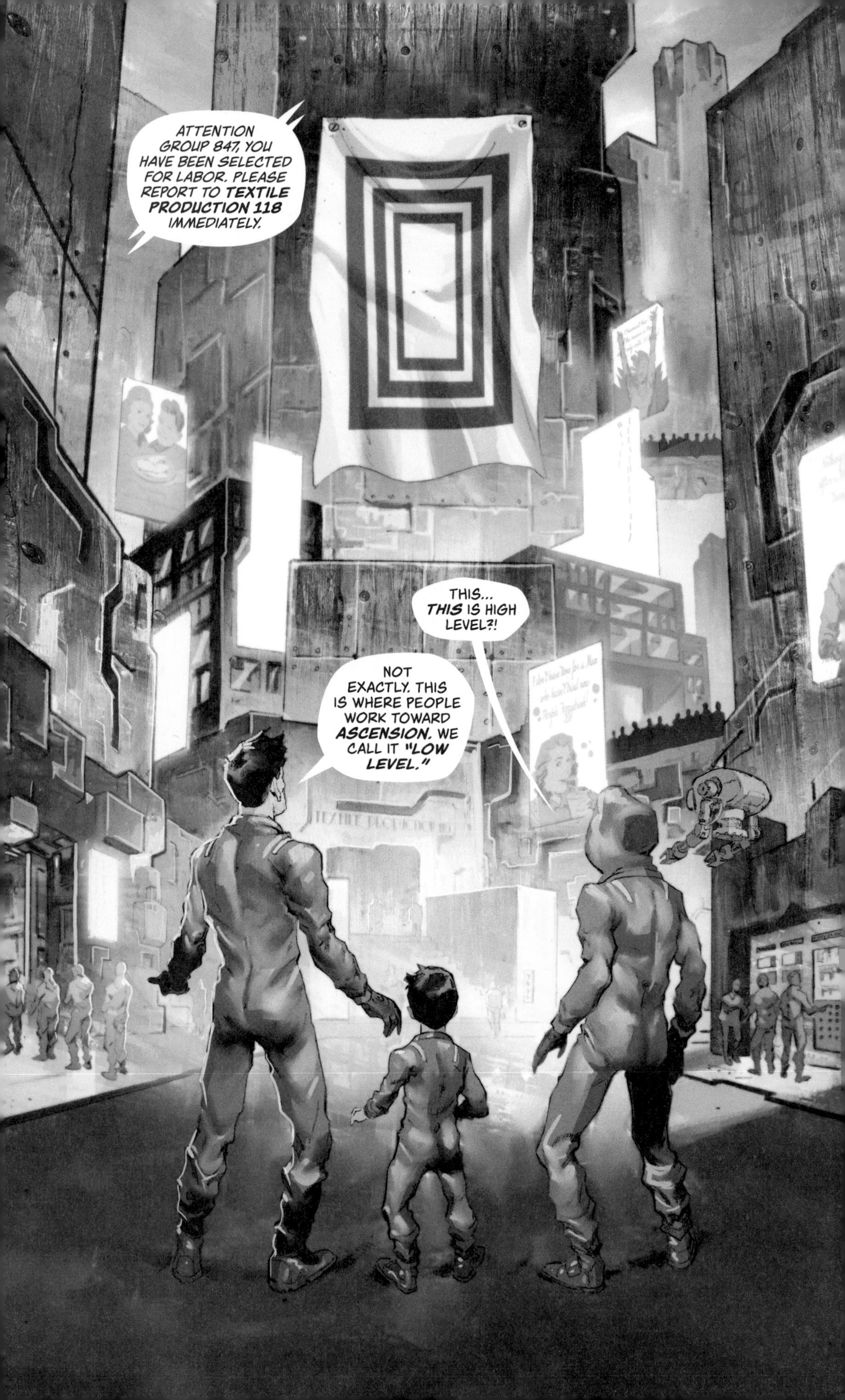
ATTENTION GROUP 847, YOU HAVE BEEN SELECTED FOR LABOR. PLEASE REPORT TO **TEXTILE PRODUCTION 118** IMMEDIATELY.
THIS... ***THIS*** IS HIGH LEVEL?!
NOT EXACTLY. THIS IS WHERE PEOPLE WORK TOWARD **ASCENSION.** WE CALL IT ***"LOW LEVEL."***

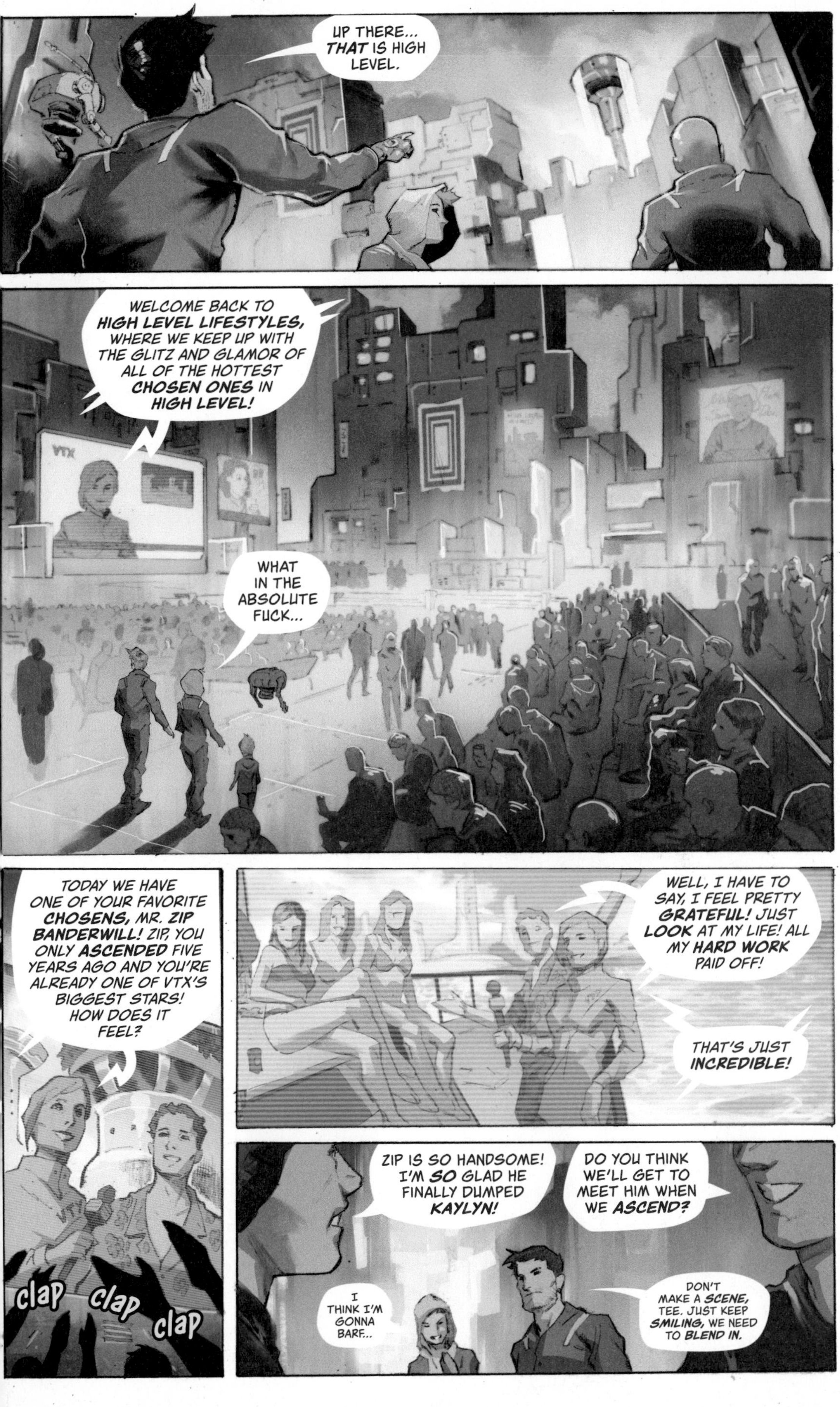
UP THERE... THAT IS HIGH LEVEL.
WELCOME BACK TO HIGH LEVEL LIFESTYLES, WHERE WE KEEP UP WITH THE GLITZ AND GLAMOR OF ALL OF THE HOTTEST CHOSEN ONES IN HIGH LEVEL!
VTX
WHAT IN THE ABSOLUTE FUCK...
TODAY WE HAVE ONE OF YOUR FAVORITE CHOSENS, MR. ZIP BANDERWILL! ZIP, YOU ONLY ASCENDED FIVE YEARS AGO AND YOU'RE ALREADY ONE OF VTX'S BIGGEST STARS! HOW DOES IT FEEL?
clap clap clap
WELL, I HAVE TO SAY, I FEEL PRETTY GRATEFUL! JUST LOOK AT MY LIFE! ALL MY HARD WORK PAID OFF!
THAT'S JUST INCREDIBLE!
ZIP IS SO HANDSOME! I'M SO GLAD HE FINALLY DUMPED KAYLYN!
DO YOU THINK WE'LL GET TO MEET HIM WHEN WE ASCEND?
I THINK I'M GONNA BARF...
DON'T MAKE A SCENE, TEE. JUST KEEP SMILING, WE NEED TO BLEND IN.

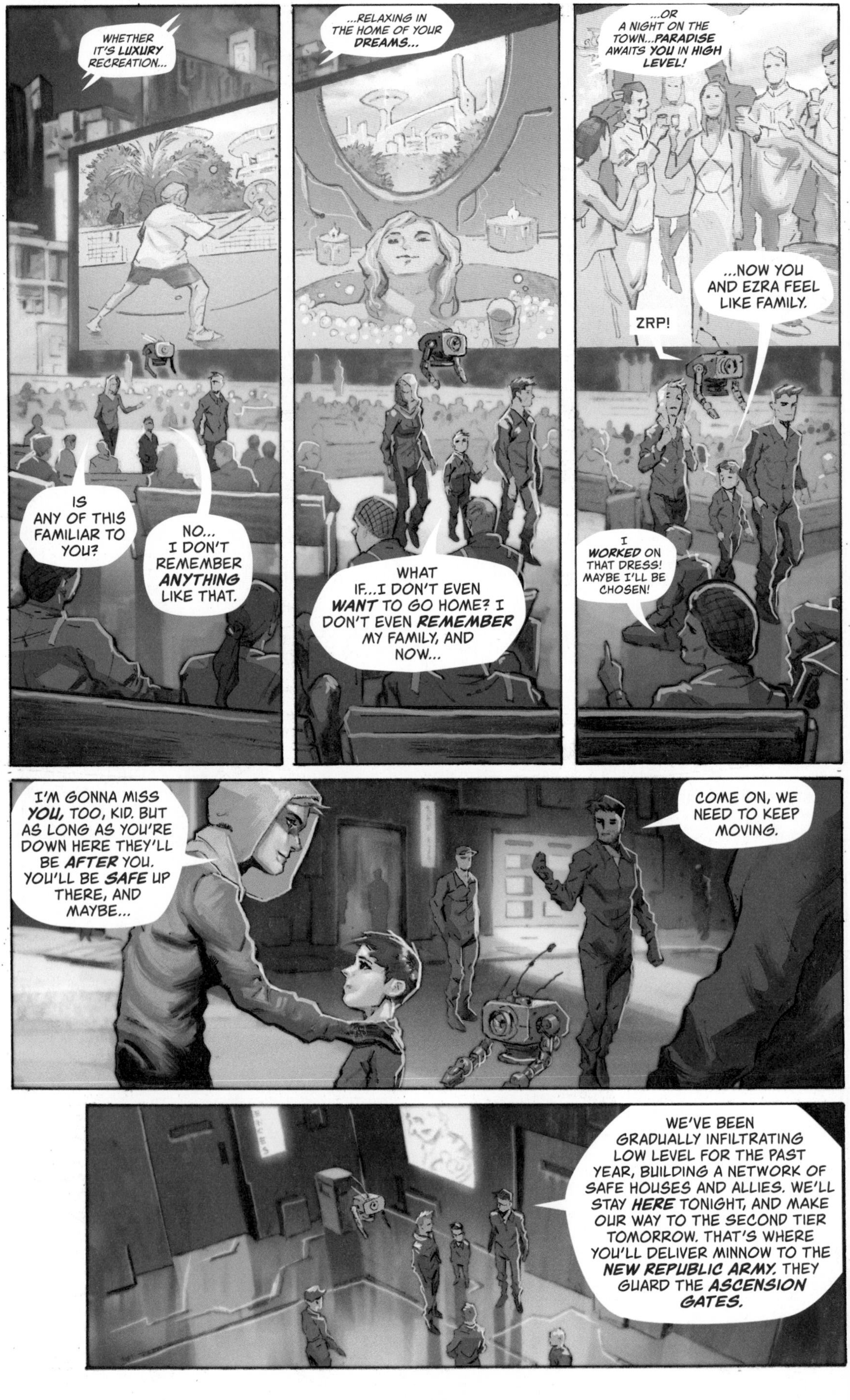
WHETHER IT'S LUXURY RECREATION...
IS ANY OF THIS FAMILIAR TO YOU?
NO... I DON'T REMEMBER ANYTHING LIKE THAT.
...RELAXING IN THE HOME OF YOUR DREAMS...
WHAT IF...I DON'T EVEN WANT TO GO HOME? I DON'T EVEN REMEMBER MY FAMILY, AND NOW...
...OR A NIGHT ON THE TOWN...PARADISE AWAITS YOU IN HIGH LEVEL!
...NOW YOU AND EZRA FEEL LIKE FAMILY.
ZRP!
I WORKED ON THAT DRESS! MAYBE I'LL BE CHOSEN!
I'M GONNA MISS YOU, TOO, KID. BUT AS LONG AS YOU'RE DOWN HERE THEY'LL BE AFTER YOU. YOU'LL BE SAFE UP THERE, AND MAYBE...
COME ON, WE NEED TO KEEP MOVING.
WE'VE BEEN GRADUALLY INFILTRATING LOW LEVEL FOR THE PAST YEAR, BUILDING A NETWORK OF SAFE HOUSES AND ALLIES. WE'LL STAY HERE TONIGHT, AND MAKE OUR WAY TO THE SECOND TIER TOMORROW. THAT'S WHERE YOU'LL DELIVER MINNOW TO THE NEW REPUBLIC ARMY. THEY GUARD THE ASCENSION GATES.

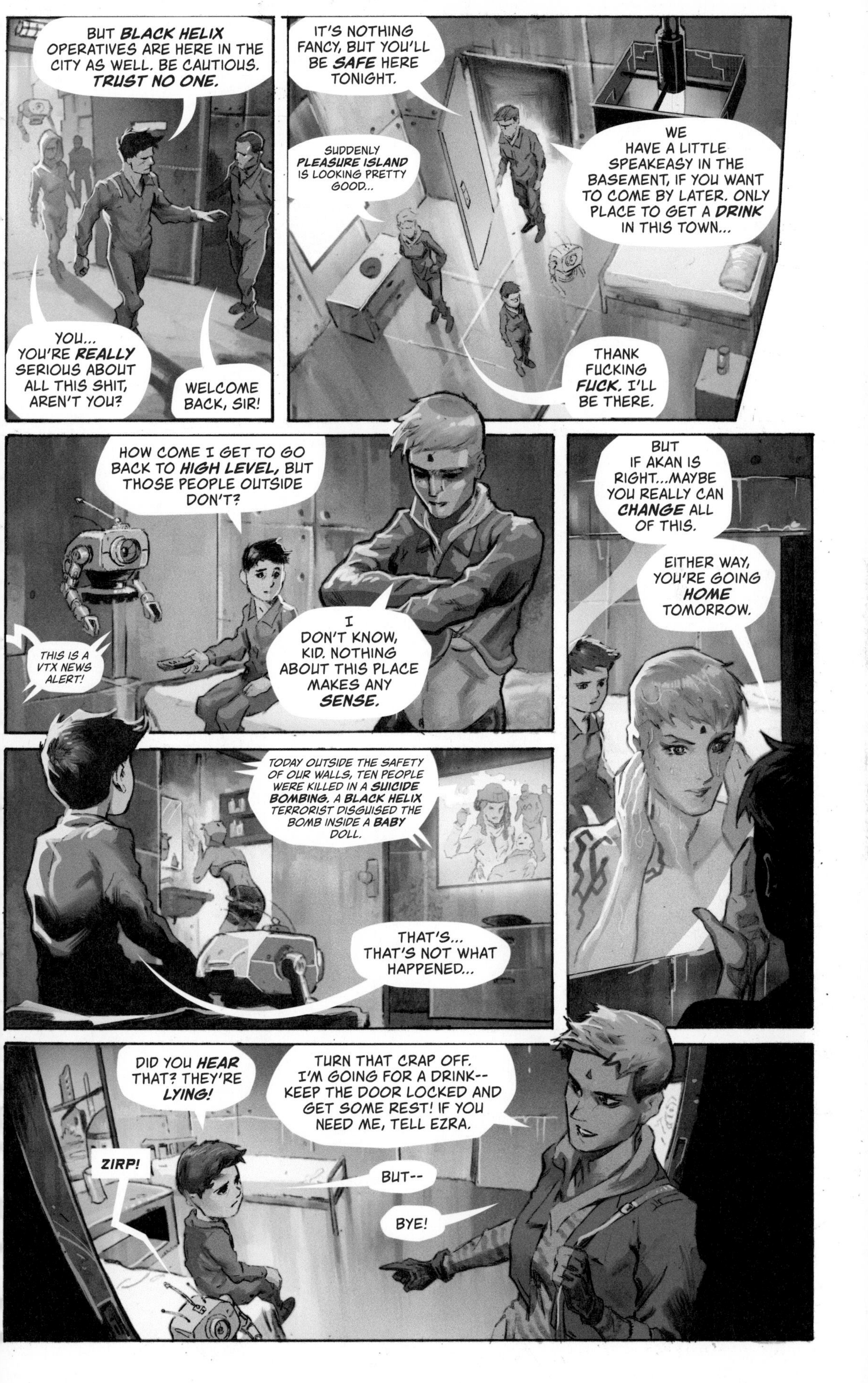

BUT BLACK HELIX OPERATIVES ARE HERE IN THE CITY AS WELL. BE CAUTIOUS. TRUST NO ONE.
YOU... YOU'RE REALLY SERIOUS ABOUT ALL THIS SHIT, AREN'T YOU?
WELCOME BACK, SIR!
IT'S NOTHING FANCY, BUT YOU'LL BE SAFE HERE TONIGHT.
SUDDENLY PLEASURE ISLAND IS LOOKING PRETTY GOOD...
WE HAVE A LITTLE SPEAKEASY IN THE BASEMENT, IF YOU WANT TO COME BY LATER. ONLY PLACE TO GET A DRINK IN THIS TOWN...
THANK FUCKING FUCK. I'LL BE THERE.
HOW COME I GET TO GO BACK TO HIGH LEVEL, BUT THOSE PEOPLE OUTSIDE DON'T?
I DON'T KNOW, KID. NOTHING ABOUT THIS PLACE MAKES ANY SENSE.
THIS IS A VTX NEWS ALERT!
BUT IF AKAN IS RIGHT...MAYBE YOU REALLY CAN CHANGE ALL OF THIS.
EITHER WAY, YOU'RE GOING HOME TOMORROW.
TODAY OUTSIDE THE SAFETY OF OUR WALLS, TEN PEOPLE WERE KILLED IN A SUICIDE BOMBING. A BLACK HELIX TERRORIST DISGUISED THE BOMB INSIDE A BABY DOLL.
THAT'S... THAT'S NOT WHAT HAPPENED...
DID YOU HEAR THAT? THEY'RE LYING!
TURN THAT CRAP OFF. I'M GOING FOR A DRINK-- KEEP THE DOOR LOCKED AND GET SOME REST! IF YOU NEED ME, TELL EZRA.
ZIRP!
BUT--
BYE!

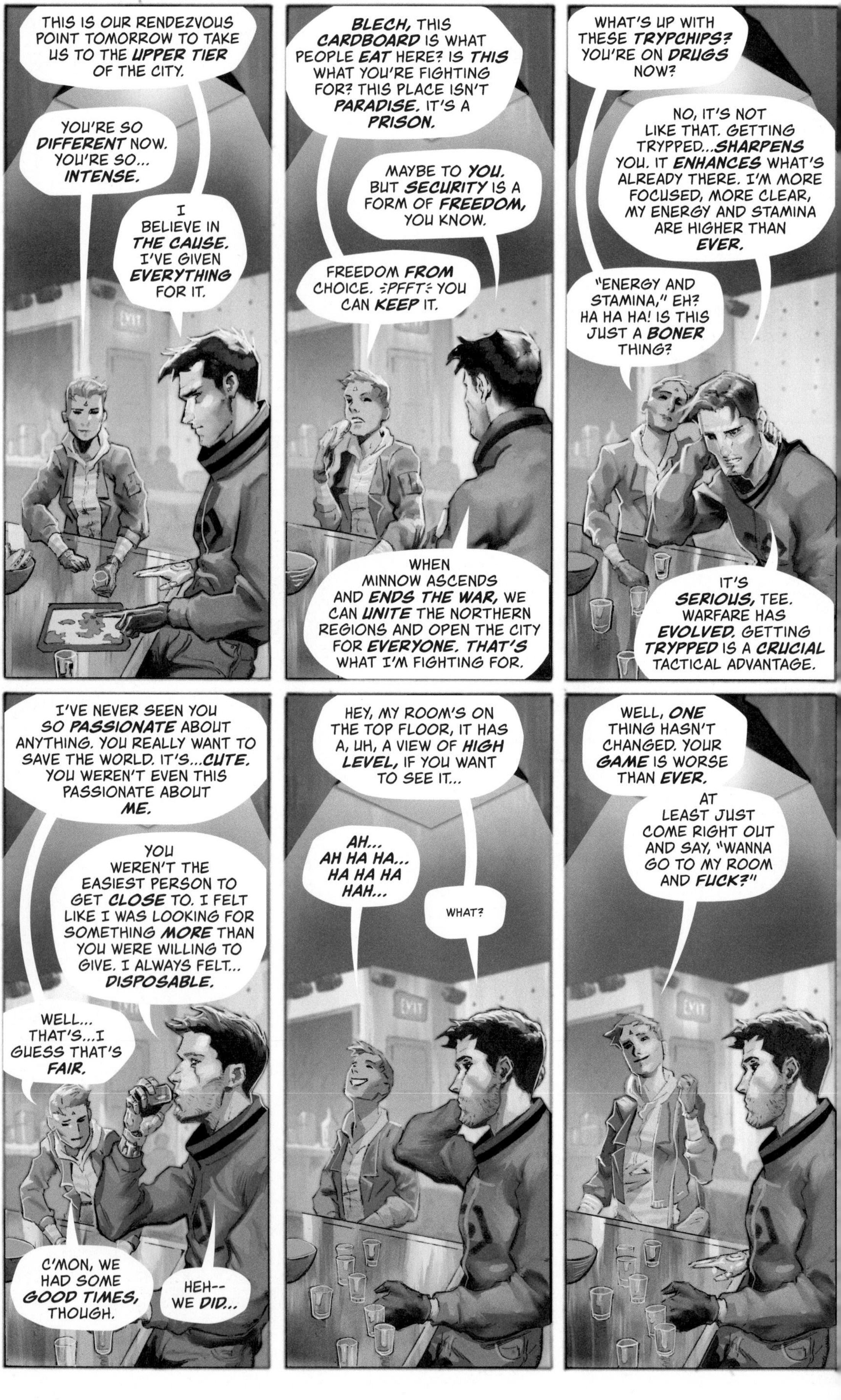
THIS IS OUR RENDEZVOUS POINT TOMORROW TO TAKE US TO THE UPPER TIER OF THE CITY.
YOU'RE SO DIFFERENT NOW. YOU'RE SO... INTENSE.
I BELIEVE IN THE CAUSE. I'VE GIVEN EVERYTHING FOR IT.
BLECH, THIS CARDBOARD IS WHAT PEOPLE EAT HERE? IS THIS WHAT YOU'RE FIGHTING FOR? THIS PLACE ISN'T PARADISE. IT'S A PRISON.
MAYBE TO YOU. BUT SECURITY IS A FORM OF FREEDOM, YOU KNOW.
FREEDOM FROM CHOICE. =PFFT= YOU CAN KEEP IT.
WHEN MINNOW ASCENDS AND ENDS THE WAR, WE CAN UNITE THE NORTHERN REGIONS AND OPEN THE CITY FOR EVERYONE. THAT'S WHAT I'M FIGHTING FOR.
WHAT'S UP WITH THESE TRYPCHIPS? YOU'RE ON DRUGS NOW?
NO, IT'S NOT LIKE THAT. GETTING TRYPPED...SHARPENS YOU. IT ENHANCES WHAT'S ALREADY THERE. I'M MORE FOCUSED, MORE CLEAR, MY ENERGY AND STAMINA ARE HIGHER THAN EVER.
"ENERGY AND STAMINA," EH? HA HA HA! IS THIS JUST A BONER THING?
IT'S SERIOUS, TEE. WARFARE HAS EVOLVED. GETTING TRYPPED IS A CRUCIAL TACTICAL ADVANTAGE.
EXIT
I'VE NEVER SEEN YOU SO PASSIONATE ABOUT ANYTHING. YOU REALLY WANT TO SAVE THE WORLD. IT'S...CUTE. YOU WEREN'T EVEN THIS PASSIONATE ABOUT ME.
YOU WEREN'T THE EASIEST PERSON TO GET CLOSE TO. I FELT LIKE I WAS LOOKING FOR SOMETHING MORE THAN YOU WERE WILLING TO GIVE. I ALWAYS FELT... DISPOSABLE.
WELL... THAT'S...I GUESS THAT'S FAIR.
C'MON, WE HAD SOME GOOD TIMES, THOUGH.
HEH-- WE DID...
HEY, MY ROOM'S ON THE TOP FLOOR, IT HAS A, UH, A VIEW OF HIGH LEVEL, IF YOU WANT TO SEE IT...
AH... AH HA HA... HA HA HA HAH...
WHAT?
WELL, ONE THING HASN'T CHANGED. YOUR GAME IS WORSE THAN EVER.
AT LEAST JUST COME RIGHT OUT AND SAY, "WANNA GO TO MY ROOM AND FUCK?"

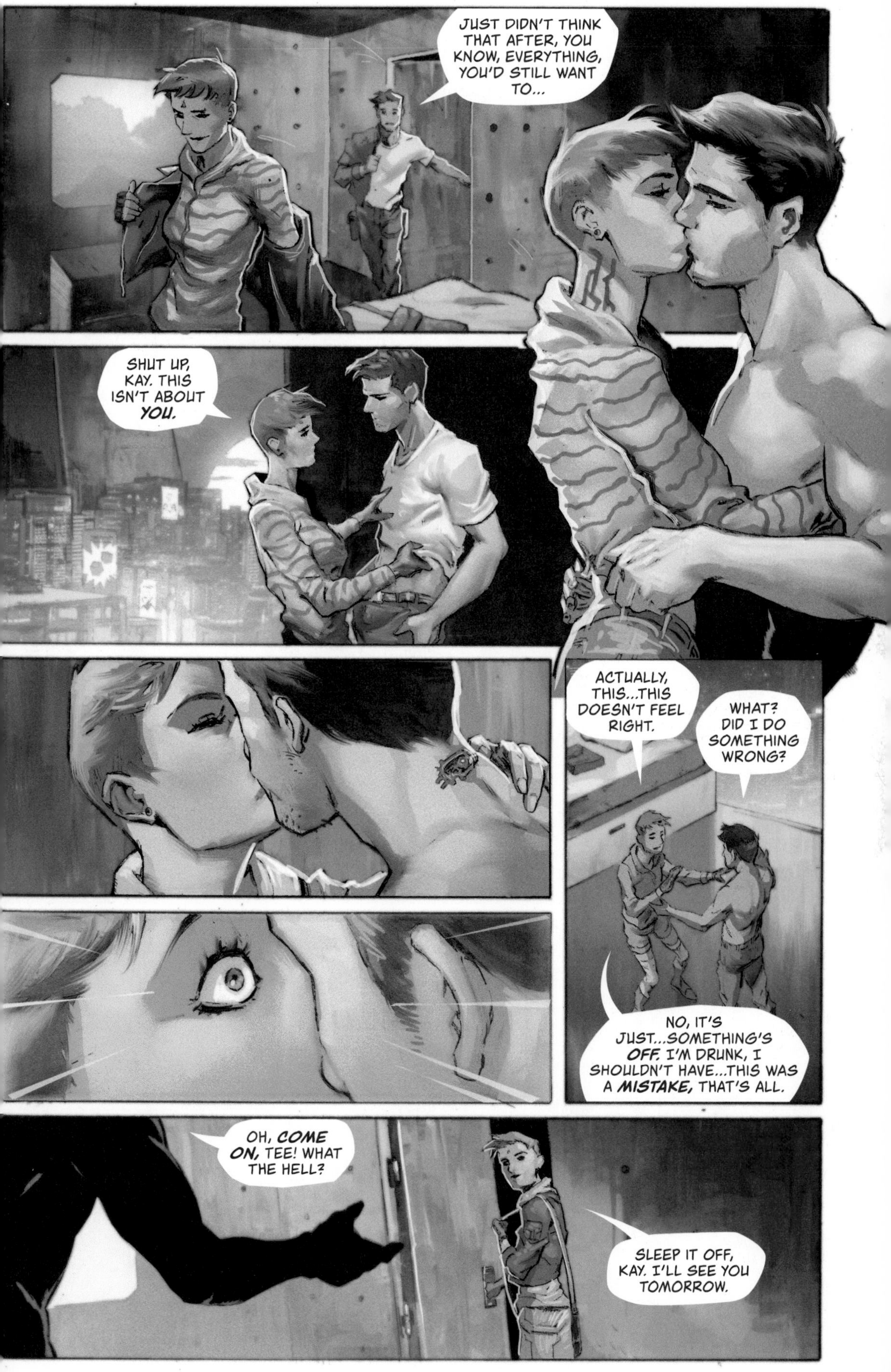
JUST DIDN'T THINK THAT AFTER, YOU KNOW, EVERYTHING, YOU'D STILL WANT TO...
SHUT UP, KAY. THIS ISN'T ABOUT *YOU.*
ACTUALLY, THIS...THIS DOESN'T FEEL RIGHT.
WHAT? DID I DO SOMETHING WRONG?
NO, IT'S JUST...SOMETHING'S *OFF.* I'M DRUNK, I SHOULDN'T HAVE...THIS WAS A *MISTAKE,* THAT'S ALL.
OH, *COME ON,* TEE! WHAT THE HELL?
SLEEP IT OFF, KAY. I'LL SEE YOU TOMORROW.

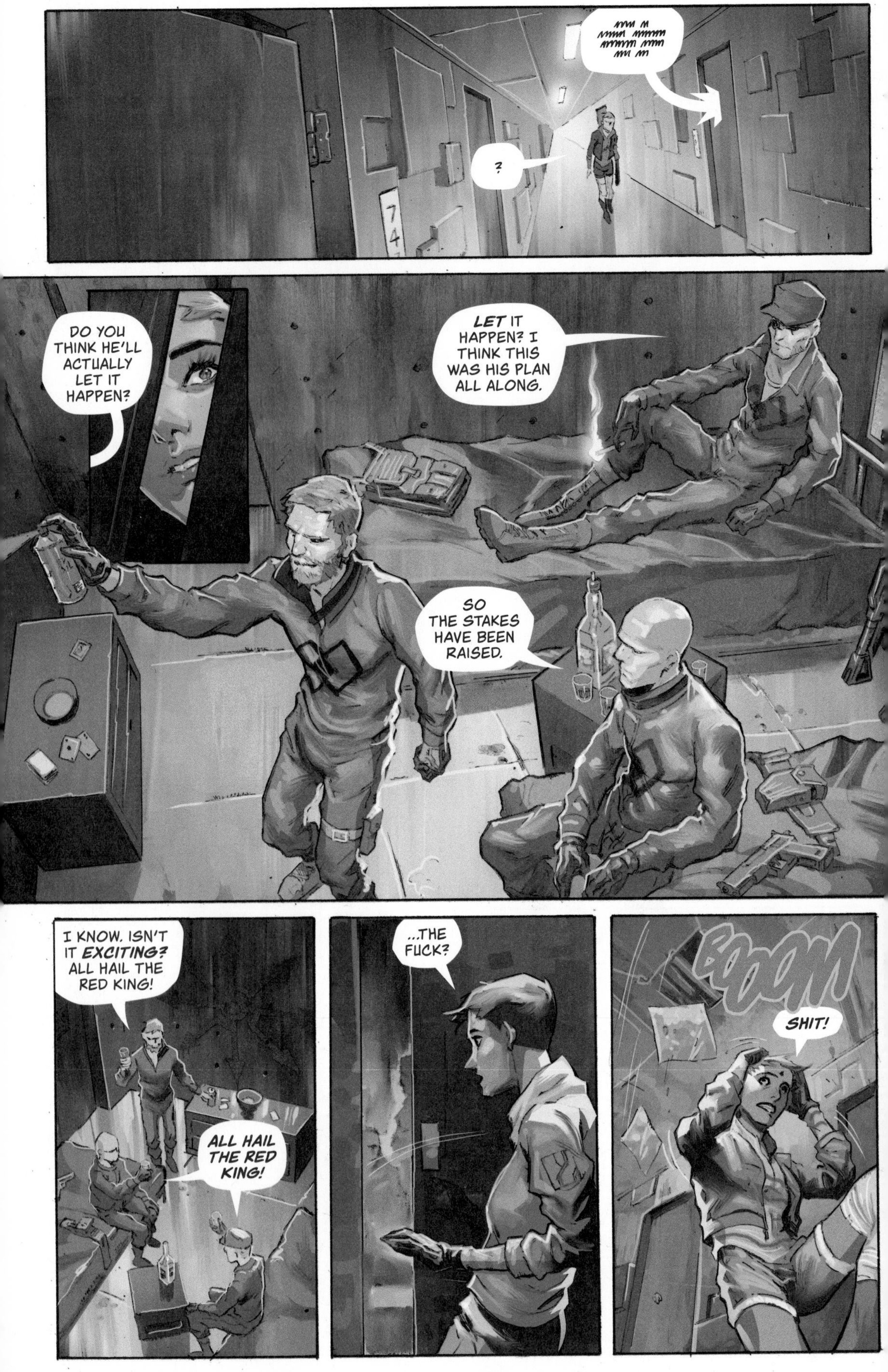
?
DO YOU THINK HE'LL ACTUALLY LET IT HAPPEN?
LET IT HAPPEN? I THINK THIS WAS HIS PLAN ALL ALONG.
SO THE STAKES HAVE BEEN RAISED.
I KNOW. ISN'T IT EXCITING? ALL HAIL THE RED KING!
ALL HAIL THE RED KING!
...THE FUCK?
BOOOM
SHIT!

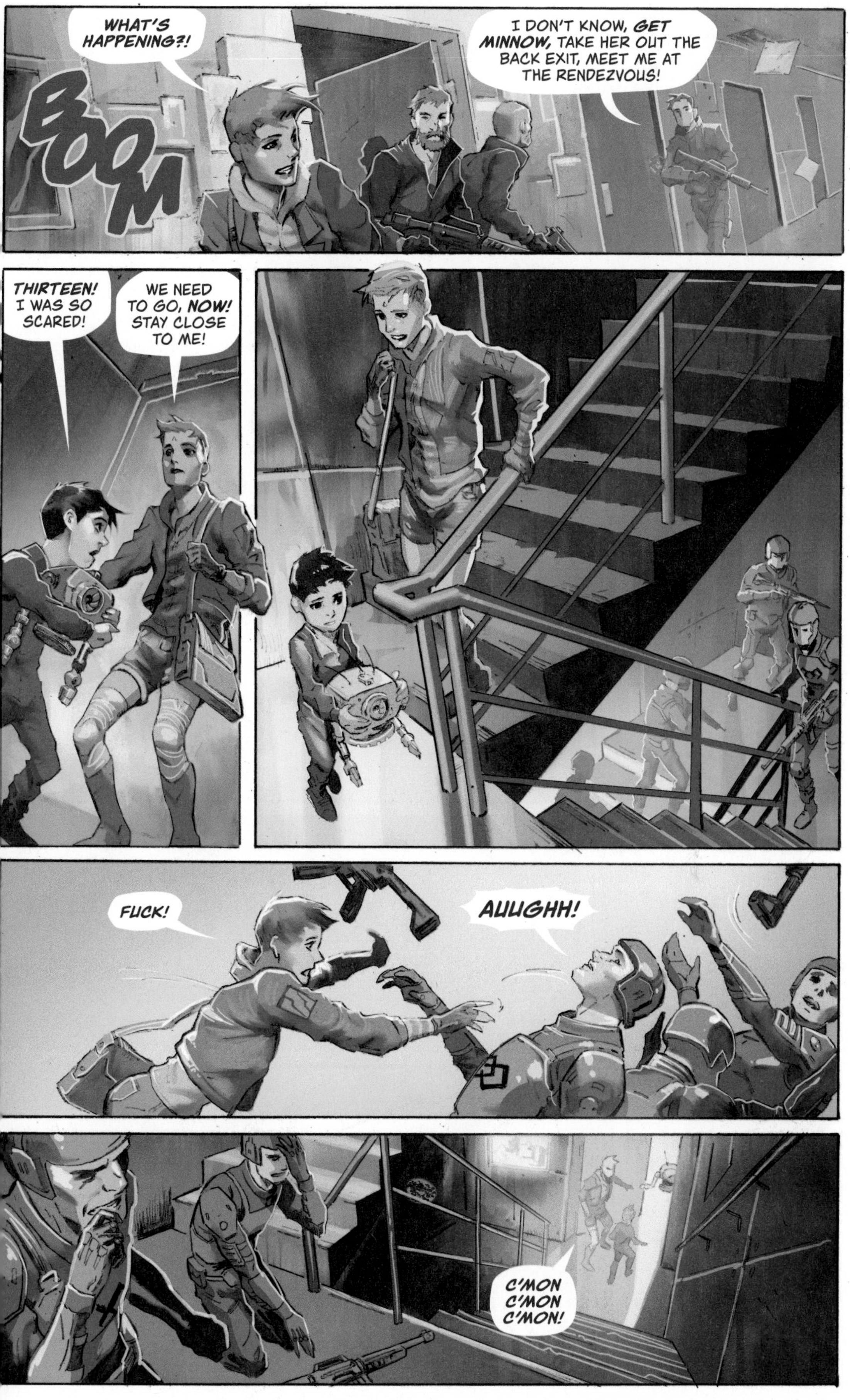
BOOM
WHAT'S HAPPENING?!
I DON'T KNOW, GET MINNOW, TAKE HER OUT THE BACK EXIT, MEET ME AT THE RENDEZVOUS!
THIRTEEN! I WAS SO SCARED!
WE NEED TO GO, NOW! STAY CLOSE TO ME!
FUCK!
AUUGHH!
C'MON C'MON C'MON!

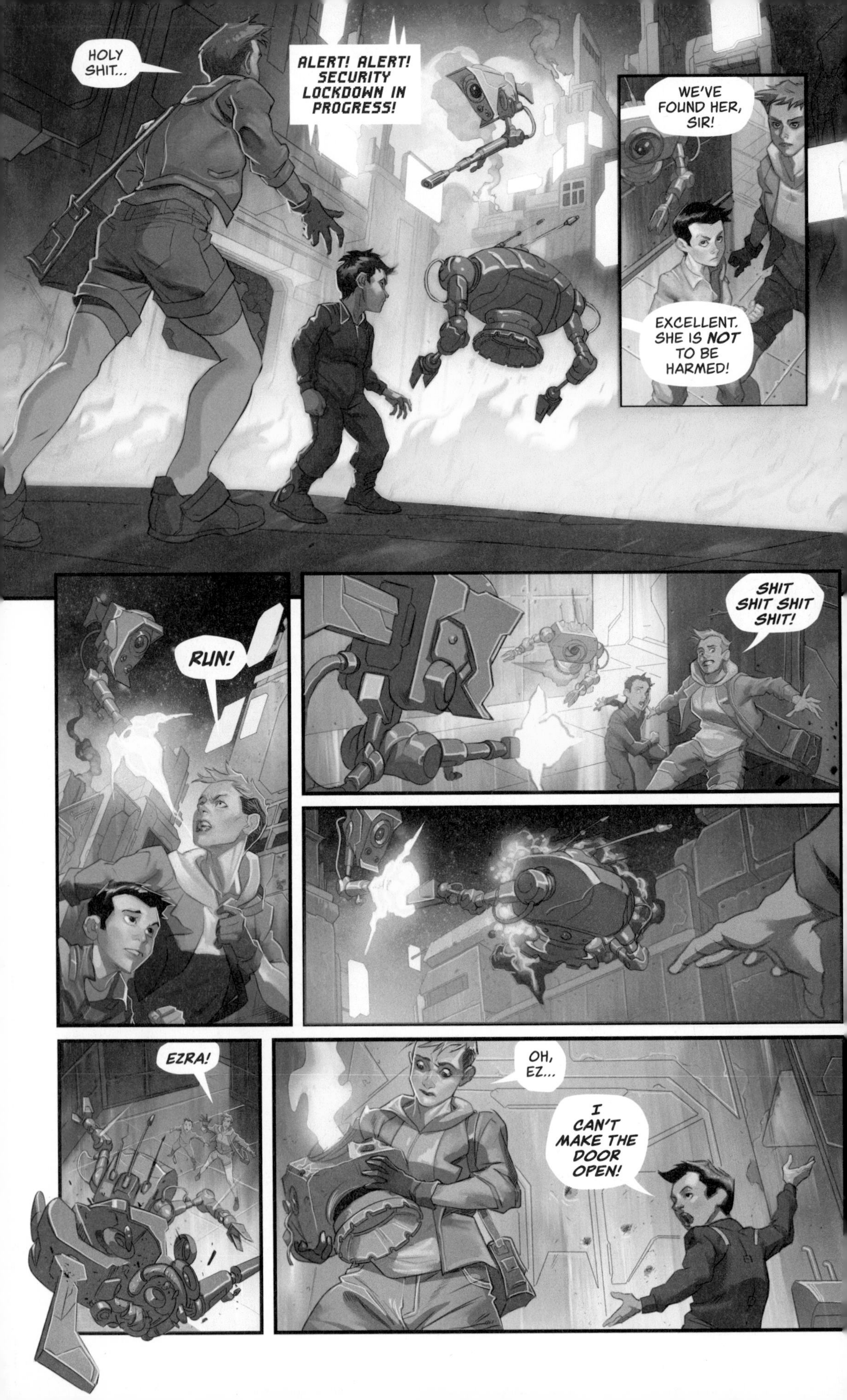
HOLY SHIT...
ALERT! ALERT! SECURITY LOCKDOWN IN PROGRESS!
WE'VE FOUND HER, SIR!
EXCELLENT. SHE IS NOT TO BE HARMED!
RUN!
SHIT SHIT SHIT SHIT!
EZRA!
OH, EZ...
I CAN'T MAKE THE DOOR OPEN!

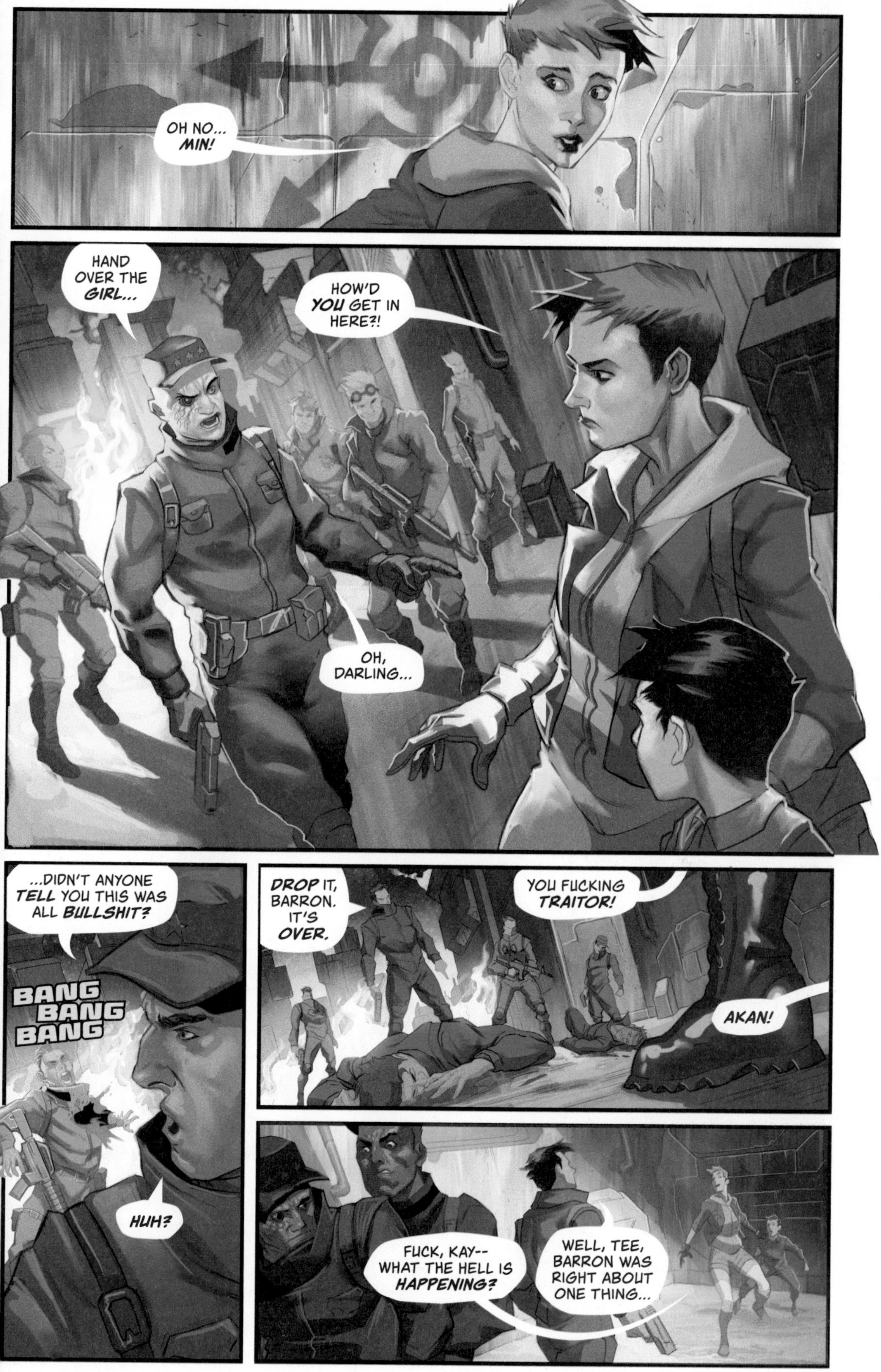
OH NO... MIN!
HAND OVER THE GIRL...
HOW'D YOU GET IN HERE?!
OH, DARLING...
...DIDN'T ANYONE TELL YOU THIS WAS ALL BULLSHIT?
BANG BANG BANG
HUH?
DROP IT, BARRON. IT'S OVER.
YOU FUCKING TRAITOR!
AKAN!
FUCK, KAY-- WHAT THE HELL IS HAPPENING?
WELL, TEE, BARRON WAS RIGHT ABOUT ONE THING...

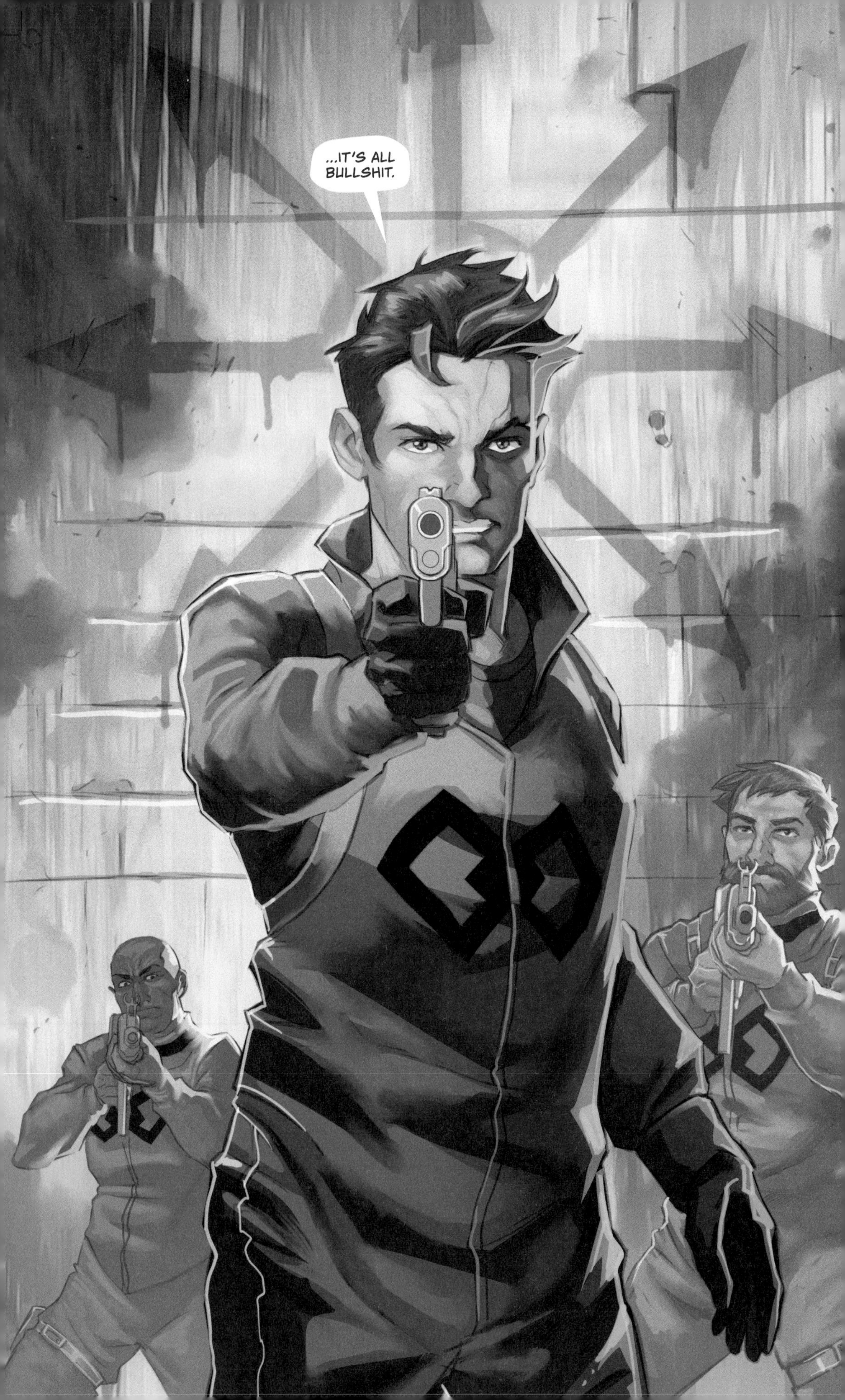
...IT'S ALL BULLSHIT.

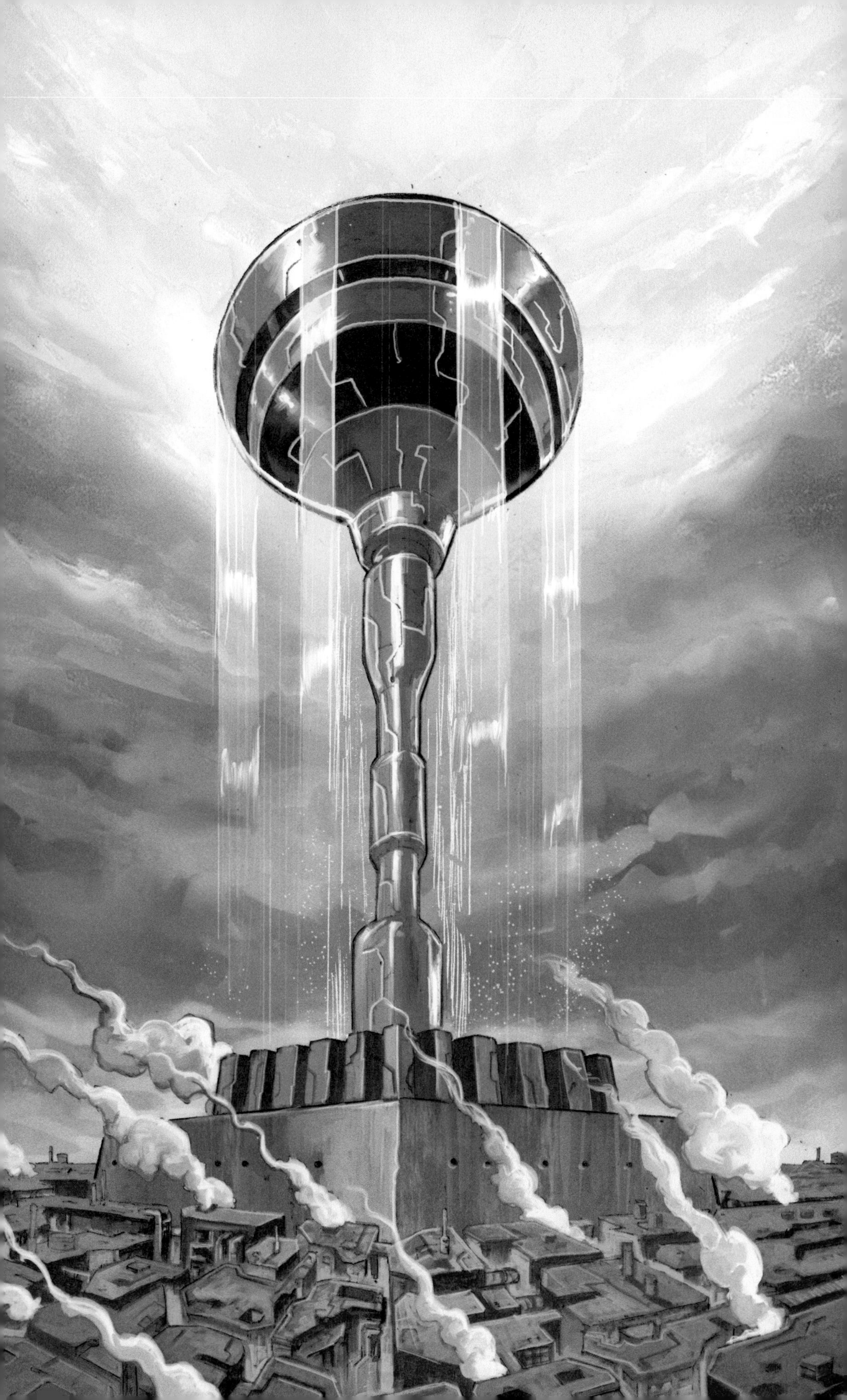

CHAPTER SIX
ASCENSION

STORY
ROB SHERIDAN

ART
BARNABY BAGENDA AND OMAR FRANCIA

COLORS
ROMULO FAJARDO JR.

LETTERING
NATE PIEKOS OF BLAMBOT®

COVER
BARNABY BAGENDA AND ROMULO FAJARDO JR.

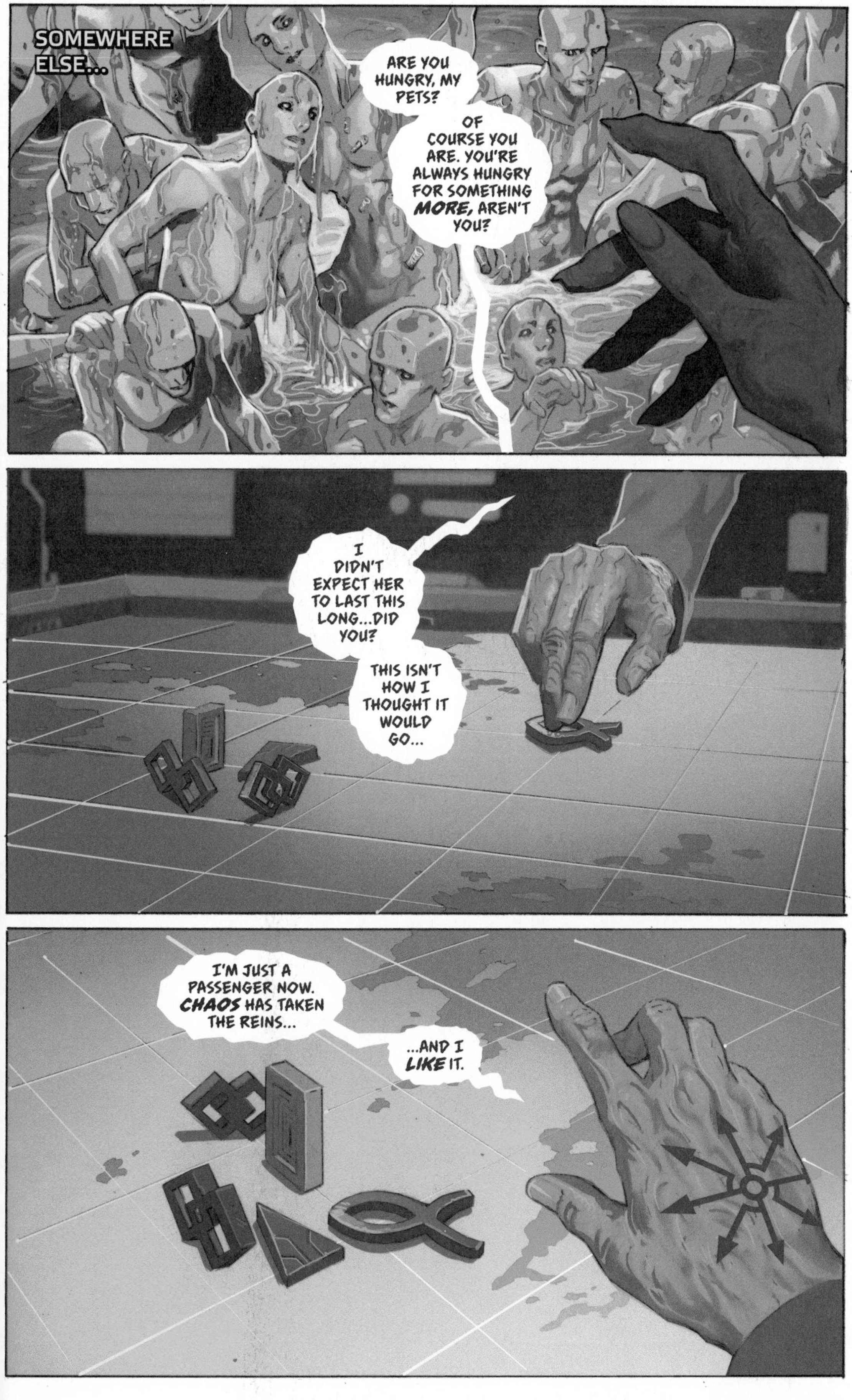
SOMEWHERE ELSE...
ARE YOU HUNGRY, MY PETS?
OF COURSE YOU ARE. YOU'RE ALWAYS HUNGRY FOR SOMETHING MORE, AREN'T YOU?
I DIDN'T EXPECT HER TO LAST THIS LONG...DID YOU?
THIS ISN'T HOW I THOUGHT IT WOULD GO...
I'M JUST A PASSENGER NOW. CHAOS HAS TAKEN THE REINS...
...AND I LIKE IT.

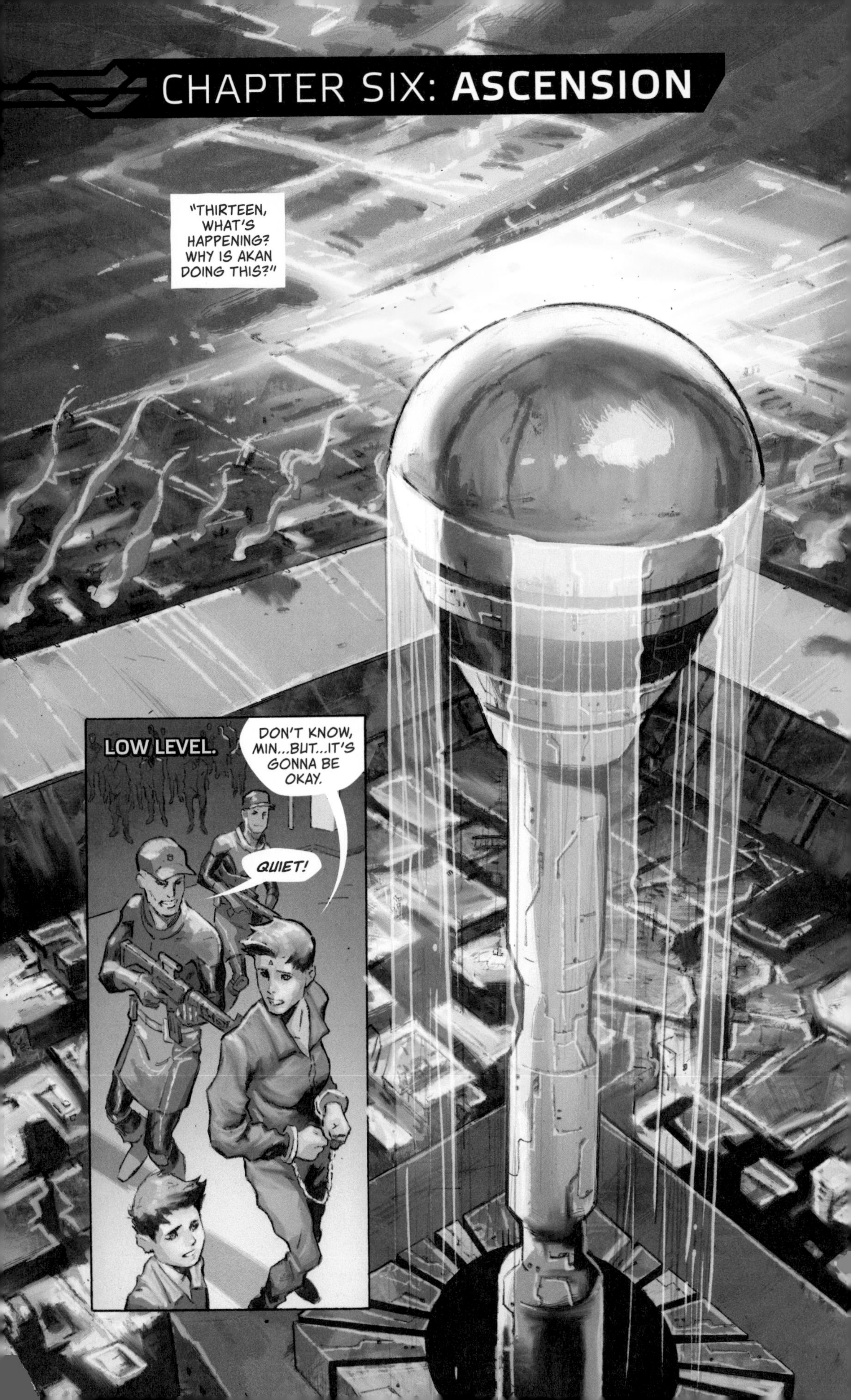

CHAPTER SIX: ASCENSION
"THIRTEEN, WHAT'S HAPPENING? WHY IS AKAN DOING THIS?"
LOW LEVEL.
DON'T KNOW, MIN...BUT...IT'S GONNA BE OKAY.
QUIET!

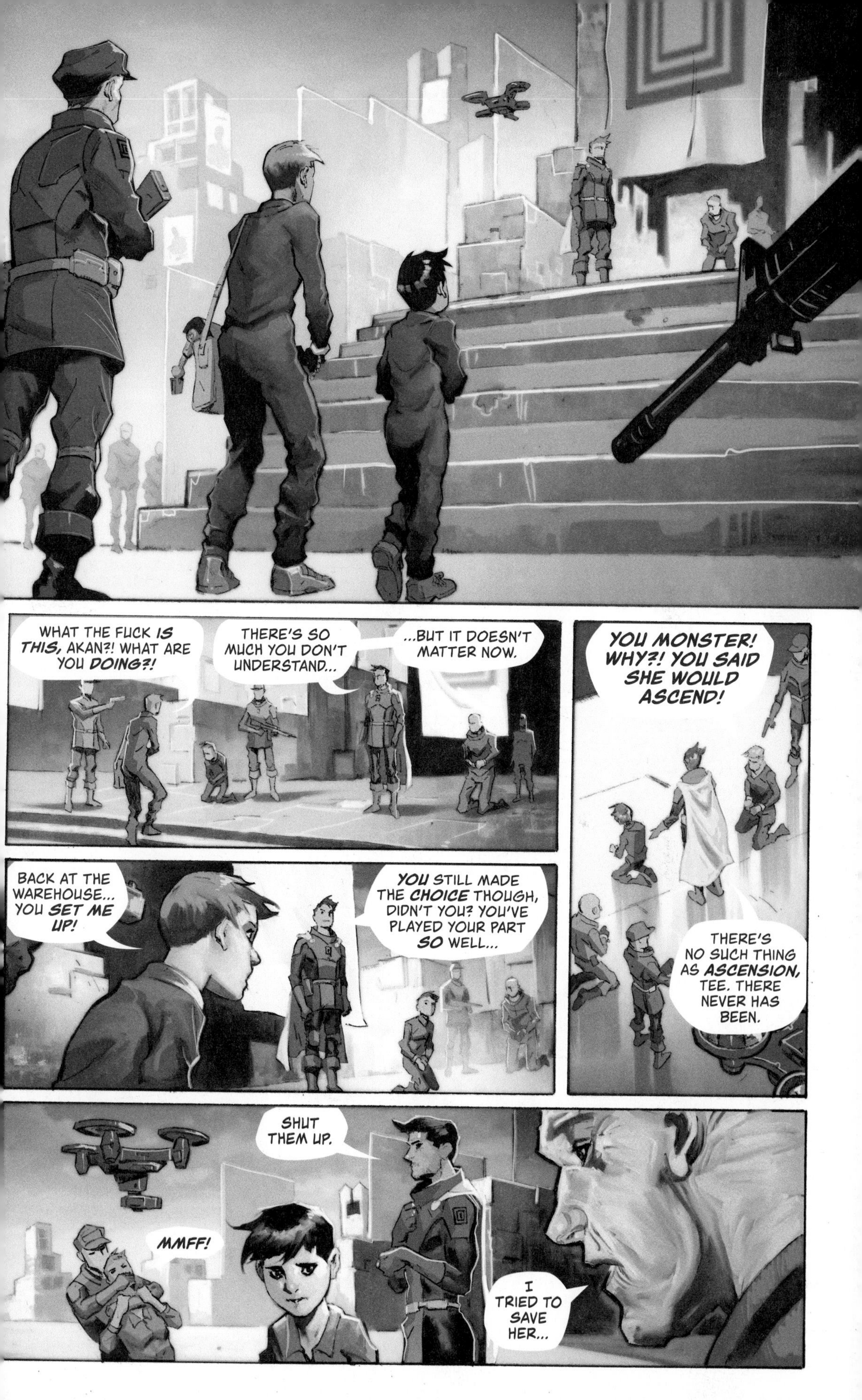
WHAT THE FUCK IS THIS, AKAN?! WHAT ARE YOU DOING?!
THERE'S SO MUCH YOU DON'T UNDERSTAND...
...BUT IT DOESN'T MATTER NOW.
YOU MONSTER! WHY?! YOU SAID SHE WOULD ASCEND!
BACK AT THE WAREHOUSE... YOU SET ME UP!
YOU STILL MADE THE CHOICE THOUGH, DIDN'T YOU? YOU'VE PLAYED YOUR PART SO WELL...
THERE'S NO SUCH THING AS ASCENSION, TEE. THERE NEVER HAS BEEN.
SHUT THEM UP.
MMFF!
I TRIED TO SAVE HER...

SIR, WE'RE TAPPED INTO VTX AND EVERY SIGNAL IN RANGE. READY ON YOUR COMMAND, SIR.

BEGIN THE TRANSMISSION.

GREETINGS FROM THE *NEW REPUBLIC ARMY.*

FOR YEARS, *WE* HAVE PROTECTED THE SACRED *ASCENSION GATES.*

AND FOR YEARS, THE TERRORISTS *BLACK HELIX* HAVE RAVAGED THE NORTH, KILLING *THOUSANDS.*

WHAT PROGRAM IS THIS?

I DON'T KNOW...

THIS MORNING, BLACK HELIX *ATTACKED* OUR WALLS. THEY WANT TO TAKE AWAY YOUR *FREEDOM* TO *ASCEND.*

DO NOT BE FOOLED BY APPEARANCES. BEFORE ME IS THE *WEAPON* BLACK HELIX HAS USED FOR THEIR REIGN OF TERROR.

THAT'S THE *GIRL*--THE ONE WHO STOPPED THE GUNS!

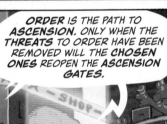

ORDER IS THE PATH TO *ASCENSION.* ONLY WHEN THE *THREATS* TO ORDER HAVE BEEN REMOVED WILL THE *CHOSEN ONES* REOPEN THE *ASCENSION GATES.*

OH NO...

LEASURE ISL

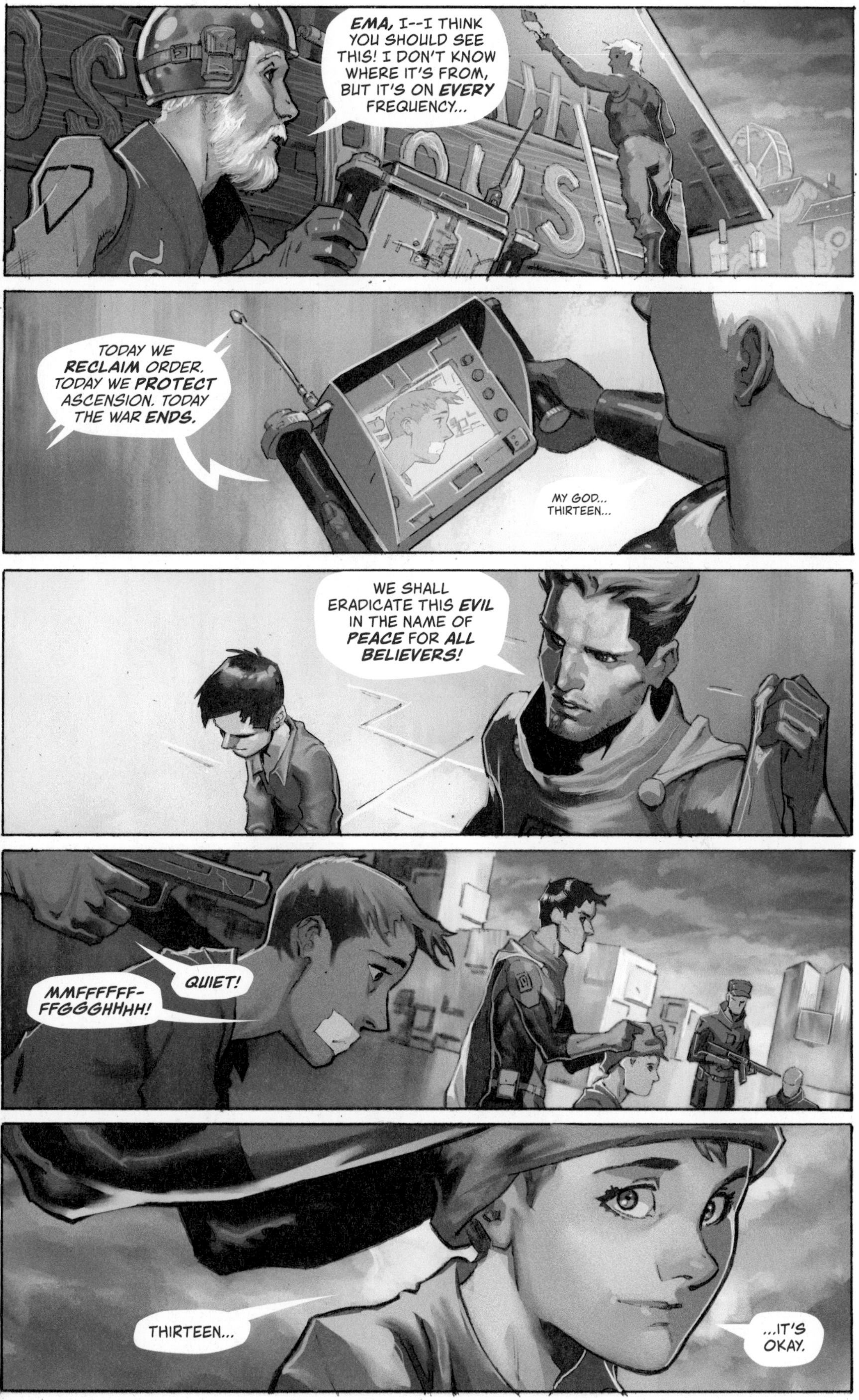
EMA, I--I THINK YOU SHOULD SEE THIS! I DON'T KNOW WHERE IT'S FROM, BUT IT'S ON EVERY FREQUENCY...
TODAY WE RECLAIM ORDER. TODAY WE PROTECT ASCENSION. TODAY THE WAR ENDS.
MY GOD... THIRTEEN...
WE SHALL ERADICATE THIS EVIL IN THE NAME OF PEACE FOR ALL BELIEVERS!
QUIET!
MMFFFFFF-FFGGGHHHH!
THIRTEEN...
...IT'S OKAY.

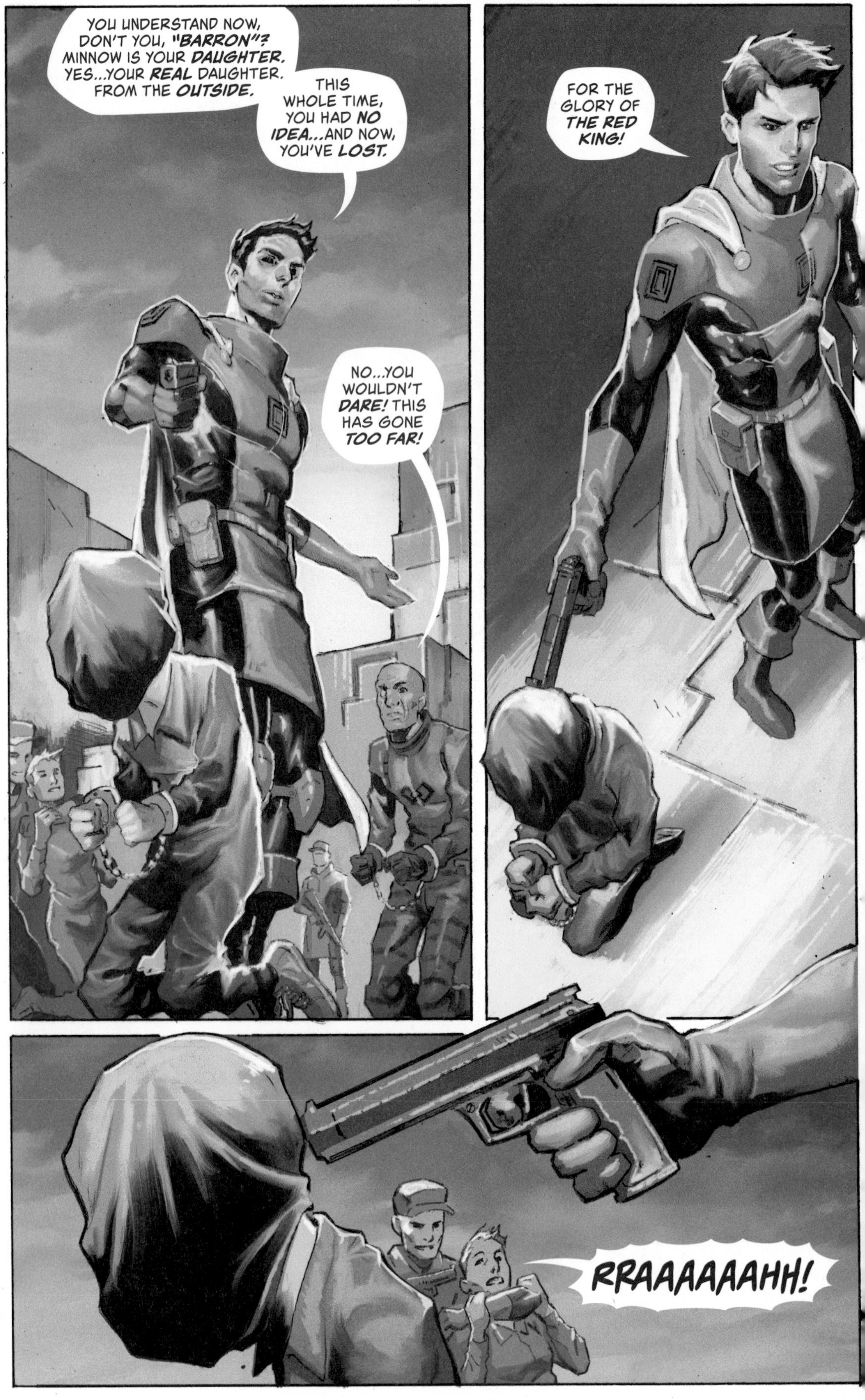
YOU UNDERSTAND NOW, DON'T YOU, "BARRON"? MINNOW IS YOUR DAUGHTER. YES...YOUR REAL DAUGHTER. FROM THE OUTSIDE.
THIS WHOLE TIME, YOU HAD NO IDEA...AND NOW, YOU'VE LOST.
NO...YOU WOULDN'T DARE! THIS HAS GONE TOO FAR!
FOR THE GLORY OF THE RED KING!
RRAAAAAAHH!

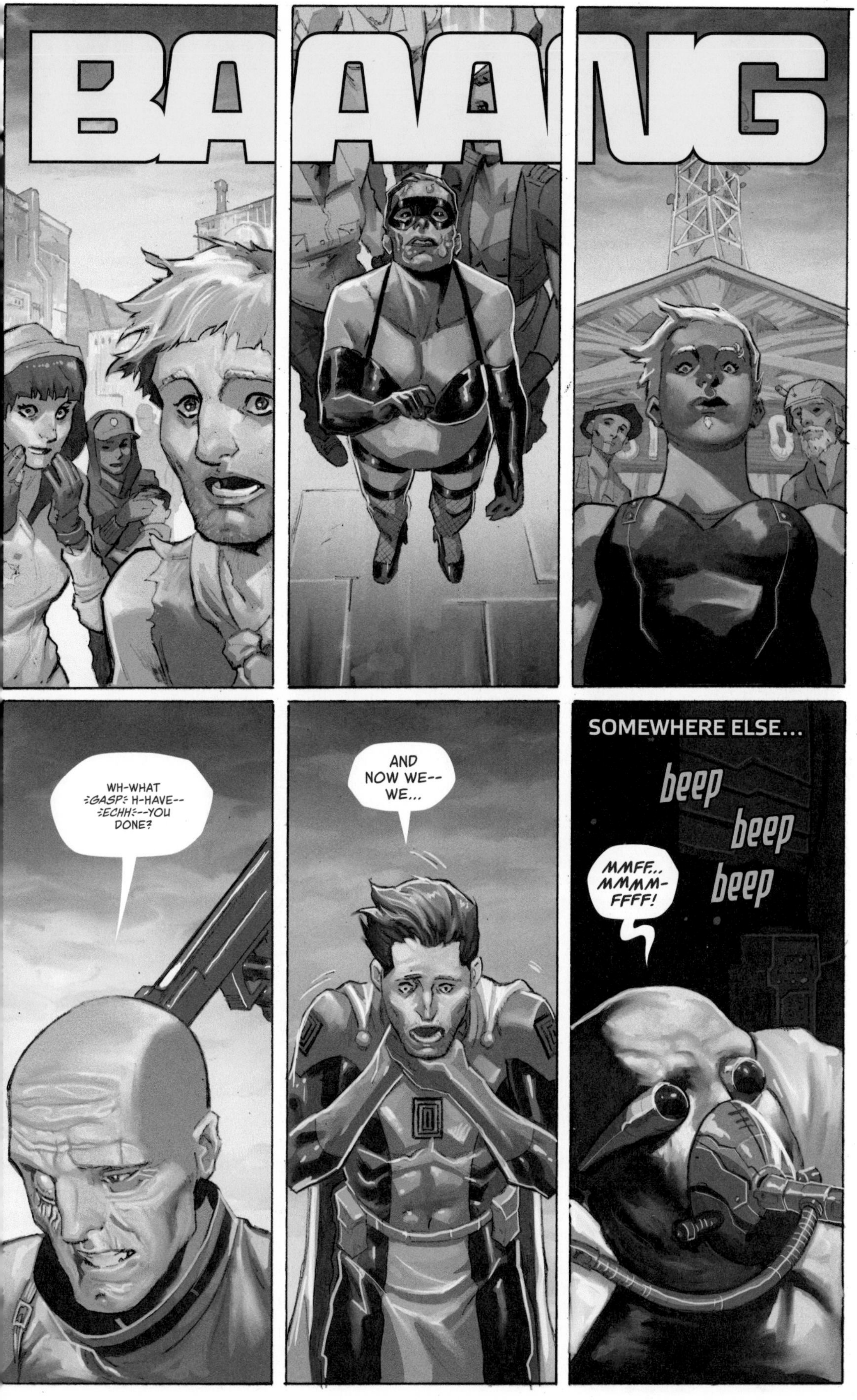
BAAANG
WH-WHAT ⸗GASP⸗ H-HAVE-- ⸗ECHH⸗--YOU DONE?
AND NOW WE-- WE...
SOMEWHERE ELSE...
beep
beep
beep
MMFF... MMMM-FFFF!

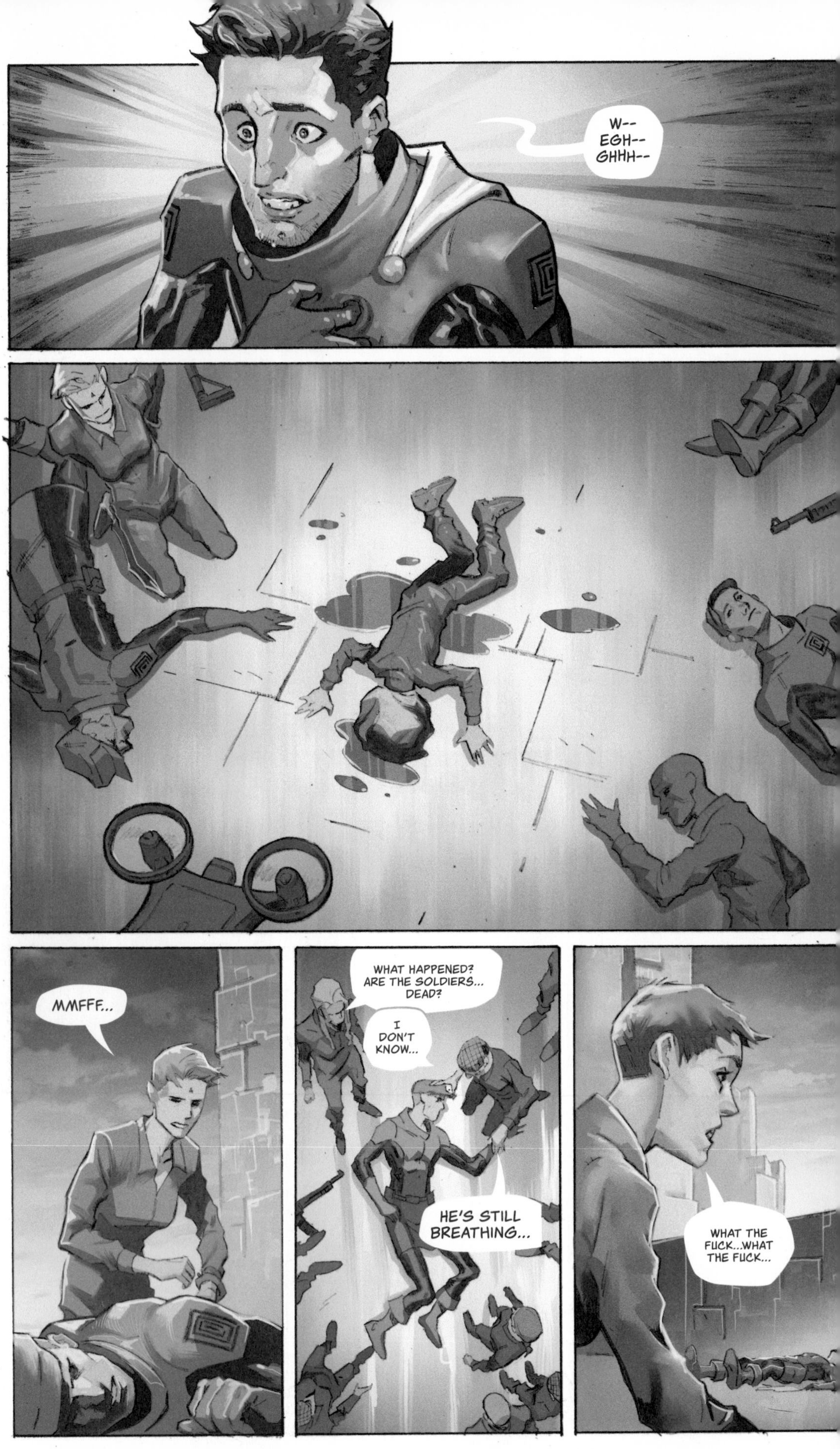
W-- EGH-- GHHH--
MMFFF...
WHAT HAPPENED? ARE THE SOLDIERS... DEAD?
I DON'T KNOW...
HE'S STILL BREATHING...
WHAT THE FUCK...WHAT THE FUCK...

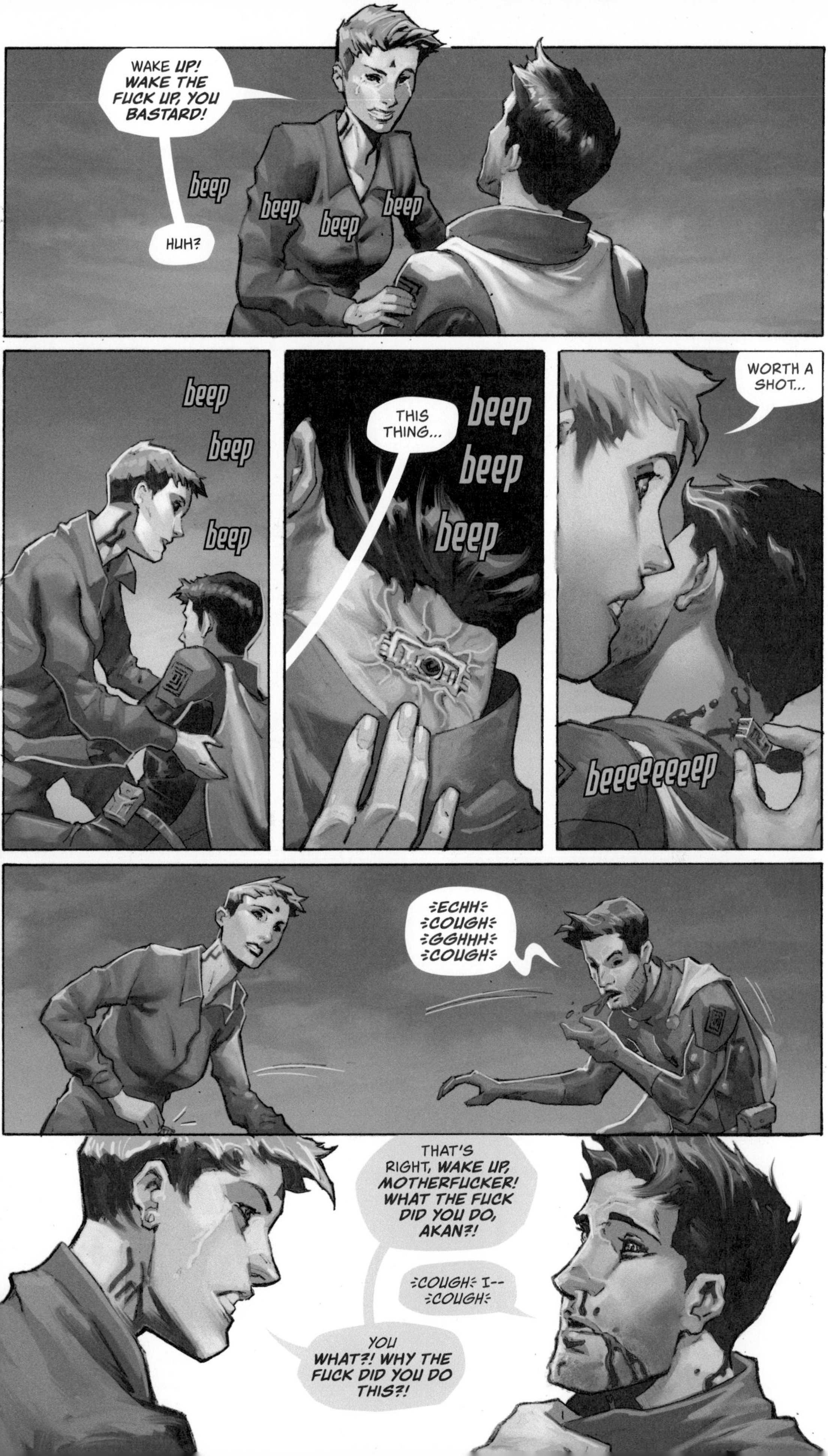
WAKE UP! WAKE THE FUCK UP, YOU BASTARD!
beep
beep
beep
beep
HUH?
beep
beep
beep
THIS THING...
beep
beep
beep
WORTH A SHOT...
beeeeeeeep
ECHH COUGH GGHHH COUGH
THAT'S RIGHT, WAKE UP, MOTHERFUCKER! WHAT THE FUCK DID YOU DO, AKAN?!
COUGH I-- COUGH
YOU WHAT?! WHY THE FUCK DID YOU DO THIS?!

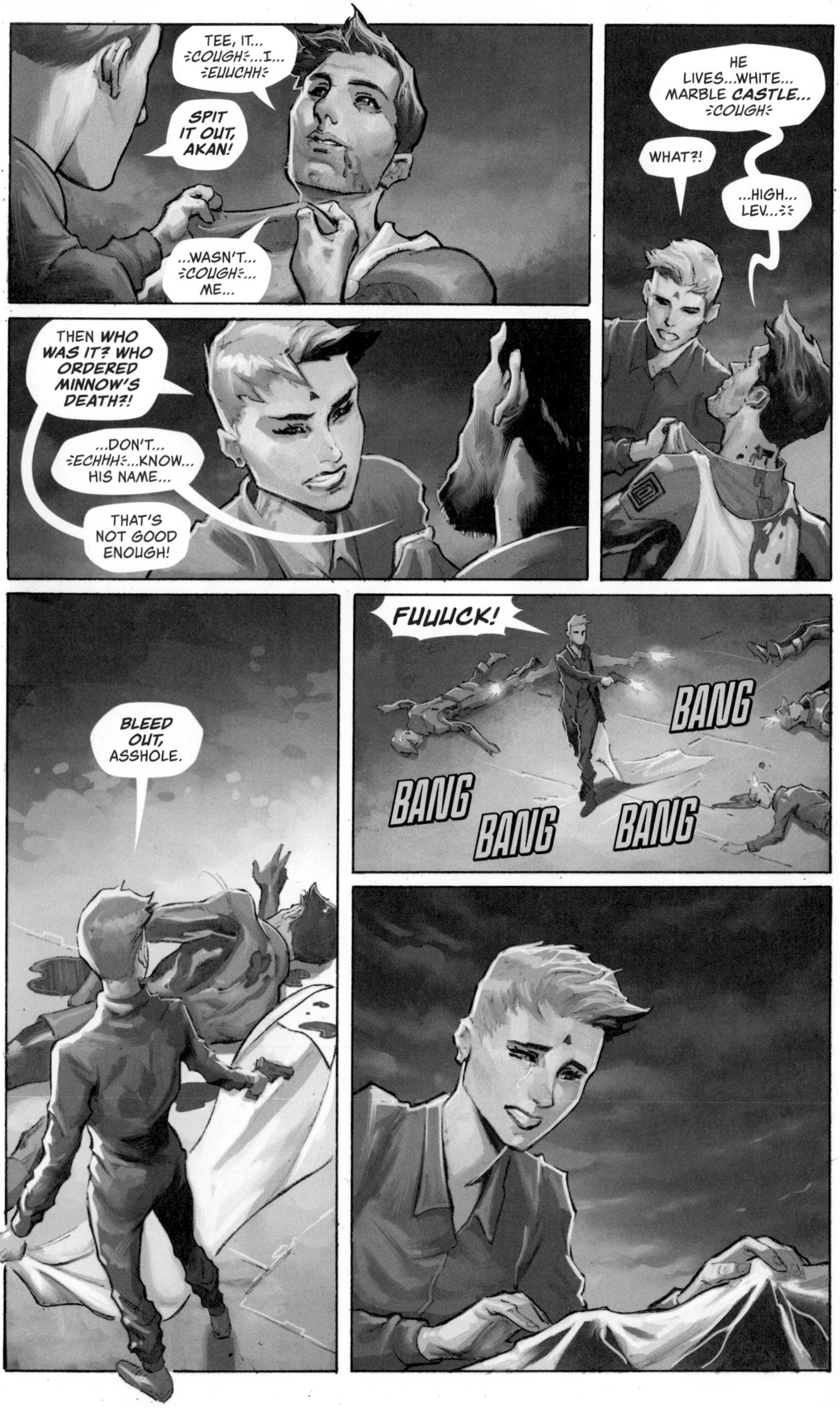
TEE, IT... =COUGH=...I... =EUUCHH=
SPIT IT OUT, AKAN!
...WASN'T... =COUGH=... ME...
HE LIVES...WHITE... MARBLE CASTLE... =COUGH=
WHAT?!
...HIGH... LEV...=
THEN WHO WAS IT? WHO ORDERED MINNOW'S DEATH?!
...DON'T... =ECHHH=...KNOW... HIS NAME...
THAT'S NOT GOOD ENOUGH!
BLEED OUT, ASSHOLE.
FUUUCK!
BANG
BANG
BANG
BANG

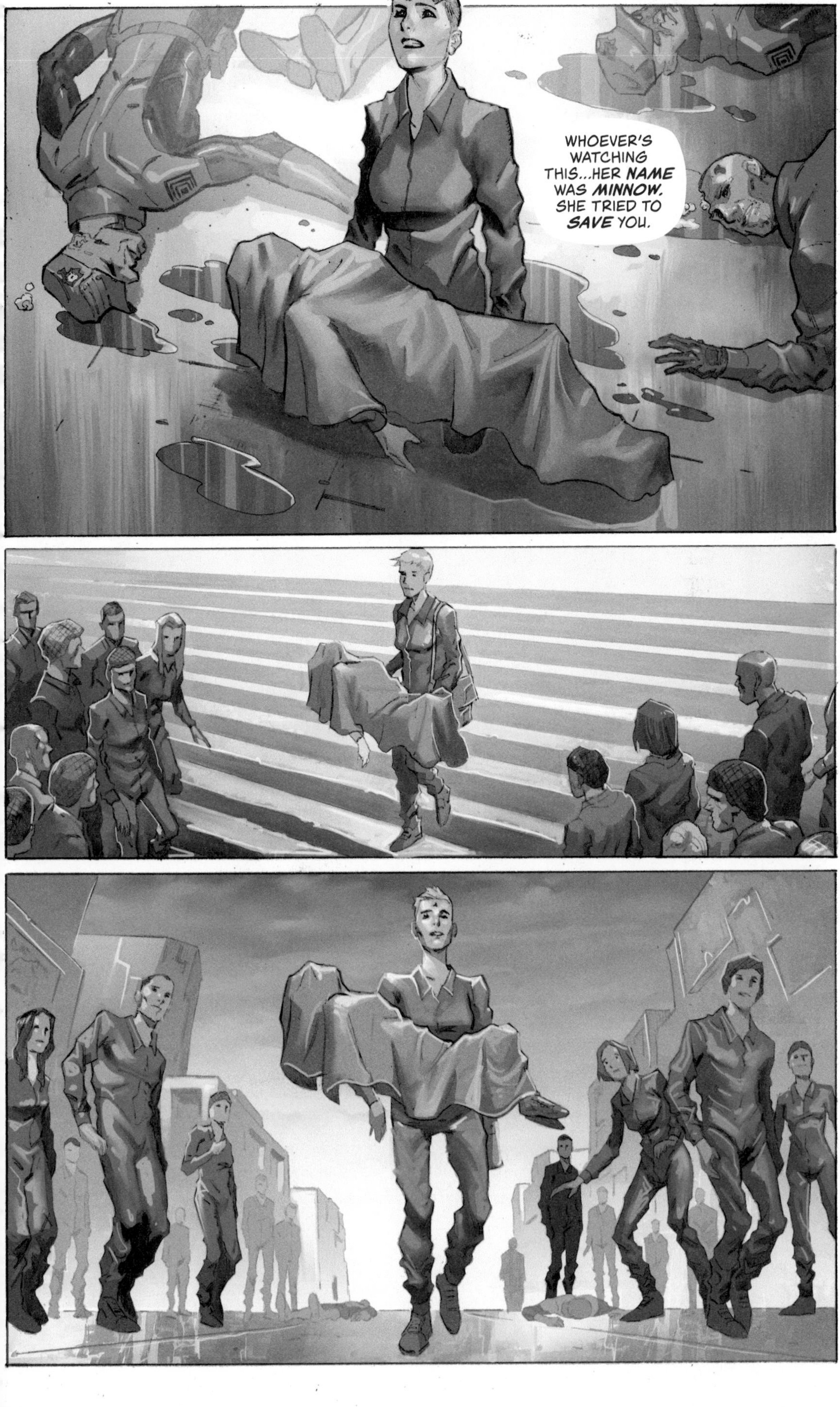
WHOEVER'S WATCHING THIS...HER **NAME** WAS **MINNOW.** SHE TRIED TO **SAVE** YOU.

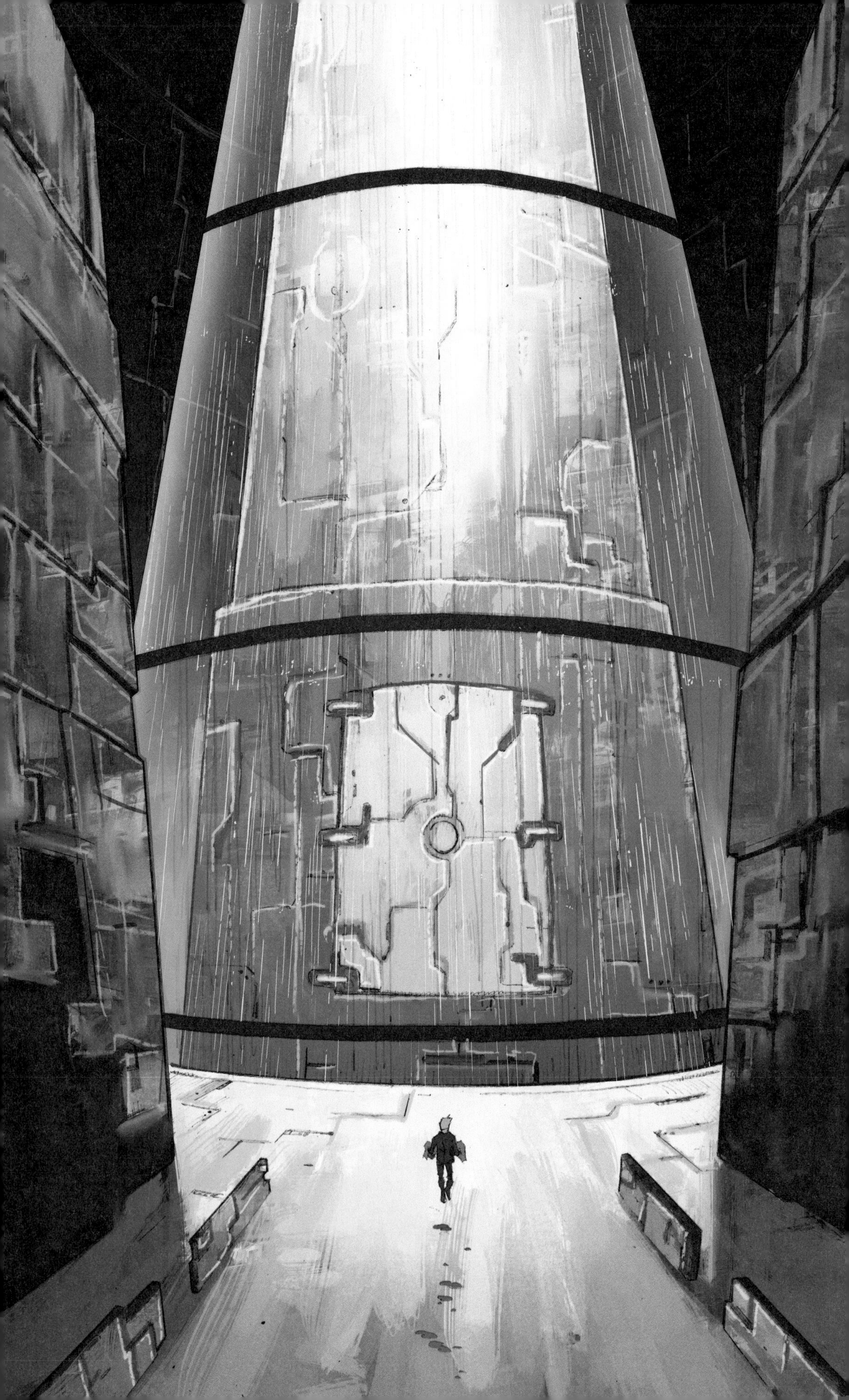

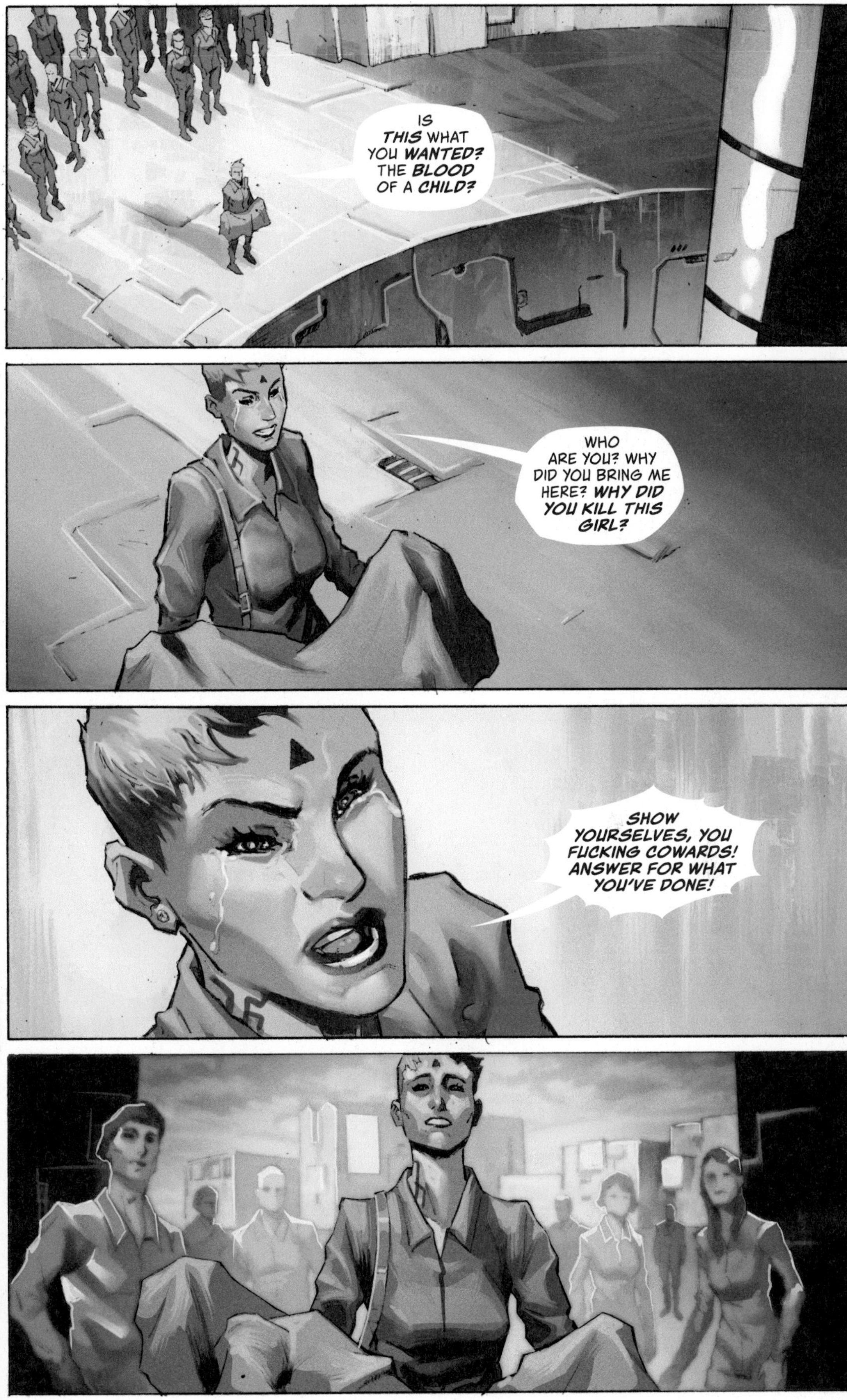
IS THIS WHAT YOU WANTED? THE BLOOD OF A CHILD?
WHO ARE YOU? WHY DID YOU BRING ME HERE? WHY DID YOU KILL THIS GIRL?
SHOW YOURSELVES, YOU FUCKING COWARDS! ANSWER FOR WHAT YOU'VE DONE!

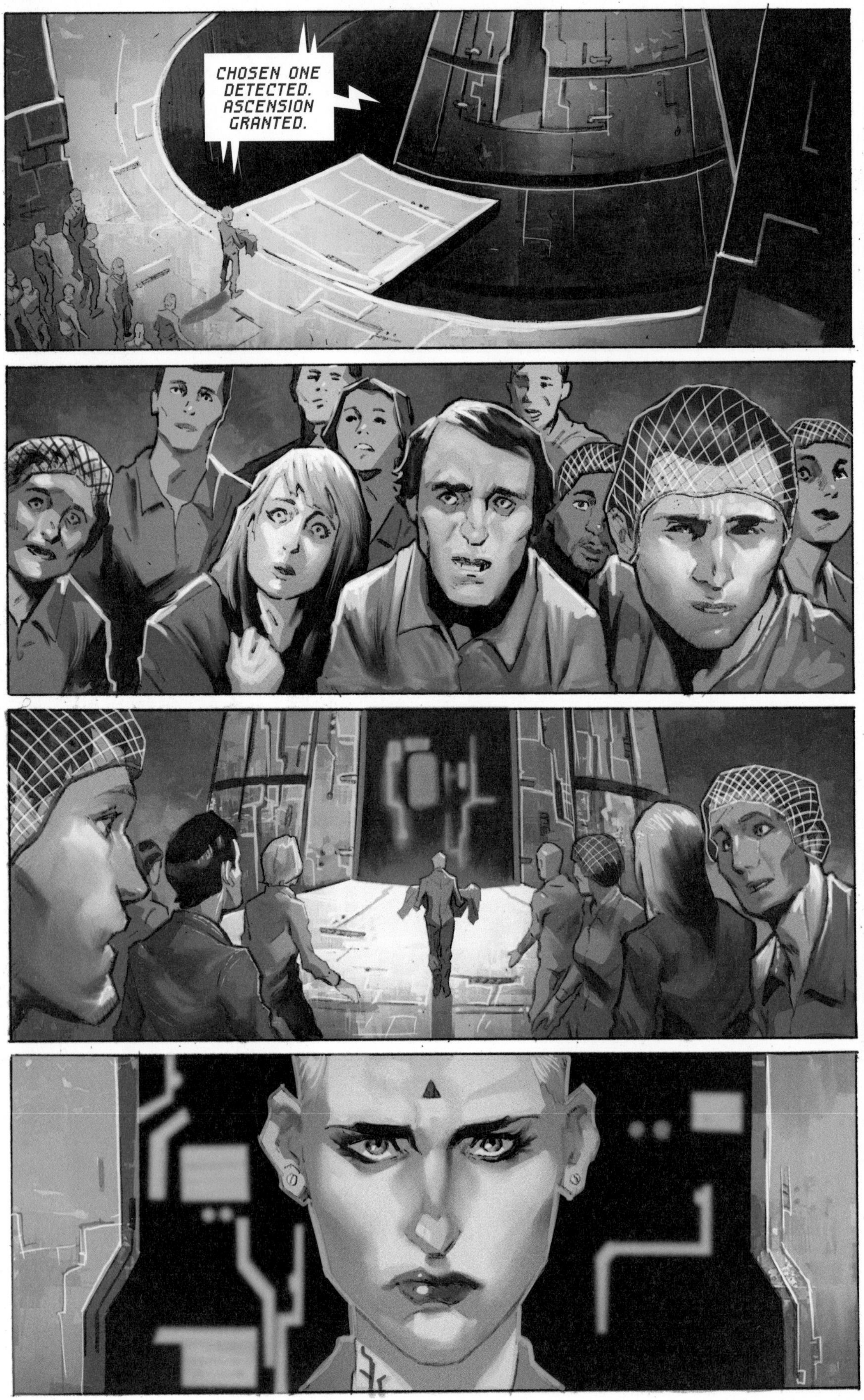
CHOSEN ONE DETECTED. ASCENSION GRANTED.

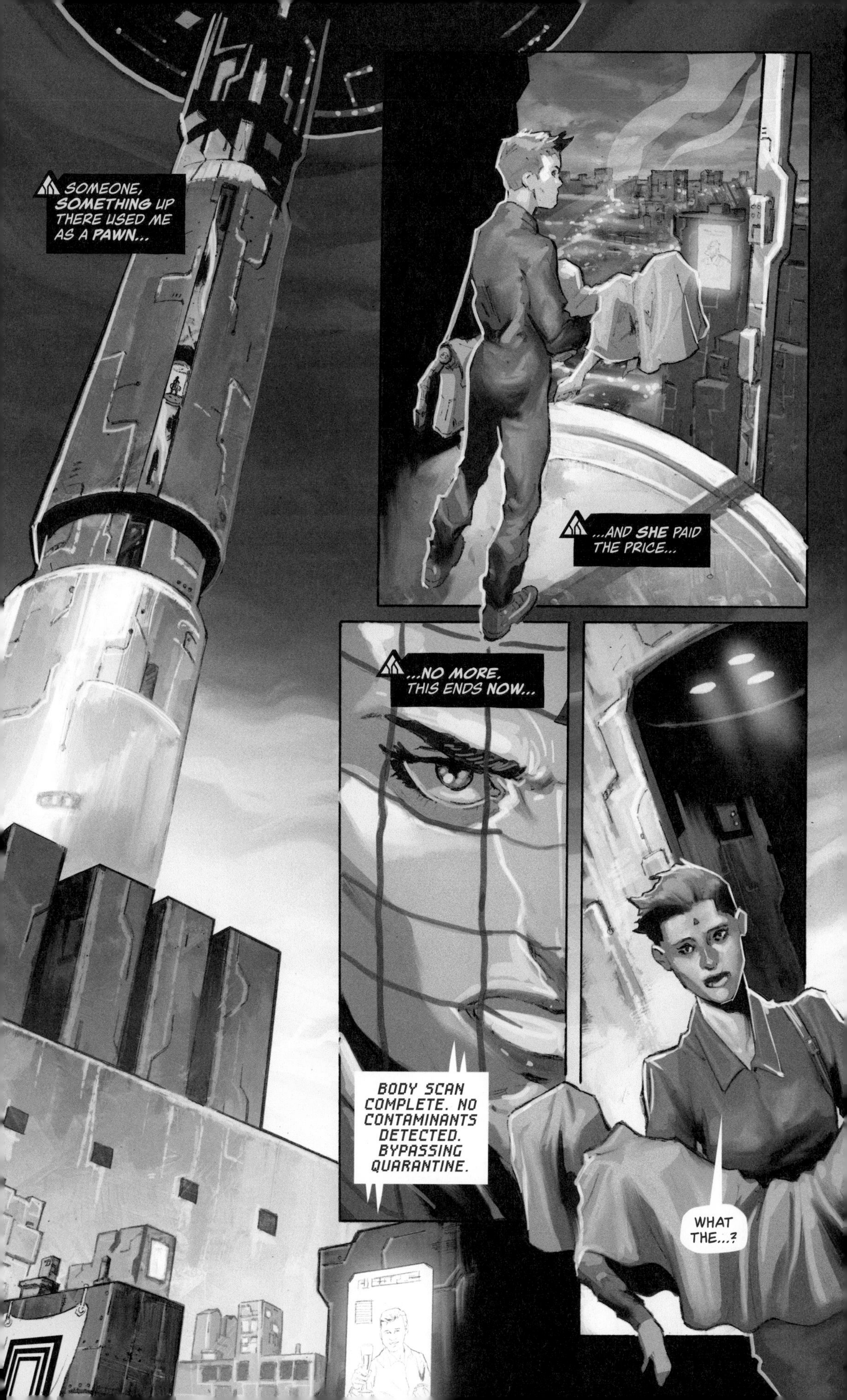
SOMEONE, SOMETHING UP THERE USED ME AS A PAWN...
...AND SHE PAID THE PRICE...
...NO MORE. THIS ENDS NOW...
BODY SCAN COMPLETE. NO CONTAMINANTS DETECTED. BYPASSING QUARANTINE.
WHAT THE...?

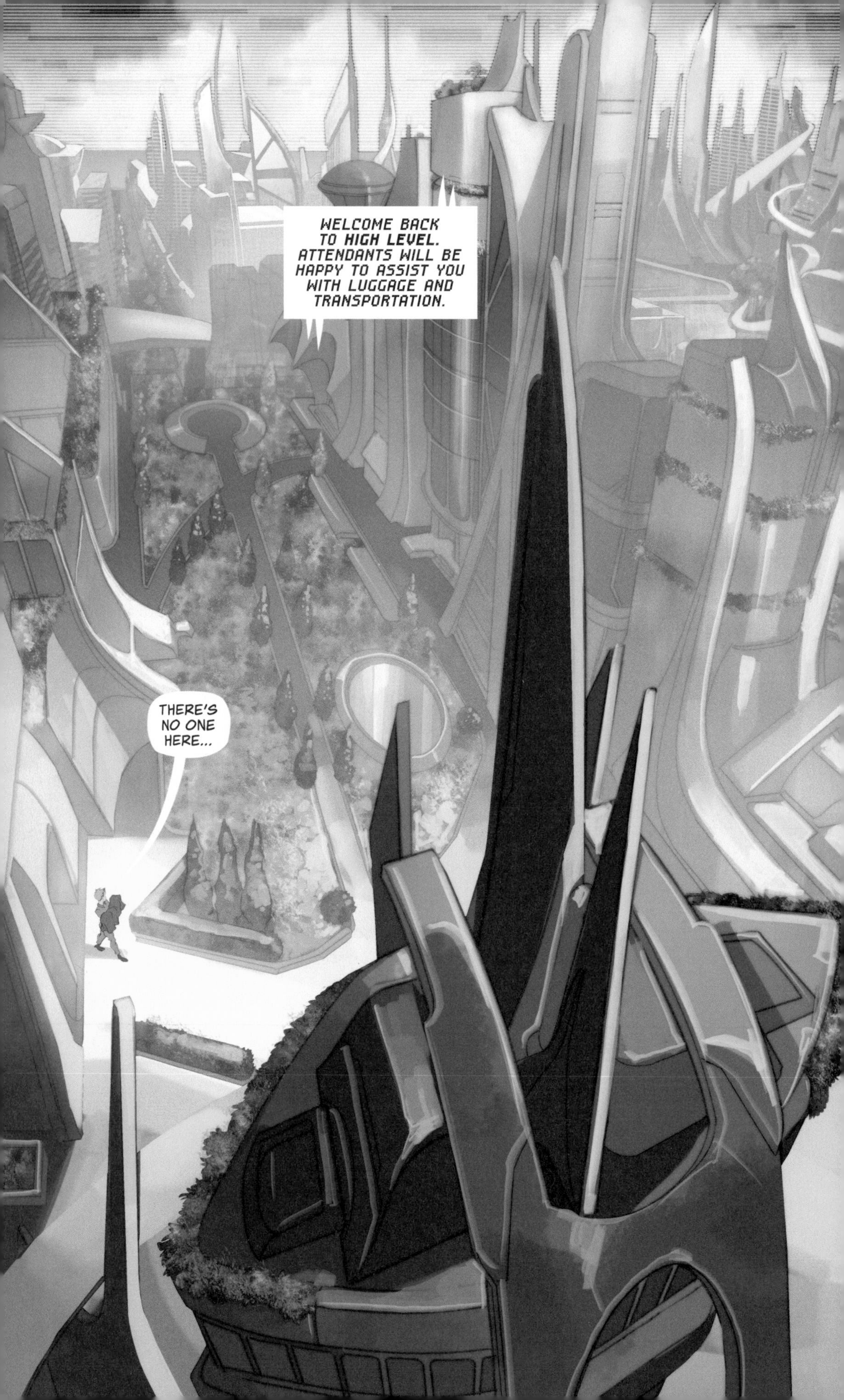
WELCOME BACK TO HIGH LEVEL. ATTENDANTS WILL BE HAPPY TO ASSIST YOU WITH LUGGAGE AND TRANSPORTATION.
THERE'S NO ONE HERE...

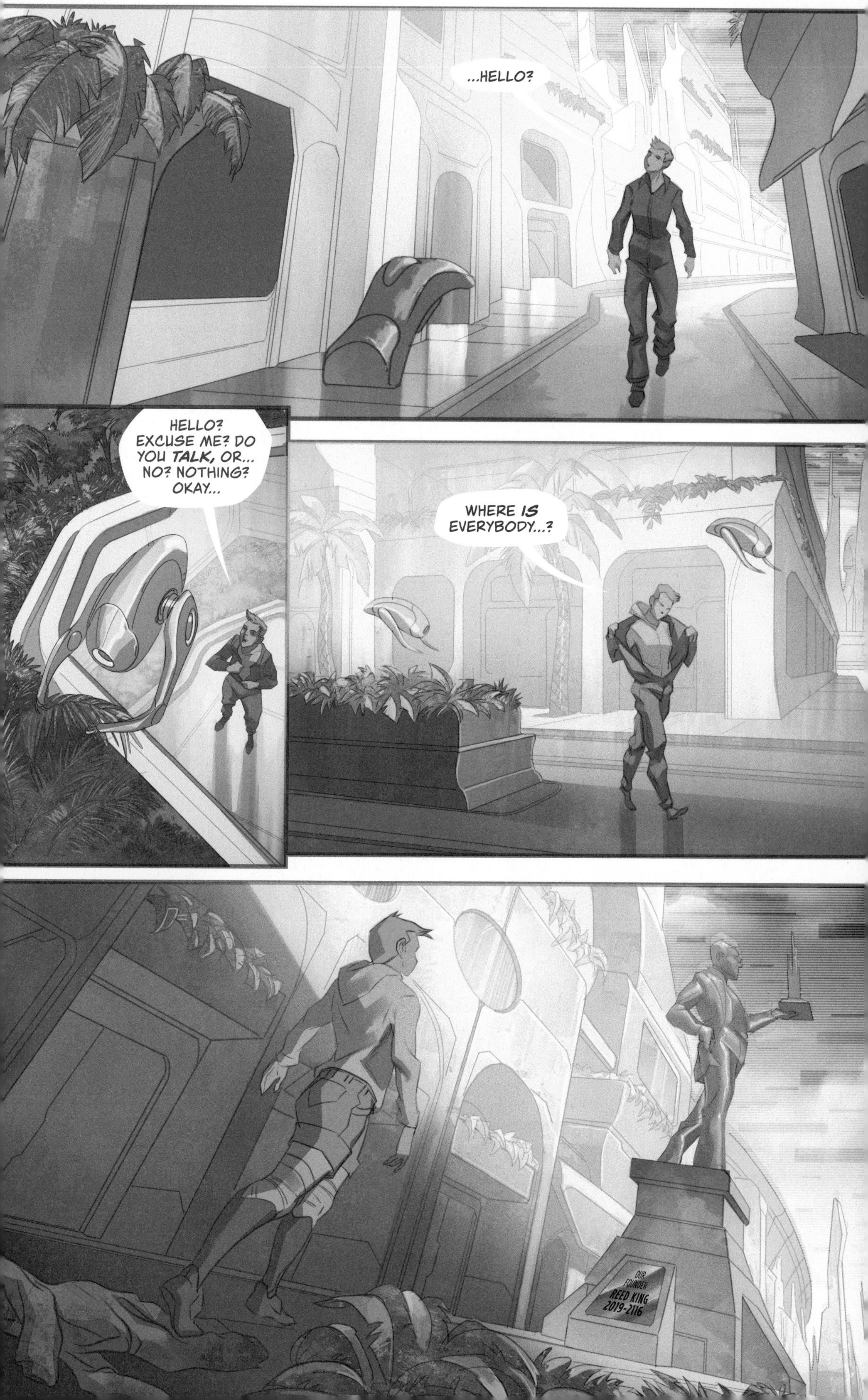
...HELLO?
HELLO? EXCUSE ME? DO YOU *TALK,* OR... NO? NOTHING? OKAY...
WHERE *IS* EVERYBODY...?
OUR FOUNDER REED KING 2019-2116

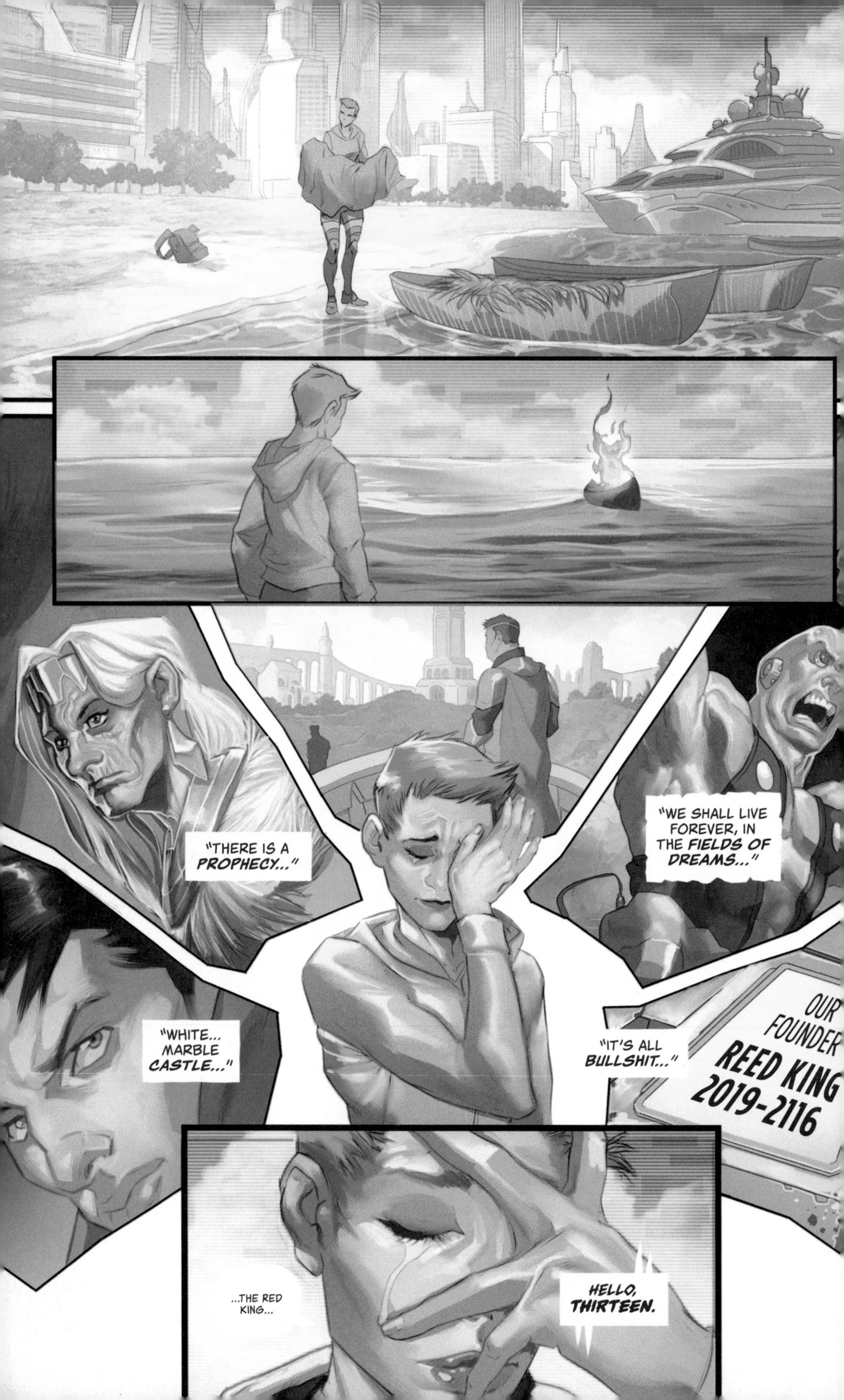
"THERE IS A PROPHECY..."
"WE SHALL LIVE FOREVER, IN THE FIELDS OF DREAMS..."
"WHITE... MARBLE CASTLE..."
"IT'S ALL BULLSHIT..."
OUR FOUNDER
REED KING
2019-2116
...THE RED KING...
HELLO, THIRTEEN.

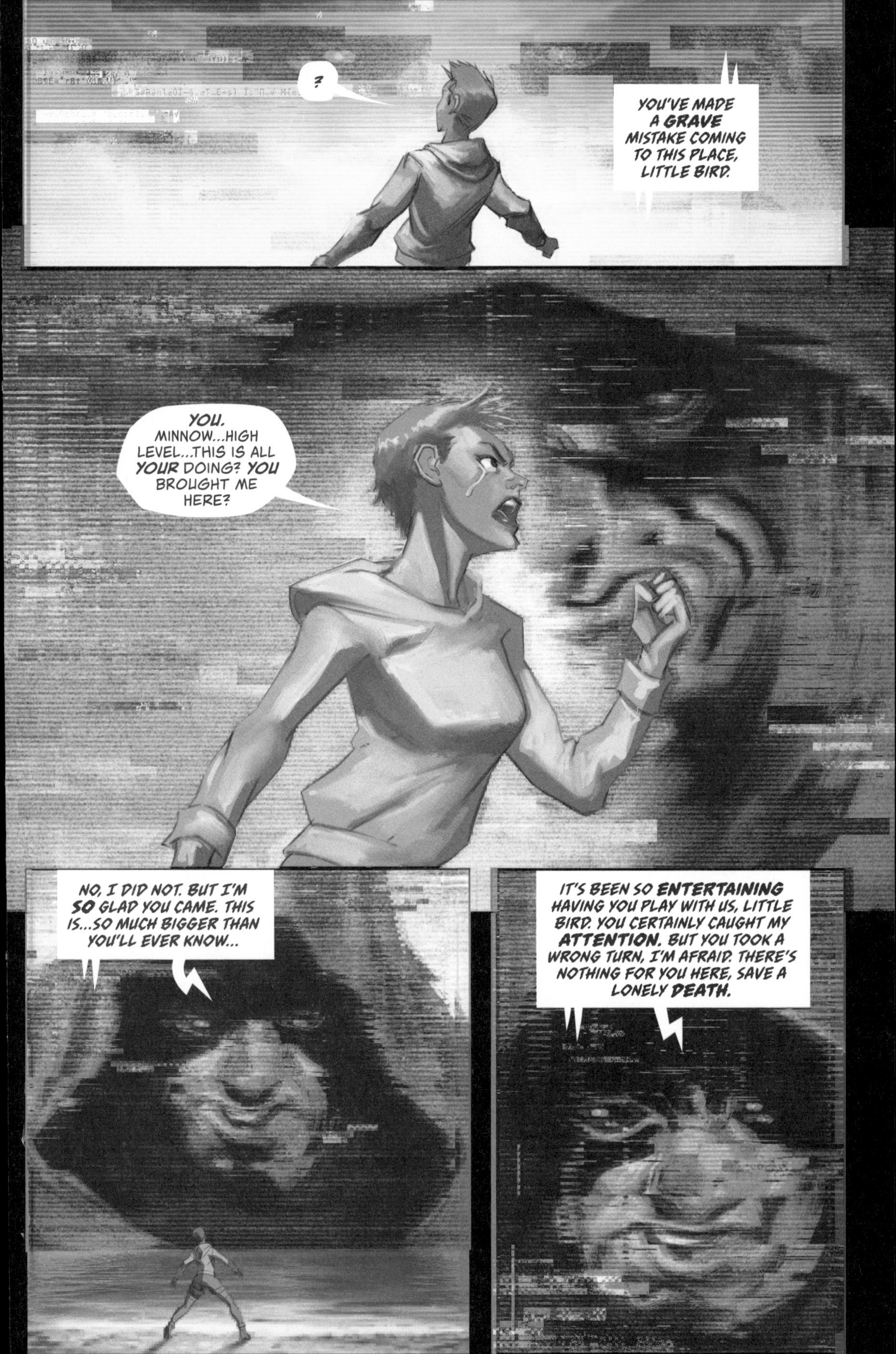
?
YOU'VE MADE A GRAVE MISTAKE COMING TO THIS PLACE, LITTLE BIRD.
YOU. MINNOW...HIGH LEVEL...THIS IS ALL YOUR DOING? YOU BROUGHT ME HERE?
NO, I DID NOT. BUT I'M SO GLAD YOU CAME. THIS IS...SO MUCH BIGGER THAN YOU'LL EVER KNOW...
IT'S BEEN SO ENTERTAINING HAVING YOU PLAY WITH US, LITTLE BIRD. YOU CERTAINLY CAUGHT MY ATTENTION. BUT YOU TOOK A WRONG TURN, I'M AFRAID. THERE'S NOTHING FOR YOU HERE, SAVE A LONELY DEATH.

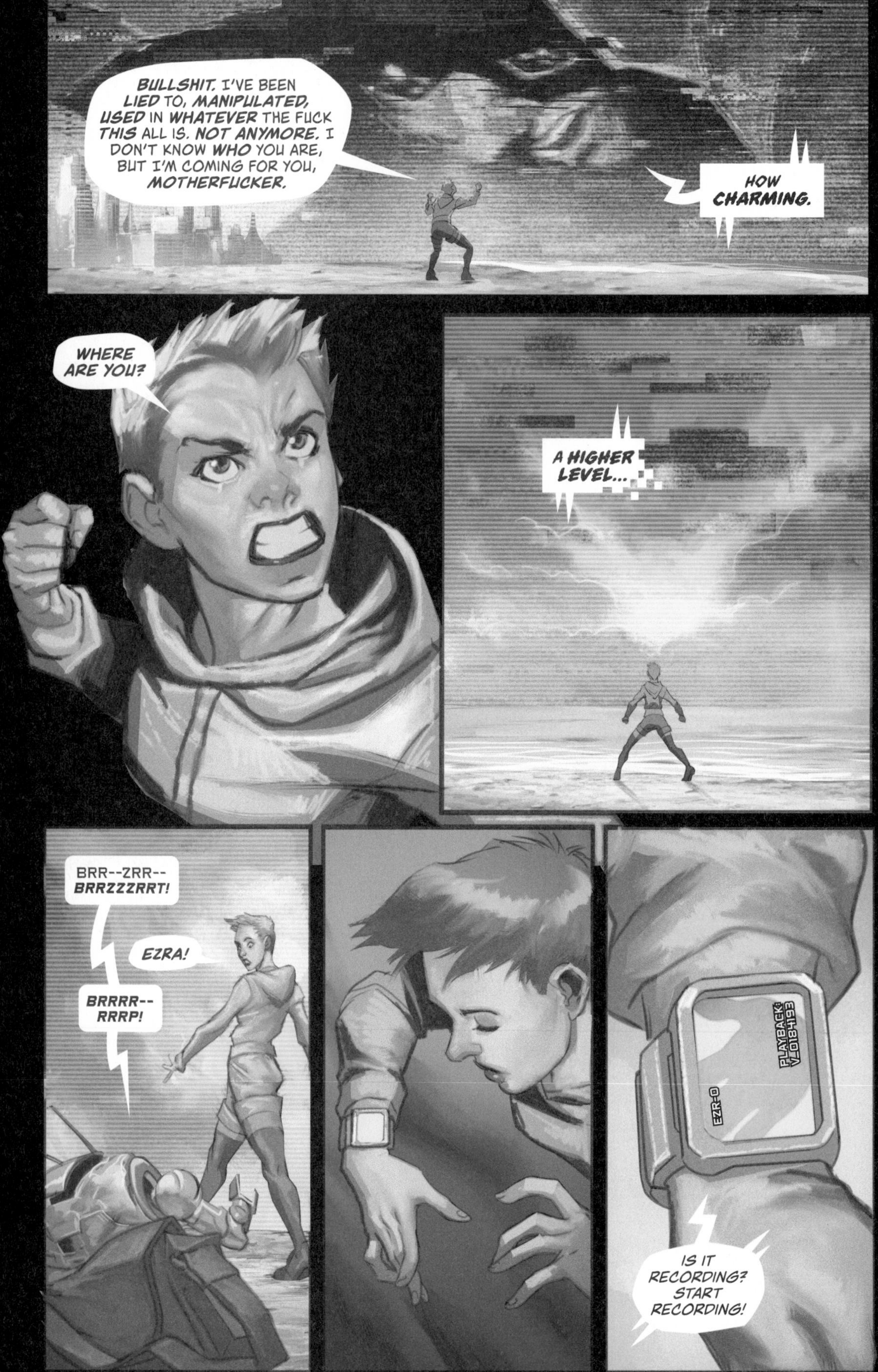
BULLSHIT. I'VE BEEN LIED TO, MANIPULATED, USED IN WHATEVER THE FUCK THIS ALL IS. NOT ANYMORE. I DON'T KNOW WHO YOU ARE, BUT I'M COMING FOR YOU, MOTHERFUCKER.
HOW CHARMING.
WHERE ARE YOU?
A HIGHER LEVEL...
BRR--ZRR--BRRZZZRRT!
EZRA!
BRRRR--RRRP!
PLAYBACK: V.0184193
EZR-0
IS IT RECORDING? START RECORDING!

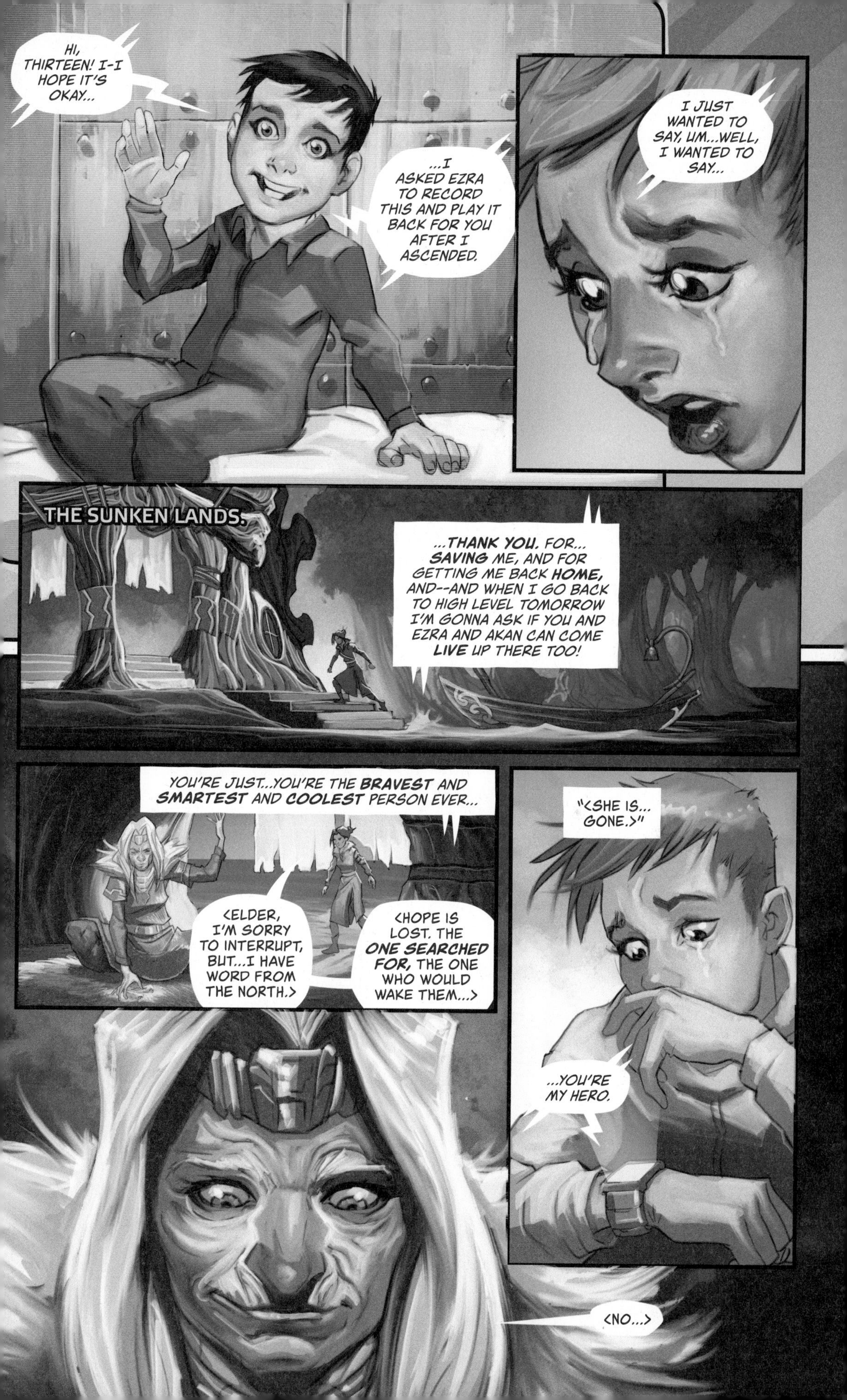
HI, THIRTEEN! I-I HOPE IT'S OKAY...
...I ASKED EZRA TO RECORD THIS AND PLAY IT BACK FOR YOU AFTER I ASCENDED.
I JUST WANTED TO SAY, UM...WELL, I WANTED TO SAY...
THE SUNKEN LANDS.
...THANK YOU. FOR... SAVING ME, AND FOR GETTING ME BACK HOME, AND--AND WHEN I GO BACK TO HIGH LEVEL TOMORROW I'M GONNA ASK IF YOU AND EZRA AND AKAN CAN COME LIVE UP THERE TOO!
YOU'RE JUST...YOU'RE THE BRAVEST AND SMARTEST AND COOLEST PERSON EVER...
<ELDER, I'M SORRY TO INTERRUPT, BUT...I HAVE WORD FROM THE NORTH.>
<HOPE IS LOST. THE ONE SEARCHED FOR, THE ONE WHO WOULD WAKE THEM...>
"<SHE IS... GONE.>"
...YOU'RE MY HERO.
<NO...>

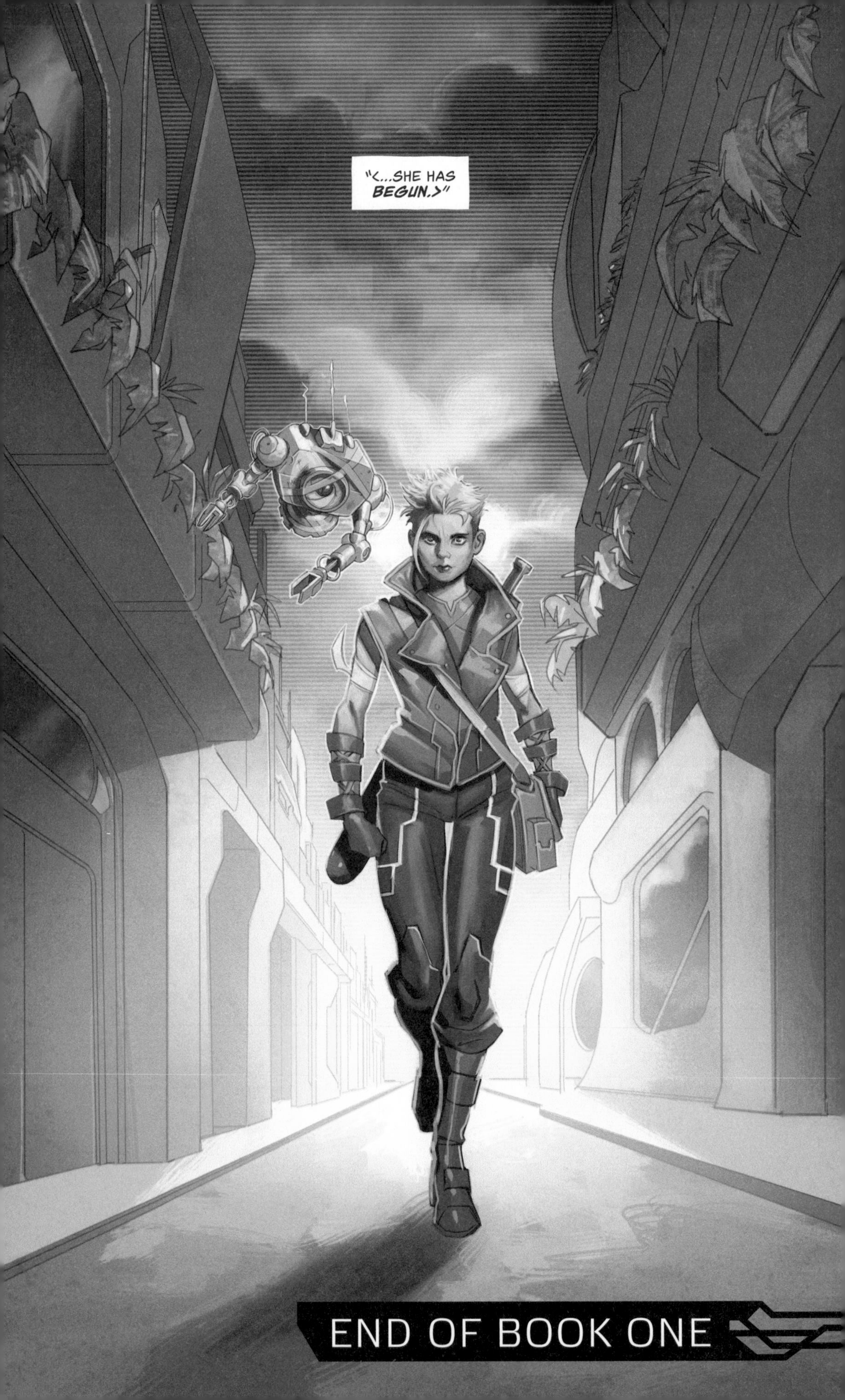
"<...SHE HAS BEGUN.>"
END OF BOOK ONE

HIGH LEVEL ENCYCLOPEDIA

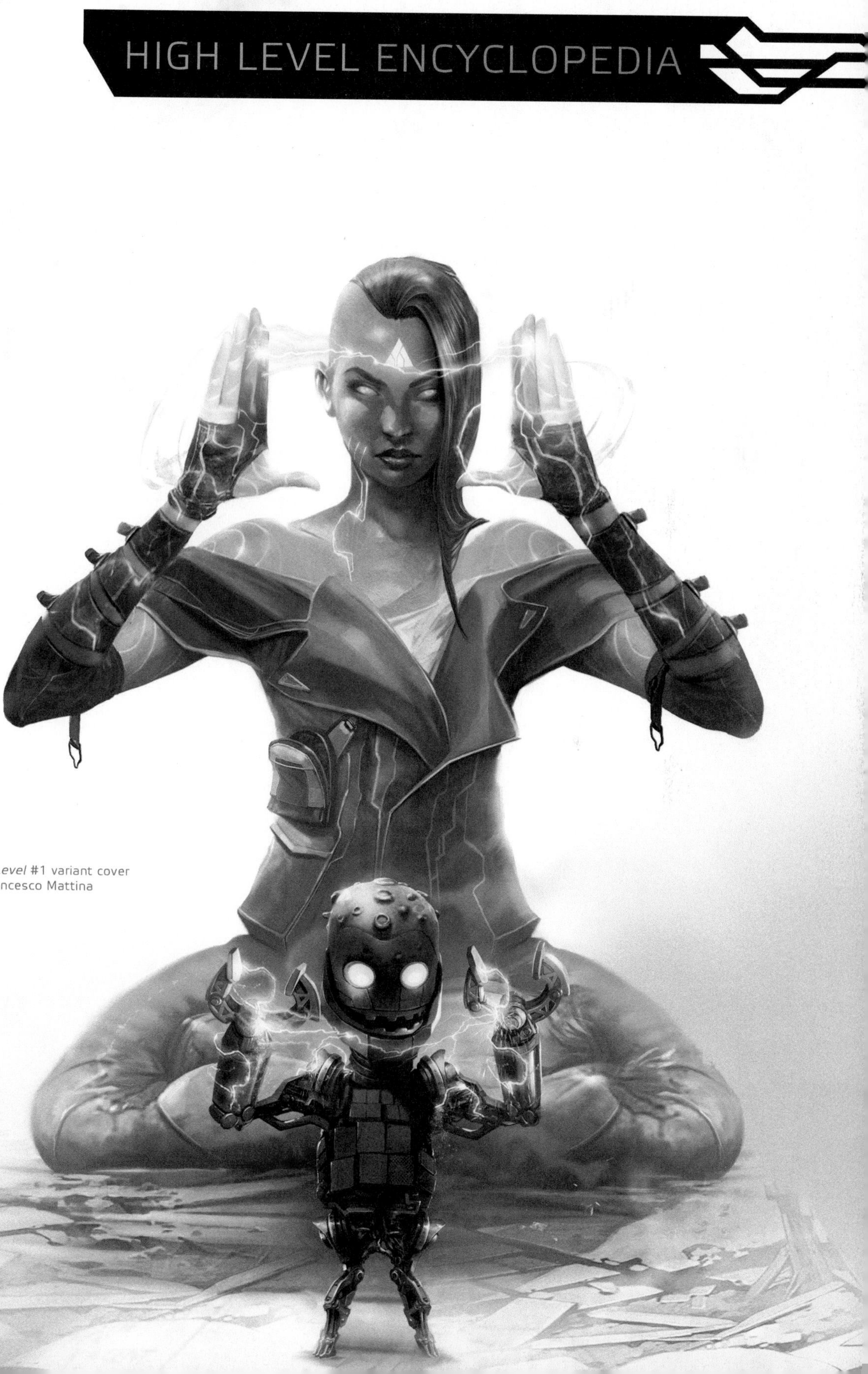

High Level #1 variant cover
by Francesco Mattina

THIRTEEN

AGE: 28
OCCUPATION: Septic Maintenance / Smuggler
HOME: Ordell Faire, Onida

A loner who keeps to herself, **Thirteen** is most comfortable at home in the solitude of her fort, an ancient hollowed-out carnival ride she's repurposed into a functional living space and workshop.

A relentless tinkerer, Thirteen spends her free time building marionettes: small robots whose movements she can control with gesture gloves. Alone and safe in her world, Thirteen guides her marionettes through intricate, meditative dances. That is, when she's not poring in fascination over ancient media she's acquired: books, music, videos, and other relics from **The Old World**.

Safe in her fort, Thirteen is in control, and that's how she likes it. Everything is exactly how she wants it to be...for now.

Thirteen makes a living towing her *Suck 'n' Pump* trailer to businesses throughout the region of **Onida Flats** day after day, emptying their septic tanks. It's a shitty job with shitty pay, but someone has to do it.

For Thirteen, though, it's the perfect cover for her secret side gig, smuggling data chips and other contraband. Thirteen's septic trailer, classified as a "vital services" vehicle, is licensed for militia-protected safe passage throughout the **Outland** regions, granting Thirteen access to highly secured establishments she wouldn't otherwise be able to penetrate.

Besides, no one would ever suspect the lowly "sewer girl"...

Thirteen concept art by Barnaby Bagenda

ORDELL FAIRE

REGION: Onida Flats
AFFILIATION: Neutral / Independent

Thirteen's home in **The Outlands**, **Ordell Faire** is an independent town built on the ruins of an ancient amusement park. Powered by bioelectric **"Supertrees,"** the people of Ordell have repurposed the old park into a thriving sustainable community in a part of the world thought to be uninhabitable.

Ordell processes its own water, generates its own electricity, and grows its own plants and herbs (via indoor hydroponics labs, using seed kits scavenged from **The Old World**). Its people are warm and expressive survivors who take pride in the creative ways they decorate their surroundings. They use the common Outland currency but primarily deal in trades. Ordell's citizens are accustomed to sharing goods and services amongst the community for the benefit of all. As with most Outland towns, Ordell is protected by a contracted local militia.

Onida Flats concept art by Barnaby Bagenda

EZRA

AGE: 3
OCCUPATION: Surveillance / Utility
HOME: Ordell Faire, Onida

Ezra is an autonomous surveillance/utility drone, built by **Thirteen** from cobbled-together parts and repurposed code. A "work in progress," Ezra is at once a learning tool for her robotics and programming and a companion for Thirteen.

Although his A.I. is still primitive, Ezra has learned to understand complex common-language commands and execute a wide range of tasks accordingly. His adaptive learning behaviors allow his brain to "grow," and Thirteen swears he seems to be growing a personality.

Ezra's camera eye transmits an A/V signal to Thirteen's devices, including her watch and the video monitors in her van. Through his eye she can assess situations, spy on targets, and clear paths to better prepare for her smuggling operations. Ezra's camera also has facial and threat recognition technology.

Ezra can't speak yet (it's on Thirteen's to-do list), but in Thirteen's lonely **Outland** travels, he makes for a damn good listener.

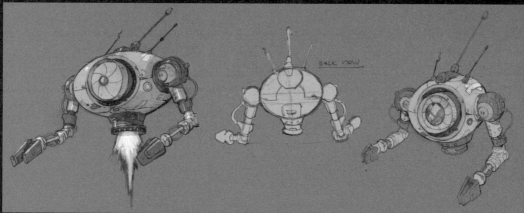

Ezra concept art by Barnaby Bagenda

AKAN

AGE: 30
OCCUPATION: Soldier, Black Helix (defected)
HOME: New Columbia, Teharon

An old flame of **Thirteen**'s, **Akan** left **Onida** four years ago after the two had a falling out. Ever the restless idealist, he traveled north in search of a higher purpose he felt he couldn't achieve in the remote town of **Ordell Faire**.

Much to Thirteen's surprise, Akan was drawn into the **Black Helix** army, one of two warring factions that have ravaged the northern regions with bitter, violent sectarian conflicts for longer than anyone can even remember.

Recently, however, Akan became disillusioned with Black Helix, opposing their violent tactics and shortsighted goals.

Defecting from Black Helix and taking **Minnow**—their prized human weapon—with him, Akan has found himself on the run from the very army he once fought for and has returned to Thirteen with a desperate plea for help.

Akan concept art by Barnaby Bagenda

EMA

AGE: 51
OCCUPATION: Merchant / Trader
HOME: Ordell Faire, Onida

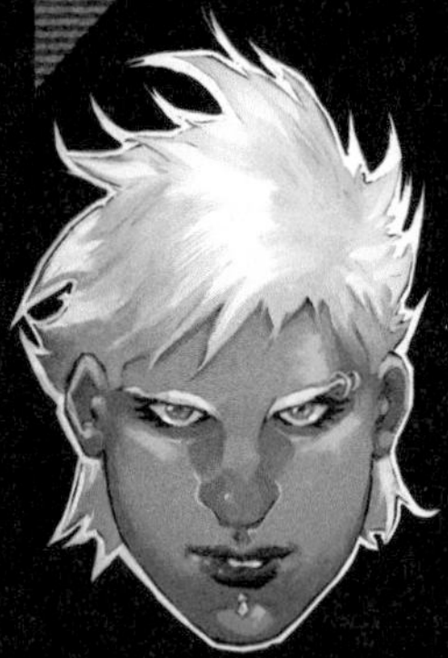

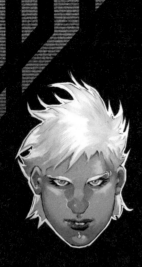

A lifelong resident of **Ordell Faire, Ema** is a level-headed leader who owns and operates **Ghost House**, a shop for used electronics, tools, robotics equipment, and unusual relics from **The Old World**.

Ema has long been a mentor to **Thirteen**, encouraging her budding interest in programming and engineering at a young age. But she's also an agent for Thirteen's clandestine smuggling work, arranging jobs through her far-reaching trade contacts in exchange for a cut of Thirteen's profits.

Ema is beloved and respected by the citizens of Ordell Faire, who often seek her advice in matters of both life and business. She is chairwoman of the town council and has been instrumental in shaping and preserving Ordell's unique culture and thriving economy for decades.

JASPER

AGE: 46
OCCUPATION: Scavenger / Trader / Cartographer
HOME: Ordell Faire, Onida

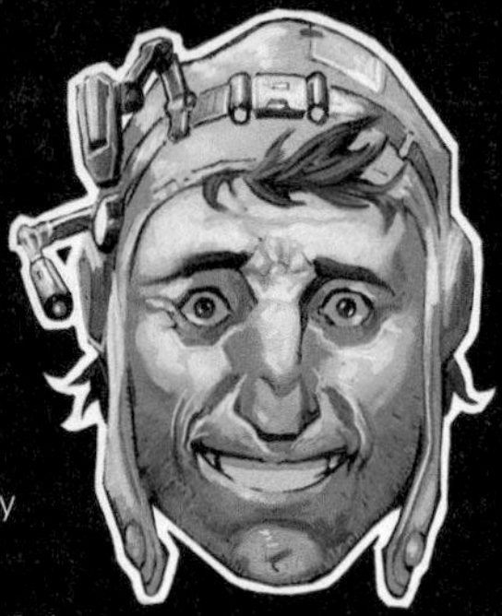

Well-known throughout the **Outland** regions as an expert scavenger and cartographer, **Jasper** is a jovial and adventurous treasure-seeker who **Thirteen** counts as one of her few friends.

Jasper has made a name for himself pillaging ancient storage pods throughout the Outland's uninhabited wastelands. The industrial-strength pods, hermetically sealed and buried underground, were left behind during **The Great Migration** generations ago and are filled with perfectly-preserved clothing, electronics, books, furniture, seed kits, and more. Jasper has profited from the abundance of the abandoned pods (which led to a thriving trade culture, and relics from the past have inspired **Onida**'s expressive style and DIY technology), but they're an increasingly scarce resource.

Foreseeing his time as a scavenger running short, Jasper's thoughts have turned to stories he heard during his travels; tales of untold wealth and comfort granted to those who "ascend" to **High Level**, and he's decided to head north to try his luck at fortune and glory in the fabled *Silver City*.

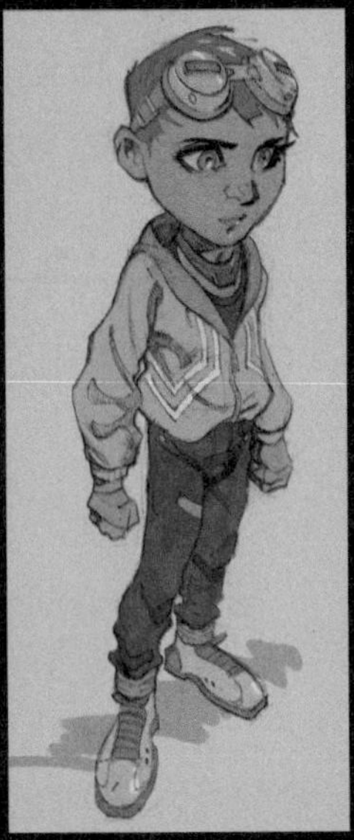

Minnow concept art by Barnaby Bagenda

MINNOW

AGE: 9
OCCUPATION: Special Ops, Black Helix
HOME: High Level

Minnow's origins are a mystery, but her mysterious "powers" (finding and opening heavily-secured ancient military facilities with her mind) have made her a valuable commodity to **Black Helix** and their leader, **General Barron**.

Used as a pawn of war for as far back as she can remember, Minnow has been torn between aggressive military leaders (led by Barron) who seek to use her as a weapon and a growing insurgency (led by **Akan**) who believe that Minnow is from **High Level** itself and that returning her home to "ascend" and prove old legends true is the key to peace.

Curious, bright, and optimistic, Minnow resents the role she's been forced to play throughout most of her life in Black Helix's violent military campaigns and desires above all else a return to a safe, stable life.

In an act of desperation, Akan has brought Minnow to **Thirteen** in hopes that his former lover will transport the child safely back to her supposed home, the mythical *Silver City*.

GENERAL BARRON

AGE: 62
OCCUPATION: General, Black Helix
HOME: New Columbia, Teharon

General Barron is the leader of **Black Helix**, one of two armies who have battled for control of the northern regions for generations.

Barron ascended the ranks of Black Helix with a ruthlessly aggressive agenda, pushing his army toward increasingly violent assaults.

Key to Barron's military success has been **Minnow**, a mysterious child from **High Level** with unexplainable "powers" that have turned her into a vital weapon for Black Helix. Barron has exploited Minnow's abilities relentlessly in his lust for power, causing some in his ranks to question the general's tactics and motivations.

Recently, a rebel group within Black Helix led by **Akan** has defected, taking Minnow from Barron. The rebels believe Minnow was sent not as a tool of war, but as an offering of peace. Akan has asked **Thirteen** to return Minnow to High Level in hopes it will end the war, but Barron will stop at nothing to reclaim his prized weapon.

NIBI OUTPOST

REGION: Nibi
AFFILIATION: Neutral / Independent

Hidden in the structure of an ancient sports arena buried under a massive landfill, **Nibi Outpost** is a dangerous smuggling den and a lawless black market that only those with permission dare approach.

Founded generations ago by **Outland** scavengers, Nibi's landfill location is advantageous both as camouflage and as a constant supply of salvage material. Unmarked waste disposal drones, widely believed to come from **High Level**, regularly dump fresh trash onto the landfill, which Nibi's child scavengers root through for useful wares.

Nibi's primary trade, however, is refurbished military-grade weapons, which are sold in its black market and smuggled out to other outposts across the Outlands. The smuggler outposts benefit from the economy of war, and the warring factions in the north often rely on smugglers for new weapons and supplies in a seemingly endless cycle of money and death.

SUPERTREES

SPECIES: Supertrees
REGIONS: Flin, Onida, Otkon, Sapson, Nibi

Generations ago, **Outland** raiders of ancient underground storage pods discovered seed kits from **The Old World** for what have since been colloquially referred to as "**Supertrees**."

The trees, which appear to have been genetically engineered during **The Great Migration**, grow rapidly and strongly, able to survive in the most extreme climates and withstand the most severe storms. Most importantly, the trees are bioelectric, generating electricity through advanced photosynthesis.

By strategically planting Supertrees and accessing their conductive sap, Outland communities have been able to thrive with off-grid electricity, from the southern wastelands all the way to the isolated metropolis of **Pleasure Island**.

Supertrees concept art
by Barnaby Bagenda

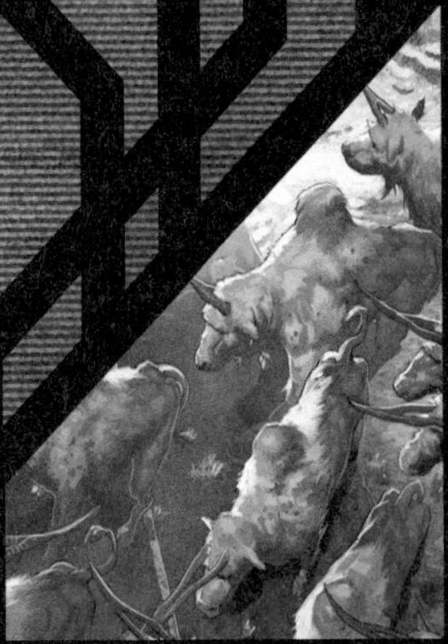

UKUDLA

SPECIES: Ukudla
REGIONS: Flin, Onida, Otkon, Sapson, Nibi, Western Territories

"**Ukudla**" is the common name given to a species of massive ungulate mammals who roam the **Outland** regions in herds that number in the thousands.

Ukudla are widely believed to have been genetically engineered and bred as a controlled, sustainable food source in **The Old World**, and were likely let free unintentionally during **The Great Migration**. Since then, the Ukudla population has thrived as the dominant animals of The Outlands, one of the few mammalian species that can survive the harsh climate conditions and food/water scarcity.

Ukudla are hunted for food by Outlanders, as one Ukudla can feed an entire village for weeks. They are, however, extremely strong, fast, and difficult to kill, and won't hesitate to gore anyone who threatens them. Attempts have been made to farm Ukudla, but few have succeeded in containing them without heavy-duty equipment.

It is rumored that the tribespeople of **The Sunken Lands** are master Ukudla hunters who worship the animals' spirits as givers of life, decorating their homes and clothing with bones from the mighty creatures.

THE SUNKEN LANDS

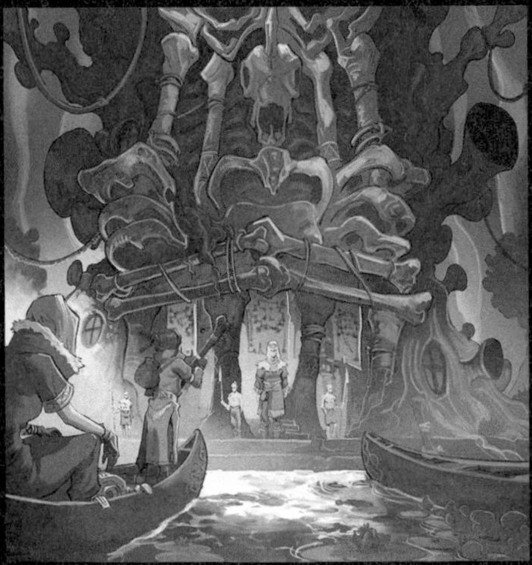

REGION: Nibi
AFFILIATION: Neutral / Independent

Little is known about the tribes who inhabit the storm-ravaged swamps along the Manitoba coast. It is theorized that they are master **Ukudla** hunters who worship water and lightning spirits, but beyond that what's said about them is vague and contradictory.

Some believe the tribes originated from **Great Migration** settlers who chose to reject technological survivalism and instead confront the anger of the earth directly, finding ways to coexist with it.

Others claim the tribespeople are heretics cast out of society, demon worshipers who practice strange rituals and despise the "heathens" of nearby **Outland** communities like **Nibi Outpost** and **Pleasure Island**.

The only thing anyone is sure about is that the tribespeople protect their land fiercely, and no one who's entered to investigate has ever returned...

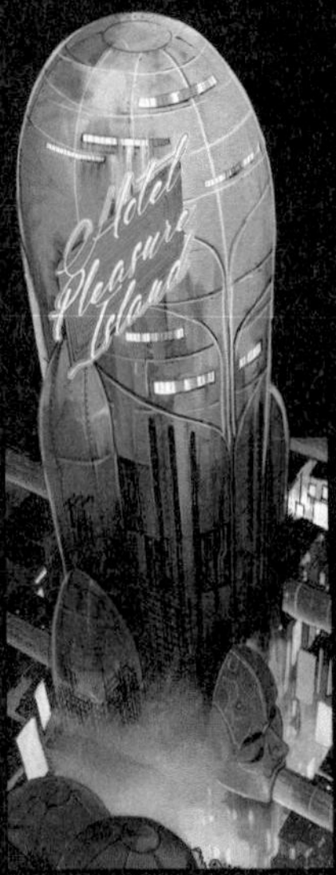
Hotel
Pleasure
Island

PLEASURE ISLAND

REGION: Nibi
AFFILIATION: Neutral / Mafia-Controlled

The only known metropolis to rise after **The Great Migration** and **Great Disruption**, **Pleasure Island** is an **Outland** oasis for sex, drugs, gambling, and any other vice one could imagine. The city was built decades ago by infamous mafia kingpin **The Room**, who envisioned it as both a playground for Outland denizens and a sanctuary for **The Changed**.

The city is a place of "free expression," where anything is allowed as long as it's consensual. Although the rules are few, punishment for breaking them is a grisly death: eaten alive by the gnashing teeth of The Room's many mouths.

Pleasure Island has been able to thrive thanks to The Room's quiet agreement with the two warring factions whose territorial conflicts rage just north of the city. Both armies are paid a handsome tax to keep the city neutral and untouched, and soldiers on leave enjoy its bars and brothels.

THE ROOM

AGE: 106
OCCUPATION: "Business Owner"
HOME: Pleasure Island, Nibi

A feared and respected crime lord, **The Room** owns and manages **Pleasure Island**, the notorious **Outland** metropolis of indulgence.

The Room are of **The Changed**, a race believed to be the result of failed **Old World** genetic experiments to "enhance" humans. The Changed are generally more intelligent and physically stronger than average humans. They process nutrients more efficiently, and are able to survive weeks without eating if necessary. They also have heightened immune systems and significantly longer lifespans, sometimes living up to 200 years.

The Changed suffer from uncontrollable and unpredictable cellular growth, creating mutated tissue that warps and distorts their bodies to varying degrees. For many the mutations are minor and merely aesthetic in nature, most commonly affecting the face. But in extreme cases the mutations can be much more aggressive and debilitating, growing new organs, limbs, bone, and teeth. As a result of their physical appearance, The Changed have been mocked, feared, and discriminated against for generations.

The Room's Changed mutations are particularly extreme and ongoing, to a degree that would normally be fatal, were it not for The Room's wealth and resources that have kept them alive with complex life support systems and cybernetic enhancements.

VALENTINA

AGE: 42
OCCUPATION: Dominatrix
HOME: Pleasure Island, Nibi

A lively and outspoken **Changed** woman, **Valentina** works as the head dominatrix at **The Blue Rose** brothel in **Pleasure Island**.

As a child, Valentina's parents sought to escape their war-ravaged home in the north and journey to **High Level** to seek safety and prosperity. They were killed in an explosion during the trip, leaving young Valentina to fend for herself in the vast slums outside High Level's walls. The gangs took her in, and by the age of twelve Valentina was working as a drug mule, running everything from narcotics to valuable medicine in and out of the slums. Eventually she was given a job that would take her to Pleasure Island, and she found herself in such awe of the city that she never went back.

Valentina is a realist who has seen the horrors of the world and has no use for faith. She's spent years building a life where she's in control, far removed from any hope of salvation promised by the *Silver City*.

BLACK HELIX

REGION: Teharon
BASE OF OPERATIONS: New Columbia, Teharon
LEADER: General Barron

Born out of the ashes of **The Blue Coalition Army** from **The Old Wars**, **Black Helix** is a militia group and protostate that has long fought against **The New Republic Army** for control of the land and resources surrounding **High Level**.

The old stories often told of The Blue Coalition as a principled people's opposition movement, but few now would likely say the same of Black Helix, save its own devoted soldiers. The militia group's tactics have grown increasingly violent over the past decades, and its motives increasingly murky. Countless towns throughout **Teharon** and **New Republic** have been ravaged and raided in Black Helix's ongoing attempts to draw Republic forces into conflicts and weaken their defenses along the New Republic border.

Black Helix's primary stronghold is the martial law city of **New Columbia**, where citizens build munitions, prepare supplies, and train to be soldiers. Dwindling resources and the toll of war have impoverished New Columbia, and many workers are growing tired of starving for the sake of a military agenda that seems less interested in helping its people than it does in raw power. Some claim there have been whispers of revolution…

LOW LEVEL

REGION: New Republic
AFFILIATION: New Republic Army

Commonly referred to as "**Low Level**," the vast walled city that surrounds the base of **High Level**'s tower has been closed off from outside entry for at least a generation.

Outside Low Level's heavily guarded walls, millions of desperate refugees who have pilgrimaged across the continent wait in impoverished shantytowns, still hoping to be granted entry into the walled city.
They die there waiting.

Inside Low Level's walls is an industrial metropolis where hundreds of thousands of men, women, and children work long hours in factories to produce goods and food for the citizens of High Level above, as well as manage their energy, water, and waste. Low Level's workers all wear identical gray uniforms, and live in small utilitarian dormitories.

Workers earn credits for their hours, which they can spend on "flair" for their uniforms (small colored buttons) or extra food from the automats. Aside from the factory-issued water and NutriPaste sustenance rations, automats offer additional "snack" food for purchase in the forms of SavorDiscs, FlavorCubes, and FizzyDrink.

Low Level's citizens understand themselves to be immensely fortunate for the safety and resources provided by the city. Billboards, announcements, and video broadcasts remind them constantly to "be grateful" for the privilege of their citizenship and reinforce the dangers and misery of the world outside their walls. The VTX video transmission network broadcasts 24/7 programming throughout Low Level, featuring news and entertainment from the glamorous city of High Level above.

All citizens of Low Level work tirelessly in hopes of being "chosen" to "ascend" to the upper city of High Level. Hard work and obedience, they are reminded, are the path to **Ascension**. Ascension ensures a life of fortune and luxury in a promised land unlike what anyone on earth has ever imagined. Although VTX broadcasts showcase recent Ascensions and citizens will swear they know someone who knows someone who ascended not long ago, when pressed on the matter no one seems to have actually witnessed an Ascension firsthand in their lifetime...

Control of Low Level has been central to the long-raging war of the Northern Regions. **The New Republic Army** has held the city for years, acting as a military security force. But recently attacks by the so-called "terrorist" army **Black Helix** have increased, causing panic amongst Low Level's citizens that the New Republic Army is anxious to quell.

NEW REPUBLIC ARMY

REGION: New Republic
BASE OF OPERATIONS: Low Level, New Republic
LEADER: Unknown

A powerful and organized security force, **the New Republic Army** controls the most valuable land in the world: the northern region of **New Republic**, home to the manufacturing powerhouse of **Low Level** and the fabled utopia of **High Level**.

The New Republic is believed to have descended from the ancient **American Nationalist Army**, an invading force of legendary might whose occupation of the northern regions during **The Great Migration** may have been the catalyst of **The Old Wars** (most of that history has been destroyed, so specifics from that time are largely conjecture). Today, however, The New Republic Army's only apparent agenda is to maintain its protection of High Level and the many natural and artificial resources it requires—which means defeating the "terrorists" **Black Helix** at all costs.

The most sacred duty of The New Republic Army is to guard the **Ascension Gates** at the base of High Level's massive tower spire. There, the high-ranking Guardian class of New Republic soldiers await word from **The Chosen Ones** on who will next be chosen. The massive Ascension Gates are surrounded by a deep chasm, where waterfalls cascade down from the city above. From a hundred miles away, the waterfalls of High Level's opulent tower can be seen shimmering majestically, sparkling in the sunlight, earning its storied nickname, *The Silver City.*

\<DATA MISSING\>

AGE: \<data missing\>
OCCUPATION: \<data missing\>
HOME: \<data missing\>

\<data missing\>

>data intercepted

>point of of origin: unknown

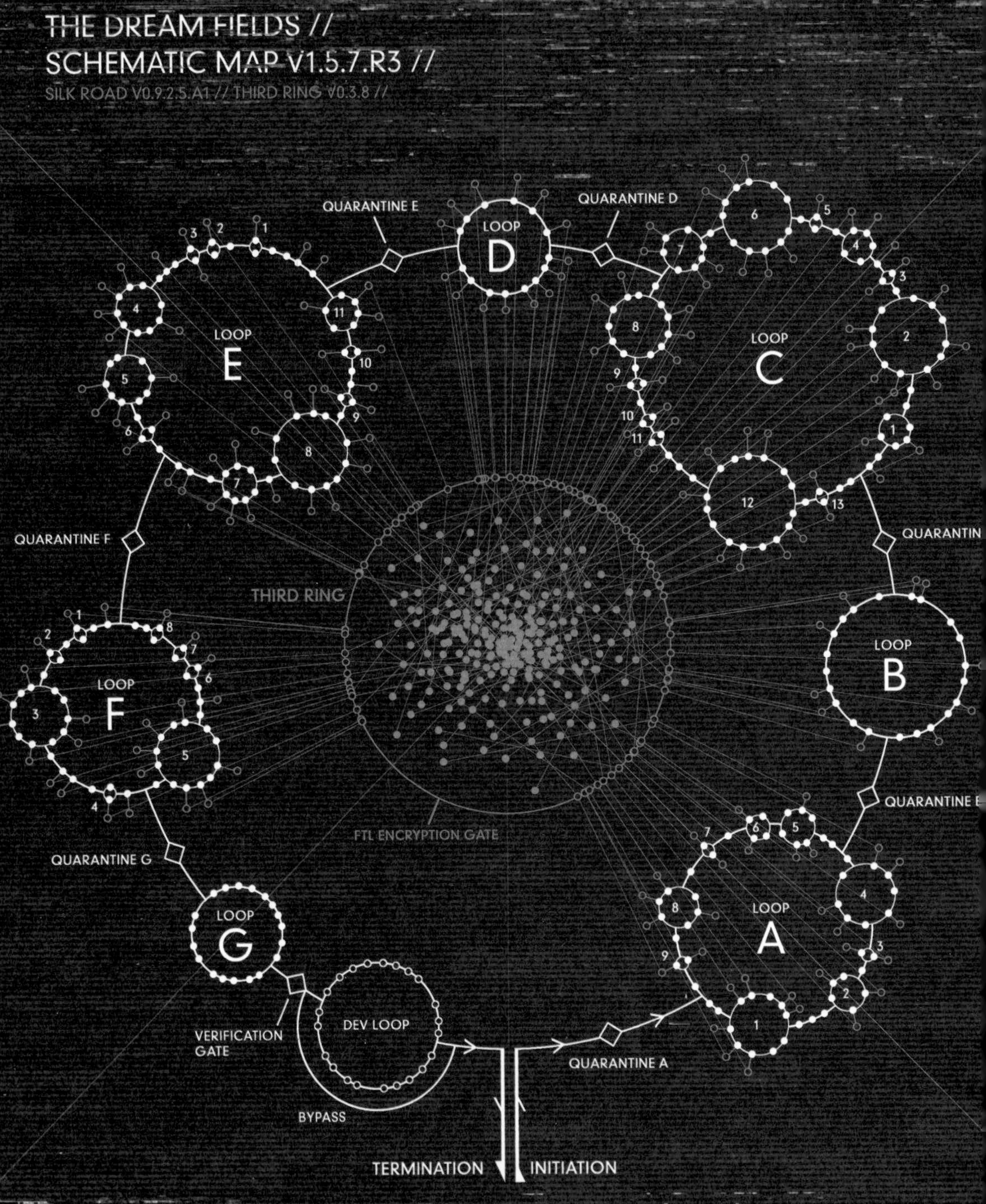

THE DREAM FIELDS //
SCHEMATIC MAP V1.5.7.R3 //
SILK ROAD V0.9.2.5.A1 // THIRD RING V0.3.8 //
QUARANTINE E
QUARANTINE D
LOOP
D
LOOP
E
LOOP
C
QUARANTIN
QUARANTINE F
THIRD RING
LOOP
B
LOOP
F
QUARANTINE B
FTL ENCRYPTION GATE
QUARANTINE G
LOOP
A
LOOP
G
VERIFICATION
GATE
DEV LOOP
QUARANTINE A
BYPASS
TERMINATION
INITIATION